Demography and Population Problems

Rajendra K. Sharma

ATLANTIC
PUBLISHERS & DISTRIBUTORS (P) LTD

Published by
ATLANTIC
PUBLISHERS & DISTRIBUTORS (P) LTD
7/22, Ansari Road, Darya Ganj, New Delhi-110002
Phones : +91-11-40775252, 40775214, 23273880, 23275880
Fax : +91-11-23285873
Web : www.atlanticbooks.com
E-mail : orders@atlanticbooks.com

Branch Office: Chennai
Phones : +91-44-48531784, 28291383
E-mail : chennai@atlanticbooks.com

Printed & bound in India by Atlantic Print Services

Preface

This book covers university syllabi in Sociology in the papers entitled: Demography; Social Demography; Population Studies; Population Problems; Vital Statistics in India etc. Analytic presentation of data derived from authentic sources; holistic approach to controversial problems; simple and easy narration with examples from Indian circumstances and questions for exercise at the end of each chapter make this work an ideal textbook for students and a reference work for the teachers.

Starting from Historical Review and discussion of the Concept, Scope and Importance of Demography, the book includes chapter on: Relationship with other Studies; Theories of Population; Methods and Sources of Demographic Data; Growth and Trends of World Population; Development of Demography in India; Structure and Characteristics of Indian Population; Population Dynamics: Mortality; Fertility: Nature, Measures and Trends; Fertility in India; Migration: Types, Measurement, Theories and Trends; Urbanisation; Labour Force; Unemployment in India; Population Problems; Family Planning and Family Welfare; and Population Policies.

Suggestions for improvement are solicited from indulgent readers.

Rajendra K. Sharma

Contents

1

Historical Review

John Graunt, an English Haberdasher, has been acclaimed as the father of demography or population studies. He published a pamphlet in London in 1662 with the title *"Natural and Political Observations Made upon the Bills of Mortality."* This pamphlet contained a quantitative analysis of mortality. It also analysed fertility and migration. The article was based upon weekly bills of mortality containing reports on burials and Christenings, in a population of half a million persons in London and suburbs. These reports used to be compiled and maintained regularly by Parish clerks since 1603. Graunt gathered the data contained in these reports during the period 1604 to 1661 and prepared a systematic and objective report. This report was monumental as the first landmark in the history of population studies. Its important characteristics were as follows:

1. Consideration of several aspects of population which are considered important today.
2. Examination of the data on mortality and fertility, pointing out their weaknesses, limitations and prejudices.
3. Observations based upon the basic data and the discovery of the biological phenomena of the excess of male births over female births in London and suburbs.
4. Estimation of the size and growth of population of London in absolute numbers.
5. Analysis of the causes of the increase in the population of London due to migration.

Thus, on the basis of data concerning mortality, Graunt pointed out that the cause of the growth of the population of London is not increasing births, since deaths outnumbered births, but a sizable migration into the city. As Graunt is supposed to be the father of population studies, it may be said to be born in the middle of the 17th century. Besides John Graunt some other contemporary English scholars made significant contributions to population studies. Among them may be mentioned Sir William Petty (1623-1687), a friend and collaborator of Graunt. He contributed what is known as 'Political Arithmetic'. He prepared life tables with Graunt. About 30 years after the publication of Graunt's observations, an English astronomer Edmund Halley (1665-1742) constructed the first empirical life-table based on the data of births and deaths. He coined the term 'Expectation of Life'. Yet another significant contribution was made by Gregory King (1648-1712), an English scholar, by estimating the population of England and Wales. Before the first census of England and Wales in 1801, this was the only estimate of their population size.

Development in Germany and Other Countries

The above mentioned works of the British demographers inspired population research in Germany, Netherlands, Sweden and other European countries. A massive book on population, consisting of nearly 1200 pages and an appendix of 68 tables was written by Johann Peter Sussmilch, a clergyman of Germany. He tried to construct mortality tables of universal applicability by combining the population data from Germany. France and Sweden. He based his studies on a large number of observations. He concluded that there is always an excess of women over men in a population. He was the first person to emphasize what is known as, "The law of large number", "Implying that the value of a finding increases along with the number of cases on which it is based."[1]

The most important conclusions and findings of Sussmilch were as follows:

1. Generally there is an excess of women over men in a population.
2. The value of population survey increases with the number of cases included by it.

1. Frank Lorimer, *The Development of Demography, op. cit.*, p. 129.

3. Men are more prone to remarry, as is clear by the frequencies of remarriages among men and women.
4. Deaths were most frequent in the first few weeks of life, and the number of deaths decline to a lower level around the age of 15.
5. There is a divine hand in the regular movements of the population.

Sussmilch studied the factors influencing fertility such as the age of marriage, disruption of marriage by death, prolonged nursing of infants, effects of various diseases, etc. In 1765, he tried to estimate the population of the world in the third edition of his book. *The Divine Order*. Like the British scholar Gregory King, Sussmilch maintained that population grows in geometric progression. His interpretations were however coloured by theology, since he saw the divine hand in the regular movements of the population.

RESEARCH IN 18th AND 19th CENTURIES

Population studies in the 17th century were made in different social strata in varied avocations. These researchers tried to discover the hitherto unknown relationships in vital processes of life and death in quantitative terms. They had a great respect of empirical observations.[1]

Thomas R. Malthus

Some scholars in the 18th centuries observed the relationship between the potentiality of population growth and available resources. They concluded that the potentialities of human population growth might surpass the resources required for its support. In 1755 Benjamin Franklin published his observations. During the same period, the Chinese writer, Hung Liang Chi pointed out that in the 18th century the growth of the means of subsistence was not in proportion to the growth of population. However, the most important essay attracting public attention, regarding population growth, was published by Thomas R. Malthus (1766-1834). Malthus, a young clergyman, attracted a great deal of attention and gave rise to much controversy by the publication of his essay, *"An Essay on the Principles of Population as it Affects the Future Improvement of Society, with Remarks on the*

1. *Ibid.*, p. 131.

Speculations of Mr. Godwin, M. Condorcet and other Writers". The main theme of the thesis propounded by Malthus was that while means of subsistence increase in arithmetical progression, population grows in geometrical progression. Therefore the growth of population is the main cause of poverty. This thesis aroused a lot of controversy everywhere. Malthus toured Scandinavian countries and studied the condition of population. He presented sufficient data to support his thesis in his book. He emphasized moral self-restraints so that population may be controlled. In the words of Peter R Cox, "Consistently, Malthus advocated 'moral restraint' (*i.e.*, absence of sexual intercourse) in order that starvation, pestilence and vice could be avoided ('Vice', it may be noted, in his view included contraceptive practices)."[1]

Development in 19th Century

In 19th century there was widespread interest in research in the field of fertility. This was particularly due to the reason that in some of the countries fertility was not stopped. While birth rate was high in Asian countries, in Europe it was not so. Towards the end of the 18th century fertility started decline in France. Initially this was considered the result of intellectual progress, order and foresight. However, when France was defeated by Prussia in 1870, concern regarding the decline of the French fertility arose. The most important developments in demographical studies in 19th century were concerning the probability theory in statistics, the beginning of census operation and the establishment of the system of civil registration. The first census in USA was held in 1790. In 1801 England and France had their first census survey. The census technique was gradually improved and the scope of census was consequently widened. The course of population growth could now be traced on the basis of census surveys of a population at regular intervals. Most of the progress in this direction was made in England by the establishment off General Registrar Office. This office was occupied by William Farr in 1839. He continued to hold this position upto 1880 and made significant contributions to the methodology of population analysis by the construction of life-tables and the study of occupational mortality. In this connection writes Peter R. Cox, "Thoroughness and a capacity for the systematic analysis of a large volume of information were desirable qualities in dealing with the new masses of figures

1. Peter R. Cox, *Demography*, 1977, p. 300.

relating to a complex of matters. Among those who possessed these and other qualities and successfully pioneered in this field in England was William Farr ...was responsible for preparing census and registration reports — he who drew the attention of the general public to the high mortality in certain districts."[1]

DEVELOPMENT IN THE EARLY 20th CENTURY

But the most important period in the development of demography is the early years of the 20th century. During this period demographers in USA, England and European countries started working in the field of fertility. In England, National Birth Rate Commission was appointed in 1916 to study the causes of declining birth rate. This question was earlier raised at the time of the census of 1911. In 1922, A.M. Carr Saunders, a biologist, published his book *The Population Problem*. This book contained a systematic statement of the problems of population size and growth. It also discussed the genetic question. Carr Saunders was professor of social sciences. There was a chair of social biology occupied by Prof. Lancelot Hogben in 1930 till 1937, after which the post was abolished. The first chair for the post of demography was created in 1938 when R.R. Kuezynski was appointed reader in Demography at the London School of Economics. After it demographical studies were gradually introduced in British universities. There was a growing concern for declining birth rate in the country. A Population Investigation Commission was appointed n 1936 in Britain under the chairmanship of A.M. Carr Saunders and with D.V. Glass as research secretary, to study the problem of birth rate and related natters. A Royal Commission was set up in 1943 to enquire into the reasons or the falling birth rate. The Commission submitted its report in 1949 which was widely appreciated.

During this period significant contributions were made in demographical studies in USA. John Durand, in his essay, Demography's Three Hundredth Anniversary, considers Walter Willcox, to be the first American Demographer. Walter Willcox, Professor at Cornell University in USA, published his statistical study of divorce in 1891. In 1920, population studies were seriously undertaken in USA. In 1925, Louis I. Dubblin and Alfred J. Lotka published a treatise on the stable population model. This

1. *Ibid.*, p. 301.

was a landmark in the development of population studies. Earlier, in 1922 a Scripps Foundation for research in Population Problems was established at Miami University with Warren Thompson as Director and P.K. Whelpton as Associate Demographer. In 1937, the Population Association of America was established at Princetoin niversity under the directorship of Frank W. Notestein. Population studies have been carried out since 1920 by the Millbank Memorial Fund of New York City. Valuable material has been published under the leadership of Clide Kiser.

Developments since the Second World War

After the Second World War demographical studies were widely undertaken in the developed countries. In USA, the Princeton Group studied the social and psychological factors affecting fertility and the practice of contraception among the Americans. An important study undertaken by this group was: "the growth of American Families". Several research studies were undertaken to study the problems of population growth, family planning and urbanization in developed countries. The growth rate of population during 1960 and 1970 in America led to the suggestion by some leading demographers to aim at zero population growth. As a result of heavy industrialization and rapid population growth the environment in Western countries had ban gradually deteriorating. This caused serious concern among demographers. In June 1972, a conference on Human Environment was held by UNO in Stockholm, Sweden, focusing attention on the study of the human population in relation to its environment or ecological system.

Besides the developed countries, there has been a spectacular progress in demography in the developing countries. For example, there has been a growing awareness of the population problem in India and programmes have been outlined for family planning and birth control. Interest in population studies can also be seen in Pakistan, Sri Lanka and the Philippines among other developing countries. The rapid decline in the mortality of the low income countries and the political emancipation of several Afro-Asian countries led to the widening of the scope of population research. The newly independent nations concentrated upon the problem of raising the standard of living of their people and therefore started with assessment of the growth, distribution and problems of population. Economic planning, planning for development and five year plans were introduced to check population growth according to the means of subsistence available. The planners realised that unprecedented fall in death rate had been responsible for accelerating the rate of population growth. During the period 1900-1950 the population of developing countries increased by 0.8%. In the next 20 years, however, it increased by 2.5%. Similarly, during the period 1900-1950 the death rate of these countries was 32, while during 1960-1970, it was 17. Therefore, during the period 1950-1970 the rate of growth of population was spectacular. For example the rate of population growth in India during 1931-1941 was 14.23%. During 1961-1971, however, it was 21.64%. Therefore, it was natural that the importance of population planning was realised everywhere. It was recognized that the rapid growth of population adversely affects the standard of living and the economic and social progress. Therefore, during 1960-1970 several nations adopted specific population policies and family planning programmes. More and more information was gathered about population through census surveys and demographic sample surveys. Several countries were helped by UNO to introduce systems of vital registration and conduct sample surveys.

Besides the developed and the developing countries, the most important role in demographical studies in 20th century has been played by UNO and other international agencies. A Population Commission was set up at UNO as a part of the legislative wing of the organization. A Population Division in the Department of Social Affairs was permanently established. The first World Population Conference was sponsored by UNO in 1954 in Rome. This was followed by similar conferences at Belgrade in 1965 and Bucharest in 1974. The year 1974 was observed as UN World Population Year. During this year several population surveys were undertaken and economic aid was given to many countries for this purpose. The proceedings of all the conferences sponsored by UNO have been published. In 1956, the Demographic Training and Research Centre (now known as the International Institute for Population Studies), was established in Bombay under the Joint Sponsorship of the Government of India and the UNO. This was particularly created for the study of population problems in the ECAFE region (now known as ESCAP region) and for the training of personnel, in this field. At present UN has set up 4 other regional centres one each at Santiago in Chile, Cairo in Egypt, Accra in Ghana and Yaounde in the Cameroon. The Economic and Social Commission for Asia and the Pacific (ESCAP), previously known as the Economic Commission for Asia and the Far East (ECAFE), is a branch of the United Nations situated in Bangkok, Thailand, and is very active in promoting regional population studies.

The other UN bodies, such as the World Health Organisation (WHO), the United Nations Economic, Social and Cultural Organisation (UNESCO), the Food and Agricultural Organisation (FAO) also continue to maintain their interest in the problems of population. The International Statistical Institute, Netherlands, has recently set up an organisation for World Fertility Survey and several such surveys in different countries are being conducted. The professional international organization of demographers, known as the International Union for the Scientific Study of Population (IUSSP), holds a meeting of all members at intervals of two to three years and publishes the proceedings and contributed papers. The contribution of the UNO is significant in the field of methodology and the techniques of population analysis. Its publications have provided data to demographers everywhere particularly the United Nations Demographic Year Book.

QUESTION FOR EXERCISE

1. Trace the history of demography and population development.

2

Demography: Concept, Scope and Importance

The term demography was first used by Guillard in 1855. However, some scholars maintain that the beginning of demography should be traced from John Graunt's essay *Natural and Political Observations made upon the Bills of Mortality*, in 1662. John Graunt defined techniques of demographic analysis. He presented what is known as analysis-approach. In contrast to it Robert Malthus presented what is known as problem approach. In the words of S.N. Agarwala, "Demography is said to have its beginning in 1662 when John Graunt published in London an article entitled, Natural and Political Observations made upon the Bills of Mortality ... John Graunt was the exponent of the 'analysis-approach'.... Thomas Robert Malthus can be said to be the leader of the 'problem-approach' in demography."[1]

VARIOUS TERMS AND THEIR MEANINGS

Generally speaking the history of demography may be traced since about three centuries back. However, quantitatively as well as qualitatively, its development may be observed only in the 20th century. Today, demography is being considered as an independent branch of knowledge. As Peter R. Cox has said, "It is sometimes argued that certain branches of population analysis should be distinguished from others by a separate title. In this connection the word 'demology' has occasionally been suggested as an indicator of the more learned branches of the subject; but

1. Agarwala, S.N., *Some Problems of India's Population*, p. 1.

this has not come into general use. Rather more commonly, the expression 'population studies' is used to indicate the simpler and more descriptive demographic work. There is, however, no sharp dividing line between the various parts of demography and these expressions are used, if at all, without much consistency."[1]

In the beginning, demography was concerned only with the enumeration of population. Gradually, it began to study population from empirical, statistical and mathematical viewpoints. Today it studies the size, the composition and distribution of population. The size includes the population at a place in different periods. The composition of population includes measurable characteristics of population such as age, sex, marital status, education, religion, caste, health, etc. These characteristics of population organization are always changing. Distribution of population may be studied according to communities and religious groups or according to fields of population. Demography studies the patterns and causes of the changes in the size, composition and distribution of population. It studies the influence of these changes upon different aspects of society. It studies the birth, mortality, marriage, migration and social mobility, quantitatively.

DEFINITION OF DEMOGRAPHY

The term demography has been derived from two Greek words meaning *Demos* or the people to draw or write. Thus literally speaking, demography is concerned about writings concerning the people. The above analysis of the present day field of demography also clarifies its meaning. The following definitions of demography will further help in the understanding of its meaning:

1. *Philip M. Hauser and Dudley Duncan*: "Demography is the study of the size, territorial distribution and composition of population, changes therein, and the components of such changes, which may be identified as natality, mortality, territorial movement (migration) and social mobility (change of status)."[2] This definition of demography is not sufficiently wide. In fact the field of demography changes according to time, place and circumstances. This point has been particularly raised by Warren S. Thompson and David T. Lewis, in their book *Population Problems* (1965).

1. Peter, R. Cox. *Demography*, p. 2.
2. Philip M. Hauser and Dudley Duncan. *The Study of Population*, p. 2.

2. *Donald J. Bogue*: "Demography is the mathematical study of size, composition and special distribution of human populations and of changes overtime in these aspects through the operation of the five processes of fertility, mortality, marriage, migration and social mobility. Although it maintains a continuous descriptive and comparative analysis of trends, in each of these processes and in their net result, its long-run goal is to develop a body of theory to explain the events that it charts and compares."[1]

3. *Spengler, Vance, Ryder, Lorimer and Moore*: Demography is an elaborate study of population. This view has been elaborated by Frank Lorimer in his book *The Nature of Demography* (1957). According to these thinkers, "Modern demography is closely related to economics, sociology, psychology, geography, mathematics, genetics, ecology and anthropology. It is thus a multi-science discipline...." This has been also accepted by UNO in its publication Determinants and Consequences of Population Trends. This definition of demography may be considered as representing the present state of affairs.

Nature of Demography

Explaining the scientific nature of demography, Irene Taeuber has pointed out, "With improved data, new techniques and the precise measurement of the demographic transition that is occurring, demography has become science rather than literature."[2] This was also emphasized by John V. Grauman when he said, "Demography is both an abstract science and applied technology." Demography today uses scientific methods, the most important of which is analysis. As S.N. Agarwala said, "Demography deals with population statistics. Population studies deal with analytical interpretation of population dynamics and composition, which covers a wider area.... We are shifting from demography to population studies."[3]

Objectives of Demography

The scientific nature of demography also becomes clear from an analysis of its objectives. Generally speaking, the following are the four objectives of demography:

---

1. Donald J. Bogue, *Principles of Demography*, 1969, p. 1.
2. Irene Taeuber. Population Studies in United States. *Population Index*. Oct. 1946, p. 254.
3. Agarwala, S.N. in "Training India's Demographers" An Interview by K.N.M. Pillai, *Span*, June 1970, p. 31.

1. To achieve knowledge of the size, organization and distribution of the population of the field of study.
2. To describe the past evolution of population in an area and its distribution in different fields.
3. To enquire into trends of population and its relationships with the different aspects of social organization in an area.
4. To predict the future demographic evolution and its probable consequences.

Thus, it is clear that demography performs all the functions characteristic of a science such as enquiry into cause-effect relationships, prediction about the future etc. It uses the scientific methods of observation and analysis. It is factual. It is universal. It is veredical. It finds out what will be on the basis of what is. Its laws are verifiable generalizations. As distinguished from normative science, it is a positive science, which studies facts both qualitatively as well as quantitatively.

SCOPE OF SOCIAL DEMOGRAPHY

The scope of social demography has been classified into two sections: Macro-demography and Micro-demography. While the former includes studies of systems, cultures and societies on a large scale, the latter studies the individual and the family as a unit of society. Thus, the latter study has smaller units and is conducted intensively. In the words of Donald J. Bogue, "It is the study of the growth, distribution and redistribution of the population within a community, state, economic area or other local area. This includes both numerical and compositional aspects and is performed by using meaningful sub-divisions of community or local areas."[1]

However, most of the population studies are conducted in the field known as macro-demography. The two fields help each other. For example, death rate is studied both from the macro and the micro standpoints. Similar is the case concerning birth rate, fertility, migration, etc. The field of demography includes the subjects which are discussed in world population conferences since 1954. The two conferences of 1954 and 1965 discussed the following subjects: fertility, death rate, migration,

1. Donald J. Bogue, Macro-Demography in D. J. Bogue, *Applications of Demography, the Population Situation in the U.S. in 1975* (Chicago), 1957, pp. 49-52.

genetic composition, future probabilities, population and means of subsistence, techniques of population measurement and the training of the demographers. Other subjects included in the scope of demography are: distribution of population, qualitative aspect of demographic data, family planning, growth of population, demographic aspects of supply of labour, demographic aspect of education, demographic aspect of housing and the demographic aspect of saving and investment. The scope of demography has further increased after 1965. The computer techniques are the contribution of this decade. In the words of Peter R. Cox: "Computer techniques, using simulation, have been developed in order that stochastic variability can be provided for in various stages. This is a rapidly growing area of demography, and prospects for future progress are almost as important as the work already done."[1]

Aspects of Social Demography

The different aspects of the study of population or social demography may be briefly described as follows:

1. Size of Population: Demography is fundamentally the study of population. Population is primarily studied in the form of its size. In India census studies of populations are undertaken after every ten years. The demographers in different countries find out the size of the population of their countries. These data are further utilised by agencies of United Nations to arrive at the size of world population. The Population Division of United Nations situated at New York studies the world population and working papers are published in this respect from time to time. Some important data are also provided by Food and Agricultural Organization (FAO) from time to time. The Department of Economic and Social Affairs of United Nations also publishes useful data from time to time.

2. Organization of Population: Population organization includes the measurable characteristics of population of community in a country during a particular period. These characteristics include age, sex, marital status, educational level, religion, caste, race and health etc. These characteristics are generally changing.

3. Population Distribution: The distribution of population is generally studied according to geographic areas. The measures of population distribution include percentage of population and

1. Peter R. Cox. *Demography* (1970), p. 8.

density of population. The factors affecting population distribution are studied as geographic, social, economic and demographic. Population distribution is also studied by classification of residence. This includes rural and urban residence. It also includes the study of urban growth or urbanisation. The measures of urbanisation include percentage of population in urban areas, ratio of urban-rural population, size and locality of residence of the median inhabitant, tempo of urbanisation, etc. Study is conducted concerning the levels and trends of world urbanization and factors effecting urban-rural population distribution. Besides, urbanization is studied in almost every country by the government agencies.

4. Fertility: An important field of demographical study is fertility. It is expressed in terms of birth rate, birth order, family size, sterility and contraception, etc. The influence of biological limits and social norms upon fertility are important. The demographer studies the reproductive span and theoretical maximum fertility. He also studies psychological, social and cultural factors affecting fertility. The psychological factors affecting fertility include Adolescent Sterility, Post-Partum Sterility and Average Interval between Successive Births, Re-productive Wastage, etc. The social and cultural factors affecting fertility include: Intermediate Variables, Intercourse Variables, Voluntary Abstinence, Foetal Mortality from Voluntary Causes (Induced Abortions), Use or Non-use of Contraceptives including Sterilisation, Norms about Intermediate Variables and Family Size, etc. Besides, basic measures of fertility and methods of conception control are also studied. The basic measures of fertility are the measures based upon performance during one year, such as the Crude Birth Rate, the General Fertility Rate, Age Specific Fertility Rate, Total Fertility Rate, Gross Reproduction Rate, Sex-Age adjusted Birth Rate, Measures based on Sex-Age Distribution, Measures based on children ever born. The methods of conception control are both male and female. The male methods of conception control include coitus interrupts, condom, male sterilisation or vasectomy, female methods of conception control, include the rhythm method — the calendar method, the temperature method, mechanical and chemical contraception — the diaphragm, chemical contraception, the intra-uterine device (IUD), oral contraception, female sterilization, advances in contraceptive technology, induced abortion, etc.

On international level demography studies levels and trends of fertility in the world, factors associated with long term decline of fertility in the developed countries, factors related to high fertility in the developing countries, differential fertility, etc.

5. Mortality: An important field of demographical study is mortality. It is measured by crude death rate and infant mortality rate. It includes the study of Sex and Age patterns of mortality, causes of death, levels and trends of mortality in a country and in the world and mortality differentials such as urban-rural and occupational, etc.

6. Migration: Migration has been classified as immigration and emigration, in-migration and out-migration. The demographer studies general trend of migration, migratory movement, place and origin of destination, gross and net migration, migration interval, migration streams, etc. The sources of data concerning migration include census surveys and population registers. The methods of measuring internal migration are direct as well as indirect. The direct measures include data concerning place of birth, duration of residence, place of last residence, etc. The indirect measures include data concerning vital statistics, survival ratio and migration. Demography studies differential migration oy age, sex, marital status and educational attainments. It studies both national as well as international migration and also migratory movement.

7. Labour Force: An important field of demographical study is the labour force. Study is made of economically active population both employed and unemployed, population that is not economically active such as home makers, students and income recipients, etc., time reference period, gainful worker concept and labour force concept and the status of labour. The sources of data for the analysis of economically active population are population census and special sample surveys. The basic measures of economic activity or labour force analysis include the crude labour force participation rate or the crude activity rate, the general labour force participation rate, the age-sex specific labour force participation rates, the standardised labour force participation rates, etc. The levels of labour force participation rates are studied both among males and females. Besides, national and international studies concerning employment, unemployment, underemployment, rural unemployment, educated unemployment, etc., are undertaken by demographers.

8. Institutional Demography: Institutional demography includes the study of demographical aspect of social institutions particularly family and marriage. The study of marriage includes marital status, mean age at marriage by census data, time trend in the age at marriage, marriage frequencies by sex, marriage age by status, marriage age by zones, marriage age by religious groups, marriage age by caste, recent increase in marriage age, difference in marriage age by residence, differences in marriage age by educational level, etc. It also studies the extent of widowhood, method of computation of widowhood age, trend in the mean widowhood age, widowhood age by religion, mean duration of fertile union, method of computation, etc.

9. Population Policy: The development of a country today very much depends upon population policy. Population growth and socio-economic development are intimately related. The study of population policy includes: philosophy and guiding principles, the magnitude of the task, organizational structure, services and supplies, education and motivation, family planning targets, family planning progress and achievement, birth averted and effect on birth rate, family planning expenditure, a complex problem, family planning progress during five year plans, etc. Population policies in different countries are developed according to local requirements. Besides, suggestions are made by world organization in this connection.

The above discussion of the scope of demography or population studies I includes only the major and established areas. The scope of demography has been constantly increasing, particularly in the last decade. Therefore, new areas of research and studies are being explored. Thus, the scope is being constantly widened.

IMPORTANCE OF DEMOGRAPHY

The importance of the study of demography is clear from the scope of this important field of study. Since the scope is constantly increasing, therefore, there is growing recognition of its importance.

Demography helps in the understanding of population problems particularly of the less developed regions of the world. It also helps in planning the population of developed and undeveloped countries. International agencies are publishing data in this connection from time to time. The importance of demographical studies is clarified by the seriousness of the implications of rapid population growth. The chief problem concerning population in a country is to control population growth in relation with the growth of health amenities, food supplies, employment, education and housing. Demographical studies point out the conditions and requirements in these areas so that future development and growth may be planned accordingly. In brief, the following points many be noted about the importance of Demography:

1. Health Planning: Persistent high fertility causes significant health ? problems, both for the mother and the child. In most of the developing countries married women are characterised by continuous nutritional drain from repeated pregnancies. Premature curtailment of breast feeding is an important cause of high infant mortality. High fertility is connected with underdevelopment of children; since demography studies fertility and connected problems, its study is a must for health planning of the country.

2. Planning of Food Supply: Planning of food supply means availability of adequate food for total population, both in quality as well as in quantity. Inadequate food supply results in growth retardation, high mortality rates, poor health, low physical activity and consequently low productivity. Therefore, food supply must grow in relation with population growth. Thus, planning of food supply requires and presupposes population studies. In a particular nation, it may not be possible to meet demands of food supply within the country. Different nations today very much depend upon other nations for food supply. Besides, undeveloped and underdeveloped countries cannot meet the demands of food supply without the help of international agencies. Therefore, Population Council and Population Division of UNO study population growth and food supply on an international basis so that help may be advanced to undeveloped and underdeveloped countries.

3. Employment Planning: Employment is an international problem these days. Unemployment and underemployment is fast growing not only in the economically backward countries but also in more developed nations. A demographic factor of considerable importance is the high dependency ratio in less developed countries such as India where four or five persons depend upon the income of one person. Therefore, employment planning requires study of population in all its aspects. It also requires study of migration, immigration and emigration which are important areas of demography. Thus, the importance of demography in employment planning is clear.

4. Educational Planning: Every nation today is concerned with providing proper education to children. The number of children, however, is constantly increasing. Therefore, educational planning for children requires demographical planning. This is also required in the case of uneducated adults. For example, in India more than l/3rd of adults are illiterate. The demographical assessment of widespread illiteracy and quantum of education required is a necessary prelude to all educational planning. The estimates about the future needs of education are also made on the basis of estimates of growth of population.

5. Housing Planning: Demand for housing increases with the increase in the size of population. Therefore data for mortality, fertility, migration and family formation provide basis for estimates of housing required. For example, according to the estimates prepared by the Economic and Social Commission for Asia and the Pacific (ESCAP), the number of persons in the age-group 15-24 in the region are likely to increase from 379 million in 1970 to 469 million by 1980, an increase of 24 per cent. These people will many and would like to establish their own homes. According to another estimate prepared by ESCAP, the percentage of the urban population in the region will increase from 25 in 1970 to 44 by 2000. The increase in the urban population of the region during this period will be from 507 million to 1551 million. According to S.N. Agarwala, taking the various demographic factors which affect housing requirements, the demand for new houses during the decade 1970-1980 will increase by 31.9 per cent or by 126 million houses. Available statistics for the ESCAP region show that less than two housing units per thousand population were built each year during the 1960s whereas the requirement was for eleven units per thousand population. In Latin America there is a deficit of 20 million housing units, whereas in the ESCAP region the estimated deficit is of 22 millions housing units in the urban areas and 125 millions in the rural areas.

6. Planning Concerning Migration: India today, is suffering from brain-drain. Data concerning persons, migrating to Western countries is necessary to estimate the extent of brain-drain. Such estimates have been made and thinking has started about methods to curb this evil. Again, large number of emigrants makes a qualitative change in the population of a country particularly because most of the emigrants are highly qualified persons and technical hands. This is particularly true of underdeveloped countries like India. Therefore data concerning emigration is gathered from time to time. Further data concerning immigration, another aspect of migration, is equally necessary since it again makes qualitative changes, in the population of the country. For example, in India a large number of poor, illiterate and famished immigrants are coming from Bangla Desh for the last several years, creating difficulties particularly in the States of West Bengal and Assam. Data concerning these immigrants have to be gathered from time to time so that some sort of restriction may be put upon it. Thus, it is clear that migration statistics are very important for the government as well as non-government agencies.

The above brief resume of the importance of demography in national planning shows its value. This is equally true on the other hand about the international scene. The international agencies of UNO therefore very much depend upon the demographical data gathered by the Population Division of UNO. This data points out problems of undeveloped and underdeveloped countries. Since today it has been widely realised that peace and prosperity is universally required, the developed nations have to constantly help the undeveloped and underdeveloped nations to meet their needs. Plans at UNO must be based upon estimates of world population. And in fact this is actually being done. For example, the 1981 State of the World Population Report from the United Nations Fund for Population Activities (UNFPA) says that if the division of the world's wealth remains the same as it is today, the developing world will end in having 90 per cent of the population while the 10 per cent population of developed countries would control 80 per cent of the wealth. The report says that the number of people in the world today stands at 4.4 billion with an annual growth rate of 1.73 per cent. This growth rate is declining and has had to be revised—in 1973, an annual growth rate of 1.95 was projected for 1975-80, the 1978 projection brought it down to 1.81 per cent and the latest assessment, made this year, has it down to 1.73 per cent.

"Such a small revision of the growth rate might appear inconsequential but its significance lies in confirming the probably irreversible downward trend in global population growth," the report says. Thus, by extrapolating the present trends, it is now estimated that the population could be just over 6 billion at the end of the century, and 10.5 billion by 2110 when growth would come to a halt.

How will the world be fed? The average amount of grain marketed in the world each year is about 1300 million tonnes. Working on an average daily need of 2,300 calories per person—ranging between 820 calories a day for a baby and 2,500 calories a day for a 16-year-old male—225 kilogrammes of grain per year are needed for every person on earth. The present average annual tonnage of 1300 million is sufficient to feed more than 6 billion people—more than one-and-half times the present population. Further, recent studies reveal that the earth can sustain the production of 25 times as much foodgrain—32 billion tonnes — every year.

Yet, in 1981, about 450 million people did not have adequate food, 1200 million did not have adequate water, sanitation or health care and over 100 million 6 to 11 year-old had no school to go to. Around one-third of the world's workforce is either unemployed or not earning enough to meet their own and their family's demands. The root of the hunger problem, therefore, is that of distribution. For example, 36 out of the 40 poorest and hungriest nations export food to North America. Africa, the hungriest continent, exports protein to Europe. From the view of the developing countries, where the need for smaller families is the greatest, demographer James Kocher wrote: "The essential change which must take place before people in low income countries want smaller families is that children must become economic liabilities rather than economic assets."

Thus, the development plans for the world, as envisaged by the different agencies of UNO are based upon projections about the future growth of population. Such projections concerning the more developed and less developed regions have been made by

Population Division of UNO, to form the basis of future economic planning and development of the world. One such projection is given below:

TABLE 2.1

United Nations Medium Variant Projections, 1970-2000

(in billions)

Region	*1970*	*1980*	*1990*	*2000*
World population	3.61	4.37	5.28	6.25
More developed regions	1.09	1.18	1.28	1.36
Less developed regions	2.52	3.19	4.00	4.89

The above table shows how demography and world population planning are interrelated. Such projections have been made in India by the national demographers. They have again and again pointed out to the need of population planning.

Planning of Medical Health in India

A joint conference of the Central Council of Health and the Central Council of Family Welfare was held from 15 June, 1981 to 18 June, 1981. This three-day conference was concerned with a National Health Policy keyed to the goal of "Health for All by 2000 AD.", through primary health care. It also discussed how to build up a health information system to provide the necessary base line data for the planning of various national health programmes. The important items on the agenda of the conference were:

1. Preparation of a plan of operation for achieving the goal of Health for All by 2000 AD.
2. A national medical and health education policy within the framework of the national health policy.
3. Reorientation of medical education in the light of the proposed national medical and health policy.
4. Consideration of the draft population policy.
5. Implementation of the school health check-up and health education programmes.
6. Ways to control communicable diseases like malaria, leprosy and TB more effectively and the control of blindness.
7. Greater involvement of the practitioners of the traditional systems of medicine and homoeopathy in the health-care system.

8. Prevention of drug abuse.
9. Ethical consideration involved in research on human subjects.
10. A long range policy relating to the integration of the modern system of medicine and the various indigenous systems.

A working group was set up by the Planning Commission as a prelude to the above conference and prepare a report on future status of health in India. The group presented its report which was published on March 25, 1981 under the title, "Health for All by 2000 AD." Here are some fragments from the group's vision of life in India in 2000 AD. when its health projections come true. Indians born in 2000 AD. can expect to have an average life span of 64 years, a 12-year leap from 52 years now. In the year 2000, the death rate will come down to 9 per 1000 from 14.1. Infant mortality will fall from 33 to 21. Most children will be immunised against the major diseases. Almost all men and women wall be given cover against major communicable diseases like malaria, leprosy and tuberculosis. All school children will get health coverage. And every Indian will get water which is safe to drink.

How much will it cost India to achieve health for all by 2000 AD? Nobody seems to know. The group has not given any estimate, but it will be a stupendous sum. The Health Ministry says that to achieve this goal, ₹ 30,000 crores will be needed for the health components in the minimum needs programme alone. Providing safe drinking water and sanitation will cost ₹ 16,000 crores. And there are many other health and family welfare programmes on which large amounts will have to be spent.

Can India really achieve health for all by 2000 — the health goal which the world accepted at Alma Ata in September, 1978? A spokesman for the Union Health Ministry says: "If not in all sectors, in the crucial sectors we can achieve the goals by more efficient use of current resources — if the political will is there, and sustained commitment which is totally lacking."

The spokesman says the best thinking about health for the all exercise is that "for the first time we have a slogan for health and a crude document which can be continually refined."

There are others who feel that the goal is achievable. The Expert Committee which produced the document "Health for All:

an Alternative Strategy," in the year 1980 said that health for all could be achieved by 2000 AD, if the right strategy was adopted.

A health expert says it is not difficult to achieve. Quite a lot of it has already been achieved by Kerala. But to achieve this goal four things will be necessary: radical changes in the administrative set-up of the health services, a firm political commitment, adequate funds and their proper spending.

But the real situation was probably summed up by Health Ministry official when this point was raised the other day: "Perfection is something to be aimed at, however difficult it may be to gain it."

The above discussion about medical care and health for all policy in India shows that much has to be done in this direction as yet. Some progress is obvious. For example, the percentage of women between the ages of 15 and 44 who practiced family planning have gone up from 8 in 1969 to 23 in 1979. Improved levels of nutrition, health and education, particularly among women is required for effective lower birth rate. So far India has got 84 million dollars family planning aid and spent the equivalent of 60 million dollars from its own resources on family planning.

QUESTIONS FOR EXERCISE

1. Define Demography and discuss its scope.
2. What are the objectives of Demography? Explain the scope and aspects of Social Demography.
3. What is the importance of Demography? Show in the context of national and international scene.
4. Write short note on Planning Medical Health in India.

3

Relationship with Other Studies

The study of human population is known as population studies or Demography. Literally speaking, population studies means studies concerned with population. The term demography, on the other hand, has been derived from the Latin term *Demos* meaning people, therefore demography is the science of population. Some scholars have distinguished between these two terms. For example, Philip M. Hauser and Otis Dudley Duncan have distinguished between what they call, "Demographic Analysis", and "Population Studies". They point out that "Demographic analysis is confined to a study of the components of population variation and change," whereas "population studies are concerned not only with population variables but also with the relationships between population changes and other variables—social, economic, political, biological, genetic, geographical and the like."[1] According to United Nations Multilingual Demographic Dictionary, the term "demography" may be used in a narrow sense, as synonymous with "demographic analysis" or "formal demography", which is "primarily concerned with quantitative relations among demographic phenomena in abstraction from their association with other phenomena."[2]

On the other hand, most of the population scholars do not favour any distinction between the terms demography and population studies. This is particularly applicable to contemporary

---

1. Philip M. Hauser and Otis Dudley Duncan (Eds.), *The Study of Population*, Chicago: the University of Chicago Press, 1959, p. 2.
2. United Nations, *Multilingual Demographic Dictionary*, Population Studies No. 29, 1958, p. 3.

scholars. For example, Donald J. Bogue criticises the artificial distinction made between demography and population studies.[1] According to Lorimer, "a demographer limited to the merely formal treatment of changes in fertility, mortality and mobility would be in a position like that of a 'formal chemist' observing the compression of mercury with no information about associated changes in temperature or the constitution of the liquid .... The concept of 'pure demography' except as the skeleton of science is therefore an illusion."[2] Therefore the study of population today is considered to be interdisciplinary and there is nothing like pure demography. In this branch of knowledge, as it is being taught in Indian universities today, hardly any distinction is made between these two terms.

Population Problems

The most important population problems have been summarised by Warren S. Thompson as follows:

1. What are the changes that are taking place in the size of the population, and how are these changes brought about? What is the significance of these changes from the standpoint of human welfare?
2. Where are people found and what are the changes taking place in their distribution in communities and in areas?
3. What kind of people are found in any given population group and how do those in one group differ from those in the other?[3]

Thus, the chief population problems are concerning the size, the distribution and the traits of population. According to John Graunt, demographical studies are natural and political observations. He dedicated his observations to (1) The President of Royal Society of Philosophers "as it relates to Natural History and as it depends on the Mathematics of my Shop-Arithmetic", and (2) a member of the Privy Council "as it relates to Government and Trade". William Petty named the newly-founded discipline, as "Political Arithmetique". Thus, demography is closely related

1. Donald J. Bogue, *Principles of Demography*, New York: John Wiley and Sons Ltd., 1969, p. 4.
2. Frank Lorimer, in Philip M. Hauser and Otis Dudley Duncan (Eds.), The Study of Population, p. 165.
3. Warren S. Thompson, *Population Problems, New York*: McGraw Hill, 1953, p. 1.

with political science, economics, mathematics and statistics. Besides, some recently developed social sciences including sociology and social psychology have very much influenced demographical studies. Demography and population studies form a part of university syllabi in Economics and Sociology. Again, Demography is also closely related with geography, anthropology and law besides the biological sciences.

DEMOGRAPHY AND BIOLOGY

Pointing out the intimate relationship between Demography and Biology Hutchinson and Devy called Biology as Biodemography. This was also supported by thinkers like Malthus. It was pointed out that the birth rate is influenced by density of population. The study of races and ethnic groups is the subject matter of both Biology and Demography. Both utilise data concerning life-span and nutrition, etc. Biological laws very much function in the field of Demography. This is particularly in the form of influence of Ecology.

Human Ecology is concerned with population, environment technique and organization. Thus, Demography is a part of the wide study of human ecology. According to P.W. Frank, "Ecology as a delimited discipline must not be expected to provide specific theoretical statements about human population. Even so, it is probable that ecology can function effectively in combination with related disciplines to produce a measure of integration for the ordering of human data."[1]

Thus, the close relationship between ecology and demography can be summed up in the following words of Otis Duncan, "Human ecology provides a general perspective, heuristic principles and concepts and specific hypotheses of first rate significance to demography."[2]

DEMOGRAPHY AND GEOGRAPHY

A particular branch of geography concerned with human ecology and behaviour is known as Human Geography. This branch is intimately related with demography. It particularly studies the distribution of population according to geographical conditions. In the words of Edward Ackerman, "Recent geographers have

1. Frank, P.W., *op. cit.*, p. 673.
2. Otis, Duncan, *The Study of Population*, p. 678

taken the cultural features of the earth, analysed them generically and genetically in their space relations and established covariant relations of cultural features with each other and with those of the physical and biotic environment. These distributional features are common both to demography and geography."[1] Therefore the distribution of population in different parts of the world is dissimilar and mostly governed by geographical conditions. In the words of G. I. Trewartha, "...numbers, densities and qualities of the population provide the essential background for all geography. Population is the point of reference from which all other elements are observed and from which they all singly and collectively derive significance and meaning." Thus, population is always studied within a definite geographical area. Pointing out the intimate influence of demography E. Ackerman, writes, "Geography can seek understanding of the evolution of earth's distributions in operation of at least eight different physical, biotic and cultural processes: movement of the soil mantle; movement of water overland; climate; biotic processes, particularly vegetative demographic movement; organizational evolution; development of resources, converting techniques and development of space adjusting techniques. Demographic movement is at the heart of these forces which influence the change in space content."[2]

DEMOGRAPHY AND SOCIOLOGY

Pointing out the areas of intimate relation of demography and sociology Davis has referred to the following areas: "(1) Fertility in connection with attitudes and social institutions; (2) Population changes in relation to social and economic change; (3) The labour force with respect to population structure and social organization; and (4) The family with regard to demographic behaviour."[3] He further points out to two other areas of study where a knowledge of sociology and demography has to be combined. These are internal migration and international migration.[4] According to Broom and Selznick, demography is one of the nine principle elements of

1. Edward Ackerman, *Geography and Demography*, a Hauser and Duncan's book: The Study of Population (1961), P. 724.
2. *ibid.*,p 124. :
3 Kingsley Davis, "*The Sociology of Demographic Behaviour*" in Robert K. Merton, Leonard Broom and Leonard S. Cottrell Jr., (Eds.) *Sociology Today: Problems and Prospects*: New York: Basic Books, 1959, p. 314.
4 *Ibid.*, p.314.

sociological analysis for the discussion of six special topics such as family, city, minorities and industrial sociology, political sociology and criminal behaviour. These authors conclude, "It, therefore, appears that along with social organization, culture, socialisation, primary groups, social stratification, associations, collective behaviour and ecology, population is an important element in sociological analysis."[1]

Thus, the intimate relation between sociology and demography may be found in the following areas:

(1) Population not only depends upon birth rate and death rate but is also influenced by socialization, education and social system. Population is the group of social beings, whereas society is formed of population.

(2) Population growth very much depends upon relationship between birth rate and death rate. Birth rate depends upon sexual intercourse between the male and female which, in its tom, is determined by social norms, customs and traditions, Therefore, population growth is not merely a biological phenomena but also a social one.

(3) Death rate is also influenced by social factors. Growth in per capita income and national income, scientific progress and equitable distribution considerably lessen death rate.

The above discussion of the intimate relation between sociology and demography should not lead us to forget their distinction. It should be remembered that whereas demographical study is mainly statistical, sociology involves qualitative analysis., In demography a society is studied as a type, whereas in sociology it is studied as a system. Therefore, one will agree with the words of Wilbert E. Moore when he says, "Treating demographic variables as exogenous to social systems involves a mode of abstraction. However, the insistence that demographic variables operate in a social matrix need not blind us to some independent variability.[2]

DEMOGRAPHY AND ANTHROPOLOGY

Treating demography as a part of anthropology, Oxford Universal Dictionary prescribes, "Demography is that part of anthropology which treats of the statistics of births, deaths, disease, etc." Physical

1. Leonard Broom and Phillip Selznick (Eds.), *Sociology*, New York : Harper and Row, 1965, p. 10.
2. Wilbert E. Moore, *Sociology and Demography*, Hauser and Duncan, *op. cit*.

anthropologists today study birth rate, death rate, migration and marriage, etc., in a particular population. They are very much concerned with the development of primates and the classification of Living Varieties. Most of the anthropologists define population variation in terms of on-going biological differentiation and gene frequency. According to them mutation, selection, gene-flow, random genetic drift and selective mating are very much a part of heredity, a subject matter of demography. Besides, contemporary anthropologists are interested in the demographical subjects of procreation, death, marriage, migration, form and organization of population, etc., since these variables are useful in the study of genetic changes.[1] In spite of this close relationship between demography and anthropology, one finds a clear distinction in their scope, methods, subject matter, attitude and what not. The anthropologists, unlike the demographers, study only some particular types of population. The demographers on the other hand, study world population in its multifarious aspects. While the approach of anthropologists is anthropological, the approach of demographers is mathematical and statistical. Therefore, the distinction between the two intimately related social sciences is obvious.

DEMOGRAPHY AND ECONOMICS

The study of population is a valuable area in the field of economics. The study of population trends and economic growth is closely related. The relationship of demography and economics is particularly explicit in the fields of population and development; manpower studies: the economics of fertility; and comprehensive economic-demographic models.[2] According to Ian Bowen the number and quality of the population that may exist on the earth in the future will very much depend upon economic opportunities and economic organisation. Population growth, size and distribution cannot be discussed rationally except in the context of economic growth or change.[3]

Demography and economics are therefore particularly related through economic variables such as rate of population growth, age, sex, educational level, profession, per capita income and

1. J.B. Birdsell, 1950, Some Implications of the Genetical Concept of Race in Terms of Spatial Analysis, *Quantitative Biology, VX, 259-314.*
2. United Nations, *The Determinants and Consequences of Population Trends, p. 7.*
3. Ian Bowen, *Economics and Demography*, London : George Allen and Unwin Ltd., 1976, p. 130.

national income, etc. All these are interconnected. Similarly education and distribution of occupations influence population. Again migration, both emigration and immigration, create widespread economic changes.

The influence of population upon economics is more glaring in developing and undeveloped countries. Its influence is not so much visible in developed countries such as USA and the countries of Western Europe. However, no one can deny that population growth creates demand and influences economic factors including labour supply, employment and investment, etc.

According to Professor Hansen, the decreasing growth of population and exploration into new areas of habitation influence the possibilities of investment in the economic market. Henderson has pointed out that population poses serious economic and social problems. It is the chief cause of retarding the pace of economic progress and the supply of labour. Therefore, G. Myrdal has considered the growth of population as the first condition for economic development. If the population constantly decreases enterprise becomes more risky and consequently, the pace of economic development becomes slow.[1] The influence of population on economic development has been analysed in the Theory of Demographic Transition. This theory was presented by Warren S. Thomson and Frank Notestein. According to this principle, as a result of economic development the growth of population has to pass through rapid increase, explosion and stability, etc. Thus, the growth of population makes far reaching economic changes. The relation between demography and economics is therefore the closest. However, the two are at present independent social sciences.

DEMOGRAPHY AND LAW

The laws of a country are also concerned with the problems of population. For example, some laws are formulated to check the overgrowth of population. The laws of population and the state laws are interrelated. Defining population laws, S. Chandrasekhar has called them as, "That body of law which relates directly or indirectly to the three basic demographic variables of fertility, mortality and migration and their various components, which in turn affect the more general problems of the size, growth and

1. G. Myrdal: *Population—A Problem of Democracy*, p. 164.

distribution of the population."[1] Further, explaining the influence of population laws, the same scholar maintains that these could relate to, "Public health and sanitation; food preparation, distribution and sale; drugs and pharmaceuticals; clinics, hospitals and medical personnel; migration, marriage, fertility, child care, and all aspects of education and the role and status of women."[2] An illustration of the influence of demography on law can be found in the Indian Medical Termination of Pregnancy Act, 1972 and other such acts concerned with fertility, etc.

DEMOGRAPHY AND MATHEMATICS

The intimate relationships of demography and mathematics is based upon the facts that population studies require qualification of data. Demography studies the size, growth, structure and components of population with the help of mathematics. The study and understanding of population, therefore, depends upon mathematical tools and models. Most of the census studies and their results are communicated in mathematical terms. This can be seen in the data concerning decennial census surveys in India.

DEMOGRAPHY AND STATISTICS

Whatever has been said about the close relationships of demography and mathematics is equally applicable to the relationships of demography and statistics. It is a historical fact that the development of demography in 19th and 20th centuries was very much a result of development of the science of statistics during this period. For example, the statistical theory of probability has been very much useful in the analysis of mortality, the actuarial science has been useful in the preparation of life-tables.

DEMOGRAPHY AND PSYCHOLOGY

Among social sciences demography is closely connected with psychology, besides sociology and economics. Questions particularly connected with reproductive behaviour are psychological questions since psychology is the science of human behaviour.

---

1. S. Chandrasekhar, *Population and Law in India*, Bombay, Blackie and Son (India) Limited, 1976 p. 51.
2. *Ibid.*, p. 50..

Family planning and regulation of fertility in a particular society is very much influenced by social and cultural environment. The family size in a community is very much determined by the social laws. Thus, population growth is very much influenced by psychological factors. In the fields of public health, mortality and migration also psychological factors are very important. Migration from rural to urban areas influences distribution of population. All these factors exhibit the close relation between demography and psychology. These sciences utilise mathematical models and statistical tools. However, the attitude and the objective as well as the scope of the two is very much different. The relationship of demography and psychology can be particularly seen in some fields of psychology such as social psychology, industrial psychology, business psychology, differential psychology and psychology of adjustment, etc. A sound knowledge of these branches of psychology will be useful in the understanding of the growth and distribution of population. It will be particularly useful in successful inducement of birth control. Therefore, modern governments do not blindly impose family planning upon the public but give psychological inducements.

QUESTIONS FOR EXERCISE

1. Distinguish between Demography and Population studies. Explain important population problems.
2. Discuss the relationship of Demography with Biology, Geography and Sociology.
3. Explain the relationship of Demography with Anthropology and Economics.
4. Show the relationship of Demography with any two of the following:

   (*i*) Law, (*ii*) Mathematics, (*iii*) Statistics, and (*iv*) Psychology.

4

Theories of Population

A theory of population is an explanation of the phenomenon of population growth. It tries to explain the rise and fall, the growth and decrease of population in different countries. It surveys the trends and analyses the causes of the various stages in the curve of population. Based upon data in one or more particular countries, a population theory seeks to generalise about the laws of population. It tries to unravel the first principles of demographical process. Though systematic theories of population have evolved very recently, theorising about population is sufficiently old. In ancient times statesmen and thinkers tried to control population according to the availability of means or to encourage it if required. The criteria for encouraging or discouraging were the military, political, social and economic issues. This is true about population theory even now. The problem of population is not worked out in vacuum. It is always considered in the context of economic, social and political issues. Of these the economic issue is the most important, since the most important problem concerning population is to meet the needs of the growing population. The history of population theories has been classified on the basis of before and after the advent of Mathus, the celebrated demographer. Thus, the periods are classified as Pre-Malthusian, Malthusian and Post-Malthusian periods. These periods show thinking about population theories. But even before these some early thinking can be discerned about population problems.

EARLY THINKING ON POPULATION

Most of the thinking in the West started with the Greek thinkers, in the Greek scheme of life, the individual was a part of the state. The purpose of marriage was procreation. Wars required a continuous demand of soldiers. Therefore, procreation was encouraged and even rewarded by Greeks and the Romans. The Spartans and the Athenians encouraged population due to expansionist policy. They also tried to avoid overpopulation and encouraged abortions and even infanticides. The idealist Greek thinkers tried to estimate optimum population. According to Plato (427-347 BC) a city state should have 5040 citizens so that highest good may be achieved. In this ideal population Plato did not include women, children and slaves. Including them the total population of an ideal city state in Plato's time was about 50,000. Plato also did not overlook the possibility that the demographic ideals may not be followed. Therefore, he recommended infanticide on the grounds of Eugenics. In order to control population and maintain its highest quality, Plato recommended selective breeding among human beings. He recommended that the age of marriage for the girls should be between 16 and 20. Marriage was made compulsory. The peculiar number of 5040, according to Jowett, is based upon numerology. According to Hutchinson, "it was simply to aid in maintaining an even division of property."[1] Plato's ideal on population, as expressed in his *Laws*, were based on the ideal of city state.

After Plato, Aristotle (348-322 BC) maintained that fast population growth leads to increase in poverty and suggested abortions and. infanticides, in order to control the size of the city state. He also proposed family planning to be prescribed by the state. Thus, the Greek thinkers insisted both on proper quantity and quality of population.

Besides Greeks, the Romans also thought over population issues. They encouraged procreation and made marriage compulsory. Those who did not marry were burdened by several disabilities.

PRESCRIPTIONS OF GREAT RELIGIONS

Most of the ancient thinkers were influenced by their religions. Religion had a hold on thinking in ancient time. Therefore, in order to understand the early thinking on population issues it is necessary to cast of glance on the prescriptions of great religions on population issues. This is particularly true about early Indian

---

1. Hutchinson, E. P., *The Population Debate: The Development of Conflicting Theory Upto 1900*. Boston: Houghton Mifflin Company, 1967, PP. 12-13.

thinking. Hindu thinking on population issues was guided by the Dharmasastras.

1. Hindu Religion: Hindus have prescribed marriage as almost compulsory. According to the Dharmasastras, no one can go to heaven without procreating a son. In order to conduct religious activities every man needed a wife by his side. The household Ashram was considered as the basis of the entire social structure. Thus, most of the males and females centred Grahastha Ashram after completing Brahmacharya Ashram. The Hindu marriage aimed at the three fold ideal: fulfilment of Dharma, procreation and sex enjoyment. Of these, procreation was considered most important. The birth of a son was the ideal but sometimes one finds prayers for the birth of a daughter since Kanyadan was also a source of religious gains. Fertility was praised and encouraged so much so that the newly married couples were blessed for having eight sons and five daughters. From the political and economic viewpoint, the Arthasastra of Kautilya has recommended large population for military and economic gains. Thus, the Hindu Shastras have everywhere encouraged growth of population. Therefore, there is hardly any wonder that in India population multiplied fast.

2. Judaism: One finds an oft quoted injunction to Adam and Eve in the sacred books of lews, "Be fruitful and multiply and replenish the earth. Thus Judaism deplores childlessness and admires fertility. It is true about the Jews even now considering the small number of their followers as compared to the number of followers of the great religions.

3. Christianity: In the world today, Christianity commands maximum number of followers. This is not only due to the greatness of Christianity but also their encouragement of fertility like any other great religion. From the moral viewpoint the Christian saints eulogised celibacy like the Hindu thinkers and marriage was sometimes regarded as a necessary evil However, as a general rule marriage was blessed by the priests.

4. Islam: The most populationistic great religion is the Islam. It is both because it prescribes polygamy and also encourages procreation. According to the Fatwa of Sheikh Abdullah Al-qualquili, "Marry the affectionate prolific woman, for I shall be proud of you among the nation."[1] The ideal of marriage was procreation. It is interesting to note that Ibn Khaldoun (1332-1460 B.C.) was of the opinion that a densely settled population helped to achieve more division of labour, more utilisation of resources and ensured military and political security. He, however, also pointed out that the vicious circle of population growth leads to luxurious living which in turn causes economic depression and ultimately depopulation.[2] The Muslim tradition recommends marriage with four women at one time, and the fifth could always be married by divorcing one of the four at short notice. Therefore, the economically well of section procreated at a high rate. The Muslim population has grown fast in almost every country, including India, due to Islam's encouragement to population growth.

PRE-MALTHUSIAN THEORIES

This period is calculated from the beginning of 16th century to the end of 18th century. It was a period of rapid thinking in all aspects of human life. Thinking on economy and population was particularly influenced by exploration of routes from West to East, discovery of America, rise of Capitalism, collapse of feudal system and the emergence of Imperial powers like British, French. Portugese and Spanish. The following landmarks can be traced in pre-Malthusian period:

1. The Mercantilist School: This has been considered as a link between medieval and modern economic thought. It aimed at increasing national wealth and power resulting in rivalry and competition. Therefore, the size of the population was considered an asset from the point of view of war, supply of labour and utilisation of national resources. Hence, as Eli Heckscher has pointed out, "An almost frantic desire to increase population prevailed in all countries.[3] The general opinion during this period favoured increased birth rates. The increase of birth rates was to be gained by procreation on the one hand and, on the other hand, by the adoption of such measures as (*a*) placing various disabilities on celibates; (*b*) encouraging marriages directly;

1. "Fatwa", Sheikh Abdullah Al-qualquili, *Muslim Attitudes towards Family Planning*, New York: The Population Council, 1967, p. 3.
2. United Nations, *The Determinants and Consequences of Population Trends*, p. 35.
3. Heckscher, Eli F. *Mercantilism*, Vol. 2 London: Allen and Unwin, 1935, p. 158.

(*c*) encouraging fertility, (*d*) making punishment for illegitimate births less severe or abolishing such punishment entirely; and (*e*) encouraging immigration and preventing emigration.[1] The most important mercantile writers included Niceolo Machiavelli (1469-1527) and Giovanni Botero (1540-1617). Of these Machiavelli has been hailed as one of the precursors of Malthus. Botero was one of the first to study population scientifically. He was convinced that food for subsistence was necessary for any population. He, however, regarded large population a source of strength .

2. The Physiocratic School: As a reaction against the mercantilist ideas and policies, the physiocratic school of economic thought evolved in France about the middle of the 18th century. This school considered land as the source of all wealth. They did not favour population increase at the cost of standard of living. They approved only such increase which may be useful to expand agricultural production. This school was founded by Quesney (1694-1774). He maintained that a large population may be desirable only if it could be comfortably maintained. Another French economic thinker Mirabeau (1715-1789) maintained that agriculture must be encouraged to feed large population desirable for the state. Similar views were expressed by Merier de la Riviere and Cantillon.

3. The beginning of the Malthusian Theory: During this period it was more and more realised that population increases more rapidly than food supply. Therefore, the earlier optimism was gradually replaced by a pessimistic view resulting in the benevolent faith in means to control population. Among the most important writers during this period were Mathew Hale (1677), Robert Wallace (1687-1771), John Bruckner (1726-1804), James Steurt (1712-1780), and Joseph Townsend (1739-1816).

MALTHUSIAN THEORY OF POPULATION

Historical Review

The most important theory in the history of demography was presented by Thomas Robert Malthus (1766-1834). Among his most important works was his famous Essay on Population entitled: *An Essay on The Principe of Population as it Affects the Future Improvement of Society, with Remarks on the Speculations of*

1. Charles Emil Stangeland, *op. cit.*, pp. 123-137.

Mr. *Godwin, M. Condorcet And Others*. This essay was published anonymously. It, however, became one of the most controversial books of modern times, and brought both honour and criticism to the author. Its importance as a landmark in the history of population can be judged by the fact that the year of its publication is reckoned as the base year for the study of population doctrines.

As is clear by the title of the Essay, it was mainly directed against the optimistic views of William Godwin, an English philosopher and Marie Jean Antonie Condorcet, a French mathematician, economist and philosopher. Therefore, it is necessary to understand the view of these two persons before understanding Malthusian theory. According to Condorcet, "All inequalities of wealth, of education, of opportunity, of sex, would soon disappear. Animosities between nations and races would be no more. All persons would speak the same language. The earth would be bountiful, without stint. All diseases would be conquered, and if man did not become immortal, the span of his life would have no assignable upper limit. The question whether production would always suffice to satisfy" the people's wants could not be answered, for the problem would not-have to be faced for ages to come, by which time man would have acquired new types of now still unimagined knowledge. In the rational age to come, men would recognise their obligations to those not yet born and to the general well-being both of their society and of all humanity and ... not to the puerile idea of filling the earth with useless and unhappy beings. At the time, a limit could be set to the population other than by premature death of a portion of those born.[1]

William Godwin published his book *Enquiry Concerning Political Justice*, in 1793, which presented a Utopian ideal of perfect society. In this society, according to him, 'There will be no war, no crimes, no administration of justice as it is called, and no government."[2] Besides this, there will be neither disease, anguish, melancholy nor resentment. Every man will see with ineffable ardour the good of all.

This Utopian thesis was challenged by Malthus. He pointed out that the tendency of the population to grow faster than the means of subsistence gradually leads to human misery and creates

1. William Petersen, *The Politics of Population*, Garden city, New York : oubleday and Company 1965, pp. 32-33.
2. *Ibid.*, p. 33.

impediments in the path of progress. He laid more emphasis on criticism of the Poor Laws in the 2nd edition of his Essay published in 1803. This edition contained substantial statistical data in support of arguments. It proposed moral constraints as a preventive against rapid growth of population. Next five years in the life of Malthus were devoted to collection of further statistical data and study of the writings of other authors. In 1826 was published the 6th edition of the work of Malthus now entitled; *An Essay on the Principle of Population or a View of its Past and Present Effects on Human Happiness, with an Inquiry into our Prospects Respecting the Future Removal or Mitigation of the Evils which it Occasions.* In 1872 was Published the 7th edition of the Essay.

The Central Theme

Malthus started his Essay by laying down two postulates: "First, that food is necessary to the existence of man." "Secondly, the passion between the sexes is necessary and will remain nearly in its present state,"[1] He argued, "Assuming then my postulate as granted, say that the power of population is definitely greater than the power in the earth to produce subsistence for men. Population, when unchecked increases in a geometrical ratio. Subsistence increases only in an arithmetical ratio. A slight acquaintance with numbers will show the immensity of the first power in comparison with the second."[2] The following propositions were put forth by Malthus, to establish his theory: "(1) Population is necessarily limited by the means of subsistence; (2) Population invariably increases where the means of subsistence increase unless prevented by some very powerful and obvious checks; (3) These checks, and the checks which repress the superior power of population and its effects on a level with the means of subsistence, are all resolvable into moral restraint, vice and misery."[3] Therefore, Malthus concluded, "Taking the whole earth — the human species would increase as the numbers 1, 2, 4, 8, 16, 32, 64, 128, 256 and the subsistence as numbers 1, 2, 3, 4, 5, 6, 7, 8, 9. In two centuries, the population would be to the means of subsistence as 256 to 8 ... "[4] Malthus recognised that the growth of population does not go unchecked. Pointing out powerful checks on the growth of

1. Malthus, *An Essay of Population*, Royal Economic Society, 1798, p. 11.
2. *Ibid.*, p. 11
3. *Ibid.*
4. Malthus, *An Essay on the Principle of Population*, 7th Edition, 1872, Book I, Chapter I.

population, he said, "The first of these, checks may, with propriety, be called the preventive check to population, and the absolute necessity of their operation in the case supposed is as certain and obvious as that man cannot live without food."[1] Now in order to check the preventive checks such as epidemics, wars and famines, Malthus suggested moral restraints as the best preventive check. He described it as, "Abstinence from marriage, either for a time or permanently, from prudential consideration, with a strictly moral conduct towards the sex in the interval. And this is the only mode of keeping population on a level with the means of subsistence which is perfectly consistent with virtue and happiness."[2] Vice was described as, "a sort of-intercourse which renders some of the women of large towns unprolific,"[3] such as prostitution and extra-marital sexual relations. The preventive checks were necessary in order to avoid positive checks which tended to shorten human life. These positive checks have been described by Malthus: "Such as unwholesome occupations — severe labour and exposure to the seasons — bad and insufficient food and clothing arising from poverty — bad nursing of children — excesses of all kinds — great towns and manufactories — the whole train of common diseases and epidemics — wars, infanticide, plague, famine."[4] Malthus was against poor laws since he considered poverty as an evil. He classified positive checks also into two categories: "The first were those brought about by natural causes and labelled as 'Exclusively misery', such as epidemics, famines etc., the other positive checks were those which mankind brought upon itself by itself such as wars and all types of excesses which could have been avoided."[5]

Evaluation of the Theory

Malthusian Theory, as we have already pointed out, has been acclaimed as an Epoch-making theory. It was a landmark in the history of population which divided the history into two periods: before it and after it. Though some of the ideas were known earlier, Malthus presented them in a larger framework. He examined the interrelationship between population growth and economic

1. Malthus, "A Summary View of the Principle of Population" in David Glass (Ed.), *Introduction to Malthus*, op. cit., p. 114.
2. *Ibid.*, p. 153.
3. *Ibid.*
4. *Ibid.*
5. *Ibid.*, p. 154.

and political developments. His style of writing was polished and authoritative with a philosophical touch. He never claimed originality but only more systematisation. According to Kenneth Smith, the success of Malthus may be attributed to the opportune circumstances and the political climate prevailing in his time.[1] Disillusioned by the French revolution, the intellectuals of his time supported his theory. His economic message was welcomed. The optimism of his predecessors paled before his realistic pessimism. According to Kenneth Smith, "Malthus offered a scientific pessimism which, gloomy and fatalistic though it was towards the hopes of the working classes, absolved the ruling classes from the need to make futile efforts on their behalf."[2] His plea for the abolition of poor laws naturally appealed to many persons. His doctrines were convenient to the rulers who were always afraid of the growing poverty.

Criticism

However, the theory of Malthus was subjected to harsh criticisms as well. Kautsky, one of his bitterest critics, accused him of plagiarism and said, "It was as correct to name the new population theory after Malthus as to name America after Amerigo Vespucci. Both did no more than to spread the news of what others had discovered."[3] It is undeniable that many of the ideas put forward by Malthus were already anticipated by Machiavelli, Sir Walter Raleigh, Francis Bacon, John Graunt, William Petty, Sir Matthew Hale, Benjamin Franklin, Saxe, Joseph Townsend, Sussmilch, Sir James Stuart, Hume, Robert Wallace, Arthur Young Archdeacon, Paley and others.[4] Some writers even used abusive language and more bitter criticisms. While criticising Malthus very harshly, Karl Marx referred to him as one who, "have taken the monastic vow of celibacy".[5] It may be noted in this connection that Malthus was married and had three children. The criticisms such as this were obviously based upon misconceptions and ignorance. However, the weakest point in the theory of Malthus was the ratio between the arithmetical and the geometrical progressions. According to Kenneth Smith this ratio was never really proved. It was pointed out that the theory that the population would double

1. Kenneth Smith, *op. cit.*, p. 33.
2. Ibid., p. 34.
3. As quoted in E. P. Hutchinson, *op. cit.*, p. 154.
4. Kenneth Smith, *op. cit.*, pp. 7-32.
5. Karl Marx, *Capital, Chicago*: Kerr, 1906, Vol. 1, pp. 675-76.

in a period of 25 years was based upon the evidence of doubtful American statistics in which the role of Immigration in the North American population was completely rejected.[1] According to E.P. Hutchinson the idea of arithmetical ratio concerning the growth of the means of subsistence was unanimously rejected by scholars. As a general rule the following points were raised as criticism against Malthusian theory:

1. As has been already pointed out, the ratio of arithmetical progression of means of subsistence and the geometrical progression of population growth was never proved.
2. In so many cases the theory of the growth of the means of subsistence in arithmetical ratio was not proved.
3. Malthus did not clearly distinguish between fecundity and fertility or the physiological capacity to reproduce and the actual reproductive performance.
4. The classification of checks on population growth as preventive and positive were cited as an example of poor classification, since they were not independent categories.
5. Malthus did not succeed in connecting positive and preventive checks with his theory.
6. Malthus placed undue emphasis on the limitation of the supply of land. Agricultural production tremendously increased through agricultural revolution in the 19th century.
7. Malthus painted a too gloomy picture of the future growth of population. According to Ralph Thomlinson, his predictions did not come out to be true due to agricultural revolution.[2]
8. Malthus underestimated the importance of industrial development in increasing means of subsistence.
9. The religious belief of Malthus, according to Ralph Thomlinson prevented him from understanding the possibility of the widespread use of contraceptives.
10. According to Eversley, Malthus did not utilise the 1831 census data of England.[3] According to him Malthus did not make any sign cant contribution to social thought.

---

1. Sydney Coontz, *Population Theories and Economic Interpretation*, London: Routledge and Kegan Paul, 1968, p. 25.
2. Ralph Thomlinson, *Population Dynamics*, New York: Random House, 1965, p. 56.
3. Eversley, B.E.C., *Social Theories of Fertility and the Malthusian Debate*, Oxford Clarendon Press, 1959, pp. 256-257.

11. One finds a contradiction in the twin role of Malthus as a scientist and as a moralist. His role as a scientist was vitiated by his attempts of opposing birth control.
12. He favoured postponement of marriage and even total abstinence.

In spite of the, above mentioned criticisms, Kingsley Davis has rightly maintained that though not empirically valid Malthusian theory was theoretically significant. His name occupies an important place in the history of population thought.[1] He was the first thinker who systematically and thoroughly applied inductive method to social science. Though by 1900 his main thesis was almost completely rejected, it was revived in the second decade of the 20th century. The wave subsided by 1934 but again revived after the 2nd World War. In evaluating the status of Malthusian theory in the history of demography, it will be best to conclude with Charles Emil Stangeland, who remarked: "Malthus's work was a great one written in an opportune time, and though it cannot lay claim to any considerable originality as far as the theories presented ate concerned, it was successful in that it showed more fully, perhaps more dearly, and certainly more effectively than had any previous attempt, that population depends on subsistence and its increase is checked by want, vice and disease as well as by more restraint or prudence."[2]

NEO-MALTHUSIANISM

Neo-Malthusians are the successors of Malthus. They were keen supporters of family planning movement. According to them Malthus was the first thinker who established that uncontrolled increase of population will Lead to poverty and therefore birth control must be popularised. Among the most important neo-Malthusian thinkers may be mentioned Mary Slopes of Great Britain and Margaret Sanger of U.S.A., besides so many supporters in Western Europe. These people popularised chemical and mechanical methods of birth control. The family planning

---

1. Kingsley davis, "Malthus and the Theory of Population." Paul F. Lazarsfeld and Morris Hosenberg (Eds.), '*The Language of Social Research*' New York: The Free press, 1955, p. 541.
2. Charles Emil Stangeland, *Pre-Malthusian Doctrines of Population: A Study in the History of Economic Theory*, New York, The Columbia University Press, 1904, p. 35.

movement gradually extended not only to the entire Western World but also to the countries of Asia and Africa continents.

According to Neo-Malthusianism, Malthus did not distinguish between sex desire and desire for children. Both these are fulfilled by the same physical organs. The sex desire also involves desire for reproduction. Neo-Malthusians however, do not accept this view. They reject the Malthusian theory that sex desire is identical with the desire for children. According to them sex desire is a natural and biological desire. It is the most powerful physical and psychological desire among the adults. Its repression leads to so many mental and physical evils. Desire for children, on the other hand, particularly depends upon social, moral and cultural values. It is not inherent but a product of socio-economic conditions. Fulfilment of sex desire is a must for normal and healthy life. The desire for children however, should be adjusted according to favourable or unfavourable circumstances. Only that woman should reproduce who is physically and mentally fit for the purpose. Males and females should be allowed to satisfy their sex desire without procreation. There is no moral evil in using chemical or mechanical means, of birth control to satisfy sex desire.

Neo-Malthusians acclaimed Malthus as their leader in family planning movement. However, the French economists did not agree with this idea. They pointed out that Malthus would have called modern means of birth control, "Unmitigated conjugal fraud". He would have declared them as anti-Christian and un-Godly. In his Essay on Population Malthus has pointed out that artificial means of birth control are much inferior as compared to natural restrictions such as self control. The Neo-Malthusians, on the other hand, maintain that in the second edition of his Essay, Malthus concluded that population cannot be controlled by moral restraint alone. Moral restraint is a means which cannot be expected to be practised by ordinary people. Therefore, in spite of himself Malthus was prepared to allow artificial means of birth control. The Neo-Malthusians have advanced the following arguments in favour of their artificial birth control movement:

1. Birth control is necessary to limit the family size in the context of available economic means, otherwise the standard of living will fall down considerably. Without limiting the family, it is impossible to bring up children properly and pay attention to their physical, mental and moral development.

2. Birth control is equally necessary to limit the burden on world economy. This has already reached its saturation point. Therefore, it has no more capacity to feed the additional growing number of world population.

3. Birth control is necessary on the ground of health and medical care as well.

4. Those who oppose the Neo-Malthusian approach maintained that birth control is unnatural. It is an undesirable interference in the working of the natural process. The sexual intercourse aims at child birth. Restriction upon child birth will therefore restrict the very aim of marriage. In answer to this objection Neo-Malthusians point out that if birth control is unnatural, the same can be said about wearing clothes since man is born nude and that is his natural condition. Then, why do we wear clothes? On the same grounds artificial birth control may be supported.

5. Another argument advanced against birth control is that it is immoral To this Neo-Malthusians point out that morality is a relative concept. Ethics is man-made. Human principles are never categorical and fixed. If a principle is useful from the social viewpoint, it may be accepted from the moral viewpoint as well Birth control is today a social necessity. It should be accepted as desirable without any sense of immorality.

History records that in spite of criticism and vehement opposition to the Neo-Malthusian theory of birth control, the message gradually spread in the West and also in the East. When Mary Stopes declared in England that women have a right to enjoy sex without child birth, she was threatened by the English Lords for what they oiled the misguiding of their women. Mary Stopes however, won her point. The feminist movement started by her not only spread over the entire British Island but also in Europe. Today, there is no controversy about the use of artificial birth control to check population growth. On the other hand, most of the governments in developing countries, like India are doing everything within their means to popularise the methods of artificial birth control. The feminist movement, spread all over the world, has also encouraged artificial birth control.

THE CLASSICAL SCHOOL OF THOUGHT

The classical theory of population was based upon the idea that the production, consumption and distribution of wealth are determined by economic laws. This school was founded by Adam Smith, followed by David Ricardo, Thomas Malthus, Nassau Senior, John Stuart Mill and J. B. Say. They were political economists and believed that economics functions better under a free and private initiative with keen competitions.

NEO-CLASSICAL SCHOOL

This school of thought placed more emphasis on mathematical economics and the analysis of the psychological background and consumer demands, decisions and actions. It was founded by William Jensons, Carl Manger and Leon Walrus. Among its notable leaders were Alfred Marshall, John Bates, Clark, Irving Fisher and Vilfredo Pareto.

Both the classical and neo-classical schools were concerned with an examination of the inter-relationships between population and production. This was a serious point of discussion. While according to some, increasing population resulted in increasing production, others maintained the opposite view. None of these views was conclusively proved due to lack of empirical and theoretical evidence. The issue appeared to be resolved by the formulation of the economic principle of diminishing returns in the second decade of the 19th century. This principle supported Malthusian theory. The classical economists accepted it as a natural law. In 19th century it was observed that the general being of the people and the population growth went hand in hand. This was contrary to Malthusian theory and the principle of diminishing return. John Stuart Mill and Henry Sidgwick pointed out that many countries would be better off with smaller numbers since their population had already reached the point of diminishing return. The economists Gray, Chanters, Bum and Wirth pointed out that increasing number of people stimulate production. Godwin, Ravenstone, Sadler, Almond, Scrope and Ricardo disproved the principle of diminishing return. According to Marshal, a neo-classical economist, this law was applicable particularly to agriculture and not to industry. It was realised that the total and the per capita production not only depend upon population but also upon resources, labour, capital and technology. It was pointed out that per capita income was inversely related to the number of population. It was the factor of capital which influenced the size and growth of the population. Thus, by the end of the 19th century, it was concluded that population variable was only one variable in the total economic system. The importance of population growth was therefore considerably diminished. 1 was even ignored by some writers. (Economic growth in the West kept pace with the population growth, negating the gloomy picture painted by Malthas. In this ferment of thinking about the relationship of population and production, the following points emerged:

1. Population is only one of the several factors affecting production, distinction and other human affairs.
2. The socio-economic phenomena in general and the effect of population phenomena in particular are far from simple.
3. A more cautious appraisal of the socio-economic role of population'is required. It has been recognised that productivity is affected by so many factors depending on the stage of economic development and the demographic situation.
4. The law of diminishing returns is applicable more to agricultural production and seldom to industrial production.
5. The population question cannot be considered only in relation to economics. It is also influenced by cultural factors. Therefore, it is a dependent variable, a product of so many influences.
6. The theory of optimum population has resolved the old debate about the consequences of large and growing population.

OPTIMUM POPULATION THEORY

The optimum population theory had its beginnings in the writings of Karl Winkelblech (1810-1865), a German Professor who classified nations into three categories according to the size of their population:

1. Under-populated nations, 2. Over-populated nations and, 3. Normal- populated nations. It was Edwin Caiman (1861-1935), an English economist, who used the concept optimum population,

as synonymous with the best possible population. According to him, at any given time, the population which can exist on a given extent of land, consistent with the greatest productiveness of industry at that time, is definite.[1] United Nations have defined the concept of optimum population, to mean the size of the population which results in the highest per capita income, the' highest productivity as measured in different manners, or the highest level of other less well-defined economic indicators, such as economic welfare, level of living, real income and, in some cases, employment."[2] While some writers have considered the concept too restrictive, most of the writers have accepted the idea. However, later developments provoked a critical re-examination of this theory. This theory Implied that the growth of population was beneficial upto a certain point, after which it becomes harmful. The following criticisms were levelled against this theory:

1. It is doubtful that the optimum point in the growth of population can ever be determined. The demographers have never agreed over this point.
2. The concept of optimum population is essentially a static concept, based upon the assumption that there is an optimum limit of technology, resources, foreign trade and social structure.

This theory was very popular in the second and third decades of the present century. It has been rightly concluded by Sauvey that this theory may be accepted not as an absolute theoretical concept but as a convenient tool.[3]

MARXIST SOCIALIST THEORY OF POPULATION

As has been already pointed out, Karl Marx-completely rejected Malthusian theory, as it did not fit in a socialist society. According to Karl Marx there can be no natural or universal law of population. According to him, "An abstract law of population exists for plants and animals only, and only in so far as man has not interfered with

1. Hutchinson, E. P., *The Population Debate: The Development of Conflicting Theories upto* 1900, p. 388.
2. United Nations, *The Determinants and Consequences of Population Trends, op. cit.*, p. 55.
3. Alfred Sauvey, *General Theory of Population, London*: Wicdenfeld and Nicolson, 1966, pp. 36-95.

them."[1] Again, "Every special historic mode of production has its own special laws of population, historically valid, within its limit alone. Thus, the population theory is peculiar to the capitalist system of production. It is inherent in the capitalist system and not in production. Engels maintained that under the capitalist system surplus population was linked with surplus capital. This state of affairs, according to socialist view, can be changed by social reorganisation. *Communist Manifesto* laid down the fundamentals of a socialist society. *Origin of the Family* emphasized the need for emancipation of women. The need of conscious control was emphasized. It was maintained that due to the superior status of women there will be slower growth of population in a socialist society. Later socialists however, supported responsible parenthood. According to them reproductive behaviour should be based upon complete harmony between the individual and the society. Since birth control contributes to the emancipation of women, it is accepted. Even abortions are permitted. The Marxist socialist theory of population is applicable to modern socialist countries of Europe where it is being practised and supported. Criticisms of this view have been obviously advanced by the thinkers of the capitalist society since in the capitalist countries the views of Marx and Lenin are not accepted.

BIOLOGICAL THEORIES OF POPULATION

Biological theories of population include: The Density Principle, The Diet Principle and other Theories. Though these theories have not been accepted by the demographers, however, a brief reference to them will not be out of context here.

The Density Principle

This principle was laid down by Michael Thomas Sadler (1730-,1835), an English political economist in his work entitled *The Law of Population.* This book presented the principle that fertility varies inversely with the density of population. The contradiction found in countries like Netherland, where both fertility and density were high, was explained by Sadler by pointing out a direct relationship between fertility and mortality. According to him, increasing fertility increases mortality which

1. As quoted in the United Nations, *The Determinants and Consequences of Population Trends, op. cit.*, pp. 46-47. '

in turn decreases fertility. This principle, however, has not been accepted by most of the demographers.

The Diet Principle

This was propounded by Thomas Doubleday (1790-1870), an English political economist in 1841, in his essay *The True Law of Population Shown to be Connected with the Food of People*. According to Doubleday poverty stimulates population growth since the diet of the poor is inadequate. On the other hand if the diet is sufficient one finds less fertility. It was pointed out that due to this principle one finds high fertility among Chinese, Irish and the Scotch and low fertility in France. Similar conclusions were reached by Josue de Castro in his book, *Geography of Hunger* in 1952, based upon the negative correlation between the protein content of the diet and the birth rate in a country. Most of the demographers, however, rejected this theory. Thomlinson remarked about Castro, "He might as well have considered the correlation between national fertility and consumption of ice cream, soda, use of washing machine or watching of television."[1]

Theory of Herbert Spencer

Herbert Spencer presented a theory of population on biological basis, in 1880. He pointed out that fertility increases in response to the progress of society. It is a great agency for the advancement of mankind. However, when population becomes excessive, it threatens the very existence of the human species. This requires control of population.

Theory of Corrado Gini

The Italian biologist Corrado Gini has recently presented a biological theory of population, known as the cyclical theory. According to Gini the population tends to follow an evolution similar to the life cycle of the individual. As the individual passes through the successive stages of development, maturation and involution, similar is the case, with the evolution of the human being. The biological theories have not been accepted as sufficient explanations of population since, as has been pointed out by social and cultural theories, social and cultural factors are equally important in the growth of population. Fertility is not a mere biological phenomena but very much influenced by social and cultural factors.

1. Ralph Thomlinson, *Population Dynamics*, p. 67.

MATHEMATICAL THEORIES

Development of mathematical techniques has encouraged formulation of mathematical laws of population growth. The mathematical approach to the study of population was first adopted by a Belgian astronomer Quetelet. Among the mathematical theories, the theory of logistic growth of population was developed 'by Verhulst. In United States it was propounded by Pearl and Reed. According to them the growth of population occurs in cycles. It was maintained that, "Within the cycle and in a specially limited area or universe, growth in the first half of the cycle starts slowly, but the absolute movement per unit of time increases steadily until the milk point of the cycle is reached. After this point, the increment per unit of time becomes steadily smaller untill the end of the cycle."[1] According to this theory, the total population follows an S-shaped curve. The law of logistic growth of population was acclaimed everywhere. It was found useful for estimating and projecting future population size. However, it was gradually widely questioned since it neglected socio-cultural and economic factors. It did not take into account the changes in the population growth which permit the population to exploit its resources effectively. It did not consider the changes in the aspirations and motivations concerning various patterns of fertility behaviour.

THEORY OF DEMOGRAPHIC TRANSITION

Demographic transition means the progress from one demographic condition to a different stage, for example in Western countries it was found that the population moved from a condition of high mortality and high fertility to conditions of low mortality and low fertility. Thus, the stage of high expansion of population itself leads to the stationary stage and *vice verse* Several demographers such as Landry in 1909 and Warren Thompson in 1929 attempted to construct a typology to describe demographic transition from conditions of high mortality and high fertility to the conditions of low mortality and low fertility. None of these demographers, however, made an attempt to explain these changes. In 1947 C. P. Blacker identified five phases of the demographic transition as follows:[2]

1. As explained in the United Nations, *Determinants and Consequences of Population Trends, op. cit.*, 52.
2. Blacker, C. P., "Stages in Population Growth", *The Eugenics Review*, Vol. 39. No. 3, October, 1947, pp. 88-101.

1. The high stationary stage characterised by high birth rates and high death rates.
2. The early expanding stage with falling birth rates but rapidly decreasing mortality.
3. The late expanding stage with falling birth rates but rapidly decreasing mortality.
4. The low stationary stage with low birth rates balanced by equally low mortality.
5. The declining stage with low mortality and deaths exceeding births.

It was Frank W. Notestein who, for the first time presented a theory of demographic transition in 1945 in a mature form with explanations for the changes in fertility. John Caldwell has therefore credited Notestein with expounding the theory of demographic transition."[1] According to Notestein, the rapid growth of population during the past three centuries was particularly due to the decline in the death rate, this decline resulted from the process of modernization. Modernization involved high standards of living, high incomes and advanced level of sanitation and medical knowledge, with the result that fertility registered a decline. By the middle of 1930 birth rates reached very low levels in Western countries. This was the result of widespread acceptance of contraceptive methods due to the ideal of small family prevalent in urban industrialised society. According to the stage of demographic evolution the population in different countries may be characterised into the following three types:

1. Incipient Decline: In this stage fertility falls below the replacement level. This stage could be seen in populations of Europe, The United States, Australia and New Zealand.

2. Transitional Growth: Notestein has explained this stage where, "Birth and death rates are still high and growth is rapid, but the decline of the birth rate is well established."[2]

3. High Growth Potentials: Notestein has defined this stage of population in these words: "Mortality is high and variable and is the chief determinant of growth, while fertility is high and

---

1. John Caldwell, "Towards a Restatement of Demographic Transition Theory", Population and Development Review, Vol. 2, Numbers 3 and 4, September/December, 1976, p. 323.
2. Frank W. Notestein, *Population: The Long View. op. cit.*, p. 41.

thus far has shown no evidence of a downward trend. In these populations, rapid growth is to be expected just as soon as technical developments make possible a decline in mortality."[1] Examples of this stage of population were pointed out in most of the countries of Asia, Africa and Latin America. According to George J. Stolnitz, "All nations in the modern era, which have moved from a traditional, agrarian-based economic system to a largely industrial, urbanised base, have also moved from a condition of high mortality and fertility to low mortality and fertility."[2]

Demographic transition has been also studied from the point of view of economic development. According to Ansley J. Coale and Edger M. Hoover, the agrarian peasant economy is generally characterised by high death rate and high birth rates. The death rates fluctuate according to the variations in harvests and the incidents of epidemics. Due to poor diet, lack of sanitation and medical and public health programmes, the death rates are usually high in peasant societies. On the other hand, the birth rate is high due to the prevalent ideals of prolific fertility reinforced by the economic advantages of having a large number of children. As the agrarian economy changes into industrial economy, levels of production and urbanisation rise, with the result that death rate falls due to better diet and medical care. Due to the acceptance of the ideal of small family in urban society the birth rates fall. This decline occurs after a time lag to the decline in the death rate. The birth and the death rates pursue a parallel downward course, though the decline of birth rate lags behind. As further deductions in the death rate are difficult to achieve, the birth rate again approaches the level of the death rate with the result that population grows slowly. While the death rates do not fluctuate, the birth rates fluctuate due to social and cultural reasons.

Some other thinkers have pointed out different stages in demographic transition. According to Donald Olen Cogwill, the population passes through the five stages known as: Primitive Cycle, Modern Cycle, Future Cycle or Baby Boom period, Probable Cycle and Population Cycle in the long run.[3] According to this

---

1. *Ibid.*,p. 41.
2 George J Stolnitz, "The Demographic Transition: From High to Low Birth Rates and Death Rates", Ronald Freedom (Ed.) *Population: The Vital revolution*, New York: Doubleday and Co. 1964, p. 30.
3 Donald Olen Cogwill: The Theory of Population Growth Cycles, *American Journal of Sociology*, L. V. 1949(163,70).

view population increases in S-Curve. Karl Sax has categorised the above mentioned stages into four stages only. According to him the second and the third stages in population growth are the stages of Population Explosion.[1] Landry has divided demographic changes into three demographic regimes on the basis of the theory of Cantillon: A Primitive Regime, An Intermediate Demographic Regime and A Modern Epoch.

Criticism of the Transition Theory

Generally speaking, the following criticisms have been advanced against the theory of demographic transition:

1. This theory was based on the experience of population changes in Western countries. But since the population growth in different countries does no follow identical patterns, therefore no theory can explain population growth everywhere. One finds so many exceptions to the rule. Thus, this theory is only a broad generalisation.

2. This theory fails to explain the phenomenon of 'The Baby Boom' in Western countries after the Second World War.

3. This theory does not provide a theoretical explanation of fertility as a force in demographic transition.

4. In fact this theory cannot be called a theory in the real sense since it neither extracts fundamental processes from a phenomenon nor identifies crucial variables.

5. This theory does not provide explanation of fertility decline nor does it identify crucial variables in it. Therefore it has no predictive value.

6. This theory cannot be applied to developing countries since the demographic stages in the Western countries are not necessarily explicit in the population growth in developing countries. In the face of the above mentioned criticisms, it may be concluded that the demographic transition theory at the best provides a framework and means for wider empirical generalisations. It cannot be considered a theory in the strict sense of the term, particularly for the explanation of the demographic growth in the developing countries.

---

1. Karl Sax, *The Population Explosion*, Headline Series 120, Foreign Policy Association, 1950, pp. 17-18.

SOCIAL THEORIES OF POPULATION

The social theories of population, as is clear by the title, explain population growth on the basis of social factor. The most important among these theories was the theory of Karl Marx which we have already discussed. Therefore, we will only present a brief outline of some important social theories of population.

Theory of Single Tax

This theory was presented by the American Economist Henry John. According to him, "The law of population accords with and is subordinate to the law of intellectual developments and any danger that human beings may be brought into a world where they cannot be provided for arises not from the ordinances of nature, but from the social maladjustments that in the midst of wealth condemn men to want." Therefore, the principle of population is subordinate to the principle of mental growth. Fecundity and fertility decrease with mental growth. There is no contradiction in the growth of population and the means of subsistence, provided the latter are controlled by the state. Therefore, the government should directly charge single tax from the users of land.

Theory of Social Capillarity

This theory was presented by Dumont (1849-1902) on the basis of his study of the growth of French population. According to Dumont, "The development of number in a nation is in inverse ratio to the development of individual." In other words as the individual develops, birth rate decreases. Dumont has called it theory of social capillarity since capillarity means the will for social progress. According to Dumont this theory of population applies to a well developed society based on rational thinking and idealism. He says, "From the moment when the imagination and the attraction of the ideal enter the scene, we find ourselves in the presence of a new principle of population." Thus, a theory of population is directly related to the stage of the growth of a society. Malthusian theory of population applies only to undeveloped and primitive societies. There is an inverse relationship in social capillarity and rate of birth. Since this force is inactive due to caste system in India, the birth rate is high. In France, on the other hand, due to political freedom and democracy, the birth rate is low. According to Dumont, "Just as a column of liquid must be thin in order to rise under the force of capillarity so must a family be small to rise in the social scale." The birth rate, due to the same reasons, is high in the villages and low in the cities. According to Dumont this theory does not apply to India where capillary power is inactive due to caste system. Thus, a rigid social structure retards social progress. Birth rate in the cities is always less than that in the villages. The reason of this distinction is the urban urge for a high standard of living. The thinking and conduct of urban people is more rational since they have better knowledge. Other factors influencing lower birth rate in the urban areas include: democracy, middle class, will to progress and higher standard of living. On the other hand, the factors leading to higher birth rate in the rural areas include casteism, old style thinking, illiteracy, ignorance and poverty, etc. According to Dumont this theory is not applicable to the societies having socialistic economy since in it an individual has limited scope of rising high. "The socialist principle of equality of function, if entirely applied, would necessarily imply the destruction of social capillarity and cause a high birth rate."

Criticism

The theory of population advanced by Dumont was an improvement upon Spencer's theory. However, the rise of a society does not depend upon nearly on lower birth rate but also upon so many social, economic and political factors. Therefore, Dumont's principle cannot be accepted as a rule.

Theory of Voluntarism

This theory was presented by Frank Fatlar in the end of the century. According to Fatlar, the main defect of Malthusian theory was its being confined to sex motive among human beings. Man, on the other hand, is a complex being very much influenced byideals, experiences, ambitions and desires, etc. Therefore, the Behaviour of a group is influenced by so many factors. Hence, no theory of population explains all the social phenomena. The Demographic changes should be explained on the basis of factors influencing society. Several psychological tendencies influence man's reproductive behaviour. Different classes exhibit different types of family environment. The poor do not pay much attention to restrict reproduction since the additional child will rather add to the family income. On the other hand, the rich do not want such increase since it will further divide the family income and property with the result that the standard of living will fall down. Therefore, Fatlar concludes that economic progress retards birth rate since the incentive shall be considerably less. Voluntarism seeks to remove lack of far sight and economy. Similar theories had been presented in U.S.A. by Arthur Hadley in 1896 and Weber in 1899. According to Arthur Twinning Hadley, "Intellectual man is more capable of birth control than emotional person. He can exercise more self restraint."

Principle of Individuality

This theory was advanced by the Italian economist Francesco S. Nitti in his book *Population and the Social System*. Nitti pointed out defects of other demographic theories including that of Malthus, Speeder, Marx and Dumont. According to him demographic progress has also led to the progress of civilization. Pointing out the factors influencing growth of population he said, "The influences of the psychical moral order and the influences of the political order, are but slight compared to influences of an economic kind .... But for a true understanding of the law of population the biological factors play important parts."

Theory of Increasing Prosperity and Pleasure

This theory was presented by Brenton. According to this theory the ideal of human life is pleasure. Reproduction rate increases among persons who have better means of pleasure. The poor class does not have so many options in pleasure seeking. They have no access to books, art and spiritual pleasures. Therefore, the only means of pleasure accessible to them is sexual intercourse. Consequently, they reproduce mofo children. On the other hand, since the rich have so many options to enjoy pleasure, therefore birth rate among them is lower.

Theory of Rationalism

This theory was presented by Ungern-Sternberg. He, for the first time, admitted that birth rate may be lower even among poor. The real cause of birth rate, according to him is not biological but psychological. As he pointed out, "The women too become masculinized (when infected by the capitalist mentality) in their search for equality Love relationship becomes business-like and matter of fact."[1] Advancing examples from Norway, Finland, etc.,

1. Roderich Von Ungern-Sternberg, *The Causes of the decline in Birth Rate within the European Sphere of Civilization*, p. 86.

he maintained that the wealth or poverty itself is not the factor determining birth rate nor is it urban or rural environment. The real factor determining birth rate is mental, it may be both among males and females. There is a correlation between economic development and lower birth rate. It is the capitalist mentality that induces low fertility. This, however, may be equally found in rural areas. Therefore, rural or urban, rich or poor do not necessarily determine birth rate.

Besides the above mentioned social theories, some other comparatively less known theories of population have been advanced by some other thinkers. They are however, susceptible to the same objections as have been already pointed out.

QUESTIONS FOR EXERCISE

1. Trace Pre-Scientific thinking on population.
2. Discuss Pre-Malthusian theories of population.
3. Explain Malthusian Theory of population.
4. Describe Neo-Malthusianism.
5. What is Optimum Theory of Population? Explain.
6. Describe Biological Theories of Population.
7. Write short note on Theory of Demographic Transition.
8. Discuss Social Theories of Population.

5

Methods and Sources of Demographic Data

The constituents of demographic data have been already pointed out in our discussion of the scope of demography in the first chapter. However, a brief review of demographic data will not be out of place, before starting a discussion of the methods and sources to arrive at these data. The demographic data, particularly, include the following:

Contents of Demographic Data

1. Birth Rate: Birth rate includes live births. Live birth is the complete expulsion or extraction from its mother of a product of conception, irrespective of the duration of pregnancy, which, after such separation, breathes or shows any other evidences of life, such as beating of the heart, pulsation of the umbilical cord, or definite movement of voluntary muscles, whether or not the umbilical cord has been cut or the placenta is attached; each product of such a birth is considered live born.

2. Death Rate: This includes both foetal death and still birth. Foetal death is death prior to the complete expulsion or extraction from its mother of a product of conception irrespective of the duration of pregnancy; the death is indicated by the fact that after such extraction the foetus does not breathe or show any other evidence of life. A still-birth is a foetal death occurring late in the gestation period, 'late' is usually defined as after 28 completed weeks of gestation.

3. Data Concerning Population Structure: These include sex structure, age structure, marital status, literacy and educational attainments. Sex structure depicts factors affecting overall sex ratio. Age structure shows the proportion of persons of various ages in the total population. Marital status shows the number of married, unmarried, males and females, widowers and widows, etc. In Demography the rate of marriage is known as nuptiality. Most of the marriages are registered to be legal, in most of the countries. Marriage has been defined by UNO as the legal union of persons of opposite sex. This has been further explained as: "The legality of the union may be established by civil, religious or other means as recognized by the laws of each country, and irrespective of the type of marriage, each should be reported for vital statistics purposes."[1] Besides literacy and educational attainments, population structure data also shows the population according to religion, rural and urban population and also the number of foreigners.

4. Fertility Data: Fertility data includes both fecundity and fertility. Fecundity is determined by rhythm method. Fecundity does not work in the conditions known as Parturition, Postpartum, Amenorrhoea and Anovulatory-Side. Fecundity depends upon lactation. It is also influenced by social taboos. Some persons are sterile and sub-fecund. Their number, however, is generally not more than 10% of the total pairs in the population. Fecundity and fertility is judged by electronic computer through a flowchart or diagram. The fertility data tell about sterility, family size, parity, conception, contraception and different types of factors affecting fertility.

5. Mortality Data: These include crude death rate, average expectation of life and birth, infant mortality rate, sex and age patterns of mortality, causes of death, levels and trends in mortality and mortality differentials.

6. Migration Data: These include immigration as well as emigration, their rate, trends and causal factors.

7. Size of Population Data: These include vital statistics. The growth and trends of population and the present size are known through census surveys.

8. Population Distribution: This data is particularly gathered on the basis of geographic areas. It also shows population distribution

1. U.N.O., *Multilingual Demographic Dictionary*, English Vol. (1958).

by classification of residence such as rural, urban, etc. Besides, it also shows trends in ruralisation and urbanization.

9. Labour Force: Data concerning labour force: shows economically active and inactive population. The former includes employed as well as unemployed and the latter includes home makers, students and income recipients. Besides, the data shows levels of male and female labour force, age specific labour force, rural and urban labour force, educated and uneducated labour force, etc.

The above discussion of the various constituents of population data show that it requires large scale and detailed surveys from time to time throughout the country. It is the necessary basis of all planning and development in a country.

METHODS OR SOURCES OF DEMOGRAPHIC DATA

The above mentioned data are obtained through three sources: Population Census, Registration of Vital Events and Sample Surveys. These may be called methods of gathering population data. These are also sources to gather population data. A brief explanation of these sources and methods will give an insight into the nature of population data.

POPULATION CENSUS

The term census has teen derived front the Latin word censere which means value or tax. In ancient times population census aimed primarily to prepare lists for taxation purposes, Thus, the scop of a census was limited to heads of families, farmers, merchants, landlords, and able-bodied men suitable for military service, etc. The modern census, however, includes every person in the state. The history of population census is very old. As much as five thousand years back the Sumerians used to count their population for taxation purposes. Evidence shows census taking in ancient Egypt, Babylonia, India, China, Palestine and Rome. In Biblical times, two censuses were undertaken, one by Moses in 1951 BC and the other by David in 1017 BC. In India *Arthashastra* of Kautilya prescribed population census in third century BC. Census operations were held during the reign of Ashoka (270 BC-230 BC). During the reign of Akbar in 16th century population data were collected. In England, William, the Conqueror ordered population census in 1085-1086. In 1449 population counting was undertaken in the city of Nuremburg. Total censuses were undertaken in some parts of Switzerland in the 15th and 16th centuries. In France Louis XIV undertook population census in 1715. Similar information may be gathered about other countries.

The modern concept of population census took shape only in the 17th and 18th centuries. Complete census at regular intervals were first made in 1665 in New France (Quebec) and Acadie (Novascotia). The first census of the USA was taken in 1870. England had her first census in 1801. By the middle of the 19th century census operations started in almost all European countries. During the period 1965-74 a total of 185 countries in the world conducted census operation.

The break up of this census operation was as follows: European countries: 37; North and South American countries: 47; Asian countries: 35; African countries: 40; and countries of the Oceania Region: 26.[1] This is a considerable improvement over the earlier report that in 1955-65, only 150 countries of the world conducted census operation.

Meaning and Scope of Census

The UNO prepared a list of useful topics to be covered by a census in 1970. It defined population census as enumerating the entire population of a country. To quote this definition, "A census of population is the total process of collating, 'compiling, evaluating, analysing and publishing demographic, economic and social data pertaining, at specified time, to all persons in a country or a well delimited part of a country."[2] Thus, the following may be called the salient features of census:

1. Each individual is separately enumerated.
2. Characteristics of each person are separately recorded. These characteristics include sex, marital status, age, religion, literacy, educational attainments, profession and economic activity, etc.
3. The census covers a well-defined area.
4. The census operations are carried at regular intervals such as in the case of decennial census in India. In UK and Japan it is conducted after every five years.

1. United Nations, *Demographic Year Book*, 1974, pp. 5-7.
2. United Nations, *Principles and Recommendations for the Population Censuses*, Statistical papers, Series M. No. 44, p. 2.

The above features of population census also clarify its scope. Operations are carried on through a questionnaire. Information is collected from each individual. The willingness and ability of the respondents is given due consideration. Therefore, topics arousing fear and prejudice are left outside the scope of census questionnaire. According to the list prepared by UNO the following topics are recommended to find place in a questionnaire: Place where found at the time of census; Total population, Place of usual residence; Locality; Place of birth; Urban and rural; Sex; Household composition; Age; Relationship to head of household; Marital status; Children born alive; Children living; Literacy; School attendance; Educational attainment; Type of activity; Occupation; Industry; Status (as employer; Employee, etc.). Besides, the following topics may also be included: Duration of residence; Place of previous residence; Place of work; Family composition; Relationship to head of family; Age at marriage; Duration of marriage; Marriage order; Citizenship; Educational qualifications; National and ethnic group; Language; Religion; Socio-economic status; Dependency; Main source of livelihood, etc.[1]

Census in India

In India schedules for the census in 1951, 1961, 1971 and 1981 have been continuously revised and reformed. The census schedules contain: (*a*) House list, (*b*) Establishment schedule, (*c*) Individual slip. This classification was particularly introduced in 1971 census. The details of this classification are as follows: In addition, a special census of degree holders and technical personnel was held in 1971 and 1981.

(*a*) *House list*: The house list is prepared 6 to 8 months prior to the census enumeration. Each house in the country, residential and non-residential was numbered for enumeration.

(*b*) *Establishment schedule*: Introduced for the first time in 1971 it covered all establishments where people work such as manufacturing, trade or other establishments. An establishment has been defined as a place where things are produced and services offered. The following particulars were collected for each establishment:

1. Name of the establishment or of the proprietor.

---

1. *Ibid.*, p. 17.

2. Whether the establishment is a government, a quasi-government, a private or a co-operative institution.
3. Numbers of persons working in manufacturing establishments.
4. The description of the production process or servicing done, type of power used in case of household industry, registered factory or unregistered workshop.
5. If a trade establishment, description of goods bought or sold, whether retail or wholesale.
6. If an establishment is used for other purposes, its description as an office, hotel, theatre, etc.

(*c*) *Individual slip*. This contained 17 items about each individual:

1. Name, 2. Relationship to head, 3. Sex, 4. Age, 5. Marital status, 6. For currently married women only: (*a*) Age at marriage; (*b*) Any child born in the last one year; 7. Birth place: (*a*) Place of birth; (*b*) Rural/Urban; (*c*) District; (*d*) State/Country, 8. Last residence: (*a*) Place of last residence; (*b*) Rural/Urban; (*c*) District; (*d*) State/Country, 9. Duration of residence in village or town of enumeration, 10. Religion, 11. Scheduled Caste or Scheduled Tribe, 12. Literacy, 13. Educational level, 14. Mother tongue, 15. Other languages, 16. Main activity: (*a*) Broad category: (*i*) Worker; (*ii*) Non-worker; (*b*) Place of work (Name of industry, trade, profession or service); (*c*) Description of work; (*d*) Class of worker, 17. Secondary work: (*a*) Broad category; (*b*) Place of work (Name of village/town); (*c*) Name of establishment; (*d*) Nature of industry, trade, profession or service; (*e*) Description of work; (*f*) Class of worker.

History of Census in India

The first census by counting heads in India was made during 1867-1872. In the words of Kingsley Davis, it was "An auspicious beginning", of census in India. The next census was taken in 1881. Since then upto 1981 census operations are being carried on once in every 10 years. In 1951 the first census was conducted in Independent India. It discussed the growth and structure of the population and the economic development. It included preparation of district census handbooks, and gathering data for smaller administrative units such as a village or an urban block. The census of 1961 was further improved. Analysis was made on a large scale. Information about tribes was collected and analysed for the first time. Reports were published concerning 1. Census Atlas — the first of its kind in the world; 2. Village monographs; 3. Fairs and Festivals; 4. Classification of Indian languages; 5. Special studies of cities having a population of more than one million; 6. Census of scientific and technical personnel; 7. Fertility surveys; and 8. Various other monographs. In 1971 census further improvements were made. A special feature of it was the use of computers for data processing. For this purpose a detailed tabulation plan was prepared. This census fixed a standard procedure which was followed in 1981 as well. The office of the Registrar General and Census Commissioner for India issued a booklet *Instructions to Enumerators for Filling up the Individual Slip.*[1] According to *Plans and Programmes of 1971 Census,*[2] the following procedure is to be adopted for census operation. This procedure was followed with some modifications in 1981.

Procedure for Census Taking

The following steps are now followed in census operation in India:

1. Fixing of the Machinery for Census Operation: Census operation in India is a Union subject incharge of the Ministry of Home Affairs. A Senior IAS Officer is appointed as Census Commissioner. For each Slate and Union Territory there is a Director of Census Operations. In every State and Union Territory thousands of enumerators are appointed with a hierarchy of officers from the enumerator to the director. The entire machinery of State administration and local self-government is involved in the process. Among the enumerators are generally included primary school teachers, Patwaries and village level workers and officers in the villages and teachers, clerks and other staff in local offices in the urban areas. The Central Government is empowered to notify and conduct a census, according to the Indian Census Act of 1948. The Act authorised the enumerators to compel the respondents to give correct answers to questions included in the schedule. It also guarantees that this information will be kept confidential and shall not be used as evidence in a court of law.

---

1. Office of the Registrar-General and Census Commissioner for India, *Instructions to Enumerators for Filling up the Individual Slip*, Faridabad: Government of India Press, 1970, pp. 1-18.
2. Registrar-General and Census Commissioner, India, *Plans and Programmes of 1971 Census*, p. 5.

2. Deciding the Scope of the Census: This is done by a conference of important census data users before the commencement of census operation.

3. Preparation of Map and Demarcation of Rural and Urban Areas: This is over the total area of census operation.

4. House Listing: A house list is prepared and each house, residential and non-residential, is numbered.

5. Training of Enumerators and Officers: This is done with a view to give each person a clear idea about his duties, responsibilities and powers.

6. Enumeration: The data of enumeration and its period is specified and advertised. The method of enumeration adopted is known as the extended *de jure* method, or "Usual Residence" method. This method was used for the first time in 1941, though incompletely. It was used in all subsequent census operations.

7. Checking and Editing: The data collected by the enumerators is now carefully checked and edited by the supervisors.

8. Provisional Totals: After a short period provisional totals of the population count are published in the newspapers.

9. Post-enumeration Check: This is an essential step.

10. Computerised Tabulation: Now tabulation through computers is done under the following main headings, prepared for all the States and Union Territories[1]: (1) General Population Tables, (2) Economic Tables, (3) Social and Cultural Tables, (4) Migration Tables, (5) Establishment Tables, (6) Fertility Tables (Sample), (7) Special Tables for Degree-Holders and Technical Personnel, and (8) Housing Tables. After the census operation the data gathered are published. This forms a useful background for preparation of plan development in the country. It is the main source of drafting five year plans. It gives an idea about social and economic conditions as well as the various problems. In brief, the following may be called the uses of a census report:

(1) It is the primary source of population data.

(2) It shows trends of population growth and change in the structure of population.

---

1. Office of the Registrar-General, India, *Registration of Births and Deaths in India*, paper presented at the ECAFE Seminar on Civil Registration and Vital Statistics, Copenhagen, Denmark, 22 July-10 August, 1968, p. 2.

(3) It contributes to our knowledge of changes in economic and industrial fields.

(4) It gives an idea of educational attainments.

(5) It provides a basis for demarcation of voting constituencies in democratic countries.

VITAL STATISTICS

Another important source of population data are vital statistics or registration of vital events. The meaning of vital statistics depends upon the meaning of vital events or vital records. Vital events mark the beginning and the end of a person's life such as birth and death. A still birth or a foetal death is a vital event. Events changing the civil status of a person such as marriage or divorce are also considered vital events. The occurrence of vital events has to be reported to the appropriate authorities by the persons concerned. Different agencies maintain records of births, deaths, still births, marriages and divorces, etc. These records are known as vital records. Since vital events happen continuously, vital records are also continually maintained. This recording of the vital events is known as the vital registration system. The statistics resulting from the compilation of vital events is known as vital statistics. Vital statistics also includes some ancillary information along with the vital events. For example, along with the record of births, it also includes such informations as date of birth, the sex of the baby, the age of the mother, the number of former children, the birth order, the residence of the mother, etc. Similarly, in recording the event of death, information is also collected about the data of death, place of death, causes of death and the age, sex and residence of the deceased. Thus, vital statistics provide a suitable basis for the measurement of changes in population.

The vital registration system is also known as civil registration. It is a tool for studying population changes. It, however, requires systematic registration and compilation. This is being done successfully in most of the developed countries of the world such as USA, Canada, UK, France, Sweden, Australia, New Zealand, Japan, etc. It is, however, far from being perfect in developing countries like India and the surrounding countries.

The registration of births and deaths in medieval Europe was mostly done by the religious bodies and the Church. The

Archbishop Toledo introduced registers for the recording of vital events in the fifteenth century. Thus, in the middle ages, the registration of vital events was the responsibility of the ecclesiastical authorities. In 1535, by an order of Thomas Cromwell, the clergy of England was required to record baptism, weddings and burials. The first systematic parish register was established in Sweden in 1608. Similar registers were established in Canada in 1610, Finland in 1628 and in Denmark in 1648. The ecclesiastical records have limited coverage and therefore limited importance. The first civil registration of vital events was established in Peru. It was introduced in the colonies of Massachusetts Bay and New Plymouth in USA, in 17th century. In civil systems, Registration was done by the government clerks and events of births, deaths and marriages were recorded without reference to ceremonies. This system was adopted in France in 1804 with the adoption of Napoleonic Code. The code was concerned with the legal and civil rights. It was established that civil rights claim depended on official registration. Therefore, the certificates of births, deaths and marriages established their legal; and civil status. In 19th century several countries in Western Europe and South' America adopted the system of secular civil registration. However upto 1662, vital records were not used for statistical purposes. This was visualised for the first time by John Graunt in 1662. He used vital statistics in his monumental works. In 1839, Dr. William Farr was appointed "Compiler of Abstracts" in the newly created General Register Office of England. He served in this capacity for 40 years, and was instrumental for the adoption of the vital registration system in so many countries of Europe.

Individual Uses of Vital Statistics

The following are the uses of registration of vital events and vital statistics to the individuals: .

1. Certificates of births, deaths, marriages, divorces, etc., are useful legal documents of legal status.
2. The identity of an individual is established by his birth certificate, which is also the best proof of his age.
3. It is also useful for establishing nationality or citizenship and for obtaining a passport.
4. It is a legal proof for establishing family relationship.

5. It is legally useful for deciding the questions of inheritance or insurance claims, etc.
6. A death certificate helps in the setting of questions of inheritance and other financial claims.
7. A marriage certificate establishes the marital status of a person and legitimacy off the children born.

National Uses of Vital Statistics

Besides the individual uses of vital statistics, the following national uses show its importance:

1. It provides data on births, marriages and divorces, etc., required for research in demography and public health.
2. Vital statistics give a population estimation.
3. Analytical studies based on vital statistics are useful for various purposes in population study. An example of such a study is the evaluation of family planning programme.
4. The death certificate besides providing data, gives information about various causes of death. These data are useful for medical science. They provide a basis for assessment of public health, a prerequisite for planning of public health programmes.
5. Vital statistics are utilised in planning physical facilities, educational facilities and many other facilities, such as provision of food supplies.
6. They provide a basis for the assessment of social, economic and health conditions of any particular society.
7. Thus, on the national scale, vital statistics provide a suitable basis for all plans of development and progress.

CIVIL REGISTRATION IN DIFFERENT COUNTRIES

According to the information given by United Nation's *Demographic Year Book*, 1974, the vital registration was virtually complete in the following number of countries in different areas of the world: Africa 12; North America 25; South America 3; Asia 9; Europe 35; Oceania 10; and USSR 1.[1] These data show that developing countries have been lagging behind in this connection. According to the same report the following countries

1. United Nations, *Demographic Year Book* 1974, pp. 19-27 and 244-254.

had vital registration covering less than 90% of population and therefore showing unreliable data: Africa 10; North America 7; South America 7; Asia 10; Europe 0; Oceania 3 and USSR 0. This shows that in Europe vital statistics are nowhere unreliable.

Civil Registration in India

The system of civil registration in India was introduced by the British in the middle of the 19th century. In 1863 the Sanitary Commissioner of the Government of India, laid emphasis upon the value of statistical data, for sanitary reforms. In 1866 the system of registration of births was available in CP. In 1873 the Bengal Births and Deaths Registration Act was adopted in Bihar and Orissa. In 1880 the importance of civil registration was emphasised by Indian Famine Commission. In 1886 the Government of India introduced the Births, Deaths, Marriages Registration Act, registration under which was, however, purely voluntary. In 1903 about 80% of Indian population was covered by the registration system. Important suggestions concerning registration was made by several commissions including Royal Commission on Agriculture 1924, and the Royal Commission on Labour 1928, etc. The progress of registration system however, almost stopped after the Second World War. In 1946 was set up the Health Survey and Development Committee with Sir Joseph Bhore as Chairman, and therefore called Bhore Committee. This Committee advanced important suggestions for the reconstruction of registration system in India. In 1960 the responsibility for civil registration was entrusted to the Registrar General and the Census Commissioner of India. In 1969 The Registration of Births and Deaths Act was passed, extending throughout the country and making registration of births, still births and deaths compulsory. Besides the Registrar General of India, each State has a Chief Registrar, incharge of the civil registration system. The statistical data collected every year is published by the Registrar General in a Volume *Vital Statistics in India*. This volume includes data on births, deaths, birth rates, death rates, age distribution, infant mortality, etc. The coverage of civil registration, however, is far from satisfactory in India due to under-reporting everywhere, particularly in rural areas. The basic reason for this deficiency is the widespread illiteracy and lack of civil consciousness in rural population. The births and deaths certificates in rural India are not required by most of the people and therefore they do not even know about it. Thus, though the 1969 Act makes failure to register births and deaths punishable, the coverage is far from satisfactory.

THE SAMPLE SURVEYS

The Demographic Sample Surveys collect population information on the basis of a sample representative of the whole population. Sample surveys are popular particularly in those countries where regular periodical censuses are not conducted. They are also valuable in countries like India where population census is taken only once in 10 years. The following may be noted as the most important advantages of sample surveys as sources of demographic data:

1. In sample surveys some death studies in population are possible by trained interviewers with carefully prepared questionnaires such as the statistics on abortions, etc.
2. The quality of the data obtained through sample surveys is better as compared to other methods.
3. Sample surveys are particularly useful to planners and administrators in assessing regional population problems.

Sample Surveys in India

In India sample surveys are being conducted by International Institute for Population Studies, Bombay, National Sample Survey, Government of India and other agencies. The following table shows the most important demographic sample surveys conducted in India recently, along with the institutes conducting them:

SELECTIVE DEMOGRAPHIC SURVEYS[1]

1. International Institute for Population Studies, Bombay.	1. Demographic study of Maharashtra. 2. Demographic study of Andhra Pradesh. 3. Demographic study of Orissa.
2. Indian Statistical Institute, Calcutta.	1. Some demographic aspects of a tribal population.

1. Agarwal, S.N., *India's Population Problems*, Tata Mc Graw Hill, New Delhi, 1977, pp. 39-40.

3. Institute of Economic Growth, Delhi.	1. Demographic study of six of a urbanising village.
4. Demographic Research Centre, Dharwar.	1. Dharwar Demographic Survey. 2. A Monograph of Kogilagiri—a village. 3. Study of Mysore State population (in Kannada).
5. National Sample Survey, Government of India.	1. NSS No. 8. Report on Preliminary Survey of Urban Unemployment (1953). 2. NSS No. 7 Couple Fertility. 3. NSS No. 14. Report on Some Characteristics of the Economically Active Population. 4. NSS No. 16. Report on Employment (1955). 5. NSS No. 17. Report on Sample Survey of Employment in Calcutta 6. NSS No. 34. Employment and Unemployment (1956). 7. NSS No. 44. A Note on Professions and Services. 8. NSS No. 52. Tables with Notes on Employment and Unemployment.
6. Indian Institute of Population Studies, Madras.	1. Demographic Survey of village near Madras.
7. Research Programmes Committee, Planning Commission, New Delhi	1. City surveys in Agra, Aligarh, Allahabad, Amritsar, Vardodra, Bhopal, Bombay, Calcutta, Cuttack, Delhi, Gorakhpur, Hubli, Hyderabad, Jaipur, Jamshedpur, Kanpur, Lucknow, Madras, Pune, Surat and Vishakhapatnam, which contain some demographic data on size, composition, age of marriage, fertility and migration.
8. Demographic Research Centre, Patna.	1. Report on Demographic Sample Survey, 1953.
9. United Nations and Government of India.	1. The Mysore Population Study.
10. Demographic Research Centre, Thiruvanthapuram.	1. Intensive village survey of Sree Kariyan. 2. A study on the demographic characteristics of certain occupational groups of Kerala. 3. Population of Kerala.

11. Gokhale Institute of Politics and Economics, Pune.	1. Demographic survey of six rural communities.
	2. Population problems in India, a regional social survey of Kolhapur city.
	3. Demographic profiles of an urban population.
12. Population Centre, Lucknow.	1. Demographic and family planning survey of six UP districts.

POPULATION REGISTERS

Another source of population data are the population registers, maintained in several countries including Sweden, Finland, Belgium, Israel, Taiwan and Korea. This register enters the name of each person in the country including the immigrants. It aims at establishing the identity of individuals and also controlling them. It is used to obtain demographic data about the size and structure of population, migration and vital events, etc.

DUAL REPORT SYSTEM

In some developing countries where Civil Registration System does not work properly, a dual report system has been adopted. This method has been in operation in some form or the other in India, Pakistan, Turkey, Liberia, Columbia, Thailand, Morocco, Philippines, Kenya, etc. In this system, each event of birth and death is enumerated by a dual report system, one the registration of births and deaths and the other the sample survey. The design is based on an appropriate number of small geographic samples. Continuous record of the events of births and deaths is maintained in each of these sample areas. Information about births, deaths and other relevant matters is collected through periodical sample surveys in retrospective effect. The data collected by both the procedures is compared and mathematically estimated to arrive at an accurate estimate. In India Sample Registration System was introduced in 1963-64, using the dual report system. In this system reliable estimates of vital rates as well as the population growth rates were used. It provided estimates of birth and death rates and population growth rates in India. Its estimates were fairly reliable. It fulfilled the need to measure short term changes in the rate of population growth. It is being used in several areas such as the national family planning programme.

INTERNATIONAL DEMOGRAPHIC PUBLICATIONS

The United Nations have published several important works concerning demography. Of these the most notable are the following:

1. Demographic Year Book: As is clear by the title, this is published yearly, and presents data concerning different countries of the world on the topics: population size, area, density, growth, characteristics, number of births and deaths, birth rate and death rate, number of marriages and marriage rate, immigration and emigration, etc. Detailed information is given on selected topics such as fertility, mortality, population census data, marriage, etc. In different issues of different years, for example the Demographic Year Book 1974 presented detailed data on mortality. Thus, this periodical is the best source for demographic data about different countries and the total world.

2. Statistical Year Book: As is clear by the title, this periodical is also published annually. It gives information on the following topics about the different countries of the world: National accounts, facilities of hospitals and availability of doctors, energy consumption, food production, educational facilities, newspaper circulation, availability of labour force, etc.

3. Epidemiological and Vital Records: This is a monthly periodical published by the World Health Organization (WHO). It gives information on public health, mortality and related matters in different countries of the world.

4. Other Publications: Besides the above mentioned regular publications, United Nations have published several important works from time to time providing valuable data about demographical conditions in different countries of the world. Of these some notable works are as follows:

1. *Demographic Trends in the World and its Major Regions*, 1950-70, New York: United Nations, Population Division, 1973.
2. *World Population Prospects*, 1965-2000, as assessed in 1968, New York: United Nations, Population Division ESA/P/WP. 37; December, 1970.
3. *Urban and Rural Populations*: *Individual Countries* 1950-1985 and *Regions and Major Areas* 1950-2000, New York : United

Nations, Population Division ESA/P/WP. 33/Rev. 1, September, 1970.

4. *Mysore Population Study*, ST/SOA/Series A-34, New York, 1961.
5. *Principles and Recommendations for National Populations Censuses*, ST/STAT/Ser/M/27, New York.
6. *Principles and Recommendations for the 1970 Population Censuses, ST/STAT/Ser M/44, New York*, 1969.
7. *Handbook of Vital Statistics Methods*, ST/STAT/Ser. F. No. 7, New York, 1954.
8. *Methodology of Demographic Sample Surveys*, New York, ST/TAO/ Sec, cl/4 119, Series M. No. 51.

QUESTIONS FOR EXERCISE

1. What are the contents of Demographic data? Describe important methods of gathering demographic data.
2. Write short note on Census in India.
3. What are Vital Statistics? Explain their uses.
4. Write short note on Civil Registration.

6

Growth and Trends of World Population

No complete and reliable estimates of world population were available before the present century. After carefully reviewing all the information available, the United Nations prepared estimates for the population of major regions of the world since 1920. The estimates given by Walter F. Wilcox and A.M. Carr Saunders for the period 1650-1900 are considered as the most authoritative region-wise estimates of world population. The history of population growth has been traced since 10,000 BC to 1975 AD as given in the table on next page. The table shows that the growth has been zig-zag and very gradual. Before 10.000 BC, at the end of the Ice Age, men were sparsely scattered over the earth. The size of human population was between 1,00,000 and 10,00,000. In 5,000 BC this population grew upto between 5 and 20 million. It is estimated that from 8,000 BC upto the beginning of Christian era, the population of the world increased at the rate of 0.06% per annum. By 1300 AD, it increased to 400 million. From 1300 AD to 1650 AD, there was an addition of only 1 million in the world population. In the next 50 years, however, one million was added. Yet another million grew during the period 1700 AD to 1750 AD. From 1750 AD however, population increased by 2 millions in the first 50 years and by 3 and 4 millions respectively during the next 50 year periods. Thus, prior to 1650 AD the growth of world population was very slow, while after 1650 AD it increased rapidly.

In 20th century the world population increased rapidly except for the period 1940-1950. The average annual growth rate during the period 1900-1950 was 0.8%. This rate rose to 1.9% during 1950-1970. During the next 20 years however, the population has increased very fast, registering on an average an annual growth rate of 2.22%.

WORLD POPULATION TRENDS

According to *the Washington Post* of November 1978, the world population trends are as follows: For the first time the world has reversed itself and has stopped growing so fast, the US Census Bureau has reported. Since 1970 the world's population has gone up 1.9 per cent annually, while in the previous 18 years it had been rising 2 per cent each year. According to the Bureau's study, funded by the Agency for International Development.

Table 6.1

The Growth of World Population from 1000 BC to 1991 AD

Year BC-AD	*Population*	*% Increase*	*Year*	*Population (Billion)*	*% Increase*
10000	1,00,000-1,00,00,000		1920	1.8	0.65
5000	50,00,000-2,00,00,000		1930	2.0	1.07
1 AD	256 million		1940	2.2	1.11
1300	400 million		1950	2.5	1.10
1650	0.5 billion	0.1	1960	3.0	1.79
1700	0.6 billion	0.1	1970	3.6	1.92
1750	0.7 billion	0.3	1975	4.0	1.89
1800	0.9 billion	0.4	1991	5.4	
1850	1.2 billion	0.5			
1900	1.6 billion	0.6			

Sources :
1. Ralph Thomlinson, *Population Dynamics*, New York: Random House, 1965, p. 13.
2. Jan O.M. Broek and John W. Webb, *A Geography of Mankind*, New York: McGraw-Hill Book Company, 1973, p. 450.
3. From 1920 to 1950, United Nations, *Demographic Year Book*, 1962, p. 124.
4. From 1960 to 1975, United Nations, *World Population Prospects as Assessed in 1973*, ST/ESA/SERA.S/60, New York, 1977, p. 90.

WORLD POPULATION TRENDS

According to *The Washington Post* of November 1978 the world population trends are as follows : For the first time the world has reversed itself and has stopped growing so fast, the U.S. Census Bureau has reported. Since 1970 the world's population has gone up 1.9 per cent annually, while in the previous 15 years it had been rising 2 per cent each year. According to the Bureau's study, funded by the Agency for International Development.

"We didn't expect a downturn in the rate of increase until the early 1980s, but its happening a decade earlier and its very significant," said Samuel Baum, the Bureau's Chief of International Demographic Statistics. The difference of a tenth of a percentage point "is not a tremendous decline. But it is important because the numbers are so high and it represents a change in direction, which is more important", Baum added. "The encouraging thing is that the direction has shifted in all regions of the world except Africa and even there a number of countries — Tunisia, South Africa, Mauritius and Reunion — have had substantial declines," he said (The latter two are islands in the Indian Ocean). Baum noted that more people are being added to the world and predicted that a growth rate of zero "will not be reached, at the earliest, until the years 2020 to 2025." The world's population, increased from 3.5 billion in mid-1967 to an estimated 4.3 billion in mid-1977, the report said, "At current (1976) vital rate, the world registers a net gain of over 2,00,000 persons each day," it said.

Baum said two trends account for the reduced rate of growth: a rapid decline in fertility and not-so-rapid decline in mortality, "People are being born at a slower rate and deaths are not going down as rapidly," he explained. The census report does not project future world population, but the World Bank has predicted it will reach six billion by 2000. The United Nations has predicted 6.3 billion by that year.

A study released recently by University of Chicago demographer Amy Ong Tsui and Donald J. Bogue projected a 5.8 billion total and said the world's population time bomb may have been defused by birth-control programmes in some of the most populous countries.

"Only 10 years ago doomsday prophesizing called for mass starvation, world chaos and possible world war by the year 2000," their study said. "If recent trends continue, the world population crisis appears resolvable."

The new census report seems to support that optimism. The report noted growth rate declines in less developed as well as developed nations. It cited Sri Lanka, where the 1966 growth rate was 2.3 per cent and the 1976 rate was 1.5 per cent. The Phillippines, Thailand and the Republic of Korea each had a decline of 0.7 per cent; Colombia had a decline of 0.6; South Africa, 0.4 and Turkey and China, 0.3. The estimate for China was made by John Aird, Chief of the Bureau's foreign demographic analysis division and was based primarily on provincial population figures that have been released since the death of Chairman Mao.

China's population was estimated to be 982.5 million, 23 per cent of the world figures. India's growth rate was 2.2 per cent in 1976 and 1977, about the same as it was in the mid-1960s.

Asia, with 2.5 billion people had 58 per cent of the world's total in 1977, the report said. Because of the sheer size of its base population, its population growth accounted for two-thirds of the world's increase. The United States had a growth rate of 0.8 per cent between 1976 and 1977 compared with 1.1 per cent between 1966 and 1967. The United States had 5 per cent of the world's population last year. North America, Europe and the Soviet Union, combined, had 23 per cent, the report showed. Africa's annual growth rate between 1975 and 1977 was 2.8 per cent. It has been rising steadily since 1950, when it was 2.1 per cent.

According to Michael Palmer's estimate, between now and the end of the century the actual number of people in the world will still increase from just over 4 billion to just over 6 billion, 90% of the extra 2 billion people will be born in the economically poor countries of the world. The world population will grow to 6196 million in the year 2000. This is an increase of 40% on the earlier estimate of 4413 million population in 1980. Of this total world population the break up between the poor world and the rich world will be 4848 million and 1348 million respectively. The poor world will increase 50% of the earlier estimate of 2332 million in 1980. On the other hand the rich world will only increase 14% of the 1980 estimate of 1181 million. Similar projections have been made by other demographers all over the world. According to S.N. Agarwala, "It took nearly two million years for the human population to reach one billion. The second billion came in a hundred years, the third in thirty and the fourth in fifteen years. At the present rate of growth, the fifth billion will be reached in eleven years and the sixth billion in only nine years."[1] According to a United Nations estimate the world population will be 6.25 billions in 2000 AD. Of this while only 1.36 will be of the more developed regions, as much as 4.89 will be of the less developed regions.[2] China and India are now contributing around 37% of increase in world population. Brazil adds more people per year than the Soviet Union. Therefore it has been concluded, "Thus, the more developed regions during the period 1965-1985, would add to their population at an average rate of 5 per cent per quinquennium, while the less developed regions would gain at an average rate of 13 per cent per quinquennium. Because of the higher rate of population growth in die less developed regions, their population in 1985 would be nearly three times that of the more developed regions (the ratio being 2.9 to 1) whereas in 1965 the ratio was only 2.2 to l."[3]

POPULATION AND DEVELOPMENT

This change in world population will considerably decrease the quality of population. It will increase the burden upon the more developed regions. Thus, it will create problems of health, food supply, employment and education, and housing. The demographers have started thinking how to maintain the pace of development with the increasing population. A recent survey of Population and Development in the Eighties by Michael Palmer presents some interesting ideas in this connection.[4]

In some population circles, the 1980s have been hailed as the Decade of New Integrations. Even if you are distrustful of these seemingly all-embracing labels, it remains a certainty that in the next few years more and more research and ideas will be devoted to the link between population and the whole process of development.

1. *Op. cit* pp. 2-3.
2. *World Population Prospects, 1970-2000 as assessed in 1973,* New York: United Nations, Population Division, ESA/P/WP. 53,1975, p. 47 (mimeographed).
3. Agarwal, S.N., *India's Population Problems,* 1977, p. 5.
4. *The Indian Express,* September 28,1979, pp. III-IV.

TABLE 6.2

UN Scenario on World Population

Each year the world's population grows by almost 90 million, an increase of 2.8 people each second. The world's population will continue to grow at least until 2050. The world's largest countries, which play a critical role in determining future population growth, are a diverse group. They range from Iran, where the average woman has 6.6 children, to Germany, where the average is 1.3.

	Population in millions) 1994	***2025*	*Years for population to double**	*Average number children/women*	*% married women contraception*
China	1,192.0	1,504.3	61	2.0	80.9
India	911.6	1,376.1	36	3.6	39.9
USA	260.8	338.3	98	2.1	69.1
Indonesia	199.7	288.5	43	3.0	47.1
Brazil	155.3	199.9	40	3.0	56.0
Russia	147.8	142.1	**	1.6	22.0
Pakistan	126.4	275.6	25	6.1	9.0
Japan	125.4	125.8	267	1.6	M.A
Bangladesh	116.6	211.3	29	4.9	31.2
Nigeria	98.1	248.0	23	6.5	3.5
Mexico	91.8	137.5	31	3.2	44.6
Germany	81.2	73.2	**	1.3	N.A
Iran	61.2	152.2	19	6.6	22.0
Egypt	58.9	97.9	31	3.9	44.8
United	58.4	62.1	261	1.6	71.0
France	58.0	58.7	162	1.7	64.0
WORLD	5,607.0	8,504.0	43	3.2	48.5
Developed countries	1,164.4	1,258.7	264	1.7	51.2
Developing countries	4.442.6	7,119.1	36	3.6	48.0

* Assuming current growth doesn't change. ** Population expected to decline.

Source: United Nations; Population Reference Bureau.

It is no more than a logical outcome of the changing perception of population from the initial focus on morbidity and mortality through the height of the so-called "population crisis" and its emphasis on the fertility factor in population growth to the present decade when population is universally recognised as an integral factor in development. Now that recognition is due to be turned into reality and population to take its full place in development programmes and policy-making.

Increased Education

Already a number of areas have been identified which illustrate the strong interplay between population and development. In the field of increased education for women, for example, there are potentially significant implications for the lowering of the fertility rate as is shown by what has happened in Sri Lanka and Kerala in India. In Kerala, where the birth rate has fallen from 39 in 1961 to 28 in 1976, the female literacy rate is twice as high as in any other state. The same story of high literacy and falling fertility can be told in Sri Lanka. Moreover, in both instances, the decline in fertility has been achieved without the classic precondition of an economic boom.

Investments and Trade Policies

Major investments and new transportation and trade policies can also have a marked effect on population factors, particularly those relating to the location of people and the growth of cities both problems which are becoming increasingly acute in many countries.

Urbanization

All over the world the move to the cities is gaining pace. In developed countries, half the population lived in urban areas in 1950; by the end of the century three-quarters are expected to do so. Similarly, in less developed regions; in Africa, the urban population tripled during 1950-1975 and will triple again by the year 2000. Individual examples are equally horrendous: Mexico City will have increased its population from 2.9 to 31.6 million in the period 1950-2000 and Greater Bombay will have jumped during the same period by over 650 per cent to 19.1 million people. It almost goes without saying that these population figures are of vital importance to those with the responsibility for planning and providing for the sendees needed to keep these "exploding" cities alive.

International Migration

International migration is equally important to the planning of manpower needs in the economy. The phenomenon of workers from South-East Europe and Asia flocking to the factories of West Germany and Northern Europe is well-established; equally significant are the figures for migrant workers in some of the states of the Middle East where economies are booming but which lack their own manpower resources: in Qatar and Kuwait 77 and 71 per cent respectively of total employment is taken up by immigrant labour. The economic consequences of these population shifts are vital also: in 1977 the total remittances to Egypt, Jordan, Morocco, Tunisia and the two Yemens met close to 30 per cent of the total value of foreign exchange earned through exports.

Labour Force

It is only through the careful analysis and marriage of population statistics and manpower needs that the necessary cooperation among developing countries in the flow of labour can be achieved. This complex relationship between population growth and manpower needs will certainly continue in the future. When the present numbers of children in the developing world start entering the labour force, the future growth of that force may well exceed the growth rate in the population as a whole. This phenomenon has, indeed, already occurred in certain countries leading to increasing numbers of unemployed and underemployed.

Two-Way Relationship

The relationship between population and development, than, is a two-way one: to take simplified examples, rapidly rising population numbers have been seen as imposing enormous strains on the environment and contributing to the depletion of the earth's natural resources. Conversely, we can see the effect greater educational opportunities can have in reducing fertility and stabilizing are reducing the birth rate.

Sheer numbers may be the raw material of demographic statistics but increasingly sophisticated analysis of those numbers has shown further-examples of the tie-up between figures and social and economic concerns. Take the growing problem of an aging population. The consequences that arise when the relative size of a population's younger members rapidly declines, as is happening particularly in the developed world are manifold:

the need to shift resources from assistance for child health and education to welfare systems for the aged; major impacts on residential and labour force mobility and the probable need for changes in political attitudes towards immigration to bolster a declining labour force.

Decline in Mortality

Then there is the effect of declining mortality rates both in advancing life expectancy and combating previously high infant death rates. Not only has this had probably profound effects on family formation attitudes and behaviour and, beyond that, for overall fertility figures but it poses a challenge to policy in public health and medical and health education. Since the potential for increasing control over death and disease is more and more divorced from the constraints of social and economic underdevelopment, there are now new opportunities to be seized in making further gains in Africa, Asia and Latin America. It is perfectly feasible to expect five-year gained or more in the life expectancy over the next decade in sub-Saharan Africa, South Asia and the Middle East.

The examples of the connection are legion and, once set out, almost so self-evident as to be in danger of being dismissed as understood and, therefore, relegated to the background: hence the need for the Decade of New Integrations.

As the recently published *State of the World Population 1979* pointed out, "Population policy is fast transcending the point where it can be regarded as a fiscal sideshow. Rather, much enhanced sophistication will be necessary in future in selecting among policy alternatives, in assessing their benefits and cost effectiveness, and in allowing for demographic development reciprocities. Not the least among the coming decade's major needs for improved demographic policy-making will be the rapid evolution of evaluative tools for analysing all these questions. Such tools might well, in time, come to constitute entire new areas of research in the social sciences and in the literature on administration."

The various members of the United Nations system are already giving attention to those aspects of the inter-relationship between population and development which fall within their respective mandates. For example, the International Labour Office is executing UNFPA-funded country projects which deal with population and employment planning as well as carrying out global and national research activities which examine the various aspects of migration and the numerous inter-reactions between production, female employment opportunities and fertility change.

THE DEMOGRAPHIC TRANSITION THEORY

The demographic transition has been defined by Ansley J. Coale and Edgar M. Hoover, when countries of Europe, North America, Australia, New Zealand and Japan evolved, "From a predominantly agrarian peasant economy to an economy with a greater division of labour, using more elaborated tools, and equipments, more urbanised, more oriented to the market sale of its products and characterised by rapid and pervasive changes in technique."[1] These countries have shown a demographic stability or the low population growth, not through high fertility and high mortality but through low fertility and low mortality. The theory of demographic transition has been also supported by Warren Thompson, C.P. Blacker and Frank Notestein. Various stages have been maintained as essential in the progress towards the demographic transition. These stages exist before, during and after the transition. These have teen explained as follows:

1. The Pre-Transitional Stage: In this stage population growth is almost static. Both birth and death rates are very high. The society has an agrarian peasant economy with a traditional organizational system. High death rates-are achieved due to wars, famines, epidemics, chronic malnutritions, etc. High birth rates are supported by social norms and customs regarding marriage and reproduction with emphasis upon prolific child-tearing. This stage shows high potential growth and lack of man's control over fertility and mortality. This stage may be pointed out in India particularly in the nineteenth century and early 20th century.

2. The Transitional Stage: This stage has been further classified into three types: Early, Mid and Late.

(*i*) *Early Transitional Stage:* In this stage death rates start decreasing but birth rates continue to remain high with the result that the population grows rapidly.

1. Ansley J. Coale and Edgar M. Hoover, *Population Growth and Economic Development in Low Income Countries*, Princeton: Princeton University Press, 1958, p. 10.

(*ii*) *Mid-Transitional Stage:* During this stage death rates continue to decline, but a decline in the birth rates also begins. However, since the birth rates are higher than the death rates, the rate of population growth is fairly high.

(*iii*) *Late Transitional Stage:* In this stage death rates continue to be low while birth rates remain moderate. Therefore the population growth is again low. In India the early transitional stage could be observed under British Rule. With the independence of the country and the effort to control diseases, etc., the country has now come to mid-transitional stage. The aim of late transitional stage is near though not yet achieved. In so many other countries however, one may see late transitional stage. This is in developed countries. The developing countries however, such as India, China, Thailand, Korea, the Philippines, Indonesia, Sri Lanka and some Latin American countries, are still in mid-transition or late transition stage.

3. Post-Transitional Stage: In this stage both birth and death rates are low. The country reaches a stage where population is almost stationary and can be changed by change in fertility. The theory of demographic transition describes in a simple manner the historical trends of population growth. However, most of the demographers have challenged its value as a demographic theory.

CAUSES OF RAPID POPULATION GROWTH

All the surveys of world population growth show that the rate of growth is very fast. Therefore, United Nations are trying everywhere to check the growth rate. The problem, however, is different in different countries, since as has been already pointed out, different countries are passing through different stages of the demographic transition. The following may be listed as the main causes of rapid population growth:

1. Fall in Mortality Level: A review of almost any country in the world shows a fall in mortality levels in 19th and 20th century. This may be seen in India in the following table:[1]

1940	1950	1960	1970
31.2	27.4	22.8	18.9

1. Office of the Registrar-General and Census Commissioner, The Population of *India*, 1974, World Population Year, CICRED Series, p. 35.

It is most explicit in the countries of Europe and North America. The fall in mortality level is firstly, due to agricultural revolution, secondly, due to industrial revolution, and thirdly, due to progress in medical sciences, public health and environmental sanitation.

2. Accelerated Growth Rates: After 1950 the world population increased rapidly due to the accelerated growth, particularly in the developing countries in Asia, Latin America and Africa. This was firstly, due to decline in the death rates, secondly, due to the prevention and control of diseases, and thirdly, due to expansion in medical and public health services.

Of the above mentioned causes the extension of technology and expansion of medical and public health services together with industrial revolution are those which cannot be checked nor their control is desirable. Therefore, the only hope lies in family planning and control of birth rates. This again will be planned according to the ratio of growth of population and the increase of means of subsistence in a particular country. Population control is particularly required in the developing and not so developed countries.

QUESTIONS FOR EXERCISE

1. Write an essay on World Population Trends.
2. Show the inter-relation of Population and Development.
3. What are the causes of rapid population growth? Explain with reference to India.

7

Development of Demography in India

The Indians knew the value of population studies since ancient times. The *Arthashastra* of Kautilya gives a detailed description of how to conduct a population, economic and agricultural census. During the reign of Akbar the great Abul Fazal compiled the *Ain-e-Akbari* containing comprehensive data on population, industry, wealth and traits of population. During the British period the system of decennial census started with the first census in 1872. This was particularly planned to understand the traits of Indian population based upon the census reports from 1872 to 1941. Kingsley Davis, the well known demographer, produced his monumental work *The Population of India and Pakistan*, which is valued even today for its contribution to the progress of population studies in India.

An important contribution to the growth of demography in India has been made by Imperial Gazetteers. The first Imperial Gazetteer was published in 1881 in 9 volumes at the instance of W.W. Hunter. In 1882 a companion volume entitled *The Indian Empire : Its History, People and Products*, was published. Revised versions of the Imperial Gazetteers were published in 26 volumes during the period 1907 and 1909. The first volume of the Imperial Gazetteer contains discussion on matters such as nutrition, early marriages, birth rate, relationship between marriage customs and birth rate, rural urban birth and death rates, differential in mortality by sex, religion, rural urban residence, infant mortality, causes of death and health conditions in European and the native army. This was the section of Public Health and Vital Statistics. It may be noted here that all these subjects form the subject matter of modern demography. However, before 1930, not much progress was made in India towards the growth of demography. The First Indian Population Conference was held in 1936 under the auspices of the University of Lucknow. At this Conference a paper entitled "Future Growth of India's Population" was presented. The Second All-India Conference on Population and the First Family Hygiene Conference was held in Bombay in 1938 and a paper on differential fertility based on field experience in Cochin State was presented. An interesting controversy regarding the rate of population growth ensued at this Conference (and was continued later between Professor B.P. Adarkar of Allahabad University and Dr. K.C.K.E. Raja of Madras Public Health Services, (who later became the Director of Demographic Training and Research Centre, Bombay) which kept the question of population growth alive. At about this time, Professor Adarkar started teaching an optional paper on "Population Problems" to the M.A. Economics students of Allahabad University.

The Second All-India Conference on Population and the First Family Hygiene Conference were jointly held in Bombay in 1938. Apart from discussing the social and medical aspects of birth control and human sexuality several other subjects related to population studies were covered. These included differential fertility, maternity and child welfare, infant mortality, housing and health, nutrition, morbidity, vital statistics, logistic law of growth of the Indian population, economic problems associated with population size and growth, such as population and unemployment, poverty and population, optimum theory of population, sociological analysis and forecast of population growth.[1] Thus, it is clear that Indian scholars were gradually taking interest in different aspects of demographical studies. The interest was formerly centred around the discussion whether India was overpopulated. Among the most important books written on this subject during this period may be mentioned *Food Planning for Four Hundred Millions* by Radhakamal Mukerjee published by MacMillan (London) in 1938. This book emphasised the need for agricultural development. It was followed by another

1. *Proceedings of the Second All India Population and First Family Hygience Conference*, Bombay: 1938, p. 309.

equally important publication India's *Teeming Millions by Gyan* Chand published by George Allen and Unwin (London), in 1939. This book discussed the population problem from the economic viewpoint.

In 1936 Enid Charles presented his book *Twilight of Parenthood.* which maintained that the population of India was slowly increasing. This aroused an interesting controversy between Dr. K.C.K.E. Raja, a public health worker, and Professor Adarkar, an economist, about the trend of future population growth in India. The two scholars maintained the opposite view. Other important books concerning population problems in India, published during this period include: *P.K. Wattal, Population Problem in India* (1916), Brij Narain, *The Population in India* (1925), B.K. Sarkar, *The Sociology of Population* (1936), S.Chandrasekhar, *India's Population Fact and Policy* (1946), D. Ghosh, *The Pressure of Population and Economic Efficiency in India* (1946).

During the period 1940 to 1956 the Government of India started taking interest in population studies. In 1944, the then Department of Education, Health and Lands set up the Population Data Committee under the Chairmanship of W.M. Yeats "to advise the Government of India on the available data relating to growth of population." The Family Planning Association of India was founded in Bombay in 1949 and it started propagating population control. In 1946, the Government of India appointed the Health Survey and Development Committee (popularly known as the Bhore Committee) to study health conditions in India and to make recommendations for their improvement. The Committee made a thorough study of the activities in the field of population, Vital and Population Statistics. One of the important recommendations of this Committee was that "the population problem should be the subject of continuous study."[1] Important field enquiries were made by the Indian Statistical Institute, in pre-independent period, under the able directorship of Prof P.C. Mahalanobis. The Institute collected data on fertility through field enquiries. In 1945, the All India Institute of Hygiene and Public Health, Calcutta conducted several field studies under the guidance of Dr. C. Chandrasekharan. In 1942 Prof N.V. Sovani of

1. Government of India, *Report on Health Survey and Development Committee*, 1946, IV Summary, New Delhi: Publication Dept. 1946, p. 82.

the Gokhale Institute of Politics and Economics, Pune, published a study entitled: *The Population Problem in India: A Regional Approach.*

POST-INDEPENDENCE DEVELOPMENTS

The following are important landmarks in post-independence growth of demography in India.

The 1951 Census

The first post-independence census report was prepared by the Census Commissioner R.A. Gopalaswami in 1951. This report covered not only the size and distribution of the population but also changes in it. Dr. Gopalaswami warned about the dangers of rapid population growth and said, "It is extremely important that the attention of the people should be focused on this factor of improvident maternity.... The occurrence of improvident maternity should evoke social disapproval as any other form of social indulgence."[1] Hearing this warning the government paid particular attention to family planning in five year plans.

In 1952, the National Family Planning Programme was launched in India to control population growth.

The National Sample Survey

In 1949 the National Sample Survey System was established to meet the need of census data and the data for the evaluation of development plans. The National Sample Survey (NSS) collected data on differential fertility, family planning knowledge, attitude and practice for rural and urban areas, internal migration, employment, etc.

Field Surveys

Some important field surveys were carried on during this period. In 1952-53 was carried out the Mysore Population Study, jointly sponsored by UNO and the Government of India. This study brought out social and cultural factors affecting fertility in India and served as a model for other fertility surveys. A notable survey on fertility and mortality, conducted by Professor V.M. Dandekar and Prof. Kumudini Dandekar in Nasik, Satara and Kolaba Districts, also contributed to a better understanding of fertility behaviour in India.

---

1 R.A. Gopalaswamy, *Census of India*, 1951, Vol. I, India, Part E-A. Report, p. 88.

Demographic Centres

The Central Family Planning Board set up in 1956, appointed a sub-committee on Demographic Studies under the chairmanship of Dr. V.K.R.V. Rao. This sub-committee recommended the establishment of four demographic research, centres in different parts of the country, where studies might be conducted in fertility, mortality and associated factors. As a result, the Demographic Training and Research Centre (now known as the International institute for Population Studies) was established in Bombay in 1956; the Demographic Research Centres in Calcutta, Delhi and Trivandrum in 1957; and the one at Dharwar was established in 1960.

International Institute for Population Studies (IIPS)

This Institute was established for training and research in population studies. It has four functions: Teaching, Research, Consultative services and Documentation. According to an assessment, in 1976-77, the institute trained 569 persons, out of which 355 were from India and 214 from various countries of the ESCAP region. The institute's library, perhaps the test in the world, has a stock of 27,500 books and 5,850 reprints. It subscribes to most of the periodicals on population and associated fields. Among the important studies of IIPS are the following:

(*i*) K.C. Zachariah, *A Historical Study of Internal Migration in the Indian Sub-continent* 1901-1931, Bombay: Asia Publishing House, 1964.

(*ii*) C. Chandrasekaran and K. Kuder, *Family Planning Through Clinics*, Bombay: Asia Publishing House, 1965.

(*iii*) S. Kono and M. Shio, *Inter-Prefectural Migration Streams Analysis*, Bombay: Asia Publishing House, 1966.

(*iv*) K.V. Ramachandran *et al., A Survey of School Children in Greater Bombay*, Bombay: Asia Publishing House, 1968.

(*v*) K.C. Zachariah, *Migrants in Greater Bombay*, Bombay: Asia Publishing House, 1968.

(*vi*) K.V. Ramchandran and G. Shantakumar, *Fertility Differentials in West Malaysia*, Bombay: International Institute for Population Studies, 1974.

Demographic Research

In 1959, the Demographic Advisory Committee was appointed by the Ministry of Health, mainly to co-ordinate research on population. The Family Planning Communication Action Research Committee was set up in 1960 to co-ordinate and promote research in family planning, communication and motivation. The two committees were merged in 1967 to form the Demographic and Communication Action Research Committee which became defunct when its term expired on November 3, 1971. This Committee was reconstituted on December 6, 1972, as the Committee on Socio-Economic Studies on Family Planning to cover the economic, sociological, educational, psychological, communicational and demographic aspects of population growth and family planning.

INSTITUTION ENGAGED IN DEMOGRAPHIC RESEARCH IN INDIA

Name of the Centre/Institution	*Areas of Research Activities*
1. Administrative Staff College, Hyderabad.	Family planning management, health management and information system.
2. Central Statistical Organization, New Delhi.	Population projections, fertility.
3. Demographic Research Centre, Bureau of Economics and Statistics, Trivandrum.	Family planning, fertility, migration.
4. Demographic Research Centre, Gokhale Institute of Politics and Economics, Pune.	Fertility, family planning, demographic surveys, inter-district migration.
5. Demographic Research Centre, Banaras Hindu University, Varanasi.	Mathematical models, small-scale sample surveys.
6. Demographic Research Centre, Indian Statistical Institute, Calcutta.	Fertility, family planning, mortality, nuptiality.
7. Demographic Research Centre, Institute of Economic Growth, Delhi.	Migration, urbanisation, fertility changes.
8. Demographic Research Centre, Institute of Economic Research, Dharwar.	Fertility, demographic surveys of cities.
9. Demographic Research Centre, Lucknow University, Lucknow.	Fertility, demographic surveys, population projections.
10. Demographic Research Centre, Patna University, Patna.	Demographic surveys, biostatistical studies, mathematical models.

Name of the Centre/Institution	*Areas of Research Activities*
11. Demographic Research Centre, Patna University, Patna.	Fertility, family planning, demographic surveys.
12. Demographic Research Unit, Jadavpur University, Jadavpur.	Mathematical models, metropolitan area studies.
13. Department of Statistics, University of Kerala, Kerala.	Fertility, fertility surveys, family growth study, population models.
14. Economics Department, Bombay University, Bombay,	Migration, economic activity analysis, sex ratio.
15. Indian Institute of Management, Ahmedabad.	Family planning management, management information and evaluation system.
16. Indian Institute of Management, Calcutta.	Family planning.
17. Indian Institute of Management, Bangalore.	Health statistics.
18. International Institute for Population Studies, Bombay.	Fertility, nuptiality, migration, family planning attitude, communication and evaluation, mortality and population simulation model.
19. Institute of Manpower Research, New Delhi.	Area manpower surveys, man-power studies.
20. National Council of Applied Economic Research, New Delhi.	Population projections, city surveys.
21. National Sample Survey, New Delhi.	Fertility, employment and unemployment, births and deaths.
22. Office of the Registrar General of India, New Delhi.	Census operations, mortality, fertility, birth registration.
23. Operation Research Group, Baroda.	Family planning and fertility surveys.
24. Planning and Evaluation Division, Ministry of Health and Family Planning, New Delhi.	Family planning programme evaluation.
25. Population Centre, India Population Project, Bangalore.	Surveys, evaluation, management studies.
26. Population Centre, India Population Project, Lucknow.	Benchmark surveys, family planning management studies, nutrition and family planning evaluation, family planning training, management information and evaluation system.
27. Population Studies Centre, Sri Venkateshwara University, Tirupati.:	Population education, cost-benefit studies.

FAMILY PLANNING COMMUNICATION ACTION RESEARCH CENTRES IN INDIA

Name of the Centre/Institution	*Areas of Research Activities*
1. All India Institute of Hygiene and Public Health, Calcutta.	KAP, evaluation, communication.
2. Council for Social Development, India International Centre, New Delhi.	Infant and child mortality, fertility and marriage.
3. Demographic Communication Action Research Centre, Institute for Social and Economic Change, Bangalore.	KAP, evaluation, city surveys.
4. Department of Psychology, University of Patna, Patna.	Attitude scale.
5. Department of Rural Economics and Sociology, Utkal University, Bhubaneswar.	Family planning communication.
6. Department of Sociology, University of Kerala, Trivandrum.	KAP, evaluation, communication.
7. Family Planning Research Unit, Indian Statistical Institute, Calcutta.	Evaluation, motivation, communication.
8. Gokhale Institute of Politics and Economics, Poona.	KAP, organizational aspects, evaluation, communication.
9. Indian Institute of Technology, Kanpur.	Family planning attitude studies.
10. Institute of Rural Health and Family Planning, Gandhigram.	Family planning training, family planning and health evaluation studies, fertility and mortality.
11. International Institute for Population Studies, Bombay.	KAP, family planning evaluation, family planning communication, cost-benefit analysis, target setting.
12. Institute for Economic and Social Change, Bangalore.	Migration, regional activities.
13. National Institute of Family Planning, New Delhi.	KAP, family planning evaluation, family planning communication.
14. Population Centre, India, Population Project, Bangalore.	Family planning, nutrition.
15. Population Centre, India, Population Project, Lucknow.	Family planning, nutrition.
16. Shri V.T. Krishnamachari Institute of Rural Health, Vadodra.	Training, evaluation, KAP, organizational aspects.

Teaching of Demography in India

Many Indian universities today have provision for teaching and research in demography. At the post-graduate level demography was taught leading to M.Sc. degree in the University of Kerala for the first time in India. In 1973 a Population Studies Centre was established at Shri Venkateshwara University, Tirupati. Since 1974 Demography is being taught at JNU. Besides, it forms a part of the syllabi as an optional paper in Economics at Agra, Aligarh, Allahabad, Varanasi, Vadodra, Mumbai, Calcutta, Gorakhpur, Gujarat, Lucknow, Meerut, Rajasthan, Saugar and other Universities. It is a part of the post-graduate courses in Sociology at Annamalai, Gorakhpur, Lucknow, Punjab, Vikram and Indore Universities. Besides, it is a part of M.Sc. Statistics courses at Agra, Annamalai, Delhi, Gorakhpur, Karnataka, Pune and other Universities. Provision has been made for lectures on demography, population problems and Vital Statistics in post-graduate teaching in Economics, Statistics and Sociology at some 14 universities. The scope of teaching of the subject is fast expanding to other universities as well. The Indian Association for the Study of Population (IASP) started publication of a journal, *Demography in India*, in 1972, with financial support from the Family Planning Foundation of India. The demand for demographers is gradually increasing in this country.

Census of India 1961

This provided a wealth of information in the field of demography for students and research workers.

Asian Population Conference

In 1963 India hosted the First Asian Population Conference in New Delhi which encouraged demographical research in India.

The Sample Registration Scheme

This scheme was initiated in 1964-65 by the Registrar General of India, to obtain reliable estimates of birth and death rate and the rates of natural growth.

Indian Association for the Study of Population

A significant forward step in the development of Demography in India was taken in 1972 with the establishment of the Indian Association for the Study of Population.

The above brief review of the progress of Demography in India will not be complete without mention of some eminent demographers whose work has been acknowledged not only in this country but also in the West. Among them may be named Radhakamal Mukerjee, Gyan Chand, S.N. Agarwala, C. Chandrasekharan, S.P. Jain and S. Chandrashekhar, R.A. Gopalaswami, P.K. Watal, Brij Narain, B.K. Sarkar, D. Ghosh among others. The formulae developed by S. Chandrashekhar in collaboration with Deming to estimate the missing events of birth from vital registration and retrospective surveys are now widely used. A new technique for evaluating and adjusting Indian age data was developed by Mr. S.P. Jain. A significant contribution was made to the technique of analysing migration data collected through a census by Zachariah. Dr. S.N. Agarwala made important contribution to research in the field of family planning. Mr. J.R. Reley, Present Director, International Institute for Population Studies has evolved a method of estimating birth and death rates and rates of natural increase from the census data. Today, a large number of studies are being undertaken in different fields of demography. There have been numerous studies covering knowledge, attitude and practices concerning family planning. These are known as KAP studies. By March 1977 nearly 450 studies were completed in the field of fertility alone. Thus, the future of demography in this country appears to be bright.

Census 1981

The latest count reveals that India is the second largest populated country in the world accounting for 15.53 per cent of the estimated world population of 3721 million. But India accounts for only 2.4 per cent of the world area.

China is on the top with one thousand million people.

The population of India is now 6,83,810,051 according to the provisional figures arrived at after the 1981 census. This shows a growth rate of 24.75 per cent which is .05 per cent less than that recorded in the 1971 census. There has been a net addition of 1,35,650,399 since the 1971 census.

With the exception of Kerala, men continue to outnumber women in the country — the ratio now is 935 females to 1000 males.

The density of population is now 221 per sq. km.

Life expectancy has risen from 46 years in 1971 to 54 years now.

Over 1.25 million field workers were mobilised to carry out the census operation — the biggest in the world. Counting supervisory personnel and staff at controlling levels the total task force that was at the census operations would be of the order of 4.5 million.

The census officer had classified eunuchs as 'males.' According to Mr. P. Padmanabha, Census Commissioner "eunuchs have been classified as males." The dictionary defines a eunuch as a "castrated male person." Prostitutes, whenever they volunteered the information, were classified as working women.

Many people who may have complained of having been missed by the enumerators may actually be fully enumerated. Often the information required was garnered from the neighbours or the servants of persons concerned.

Assam, Gujarat, Tripura and Mizoram have the distinction of always registering average higher than the all-India averages — from the 1901 census right through to 1981.

Though their population is small, the highest growth rates have been registered by Chandigarh at 74.95; Andaman and Nicobar Islands at 63.51 and Delhi at 52.41.

Women continue to outnumber men in Kerala.

In 1971 there were 161,673 more women in the State. But in 10 years the number has gone upto 427,295, according to provisional population figures announced.

The men in 1981 accounted for 12,487,961 as compared to 10,587,581 in 1971. There were 12,915,256 women by March 1 this year compared to 10,759,524,10 years earlier.

The total population of Kerala as on March 1, 1981 was 25,403,217. In 1971 it was 21,347,375.

On the adverse female ratio — which is found only in India, Pakistan and Bangladesh — there is little evidence to support the view that female infants die due to deliberate neglect. On the other hand, there are certain diseases that selectively kill more women than men.

The females now number 330,462,802 and the males 353,347,249.

The population has doubled since independence. It may again double itself by 2001 unless the present trend of a declining growth rate is not only kept up but improved upon, in which case the projections are of the order of 950 million.

Uttar Pradesh has the highest population with 110,858,019, Bihar has 69,823,154; Maharashtra 62,693,898; West Bengal 54,485,560, and Andhra Pradesh 53,403,619.

Delhi has the highest density of population: 4178 per sq. km. The lowest is Arunachal Pradesh with seven persons per square km. The highest female to male ratio is in Kerala at 1034 to 1000 while the most adverse is in Andaman and Nicobar Islands where there are 761 females to 1000 males.

The literacy rate is now 36.17 — for females it is 24.88 and for males 46.74. These figures do not include Jammu and Kashmir.

While the 1901 census showed that there were 1466 literate males for every 100 females, the 1981 head-count revealed 201 literate males for every 100 females.

Kerala continues to be the most literate state in the whole country with literacy rate of 69.17 per cent.

The next seven places are taken by union territories with Chandigarh reporting 64.68 per cent rate, Delhi 64.06 per cent, Mizoram 49.50, Goa 55.86, Lakshadweep 54.72, Pondicherry 54.23 and Andaman and Nicobar Islands 51.27 per cent.

The literacy percentage has increased in all the states and union territories since the last census.

For the country as a whole the literacy has been estimated at 36.17 per cent compared to 29.45 in 1971 and 24.02 per cent in 1961.

With 9,165,650 persons, Calcutta is the most thickly populated city in the country, according to 1981 census figures.

Greater Bombay comes next with 8,202,759 followed by Delhi with 5,227,730 and Madras 4,276,635.

Men outnumber women in all the 12 cities, where the population is above one million.

In all the four metropolitan cities, the literacy percentage was above 60 per cent with Greater Bombay at the top with 68.16 per cent. Sex-wise also Bombay accounts for literates — males 74.43 per cent and females 60.58.

The other eight cities with a population of over 10 lakhs are:

Bangalore	2,913,537	Hyderabad	2,565,536
Ahmedabad	2,515,195	Kanpur	1,685,308
Nagpur	1,297,977	Pune	1,685,266
Jaipur	1,004,660	Lucknow	1,006,943

The provisional population totals are as follows:

TABLE 7.1

Census Figures— 1981

	Persons	*Mates*	*Females*
1	2	3	4
India	68,38,10,051	35,33,47,349	33,04,62,802
States			
Andhra Pradesh	5,34,03,619	2,70,35,531	2,63,68,088
Assam (x)	1,99,02,826	1,04,72,712	94,30,114
Bihar	6,98,23,154	3,58,65,467	3,39,57,687
Gujarat	3,39,60,905	1,74,84,540	1,64,76,365
Haryana	1,28,50,902	68,46,153	60,04,749
Himachal Pradesh	42,37,569	21,31,312	21,06,257
Jammu & Kashmir	49,81,600	30,62,200	29,19,400
Karnataka	3,70,43,451	1,88,69,494	1,81,73,957
Kerala	2,54,03,217	1,24,87,961	1,29,15,256
Madhya Pradesh	5,21,31,717	2,68,56,752	2,52,74,965
Maharashtra	6,26,93,898	3,23,41,115	3,93,52,783
Manipur	14,33,691	7,27,108	7,06583
Meghalaya	13,27,874	6,78,833	6,48,991
Nagaland	7,79,981	4,14,231	3,59,050
Orissa	2,62,72,054	1,32,53,523	1,30,18,531
Punjab	1,66,69,755	88,40,234	78,29,521
Rajasthan	3,41,02,912	1,77,49,282	1,63,53,630
Sikkim	3,15,682	1,71,959	1,43,723
Tamil Nadu	4,82,97,456	2,44,20,228	2,38,77,228
Tripura	20,60,189	10,57,714	10,02,475
Uttar Pradesh	11,08,58,019	5,87,80,640	5,20,77,379

	Persons	Mates	Females
1	2	3	4
West Bengal	5,44,85,560	2,85,05,151	2,59,80,409
Union Territories			
Andaman and			
Nicobar Islands	1,88,254	1,06,889	81,365
Arunachal Pradesh	6,28,050	3,35,941	2,92,109
Chandigarh	4,50,061	2,54,208	1,95,853
Dadar and Nagar			
Haveli	1,03,677	52,514	51,163
Delhi	61,96,414	34,22,550	27,73,864
Goa, Daman & Diu	10,82,117	5,46,260	5,35,857
Lakshadweep	40,237	20,367	19,870
Mizoram	4,87,774	2,51,988	2,35,786
Pondicherry	6,04,136	3,04,342	2,99,794

TABLE 7.2

Total Literates

	Persons	Males	Females
India	23,79,91,232	15,88,37,215	7,91,54,717
States			
Andhra Pradesh	1,59,89,266	1,05,78,388	54,10,878
Assam	—	—	—
Bihar	1,81,63,410	1,35,51,736	46,11,674
Gujarat	1,48,58,075	95,34,470	53,23,605
Haryana	46,05,649	32,71,047	13,34,602
Himachal Pradesh	17,77,201	11,15,973	6,61,228
J and K (+)	—	—	—
Karnataka	1,42,28,947	91,71,677	50,57,270
Kerala	1,75,71,819	92,44,609	83,27,210
Madhya Pradesh	1,45,02,063	1,05,74,919	39,27,144
Maharashtra	2,96,95,721	1,50,46,963	1,06,48,758
Manipur	6,01,943	3,85,123	2,16,820

	Persons	*Males*	*Females*
Meghalaya	4,41,077	2,51,056	1,90,021
Nagaland	3,24,700	2,03,643	1,21,057
Orissa	89,64,625	62,16,037	27,48,588
Punjab	67,91,547	41,18,415	26,73,132
Rajasthan	82,01,615	63,50,945	18,50,670
Sikkim	1,06,780	75,066	31,714
Tamil Nadu	2,21,11,593	1,39,65,132	81,46,461
Tripura	8,56,688	5,39,932	3,16,756
Uttar Pradesh	3,03,58,013	2,28,45,887	75,12,126
West Bengal	2,22,71,867	1,43,91,808	78,80,059
Union Territories Andaman & Nicobar	96,520	62,470	34,050
Arunachal Pradesh	1,26,185	94,002	32,183
Chandigarh	2,91,091	1,74,953	1,16,138
Dadra and Nagar Haveli	27,578	19,007	8,571
Delhi	37,83,611	23,25,804	14,57,807
Goa, Daman & Diu	6,04,489	3,53,832	2,50,657
Lakshadweep	22,018	13,233	8,785
Mizoram	2,90,241	1,66,296	1,23,945
Pondicherry	3,27,600	1,94,792	1,32,808

CENSUS 1991

India's population, as on 1 March 1991 stood at 846.30 million (439.23 million males and 407.07 million females). This includes the projected population of 7.72 million of Jammu and Kashmir. The second largest populous country, India is the home of 16 per cent of world's population. The country, however, accounts for 2.42 per cent of the total world area.

The population of India as recorded at each decenial census from 1901 has grown steadily except for a decrease during 1911-21. In absolute terms the country's population has increased by 161.12 million during the decade 1981-91. This is ten times the population of Australia and is more than the population of Japan. An encouraging feature revealed by the provisional results is the decline in growth rate of the population in the last decade compared to 1971-81. It marginally decreased from 24.66 per cent recorded in 1971-81 to 23.85 per cent during 1981-91.

In most states the growth rate declined during the decade. However, Andhra Pradesh, Arunachal Pradesh, Madhya Pradesh, Maharashtra, Nagaland, Tripura, West Bengal, Daman and Diu, Lakshadweep and Pondicherry which account for one-third of the country's population, recorded increase in growth rate. Nagaland registered the highest growth rate of 56.86 per cent while Kerala the lowest 13.98 per cent.

Most Populous

Uttar Pradesh continued to be the largest state, population-wise with 16.44 per cent people of the country living there (139,112,287), followed by Bihar with 10.21 per cent (86,374,465) and Maharashtra with 9.33 per cent (78,937,187), West Bengal occupied fourth place accounting for 8.04 per cent (68,077,965) of the country's population followed by Andhra Pradesh with 7.86 per cent (66,508,008).

Bombay metropolis continued to be the most populated city of the country with urban population of 12.60 million, Calcutta taking the second place having 11.02 million. Delhi ranks third with a population (urban) of 9.42 million followed by Madras 5.42 million.

Population Density

One of the important indices of population concentration is the density of population. It is defined as the number of persons per square kilometre. The population density has gone up from 216 in 1981 to 267 persons in 1991. In 1901 it was 77 persons. Among the union territories Delhi has the highest density of 6,352 persons per sq. km. followed by Chandigarh (5,632). Lakshadweep which has the smallest population size is the fourth most densely populated area with a density of 1,616 persons per sq. km. Pondicherry ranks third (1,642) followed by Daman and Diu (907). Arunachal Pradesh is the most sparsely populated area of the country with 10 persons per square kilometre.

The ten heavily populated districts of the country are Calcutta, Madras, Greater Bombay, Hyderabad, Delhi, Chandigarh, Mahe,

Haora, Kanpur City and Bangalore. All of them have density of above 2,000 persons per square kilometre and 5.01 per cent of the country's population lives in these districts. The average density of these ten districts is 6,888.

Sex Ratio

In any study of the population, analysis of the sex composition plays a vital role. The sex composition of the population is affected by the differentials in the mortality conditions of males and females, sex selective migration and the sex ratio at birth.

Sex ratio is defined as the number of females per 1000 males. In India it has generally been adverse to women. The ratio has also declined over the years except in 1981 when it slightly improved to 934 from 927. In 1991, there has been a fall by seven points to 927 per thousand males. But Kerala represented a different spectrum. The state has a higher number of females than males, 1,036 females for thousand males.

In the Indian context, a sex ratio of 950 and above can be considered as favourable to females. The states and union territories coming under this category besides Kerala and Himachal Pradesh (976), Andhra Pradesh (972), Goa (967), Karnataka (960), Manipur (958), Orissa (971), Tamil Nadu (974), Dadra and Nagar Haveli (952), Daman and Diu (969) and Pondicherry (979). Chandigarh accounted for the lowest number of females per thousand male with 790.

Literacy

For the purpose of census, a person is deemed as literate if he or she can read and write any language with understanding. In the 1991 census, the question on literacy was canvassed only for population aged seven years and above, unlike earlier censuses which took into account population of five years and above for this purpose.

The final results reveal that there has been an increase in literacy in the country. The literacy rate in the country (excluding Jammu and Kashmir) is 52.21 per cent (64.13 for males and 39.29 for females).

For the population aged seven years and above the literacy rate has increased by 8.54 percentage points. The increase in male and female literacy rates are of the order of 7.63 and 9.44 points respectively.

FUTURE PROSPECTS

India's population was 900.54 million in 1993, with a growth rate of 2.1 per cent per annum during 1985-93, according to the latest World Bank Atlas, reports PTI.

The World Bank puts the Indian expectation of life at 61 years in 1992, total fertility (births per woman — 1992 figure) at 3.7, infant mortality rate per 1,000 live births in 1992 at 79, percentage of underweight children due to

CENSUS 91 POPULATION OF STATES

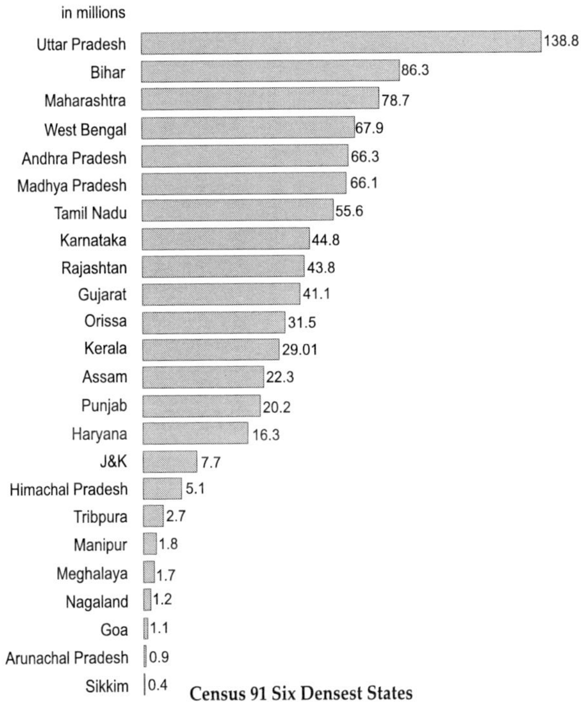

Census 91 Six Densest States
population/sq km

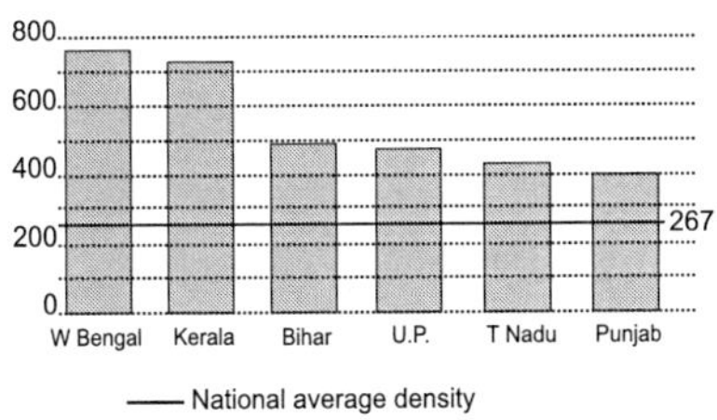

malnutrition during 1985-92 at 63, illiteracy rate in 1990 at 52 per cent female labour force as a percentage of the total in 1993 at 25.

INDIA 1991

Total Population	843,930,861
Male	437,597,929
Females	406,332,932
Absolute Increase in Population (1981-91)	160,601,764
Decadal Growth Rate (Per cent) (1981-91)	23.50
Density (Persons Per sq. km.)	267
Sex Ratio (Females Per 1000 Males)	929
Literacy Rate (Per cent) Total	52.11
Males	63.86
Females	39.42
Birth Rate (Per Thousand person)	27.4
Death Rate (Per Thousand Person)	9.4

TABLE 7.3

Population of India, 1901-1991

Year	*Population*	*Decadal Variation*		*Annual exponential growth rate (per cent)*
		Absolute	*Per cent*	
1901	238,396,327	—	—	—
1911	252,093,390	+ 13,697,063	+ 5.75	0.56
1921	251,321,213	- 772,177	- 0.31	- 0.03
1931	278,977,238	+ 27,656,025	+ 11.0	1.04
1941	318,660,580	+ 39,683,342	+ 14.22	1.33
1951	361,088,090	+ 42,420,485	+ 13.31	1.25

Year	Population	Decadal Variation		Annual exponential growth rate (per cent)
		Absolute	Per cent	
1961	439,234,771	+ 77,682,873	+ 21.51	1.96
1971	548,159,652	+ 108,924,881	+ 24.80	2,20
1981	683,329,097	+ 135,169,445	+ 24.66	2.22
1991	843,930,861	+ 160,601,764	+ 23.50	2.11

TABLE 7.4

Density of Population, India, 1901-1991

Year	Density Per Square Km
1901	77
1911	82
1921	81
1931	90
1941	103
1951	117
1961	142
1971	177 +
1981	216 + +
1991	267 + +

TABLE 7.5

Sex Ratio (Female Per 1000 Males), India, 1901– 1991

Year	Sex Ratio
1901	972
1911	964
1921	955
1931	950
1941	945
1951	946
1961	941

Year	Sex Ratio
1971	930
1981	934
1991	929 +

TABLE 7.6

Literacy Rate, India, 1901– 1991

Year	Persons (per cent)	Males (per cent)	Females (per cent)
1951	18.33	27.16	8.86
1961	28.31	40.40	15.34
1971	34.45	45.95	21.97
1981	43.56	56.37	29.75
	(41.42)	(53.45)	(28.46)
1991	52.11	63.86	39.42

TABLE 7.7

Number of Literates and Illiterates Among Population Aged Seven Years and Above, India, 1981–1991

Literates/ Illiterates	*Persons (million)*	*Males (million)*	*Females (million)*
Literates			
1981	233.94	156.95	76.99
1991	352.08	224.29	127.79
Increase in	118.14	67.34	50.80
1991 over 1981 Per cent increase	50.5	42.9	66.0
Illiterates			
1981	301.93	120.90	181.03
1991	324.03	126.69	197.34
Increase in 1991 over 1981	22.10	5.79	16.31
Per cent increase	7.3	4.8	9.0

TABLE 7.8

Population and Growth Rates in States/UTs 1971-81 & 1981-91

Sl. No.	*India/State/ Union Territory*	*Total population*		*Growth rate*	
		1981	1991	1971-81	1981-91
	India	683329,097	843,930,861	+ 24.66	+ 23.50
States					
1.	Andhra Pradesh	53,549,673	66,304,854	+ 23.10	+ 23.82
2.	Arunachal Pradesh	631,839	858,392	+ 35.15	+ 35.86
3.	Assam	18,041,248	22,294,562	+ 23.36	+ 23.58
4.	Bihar	69,914,734	86,338,853	+ 24.06	+ 23.49
5.	Goa	1,007,749	1,168,622	+ 26.74	+ 15.96
6.	Gujarat	34,085,799	41,174,060	+ 27.67	+ 20.80
7.	Haryana	12,922,119	16,317,715	+ 28.75	+ 26.28
8.	Himachal Pradesh	4,280,818	5,111,079	+ 23.71	+ 19.39
9.	Jammu & Kashmir	5,987,389	7,718,7004	+ 29.69	+ 28.92
10.	Karnataka	37,135,714	44,817,398	+ 26.75	+ 20.69
11.	Kerala	25,453,680	29,011,237	+ 19.24	+ 13.98
12.	Madhya Pradesh	52,178,844	66,135,862	+ 25.27	+ 26.75
13.	Maharashtra	62,784,171	78,706,719	+ 24.54	+ 25.36
14.	Manipur	1,420,953	1,826,714	+ 32.46	+ 28.56
15.	Meghalaya	1,335,819	1,760,626	+ 32.04	+ 31.80
16.	Mizoram	493,757	686,217	+-48.55	+ 38.98
17.	Nagaland	774,930	1,215,573	+ 50.05	+ 56.86
18.	Orissa	26,370,271	31,512,070	+ 20.17	+ 19.50
19.	Punjab	16,788,915	20,190,795	+ 23.89	+20.26
20.	Rajasthan	34,261,862	43,880,640	+ 32.97	+ 28.07
21.	Sikkim	316,385	403,612	+ 50.77	+ 27.57
22.	Tamil Nadu	48,408,077	55,638,318	+ 17.50	+ 14.94
23.	Tripura	2,053,058	2,744,827	+ 31.92	+ 33.69
24.	Uttar Pradesh	110,862,512	138,760,417	+ 25.49	+ 25.16
25.	West Bengal	54,580,647	67,982,732	+ 23.17	+ 24.55

Sl. No.	*India/State/ Union Territory*	*Total population*		*Growth rate*	
Union Territories					
1.	A & N Islands	188,741	277,989	+ 63.93	+ 47.29
2.	Chandigarh	451,610	640,725	+ 75.55	+ 41.88
3.	Dadra & Nagar Haveli	103,676	138,542	+ 39.78	+ 33.63
4.	Daman & Diu	78,9–81	101,439	+ 26.07	+ 28.43
5.	Delhi	6,220,406	9,370,475	+ 53.00	+ 50.64
6.	Lakshadweep	40,249	51,681	+ 26.53	+28.40
7.	Pondicherry	604,471	789,416	+ 28.15	+ 30.60

TABLE 7.9

Decadal Variation in Population, Change in Decadal Variation and Average Exponential Growth Rate of Population 1971-1981 & 1981–1991

India/State/ Union Territory	*Decadal variation in population (per cent)*		*Change in the growth rate*	*Rate of change of the growth rate*	*Average annual exponential growth rate*	
	1971-81	1981-91	(Col 3-2)		1971-81	1981-91
1	2	3	4	5	6	7
India	24.66	23.50	– 1.16	– 4.70	2.22	2.11
States						
1. Andhra Pradesh	23.10	23.82	0.72	+3.12	2.10	2.14
2. Arunachal Pradesh	35.15	35.86	+ 0.71	+ 2.02	3.04	3.06
3. Assam	23.36	23.58	+ 0.22	+ 0.94	2.12	2.12
4. Bihar	24.06	23.49	– 0.57	– 2.37	2.17	2.11
5. Goa	26.74	15.96	– 10.78	– 40.31	2.37	1.48
6. Gujarat	27.67	20.80	– 6.87	– 24.83	2.46	1.89
7. Haryana	28.75	26.28	– 2.47	– 8.59	2.55	2.33
8. Himachal Pradesh	23.71	19.39	– 4.32	– 18.22	2.15	1.77
9. Jammu & Kashmir	29.69	28.92	– 0.77	2.59	– 2.58	2.58
10. Karnataka	26.75	20.69	– 6.06	– 22.65	2.39	1.88

India/State/ Union Territory	Decadal variation in population (per cent)		Change in the growth rate	Rate of change of the growth rate	Average annual exponential growth rate	
	1971-81	1981-91	(Col 3-2)		1971-81	1981-91
11. Kerala	19.24	13.98	– 5.26	– 27.34	1.77	1.31
12. Madhya Pradesh	25.27	26.75	+ 1.48	+ 3.86	2.27	2.37
13. Maharashtra	24.54	25.36	+ 0.82	+ 3.34	2.21	2.26
14. Manipur	32.46	28.56	– 3.90	– 12.01	2.83	2.51
15. Meghalaya	32.04	31.80	– 0.24	– 0.75	2.80	2.76
16. Mizoram	48.55	38.98	– 9.57	– 19.71	3.99	3.29
17. Nagaland	50.05	56.86	+ 6.81	+ 13.61	4.09	4.50
18. Orissa	20.17	19.50	– 0.67	– 3.32	1.85	1.78
19. Punjab	23.89	20.26	– 3.63	– 15.19	2.16	1.85
20. Rajasthan	32.97	28.07	– 4.90	– 14.86	2.87	2.47
21. Sikkim	50.77	27.57	– 23.20	– 45.70	4.14	2.43
22. Tamil Nadu	17.50	14.94	– 2.56	– 14.63	1.63	1.39
23. Tripura	31.92	33.69	+ 1.77	+ 5.55	2.79	2.90
24. Uttar Pradesh	25.49	25.16	– 0.33	– 1.29	2.29	2.24
25. West Bengal	23.17	24.55	+ 1.38	+ 5.96	2.102	2.20
Union Territories						
1. A & N Islands	63.93	47.29	– 16.64	– 26.03	4.98	3.87
2. Chandigarh	75.55	41.88	33.67	– 4.57	5.67	3.50
3. Dadra & Nagar Haveli	39.78	33.63	– 6.15	– 15.46	3.38	2.90
4. Daman & Diu	26.07	28.43	+ 2.36	+ 9.05	2.32	2.50
5. Delhi	53.00	50.64	– 2.36	– 4.45	4.29	4.10
6. Lakshadweep	26.53	28.40	+ 1.87	+ 7.05	2.37	2.50
7. Pondicherry	28.15	30.60	+ 2.45	+ 8.70	2.50	2.67

QUESTIONS FOR EXERCISE

1. Describe the development of population in India.
2. Describe the trend of Indian population according to Census 1991.

8

Structure and Characteristics of Indian Population

The most important aspect in Demography is the study of the structure and characteristics of the population. This includes the personal, social and economic characteristics including age, sex, race, nationality, religion, language, marital status, family composition, literacy and educational attainments, employment status, occupation and income, etc. Each population may be classified into different groups, according to the above mentioned characteristics. For example, Indian population may be classified into males and females; Indians and foreigners; literate and illiterate; employed and unemployed; children, youth and old; Hindu, Muslim, Christians, Sikhs, Jains, etc.; married and unmarried; single or joint family; and groups speaking more than a dozen languages recognized by the Constitution. Similar characteristics may be observed in any other population group. Again, these characteristics are not fixed once for all. They are constantly changing over the period of time. For example, in 1961 the population of children in India was 41.08 per cent, whereas this rose to 42.10 in 1971. Thus, the number of young dependents increased over the period of time. Similarly, while in 1961 the percentage of literacy in India was 24.02%, in 1971 this increased to 29.46%, with further increase in 1981. These characteristics, again, do not show the same proportion throughout the country. For example, in India literacy has been always very high in Kerala as compared to other parts of the country. Similar comparisons can be made in the population structure of different countries.

For example, in 1970 the percentage of the age group 15 in India was 42.10% while in USA it was only 28.50%. This shows that the characteristics of population in USA are better than that in India. As a general rule the population characteristics of the developed countries are always better than those of the developing and undeveloped countries. In other words, the level of development of a country may be judged by the characteristics of population structure. For example, the percentage of females, children, illiterates, unhealthy, sick, old and disabled persons in a population shows the backwardness of society. It is not only a symptom of backwardness but also a cause which leads to further backwardness and hampers attempts to progress. This may be particularly studied in the case of the characteristics of Indian population which has the higher percentage of children, old, sick, disabled, other dependent, unemployed, illiterate people in the population. Any progress may be judged with the criteria of these characteristics. It is obvious that these characteristics hinder economic and social development.

Uses of Population Characteristics

The above discussion, incidentally, shows the uses of the study of population structure and characteristics. The following uses are more important:

1. It helps in judging the quality of the population.
2. It helps in making comparisons and identifying the level of development.
3. It is useful in the preparation of inventories of human resources necessary for all developmental planning.
4. It gives data concerning births and deaths, age and sex distribution, etc., useful for various purposes.
5. It provides material for the study of social changes.
6. It provides data for the study of present economic structure as well as the possibilities of future growth.
7. It provides data concerning health of people in the country so that planning may be made in this direction.
8. It presents an outline of the most glaring social and economic problems which may be given priority for solution.

Thus, it is clear that the study of structure and characteristics of population is a prelude to all successful planning for development.

Types of Characteristics

It may be noted here that while some of the characteristics of a population cannot be changed such as nationality, other characteristics do change over different planes and periods of time such as education, marital status, etc. Of these two types of characteristics, the former are known as ascribed and the latter achieved. Thus, ascribed characteristics are biologically or culturally assigned. For example, Indians belong to Aryan race in the North and Dravid in the South. The racial characteristic is biologically inherited and cannot be changed. The Blacks do not become Whites over a period of time. The achieved characteristics, on the other hand, are those which are open to the choice of the individual such as marital status, educational attainments, occupation, etc. In India nationality, religion, caste, mother tongue, etc., may be included in the former category. Age, sex, race and mother tongue are ascribed characteristics everywhere. Sex and age are the basic biological characteristics. They influence social, economic and political structure. They particularly influence birth and death rate, migration (both emigration and immigration), marital status, compositions of family, manpower, national income and national production, educational and medical provisions and housing, etc. Planning for development in different fields such as education, housing, employment, health, manpower, etc., is made on the basis of data concerning sex and age structure. For example, the number of male and female population in a particular period determine the number of educational institutions, teachers, text books, laboratory equipments, playgrounds, etc., needed for future planning. Similar examples may be given about the use of population characteristics in planning.

Importance of Sex and Age Characteristics

The above discussion shows the importance of sex and age characteristics in a population. The following points may be noted in this connection:

1. They provide data on fertility, mortality, migration, marital status and economic characteristics.
2. According to Ralph Thomlinson, sex and age characteristics are, "visible, indisputable and convenient indicators of social status."[1] Each individual is ascribed a status in society on the basis of sex and age.

1. Thomlinson, Ralph, *Population Dynamics*, New York: Random House, 1965, p. 428.

3. These characteristics are determined by the role of a person in society and social institutions. These roles, of course, change according to culture and even in the same culture over a period of time. However, they are found in every culture in every period and accepted by the society everywhere. Thus, for example, in patriarchal societies the status of male is high and his roles are generally outside the home. The same may be said about females in a matriarchal society. In the modern industrial societies, however, the roles of males and females are not so much definite. The women are getting more and more employment outside the home. However, house-keeping is generally a feminine occupation though she may be helped by the male occasionally. Similar examples of roles according to age may be found in different societies. While the more traditional types of societies are age-oriented with elder men working as guides, the more modernised societies have what is known as youth-oriented culture. One even finds youth cults in so many Western societies.

SEX STRUCTURE

The most important characteristic of population is the sex structure. This is known by the percentage of males in the population, in other words, masculinity proportion. The sex ratio is expressed in the number of males per 100 females or the number of females per 100 males. For example, in the year 1971 the urban sex ratio of males in some of the countries of the world was: India 116.6, Indonesia 110.0, Nepal 117.3, Sri Lanka 112.5, UK 93.6, Germany 84.1.[1] The corresponding sex ratio in rural areas was almost everywhere lower as compared to the urban areas. This means that there is a higher number of males over females in urban areas and not so higher in number in rural areas. This is particularly due to the fact that migration from rural to urban is generally in terms of the male population. Again, the percentage of the ratio has been changing in different periods in the same country.

TABLE 8.1

	1971	1981	1991
Total	547,367,926	683,810,051	843,930,861
Males	283,252,214	353,347,349	437,597,929
Females	264,115,712	330,462,802	406,332,932

1. United Nations, *Demographic Year Book*, 1974, pp. 108-113 and pp. 198-215.

According to the 1971 census the sex ratio was 107.5, *i.e*, there were 107.5 males for every 100 females in India.

According to a study the sex ratios of population in Indian cities with one million or more population in 1971 was as follows[1]:

TABLE 8.2

City	*Sex Ratio (M÷F) × 100*
Calcutta Urban Agglomeration	142.6
Greater Bombay	139.6
Delhi Urban Agglomeration	125.3
Madras Urban Agglomeration	110.7
Hyderabad Urban Agglomeration	109.1
Ahmedabad Urban Agglomeration	120.5
Bangalore Urban Agglomeration	114.4
Kanpur Urban Agglomeration	131.2
Pune Urban Agglomeration	116.2

The above table shows that sex ratio in urban areas is favourable to males. Quite a different picture is however projected by some urban areas in Europe and USA. This is particularly due to female dominated internal migration in these countries as against the male dominated internal migration in India. Most of the males in India, while migrating from rural to urban areas, leave their families in the country due to the paucity of residences in cities. The migratory labour force is mainly constituted by the males. This migratory character also changes the sex ratio in urban population in India. It has been always higher than that of rural population. As is clear by the table given above some Indian cities like Calcutta, Bombay, Delhi, Kanpur, etc., shows unusually high sex ratios in favour of males.

In the country as a whole there are more males than females in Indian population. In 1961 the number of females per thousand males was 941 whereas in 1971 it was 930. Table 8.3 shows sex ratio in India in different States and Union Territories in 1961 and 1971.[2]

1. Computed from Census of India 1971, Series 1—India, Part II-A (*i*) *General Population Tables*, pp. 241-250.
2. *Census of India*, 1971, General Population Tables, Series 1—India, Part II-A (i), pp. 131-134.

TABLE 8.3

Sex Ratio in India, 1961 and 1971

State/Union Territory	*Sex Ratio*		*State/Union Territory*	*Sex Ratio*	
	1961	*1971*		*1961*	*1971*
India	941	930	Sikkim	904	863
States			Tamil Nadu	992	978
Andhra Pradesh	981	977	Tripura	932	943
Assam	872	897	Uttar Pradesh	909	879
Bihar	994	954	West Bengal	878	891
Gujarat	940	934	*Union Territories*		
Haryana	864	867	Andaman and		
Himachal Pradesh	938	958	Nicobar Islands	617	644
Jammu & Kashmir	878 878	879	Arunachal Pradesh	894	861
Karnataka	959	957	Chandigarh	652	749
Kerala	1022	1016	Dadra & Nagar Haveli	963	1007
Madhya Pradesh	953	941	Delhi	785	801
Maharashtra	936	930	Goa, Daman &		
Manipur	1015	980	Diu	1071	989
Meghalaya .	936	942	Laccadive,		
Nagaland	933	871	Minicoy and Amindivi		
Orissa	1001	988	Islands	1023	978
Punjab	864	865	Pondicherry	1013	989
Rajasthan	908	911			

TABLE 8.4

State-wise Sex Ratio (Females Per 1,000 Males), 1901-1991

Sl. No.	*India/State/ Union Territory*	*1901*	*1911*	*1921*	*1931*	*1941*	*1951*	*1961*	*1971*	*1981*	*1991*
1	2	3	4	5	6	7	8	9	10	11	12
India *States*		972	964	955	950	945	946	941	930	934	929
1.	Andhra Pradesh	1985	1992	1993	1987	1980	1986	1981	1977	1975	1972
2.	Arunachal Pradesh	*		*	*	*	*	894	961	862	861
3.	Assam	919	915	896	874	975	868	869	896	910	925
4.	Bihar	1054	1044	1016	994	996	990	994	954	946	91
5.	Goa	1091	1108	1120	1088	1084	1128	1066	981	975	969
6.	Gujarat	954	946	944	945	941	952	940	934	942	936
7.	Haryana	867	835	844	844	869	871	868	867	870	874
8.	Himachal Pradesh	884	889	890	897	890	912	938	958	973	996
9.	Jammu & Kashmir**	842	876	870	865	869	873	878	892	823	
10.	Karnataka	983	981	969	965	960	966	959	957	963	960
11.	Kerala	1004	1008	1022	1027	1028	1022	1016	1032	1040	
12.	Madhya Pradesh	990	986	974	973	970	967	953	941	932	
13.	Maharashtra	978	966	950	947	949	941	936	930	937	936
14.	Manipur	1037	1029	1041	1065	1036	1015	980	971	961	

Sl. No.	*India/State/ Union Territory*	*1901*	*1911*	*1921*	*1931*	*1941*	*1951*	*1961*	*1971*	*1981*	*1991*
1	2	3	4	5	6	7	8	9	10	11	12
India *States*		972	964	955	950	945	946	941	930	934	929
15.	Meghalaya	1036	1013	1000	971	966	949	937	942	954	947
16.	Mizoram	1113	1120	1109	1102	1069	1041	1009	946	919	924
17.	Nagaland	973	993	992	997	1021	999	933	871	863	890
18.	Orissa	1037	1056	1086	1067	1053	1022	1001	988	981	972
19.	Punjab	832	780	799	815	836	844	865	879	888	
20.	Rajashthan	905	908	896	907	906	921	908	911	919	913
21.	Sikkim	916	951	970	967	920	907	904	963	835	880
22.	Tamil Nadu	1040	1042	1029	1027	1012	1007	992	978	977	972
23.	Tripura	874	885	885	885	886	904	932	943	946	946
24.	Uttar Pradesh	937	915	909	904	907	910	909	879	885	882
25.	West Bangal	945	925	905	890	852	865	878	891	911	917
Union Territories											
1.	A & N Islands	318	352	303	495	574	625	617	644	707	820
2.	Chandigarh	771	720	743	751	763	781	652	749	769	793
3.	Dadra & Nagar Haveli	960	967	940	911	925	946	963	1007	974	953

Sl. No.	India/State/ Union Territory	1901	1911	1921	1931	1941	1951	1961	1971	1981	1991
1	2	3	4	5	6	7	8	9	10	11	12
India *States*		972	964	955	950	945	946	941	930	934	929
4.	Daman & Diu	995	1040	1143	1088	1080	1125	1169	299	262	272
5.	Delhi	862	793	733	722	715	768	785	801	808	830
6.	Lakshadweep	1063	987	1027	994	1018	1043	1020	978	975	944
7.	Pondicherry	N.A.	1098	1053	N.A.	N.A.	1030	1013	989	985	982

* In Arunachal Pradesh the Census was conducted for the first time in 1961. Hence, sex ratio for the earlier census is not available.

** The sex ratio for Jammu & Kashmir is based on projected population.

Due to certain reasons which will be discussed in due course, the sex ratio in India has been male dominated since the beginning of the 20th century. This trend has been increasing from 1901 to 1991 as is clear by the following table:

TABLE 8.5

Percentage of Male Population

Census Year	*Sex Ratio*	*Census Year*	*Sex Ratio*
1901	102.9	1951	105.7
1911	103.8	1961	106.3
1921	104.7	1971	107.5
1931	105.3	1981	106.6
1941	105.8	1991	107.1

TABLE 8.6

Female Population Per Thousand Males

Census year	*Female/thousand Male*
1921	955
1931	950
1941	945
1951	946
1961	941
1971	930
1981	934
1991	927

STATUS OF WOMAN: WORLD'S MAN FRIDAY[1]

- In the Himalayan region, a pair of bullocks toil annually for 1,064 hours, a man for 1,212 hours and a woman for 3,485 hours on a one-hectare farm.
- With men migrating first in search of livelihoods, the number of households headed by women has gone up from 20 per cent to 45 per cent.
- The alarming current sex-ratio of 927 females per 1000 males is even lower than the 1971 ratio of 930.

1. Article by Bhavana Padiyath, January 5, 1995, *The Times of India*, New Delhi.

- Globally, women do two-thirds of the work, earn one-third of the income and own one-tenths of the total resources.
- The death rate for females has declined to 9.8 per 1,000, and the sex differential in the infant mortality rate has been bridged with the decline in the rate for females from 129 per 1000 in 1978 to 79 in 1992.
- There is also a decline in the maternal mortality rate, which stood at 286 per 1000 in 1988.
- The 30 per cent reservation for women in seats to all local bodies will introduce around 800,000 poor women to public offices in rural areas alone.

These are some of the gender issues highlighted by the draft of India's Country Paper to be presented at the fourth World Conference on Women at Beijing next year. The draft, awaiting finalisation by the department of women and child development, was presented at the inter-ministerial meeting at Jakarta earlier.

Calling for a review of the development framework, the paper calls for the recognition of women as a part of the complexity called "development structures", through an equal allocation of resources and investment targets. Out of 96 countries recently surveyed by the International Research and Training Institute for the Advancement of Women, only in six countries including India, were women's issues accorded a place in the text of the development plan.

Analysing the structures and causes of poverty, the paper concludes that women are central to the success of poverty-alleviation efforts, and raising female earning power through efforts at the regional level could prove critical to demographic planning, child survival, increase in labour productivity and economic growth.

Approximately 35 per cent of the households below the poverty line are headed by females. The new economic liberalisation policy would have to be considered in the light of this gradual 'feminisation' of poverty, especially in a scenario where women have little access to productive resources, such as land or capital, the paper emphasises.

It calls for measures to ensure that the burden of unemployment generated by the structural adjustment programme does not fall disproportionately on the shoulders of women, particularly in the informal sector.

Nearly 84 per cent of all economically active Indian women are involved in agriculture or allied activities. The reallocation of forest resources away from the needs of local communities into the hands of urban and industrial India has increased the length of the working day for tribal and nomadic women in terms of fuel, fodder, water, and food garnering activities.

"Degradation of the environment with its negative impact on women call for reversal... by re-establishing the symbiotic relation between nature and mankind and by capturing the perspectives of poor women in this regard," the paper observes. The paper attributes the improvement in women's health status despite inhibitory cultural norms, and draws attention to the increase in the life expectancy for females at birth to 58.1 during 1986-90 as compared to 31.6 in 1951. Gaps in health care and the enlargement of women's reproductive choice have been identified as key issues to be addressed in the area of health.

Women continue to be marginalised on the employment front, though their participation increased from 19.7 per cent in 1981 to 22.3 per cent in 1991. Only four per cent of all employed women work in the organised sector, which provides social security. Within the organised sector, they are in the minority, accounting for a mere 14 per cent. At the other end, women account for 90 per cent of marginal workers in the economy.

Causes of Males Dominated Sex Ratio in India

The following factors have been indentified as responsible for the unusual pattern of a higher number of males than females in the total Indian population:

1. Differential Enumeration: The lower percentage of females in Indian population may be partially attributed to the unequal enumeration of males and females in census counting. Since in the rural areas census counting is not very much scientific and the enumerators are seldom allowed to directly meet the females, it is possible that a number of females may remain uncounted. However, most of the demographers agree that this cannot explain more than a very small part of the numerical imbalance.

2. Sex Ratio of Births: According to the study conducted by Ramachandran and Deshpande, the ratio of births in maternity homes was 106 in favour of males and there was not much regional variation.[1] According to the Sample Registration Scheme, in 1961 the sex ratio of births in rural India was 107.8. According to the survey conducted by Vital Statistics Division of the Government of India, the sex ratio of the projected population for 1971 was 107.1 while it was assumed to be 108. Actually the sex ratio in 1971 was 107.5. This shows that the low percentage of females in Indian population is not due to more male births but other reasons.

3. Higher Female Mortality: Demographic data for urban India in 1969 indicates higher death rates for males at all ages of infant life, with an exception of age of 29 days to 6 months for which the death rate for females is higher. Therefore, it cannot be said that there is a tendency of higher natural mortality of females in India. However, it has been found that female mortality is higher, if not due to natural reasons, then due to social reasons. Scholars have pointed out time and again that the status of the female in Indian society has been always considered lower than that of the males. The Khanna Study and the National Sample Survey reveal a higher female death rate pattern.[2] Numerous KAP studies have shown that in India parents show strong preference for male children. Studies have shown differential treatment to sick male and female children particularly in the rural areas. Maternal mortality has been shockingly high in rural areas due to the same reasons. Therefore, it may be concluded that the most important reason for lower female ratio in Indian population is the higher mortality of female children as well as mothers.

4. Male Dominated Emigration: It can be easily accepted that international migration in India is male dominated. This, however, cannot be said to be a very important point since not many people emigrate from India to outside countries.

From the discussion of the above mentioned probable causes of male dominated sex ratio in India, it is clear that the most important factor is the lower social status of Indian women, resulting into insufficient medical aid and nutritive provisions.

---

1. K.V. Ramachandran and Vinayak Deshpande, "The Sex-Ratio at birth in India by Regions," *The Milbank Memorial Funds Quarterly*, Vol. 42, No. 2. Part I, April 1964, pp. 84-85.
2. Praveerrn Visaria, *The Sex Ratio of the Population of India*, Census of India, 1961, Vol. 1, Monograph No. 10, p. 45.

FACTORS DETERMINING SEX RATIO

The sex ratio of a country is determined by the following factors:

1. Sex Ratio at Birth: An examination of the sex ratios of registered births for a number of countries over a considerable period shows that the sex ratio of births generally remains in favour of male babies.[1] The average sex ratio is 105 male babies per 100 female babies. This average varies between 101.2 to 106.6 in different countries. For example, it is 106.7 in Ireland and Norway. It is more than 106.0 in Canada, Belgium, Poland, Romania and UK. On the other hand, South Africa shows 106.7 ratio, the lowest in the world. Sex ratio at birth is generally determined biologically, probably due to nature's balance in favour of males. Sex ratio at birth depends upon sex ratio at the time of conception and sex ratio due to deaths. It has been found that foetal deaths are generally higher in male babies. Sex ratio is also partly determined by demographic factors such as the age of mothers and the order of live births. There appears to be an inverse correlation between the age of the mother and the birth order of the child and sex ratio at birth. Comparatively more male babies are found among the first and second born children. Lower ages of mothers generally lead to the birth of female babies. Thus, there is a negative correlation between the age of the mother and the sex ratio of the births.

2. Sex Ratio of Diseased Persons: Differential mortality is an important factor determining sex ratio. It has been found by some studies that in a number of countries more than one hundred males die per 100 females.[2] The male foetus is biologically more delicate than the female foetus. Therefore, there is a higher proportion of male babies in still birth. Even after birth, the male baby continues to be at a disadvantage. In most of the countries, the crude death rates for males are higher than those for the females. Again, the expectation of life at birth for females is almost universally higher than that of the males.[3] India and Pakistan are exceptions to this rule. In developed countries the death rates are higher for males

1. Praveen M. Visaria, "Sex Ratio at Birth in Territories with a Relatively Complete Registration", *Euguenics Quarterly*, Vol. 14, No. 2, June 1967, pp. 134-135.
2. Registrar-General of India, *Sex Composition in India*, SRS Analytical Series No. 4, 1972, pp. 23-24.
3. United Nations, *The Determinants and Consequences of Population Trends, op. cit.*, p. 115.

than the females, in every age group. The overall mortality for males is therefore generally higher. This results into imbalance in sex ratio. As the age advances, the sex ratio exhibits an increasing number of females. In all the regions of the world the sex ratio is favourable to females above the age group of 65. The same can be said about other age groups. Some causes for this tendency include male deaths during wars, reflected in sex ratios in most of the countries in post-war period.

3. Sex Ratio of Net Migrants: Yet another factor affecting sex ratio is the sex ratio of net migrants. Migration is generally sex selective. For example, in India it is male dominated. Internal migration is also sex selective. While it has been male dominated in India, it is female dominated in many European countries as well as in USA.

All the above mentioned three factors determine sex ratio in different countries. As has been already pointed out, the picture in the West, particularly about migration, is different from the East. Besides the biological factors, social and cultural factors have also been influential.

AGE STRUCTURE

According to the United Nations age is, "The estimated or calculated interval of time between the date of birth and the date of census, expressed in completed solar years."[1] It has been recommended that the information on age should be collected by asking the date of birth of the individual in terms of day, month and year of the last birthday. This information obviously provides more accurate data. However, in countries like India, not many people keep a record of their birth, therefore information on age is collected by asking about "the age completed on the last birthday."[2] This is particularly true in the case of illiterate and semi-literate people. Many of them do not know their age. If questioned, they tell it by guess which may be wrong even by a decade. Again, due to absence of proper provision for registration of births in rural areas birth certificate cannot be used to know the age. Since most of the people do not need birth certificates at any time in their lives, therefore nobody cares to get it. It has been found that there is a general tendency among Indians to report

1. United Nations, *Principles and Recommendations for the 1970 Population Censuses*, Statistical Papers, Series M. No. 44,1967, p. 41.
2. *Ibid*., p. 18.

their age in numbers ending with 0 or 5, resulting in concentration of population at a certain age in census data. Further mistakes might be committed due to carelessness on either part or deliberate mischief. In order to rectify these possibilities of errors, the demographers try to determine the nature and magnitude of errors and make necessary adjustments. According to 1971 census age data in India it was found that the figures for the ages 9, 10 and 11 were respectively 5,976,600; 10,548,600; and 4,666,600 respectively. This clearly shows the tendency of preferring the 0 digit as mentioned above.

Analysis of Age Data

For Demographic purposes age data is classified in five-year age groups such as 0-4, 5-9, 10-14, 15-20, 20-24 and so on. Thus classified, the age data are used for analysis of the age structure in any population. The age structure is generally studied with the help of per cent distribution or age pyramid. Other measures used for the purpose are the average age and a few other indices. The simplest measure of age structure is the percentage distribution. It indicates the number of persons in an age group, taking the total number of persons as one hundred. This helps in arriving at an idea about the age structure of any population. It may be also useful to compare the age structures of two or more populations at a point of time. This is particularly true in the case of Age-Sex histograms or Age-Sex pyramids as shown in the following Age-Sex table of Indian population in 1971. This may be compared with data from other census reports.

An important measure in the analysis of age structure is known as the dependency ratio. This indicates the number of dependents per 100 workers. It may be computed on the basis of three broad age groups. Suppose these age groups are: 15-59, 15-64 and 15-60, in this data those having age below 15 are young dependents while those above 60 or 65 are old dependents. The dependency ratio, computed is as follows:

Age Groups: 0-14, 65+ and 15-64.

Formula: $\text{Dependency Ratio} = \dfrac{P_{0-14} + P_{65} +}{P_{15-64}} \times K$

where $P_{0\text{-}14}$, $P_{65}+$, and $P_{15\text{-}64}$, denote the populations in the age groups 0-14, 65+ and 15-64 respectively and where K is 100.

Thus, in 1971, the dependency burden for India was as follows:

$$\text{Dependency Ratio} = \frac{230,416+15,060}{301,703}\times 100$$

$$= 81.36.$$

$$\text{Young Dependency Ratio} = \frac{230,416}{301,703}\times 100$$

$$= 76.37$$

$$\text{Old Dependency Ratio} = \frac{15,060}{301,703}\times 100$$

$$= 4.99$$

Total Dependency Ratio = Young Dependency Ratio + Old Dependency Ratio

Hence 81.36 = 76.37+4.99

Age Structure in India

The following table shows the distribution of population in India according to age groups in 1971[1].

TABLE 8.7

Population Distribution According to Age Group (1971)

Age Group	Population (in Thousands)	Percentage
0–4	87,940	16.07
5–9	77,445	14.15
10–14	65,031	11.88
15–19	53,986	9.87
20–24	47,100	8.61
25–29	41,642	7.61
30–34	36,815	6.73
35–39	31,824	5.58
40–44	26,700	4.88
45–49	21,907	4.00
50–54	17,458	3.19
55–59	13,861	2.53
60–64	10,410	1.90
65–69	6,870	1.26
70+	8,190	1.50
Not Available	771	—

1. Computed from Census of India 1971, Series I, India,. Miscellaneous Studies Paper 2 of 1977, *Age and Life Tabtes* (One per cent sample), pp. 8-9.

As is clear by the table given above the age structure in Indian population shows all the characteristics of developing countries. In most of the developing countries the percentage of population in various age groups is as follows: 15 years 40%; 15-55 years 55%; above 56 years 5%. In Indian population one finds the following percentage in age structure: less than 14, 43%; 14-34 years 32%; 35-59 years 20.5%; more than 60 years 4.5%. The percentage of working population includes age group 14-59. The people above and below these age groups are dependent population. On an average the working population in India constitutes considerably lower percentage as compared to those in the developed countries. 54% of the population in India depends upon 46% of the population in the productive ages between is and 50. This shows that the dependency ratio in this country Is far more than those in other countries. This reduces savings and investments and inhibits the rate of economic and social advancement. Since an increasingly large number of persons continue to enter the working ages, the problem of unemployment worsens. Before the beginning of 1st Five Year Plan, the number of unemployed persons in India was 3 and a half million, at the end of 3rd Five Year Plan, the number of unemployed persons increased to 10 million. As compared to the age structure in 1961 census, the pattern has not changed in 1971 and 1981. Therefore the conclusions given above are equally applicable to the age structure in the present population.

TABLE 8.8

Age Structure Projections (As on 1 March)

Per cent

Age Group	*1980*	*1985*	*1990*	*2000*
0–4	48.38	13.91	12.85	10.66
5–14	25.54	24.34	23.15	20.95
15–59	54.07	55.51	57.51	60.80
60 plus	6.21	6.24	6.49	7.59
Total	100.00	100.00	100.00	100.00

Source: Five Year Plan 1985—1990.

The following table (table 8.9) showing the age distribution in population in some of the countries of the world shows the difference between the developed and developing countries in this connection[1]. The table shows that Sweden has the lowest

1. Computed from United Nations, *Demographic Year Book*, 1972, pp. 159-209.

percentage of persons under the age of 15 while Kenya has the highest percentage. Again, Sweden has the highest percentage of persons above 65 years, while this percentage is lowest for Fiji. Thus, the developing countries have high percentages of children below 15 and low percentages of persons above 65 years of age. The percentage of working population in the developing countries, ranges from 46.8% to 55.7%. On the other hand in developed countries the working population ranges from 61.6% to 69.0%. They have smaller population below the working age group ranging from 20.8% to 28.8%. The percentage of elderly persons however, is higher, ranging from 7.0% to 13.7%. The dependency ratio in the developed countries is much lower as compared to the developing countries. While the dependency ratio in developing countries is 80.5%, in the developed countries it is only 57.0%. The pyramids made of the population structure of developing and developed countries therefore exhibit

TABLE 8.9

Age Distribution in Some Countries

Country	*0-14*	*15-64*	*65+*	*Dependency Ratio*
1	2	3	4	5
Kenya (1969)	48.38	46.25	5.37	116.22
Ghana (1970)	46.92	49.44	3.64	102.26
Iran (1971)	47.15	49.73	3.12	101.08
Fiji (1966)	46.75	50.85	2.40	96.63
Pakistan (1968)	45.93	50.91	3.16	96.42
India (1971)	42.10	55.14	2.76	81.36
Sri Lanka (1963)	41.75	54.64	3.61	83.02
Chile (1970)	39.58	51.68	4.74	79.60
United States (1970)	28.50	61.63	9.87	62.25
France (1968)	23.75	62.84	13.41	59.14
Sweden (1970)	20.82	65.44	13.74	52.81
United Kingdom (1971)	23.92	62.98	13.10	58.78
Japan (1970)	23.93	69.00	7.07	44.93
Australia (1971)	28.77	62.88	8.35	59.04
Developing Countries (1970)	40.8	55.4	3.8	80.5
Developed Countries (1970)	26.7	63.7	9.6	57.0

very much different shape. While the pyramids of developing countries show broad basis and steeply sloping sides, the pyramids of the age structure of developed countries are almost rectangular in shape with a slide sloping at the older ages. It is ironical to observe that old countries have much more young population than the new countries and the new countries have much more old population. It has been observed that the age structure of the developed countries has considerably changed over the years, while it is not so in the case of developing countries. As has been pointed out, the age structure in the last three census reports in India is almost the same. On the other hand in Sweden the proportion of children under 15 and the old persons above 64 was 33.25 and 5.2 in 1860, in the beginning of the 20th century it was 32.5 and 8.4 respectively. Similar changes may be observed in the age structure of population of other developed countries such as USA, France, England, Norway, Russia, Germany and other European countries. The age structures of the populations of the developing countries have changed very slightly. Thus, a substantial difference exists in the structures of the developing and the developed countries. Similar is the case about the dependency ratio.

The process of the decrease of children and increase of old person in a population is known as the aging of population. This is applicable in the case of developed countries. It should be noted that aging of a population is not a continuous process. It has also its downward curves. However, it has come to be established in the case of developed countries.

Factors Determining Age Structure

The age structure of a population is determined by the following factors:

1. Fertility: During the 1950s, researches of various demographers such as V.G. Valaorus (1950), Frank Lorimer (1951), Alfred Sauvey (1954), Ansley Coale (1956), and the United Nations (1958), demonstrated that the aging of the population in most of the Western countries is due to a decline in the fertility rates. The increase in the proportion of the old people and persons in the medium age was a product of falling birth rate. However, it was realised later on that mortality is an equally important factor. In the economically developed countries aging of population is particularly due to declining fertility. On the other hand, increased fertility has checked the aging of population in developing countries.

2. Mortality: It has been now realised that mortality is an equally important factor in the determination of age structure in a population. It effects the age distribution though to a much lesser extent than fertility. It has been demonstrated that reductions in mortality have resulted in a younger age distribution. The medium age of Indian population has dropped because of the decline in mortality. The same has been observed in Latin America during the period 1930-1960. The decline in mortality rate is particularly due to improvement in health and medical services and technology. While it has led to survival of children, it has also prolonged life in the older generation. This has led the French demographer Bourgeois Pichat to calculate that if fertility in France has remained unchanged from 1776 to 1951, while mortality declined according to the actual pattern, the population in 1951 would still have been a young population. The decline in mortality leads to younger age group in a country passing from high levels of mortality to low levels. On the other hand, if the mortality level is already low and the expectation of life is nearly 70 years there is not much scope for increase in young population. This leads to aging of the population as found in developed countries.

The above discussion shows that the fertility and mortality together effect the age structure of a population.

3. Migration: The effects of fertility and mortality are however changed considerably by the effects of migration, particularly the age distribution of the net migrants and volume of net migration. For example, if the proportion and number of young adults is large among the net migrants, the aging of the population is retarded. On the other hand, the aging process tends to get accelerated if the net migrants include persons above 30 years of age. The influence on age structure of a population is effected both by international as well as internal migration. For example internal net migration has influenced age-sex distribution in the population of Andaman and Nicobar Islands in India.

4. War: As has been clearly shown by the last two great World Wars, the age-sex structure of a population is considerably effected by war. War casualties mainly include males in the younger age groups. War also adversely affects fertility since most of the males in the participating countries are separated from their wives for a long period. This also leads to "babyboom" in post-war period since it leads to more marriages and more sexual activity. The age-sex pyramid shows smaller sized cohorts dining the war and bigger sized cohorts after the war.

MARITAL STATUS

Marital status, as is clear by the term, shows the status of a male or female with reference to matrimony. It shows whether a person is married or unmarried. The marital status is studied in demographic surveys. It is also obtained by periodic national census collecting information regarding marital status of each individual about a certain age. Each country collects data regarding marital status in the world which are compiled by the United Nations, in its yearly publications, *The Demographic Year Book*. According to the United Nations the marital status should be classified in the following 5 categories: Single (never married), married and not legally separated, widowed and not remarried, divorced and not remarried and married but legally separated.[1]

According to this classification the following table shows the distribution of females in India by age and marital status us in 1971:

TABLE 8.10

Distribution of Females According to Age Groups 1971

Age Group	Unmarried	Married	Widowed	Separated or Divorced
10–14	88.24	11.66	0.06	0.04
15–19	42.95	56.33	0.34	0.38
20–24	9.06	89.40	0.90	0.64
25–29	1.95	95.56	1.85	0.64
30–34	0.85	94.53	3.95	0.67
35–39	0.54	91.76	6.99	0.71
40–44	0.58	84.57	14.19	0.66
45–49	0.43	78.50	20.43	0.64
50+	0.42	45.26	53.92	0.40
All Ages	21.94	65.04	12.55	0.47

1. Computed from Census of India, 1971, Series I—India, Part II Special, *All India Census Tables* (Estimated from one per cent Sample Data), pp. 118-120 (Mimeographed).

The distribution population by marital status in the 1971 census is available on sample basis. It shows that almost 50% of the people in India have been returned, as never married. This may be due to the reason that all the persons below 10 years of age who have not married have been included under this category under instructions from' the Census Commissioner. 44% of the people have been recorded as married. 6% have been recorded as widowed. The proportion of divorced or separated is very negligible since marriage in India is generally considered a sacrament. A higher percentage of males has been returned as never married. It is so since males marry later than the females. The high proportion of widows as compared to the widowers may be due to the fact that more widowers remarry. The following table-shows the percentage distribution of the population by sex and marital status, in 1971[1]:

TABLE 8.11

Distribution of Population by Sex and Marital Status 1971

	Never Married	*Married*	*Widowed*	*Divorced or Separated*
Persons	50.41	43.55	5.78	0.26
Males	55.27	41.58	2.96	0.19
Females	45.20	45.67	8.80	0.33

The above data may be compared with the marital status distribution in other countries to judge the quality of Indian population. In India the universality of marriage custom and the child marriages influence marry status. On the other hand, in countries like Ireland persons marry at a very to be age and so many persons never many. Therefore, there is bound to be a difference between the marital status of persons in such countries. As a general rule in West there is more prevalence of marrying late and also not marrying as compared to the countries in Asia and Africa.

The following table (8.12) showing distribution of females in selected countries by marital status gives a comparative picture of the condition in developing and developed countries.[2] While

1. *Pocket Book of Population Statistics,* New Delhi Office of the Registrar General, 1972, pp. 78-79.
2. Computed from United Nations: (1) *Demographic Year Book,* 1973, p. 425 and 434; *Demographic Year Book,* 1969, p. 256.

India and Pakistan are developing countries, United States and Ireland are included in developed countries.

The table shows that while in India maximum marriages take place between 20 and 24 age group, in USA and Ireland it is in the 25-29 age group in which very few marriages take place in India, While most of the people are unmarried in more developed countries in 15-19 group, in India and Pakistan most of the people are married by this age. On the other hand, while the percentage of divorced and separated is almost negligible in India and Pakistan they show a sizable number in more developed countries. These

TABLE 8.12

Distribution of Females by Marital Status

Country	*Marital Status Age Group*	*Unmarried*	*Currently Married*	*Widowed*	*Divorced and Separated*
Indian	15–19	42.95	56.33	0.34	0.38
(1971)	20–24	9.06	89.40	0.90	0.64
	25–29	1.95	95.56	1.85	0.64
Pakistan	15–19	68.60	31.10	0.13	0.17
(1968)	20–24	18.04	80.99	0.41	0.56
	25–29	5.60	92.24	1.44	0.72
United States	15–19	88.12	10.76	0.24	0.88
(1970)	20–24	36.28	57.90	0.68	5.14
	25–29	12.16	70.15	1.05	7.64
Ireland	15–19	98.40	1.59	0.01	—
(1966)	20–24	74.78	25.15	0.07	—
	25–29	37.75	61.99	0.26	—

tendencies make a difference in the social and economic quality of the population. In India the data on marital status was collected from the Census 1881 onward. The universal pattern of marital status of Indian women even according to 1971 census show that by the age of 39 almost all the Indian women are married. The high percentage of married females in the age groups 10-14 and 15-19 are evidence of the prevalence of child marriages. As regards the marital status according to rural urban distinctions, it is particularly marked in the age group 10-14. In this age group while 14% of the rural females are married, this percentage for urban females is only 3.97. In the age group 15-49 the percentage of never married in urban areas is almost double of those in rural areas. It should not be presumed that the marital status of Indian women as been constant. Several changes have occurred over a period of 20 years, since the census 1951 to 1971. A decline in mortality rates had led to increased number of widowed, divorced and separated women. The percentage of never married women has increased over the years while child marriages are on the decline. The table 8.13 at next page gives the distribution of females of age 15-44 in India by marital years in the period 1951-1971.[1]

Age at Marriage

It is difficult to find out actual data concerning age at marriage in India since marriages are not registered. However some demographers have calculated the mean age at first marriage in India. According to S.N. Agarwala, "The figures show that females marrying at the age of 12.5 years on the average in 1891, began marrying at the age of 17.1 years in 1971; similarly, the males

TABLE 8.13

Distribution of Females by Marital Status in India

Marital Status Census Year	Unmarried	Currently	Widowed and Divorced	Total
1951	8.22	82.81	8.97	100.00
1961	7.44	85.81	6.75	100.00
1971	11.00	84.50	4.50	100.00

who were marrying at the age of 19.6 began marrying at the age of 22.5 years. Thus, the female marriage age has increased by 4.6 years over the period of eighty years, that is, at an average rate of 0.58 years every ten years. The male age at marriage, on the other hand, has increased by 2.9 years only over the eighty-year period. The increase in the female age at marriage is largely because of the reduction in child marriages. For example, while in the 1891-1901 decade, 46 per cent of the girls in the age group 10-15 were married, only 20 per cent of this age group got married in the 1951-61 decade. Again, while 11 per cent of the girls in

1. Census of India 1951, Vol. I, A-II, *Demographic Tables*, pp. 171-175.

the age group 5-10 were married in the 1891-1902 decade, the corresponding percentage was negligible in the 1961-71 decade."[1]

Age at Widowhood

According to the census 1911, the percentage of widows in female population was 17. It declined to 15.5 in 1931 and 8.8 in 1971. In spite of no legal restrictions to widow remarriage, it is not very much prevalent due to social stigmas. This stigma differs in different Hindu castes. In lower castes remarriage is more prevalent. It has been estimated that the mean age at widowhood in the age group 15-45 was 34 years in 1951-61 decade. In 1941-51 decade it was around 33 years. Still earlier, in 1911-21 decade it was around 30 years. The 1971 census works it out to 35.2 years. This is particularly due to improvement in mortality. According to some studies, almost 1/4th of widows get remarried. Of these most are below the age of 20. Very few widows above 30 get remarried.

LITERACY AND EDUCATIONAL ATTAINMENT

A significant characteristic of population is literacy and educational attainment. This characteristic shows the level of development in a country. According to the United Nations, literacy can be defined as the ability of a person to read and write with understanding a short simple statement on his every day life.[2] Thus literacy is the ability to read and write with understanding. No person without understanding can be called a literate. It has been recommended by the United Nations that the information on literacy should be collected from only those who are either 10 years of age or above. It is so since the ability to read and write is not achieved until one has had some schooling. The most important source of literacy data is the national census. It is collected during census operations in all the countries of the world. The United Nations compiles information on literacy and educational attainment for all the countries of the world in the annual publication *The Demographic Year Book*. In order to calculate the level of literacy in a population the following formula is used:

$$\text{Crude Literacy Rate} = \frac{L}{P} \times K$$

1. Agarwala, S.N., *Age at Marriage in India*, Allahabad: Kitab Mahal, 1962, p. 296.
2. United Nations, *Principles and Recommendations for the 1970*, Population Census, *op. cit.*, p. 50

where L and P indicate the number of literate persons in the population and the total population respectively, and K is equal to 100. Using this formula, the Crude Literacy Rate for the population in 1971 may be computed as follows:

$$\text{Crude Literacy Rate (India, 1971)} = \frac{1,607,031}{5,454,958} \times 100.$$

The Crude Literacy Rate of 29.46, based on one per cent sample data of the 1971 Census, indicates that, in 1971, 29.46 per cent of the Indian population was literate, and that 70.54 per cent was illiterate.

Literacy in Developed and Developing Countries

The following table shows the level of education in developed and developing countries.[1]

Table 8.14

Levels of Education in Developed and Developing Countries

Level of Education		*Number of Pupils Enrolled (000's)* 1960	1970	1980	*Average Rates of* 1960-70	*Annual Growth* 1970-80
Developed Countries	Primary	124,010	138,201	125,415	1.1	– 1.0
	Secondary	47,131	70,169	81,282	4.1	1.5
	Higher	9,824	21,103	30,807	7.9	3.9
	Total	180,965	229,473	237,504	2.4	0.3
Developing Countries	Primary	122,006	204,452	295,515	5.3	3.8
	Secondary	21,480	51,609	98,323	9.2	6.7
	Higher	2,630	7,036	16,391	10.3	8.8
	Total	146,116	263,097	410,229	6.1	4.5

The ninth issue of "One World" focuses on the crucial problem of education in developing countries, which make up the majority-of the world population. The articles contributed to this issue stress three aspects of this problem:

1. *Education is the basis of development:* EXCELSIOR (Mexico) argues that education provides the indispensable foundations for scientific, technological and cultural progress.

1. Boris Kluchnikov, Director, Division of Educational Policy and Planning, UNESCO. The Future of Education, *Indian Express*, World Community Supplement, July 10, 1981.

2. There is an acute crisis in education in most third world countries, and this crisis is, according to LE SOLEIL (Dakar), a tragic reflection of the crisis of development which is presently more acute than ever in most developing countries.

3. POLITIKA (Belgrade) recalls the remarkable progress achieved at all levels of education in Yogoslavia since the Second World War, but nonetheless points to "short-circuits" between the aspirations of the young and the needs of the country, and in particular to the lack of interest in manual trades. The same problem is vividly illustrated by the remarkable psychological study contributed by ZYCIE WARSZAWY, expressing the aspirations and frustrations of young Poles.

On the other hand, newspapers from developing countries, DAWN (Karachi), INDIAN EXPRESS (New Delhi), LE SOLEIL (Dakar), and even EXCELSIOR (Mexico), express their consternation at the dramatically inadequate yield of the educational efforts, which were made in their countries, even when these efforts were intensive.

Such inadequate results are not only due to lack of financial means, cultural, ideological and structural factors are in fact far more determining. Several papers stress in this connection the fact that their educational systems are inherited from colonial powers more intent on perpetuating their empire than democratising education or respecting the indigenous cultures.

This inheritance is heavy. English and French, for example, remain the indispensable languages for communication and higher education, yet also perpetuate the elitist structure of the educational system. The elites vehicle models of thought, behaviour and consumption do not correspond at all to the needs of the majority of the population. EXCELSIOR furthermore calls attention to the importance of cultural penetration in Mexico. This nation's economy and education are in a state of dependence which, although not complete, engenders submission and passivity.

To meet the needs and cost of education which are everywhere staggering, financial means are dramatically inadequate. The third world countries are literally beset by a host of necessities, and in particular that of defense, which is aggravated by the generalised (world) arms race. The aid which developing nations receive for education from the industrialised countries represents only 9 per cent of the amount they invest in this field. And 80 per ant of this aid goes to higher education.

The conclusions which may be drawn from these views are clear. Education runs against overwhelming obstacles in developing countries. These obstacles can be overcome only if there is an effective solidarity between rich and poor nations. This solidarity is indeed the fundamental aim of a new international economic order which implies, on the part of the rich and powerful nations, less egoism and the will to curb their natural tendencies to cultural and economic domination.

In order for education to become accessible to all, it must be realised that it constitutes the surest investment towards development. Education cannot remain the privilege of an elite. Every human being has an inalienable right to education, as to health, freedom, or security. This right will become reality only when the means of defending and exercising it will be given to all, through a vast joint and generous effort of all the members of the world community.

The following table shows the projected level of education in developed and developing countries. This has been taken from Unesco Statistical Office 1981:

TABLE 8.15

Projected Level of Education in Developed and Developing Countries

	Level of Education	Number of pupils enrolled (000's) 1980	1990	2000	Average Rates of 1980-90	Annual Growth 1990-2000
Developed	Primary	125,415	128,634	131,730	03	0.2
Countries	Secondary	81,282	79,768	87,066	0.2	0.9
	Higher	30,807	32,203	35,271	0.4	0.9
	Total	237,504	240,605	254,067	0.1	0.5
Developing	Primary	295,515	397,392	484,487	3.0	2.0
Countries	Secondary	98,323	163,360	236,886	5.2	3.8
	Higher	16,391	28,352	42,988	5.6	4.2
	Total	410,229	589,104	764,261	3.7	2.0

Literacy in India

The first information about literacy in India was provided by Indian Census 1871. Since then literacy is computed by each population census. During the period 1891-1931 literacy increased slowly from 5.4 to 9.5. Therefore, it increased faster after independence, slowing 16.7 in 1951, 24.0 in 1961 and 29.5% in 1971. In 1981 the total number of literates in country was computed as 23,79,91,932 which included 15,88,37,215 males and 7,91,54,717 females. This shows a literacy rate of almost 40%. While the proportion of literate females among the total literates was formerly less than half in 1971, in 1981 it is more than half. Among females the percentage of illiteracy in 1971 was 58% in urban areas and 87% in rural areas. The corresponding male percentages of illiterates were 39 and 66 respectively. Among literates females about 88 per cent were found educated upto the matriculation level. According to the 1971 Census data literacy in different age groups was: 10-14, 60%; 15-19, 63%; 20-24, 60% for males. The corresponding percentage for female literacy in these age groups was 38, 37 and 28% respectively. Literacy is very low in rural areas as compared to urban areas, registering total number of illiterates in rural areas as 72.7% (61.2 male; 84.9 female) and 40.3% (30.5 male and 52.0 female) percentage in urban population. The percentage of educational attainments of matriculation and above was 2.2% in rural and 14.0% in urban areas. In 1971 and 1981 census among Indian states Kerala has shown the highest literacy rate followed by Tamil Nadu and Maharashtra. The lowest literacy rate was observed in Jammu and Kashmir. Among the Union Territories, Chandigarh returned the highest proportion of literates while the lowest literacy rate was observed in Arunachal Pradesh. These data concerning the state of literacy show some improvement in the total condition. However, it is far from satisfactory.

Educational attainment of males and females is a still more important population characteristic since the progress of a country depends upon educational attainment of its population. It is a very important criteria of distinction between developed and developing countries. The educational attainment in the former are much higher than those in the latter. The following table of distribution of the educational attainment of males and females of age 15 and above in India shows that it is still classified in the lower rung of developing countries:[1]

1. Computed from Registrar General Census and Commissioner of India, *Pocket Book of Population Statistics*, Census Centenary, 1972, New Delhi, pp. 70-73.

TABLE 8.16

Percentage of Literates to Estimated Population Aged 7 Years and Above, 1991

India/State/ Union Territory	1981 Persons	1981 Males	1981 Females	1991 Persons	1991 Males	1991 Females
1	2	3	4	5	6	7
India*	43.56	56.37	29.75	52.11	63.86	39.42
States						
1. Andhra Pradesh	35.66	46.83	24.16	45.11	56.24	33.71
2 Arunachal Pradesh	25.54	35.11	14.01	41.22	51.10	29.37
3. Assam	N.A	N.A	N.A	53.42	62.34	43.70
4. Bihar	32.03	46.58	16.51	38.54	52.63	23.10
5. Goa	65.71	76.01	55.17	76.96	85.48	68.20
6. Gujarat	52.21	65.14	38.46	60.91	72.54	48.50
7. Haryana	43.85	58.49	26.89	55.33	67.85	40.04
8. Himachal Pradesh	51.17	64.27	37.72	63.54	74.57	52.46
9. Jammu & Kashmir	32.68	44.18	19.55	N.A	N.A	N.A
10. Karnataka	46.20	58.72	33.16	55.98	67.25	44.34
11. Kerala	81.56	87.74	75.65	90.59	94.45	86.93
12. Madhya Pradesh	34.22	48.41	18.99	43.45	57.43	28.39
13. Maharashtra	55.83	69.66	41.01	63.05	74.84	50.51
14. Manipur	49.61	64.12	34.61	60.96	72.98	48.64
15. Meghalaya	42.02	46.62	37.15	48.26	51.57	44.78
16. Mizoram	74.26	79.37	68.60	81.23	84.06	78.09
17. Nagaland	50.20	58.52	40.28	61.30	66.09	55.72
18. Orissa	40.96	56.45	25.14	48.55	62.37	34.40
19. Punjab	48.12	55.52	39.64	57.14	63.68	49.72
20. Rajasthan	30.09	44.76	13.99	38.81	55.07	20.84
21. Sikkim	41.57	52.98	27.35	56.53	64.34	47.23
22. Tamil Nadu	54.38	68.05	40.43	63.72	74.88	52.29
23. Tripura	50.10	61.49	38.01	60.39	70.08	50.01
24. Uttar Pradesh	33.33	47.43	17.18	41.71	55.35	26.02
25. West Bengal	48.64	59.93	36.07	57.72	67.24	47.15
Union Territories						
1. A & N Islands	63.16	70.28	53.15	73.74	79.68	66.22
2. Chandigarh	74.81	78.89	69.31	78.73	82.67	73.61
3. Dadra & Nagar Haveli	32.70	44.69	20.38	39.45	52.07	26.10
4. Daman & Diu	59.91	74.45	46.51	73.58	85.67	61.38
5. Delhi	71.93	79.28	62.57	76.09	82.63	68.01
6. Lakshadweep	68.42	81.24	55.32	79.23	87.06	70.88
7. Pondicherry	65.14	77.09	53.03	74.91	83.91	65.79

Note: *Literacy rates for 1981 exclude Assam where the 1981 Census could not be held and the literacy rates for 1991 exclude Jammu & Kashmir where the 1991 Census is yet to be conducted. *The literacy rates for India for 1981 and 1991, excluding Assam and Jammu and Kashmir works out as under:*

	Persons	*Males*	*Females*
1981	43.66	56.49	29.84
1991	52.07	63.90	39.31

The 1991 figures are provisional.

TABLE 8.17

States and Union Territories Arranged in Descending Order of Literacy Rate among Persons, Males and Females, 1991

	Persons		Males		Females	
Rank	*State/Union*	*Literacy rate (per cent)*	*State/ Union*	*Literacy rate (per cent)*	*State/ Union*	*Literacy rate (per cent)*
1	2	3	4	5	6	7
1.	Kerala	90.59	Kerala	94.45	Kerala	86.93
2.	Mizoram	81.23	Lakshadweep	87.06	Mizoram	78.09
3.	Lakshadweep	79.23	Daman & Diu	85.67	Chandigarh	73.61
4.	Chandigarh	78.73	Goa	85.48	Lakshadweep	70.88
5.	Goa	76.96	Mizoram	84.06	Goa	68.20
6.	Delhi	76.09	Pondicherry	83.91	Delhi	68.01
7.	Pondicherry	74.91	Chandigarh	82.67	A & N Islands	66.22
8.	A & N Islands	73.74	Delhi	82.63	Pondicherry	65.79
9.	Daman & Diu	73.58	A & N Islands	79.68	Daman & Diu	61.38
10.	Tamil Nadu	63.72	Tamil Nadu	74.88	Nagaland	55.72
11.	Himachal Pradesh	63.54	Maharashtra	74.84	Himachal P.	52.46
12.	Maharashtra	63.05	Himachal P.	74.57	Tamil Nadu	52.29
13.	Nagaland	61.30	Manipur	72.98	Maharashtra	50.51
14.	Manipur	60.96	Gujarat	72.54	Tripura	50.01
15.	Gujarat	60.91	Tripura	70.08	Punjab	49.72
16.	Tripura	60.39	Haryana	67.85	Manipur	48.64
17.	West Bengal	57.72	Karnataka	67.25	Gujarat	48.50
18.	Punjab	57.14	West Bengal	67.24	Sikkim	47.23
19.	Sikkim	56.53	Nagaland	66.09	West Bengal	47.15
20.	Karnataka	55.98	Sikkim	64.34	Meghalaya	44.78
21.	Haryana	55.33	Punjab	63.68	Karnataka	44.34
22.	Assam	53.42	Orissa	62.37	Assam	43.70

23. Orissa	48.55	Assam	62.34	Haryana	40.94
24. Meghalaya	48.26	Madhya Pradesh	57.43	Orissa	34.40
25. Andhra Pradesh	45.11	Andhra Pradesh	56.24	Andhra Pradesh	33.71
26. Madhya Pradesh	43.45	Uttar Pradesh	55.35	Arunachal P.	29.37
27. Uttar Pradesh	41.71	Rajasthan	55.07	Madhya Pradesh	28.39
28. Arunachal Pradesh	41.22	Bihar	52.63	D & N Haveli	26.10
29. D & N Haveli	39.45	D & N Haveli	52.07	Uttar Pradesh	26.02
30. Rajasthan	38.81	Meghalaya	51.57	Bihar	23.10
31. Bihar	38.54	Arunachal P.	51.10	Rajasthan	20.84

Note : Excludes Jammu & Kashmir where the 1991 Census is yet to be held. . The figures are provisional.

TABLE 8.18

Educational Attainment 1971

Educational Attainment	Total Population	Males	Females
Literate without Educational Level	25.05	24.67	26.03
Primary	32.24	30.44	37.05
Middle	22.78	23.32	21.34
Matriculation or Higher Secondary	16.06	17.32	12.68
Non-Technical Diploma or Certificate Not Equal to Degree	0.17	0.18	0.15
Technical Diploma or Certificate Not Equal to Degree	0.38	0.40	0.35
Graduate and Above	3.32	3.67	2.40
All Educational Attainments	100.00	100.00	100.00

TABLE 8.19

Literacy Rate 1951-1991

Year	*Person*	*Male*	*Female*
1	2	3	4
1951	18.33	27.16	8.86
1961	28.31	40.40	15.34
1971	34.45	45.95	21.97
1981	43.56	56.37	29.75
	(41.42)	(53.45)	(28.46)
1991	51.21	64.13	39.29

RELIGIOUS COMPOSITION

A very important characteristic of a population is religion since it influences various types of demographic behaviour. This is particularly important in Asian countries and the countries of Indian sub-continent. The analysis of different census data has revealed the tendency of the growth of non-Hindu population faster than the Hindu population. In almost all the last census reports this has been confirmed. And yet the Hindus constitute almost 80% of the total population. Muslim's rank II with almost 12% of the total population. Christians form 2.6% and the rest is covered by other religious groups. The growth rate of the percentage of population of various religions in India is clear by the table given below :[1]

TABLE 8.20

Population According to Religion

	7961		1971		1981		1991	
Religious group	Number (million)	% to total	Number (million)	% to total	Number (million)	% to total	Number (million)	% to total
Hindus	366.5	83.5	453.3	82.7	549.7	82.6	672.6	82.41
Muslims	46.9	10.7	61.4	11.2	75.6	11.4	95.2	11.67
Christians	10.7	2.4	14.2	2.6	16.2	2.4	18.9	2.32
Sikhs	7.8	1.8	10.4	1.9	13.1	2.0	16.3	1.99
Buddhists	3.2	0.7	3.8	0.7	4.7	0.7	6.3	0.77
Jains	2.0	0.5	2.6	0.5	3.2	0.5	3.4	0.41
Other[1]	1.6	0.4	2.2	0.4	2.8	0.4	3.5	0.43
Total	439.2	100.0	548.2	100.0	665.3	100.0	816.21[2]	100.00

Source: Census of India 1981, Series I — Paper I of 1995 (Religion), Paper I of 1991 (Religion).

1. Including unclassified persons.
2. Excludes Assam and J & K.

Note : 1981 data do not include Assam.

ETHNIC COMPOSITION

Besides religion ethnic composition includes language. In India at the time of 1961 Census it was found that the population spoke as many as 1,652 mother tongues. Of these the Indian Constitution

1. *Census of India*, 1971, Paper No. 1972.

has recognised 14 major languages with Hindi as the National Language. According to 1971 Census Hindi is spoken by 162.6 million people or by about 30% of the Indian population. Along with English, Hindi is an official language in most of the states. The percentage of Sanskrit speaking people was almost negligible. In census 1981 the position of Hindi has not much improved particularly due to encouragement to regional languages in different states of the country and not much encouragement to propagation of Hindi. The status of Urdu has however somewhat improved with the increase in the Muslim population in the country. The following table shows the percentage of persons speaking the major languages in India in 1971 and 1981.

TABLE 8.21

Population According to Language

Languages	*Population (Crores)*		*Per cent*	
	1971	*1981*	*1971*	*1981*
1	2	3	4	5
Hindi	208.5	264.5	38.0	42.9
Bangla	44.8	51.3	8.2	8.3
Telugu	44.8	50.6	8.2	8.2
Marathi	41.8	49.5	7.6	8.0
Tamil	37.7	3.8	6.9	0.6
Urdu	28.6	34.9	5.2	5.7
Gujarati	25.9	33.1	4.7	5.4
Malyalam	21.9	25.7	4.0	4.2
Kannada	21.7	25.7	4.0	4.2
Oriya	19.9	23.0	3.6	3.7
Punjabi	14.1	19.6	2.6	3.2
Assamia	9.0	0.1	1.6	0.01
Sindhi	1.7	2.0	0.3	0.3
Kashmiri	2.5	3.2	0.5	0.5

QUESTIONS FOR EXERCISE

1. Define population characteristics and describe their uses, types and importance.
2. Discuss and describe age and sex characteristics of population in India. What are the causes of males dominated ratio.

3. How will you analyse Age Data? What factors determine age structure? Discuss the importance of Age structure in population.
4. Describe mental status and its significance in Indian population.

9

Population Dynamics: Mortality

Population change has been defined in terms of mortality, fertility and migration. In this chapter mortality will be discussed followed by fertility and migration in the next chapters. According to the United Nations mortality is the percentage of death in the population. Death has been defined by the World Health Organisation as follows: "Death is the permanent disappearance of all evidence of life at any time after birth has taken place (post-natal) cessation of vital functions without capacity of resuscitation."[1] This definition however, postulates that death can occur only after live birth. Therefore, mortality is closely linked with live birth. The United Nations has defined live birth as follows: "Live birth is the complete expulsion or extraction from its mother of a product of conception, irrespective of the duration of pregnancy, which, after such separation, breathes or shows any other evidence of life, such as beating of the heart, pulsation of the umbilical cord, or definite movement of voluntary muscles, whether or not the umbilical cord has been cut or the placenta is attached; each product of such a birth is considered live-born."[2]Death prior to a live birth is not included in mortality. It is known as still birth.

---

1. United Nations, Statistical Office, *Principles for a Vital Statistics System*, Statistical Papers, Series M. No. 19, New York 1953, p.6
2. *Ibid.*, p. 6.

Sources of Data

The above explanation of the concept of mortality implies sources of data about it. An important source of data is the registration of vital event. This, however, is very inadequate in developing countries except in some major cities. It is only rarely that mortality data are gathered through census. On the world level *The Demographic Year Book* of the United Nations provides data on mortality including number of deaths, death rates, death by age and sex, infant deaths, infant mortality rates, causes of death, etc. Statistical report of the World Health Organisation also provides information on mortality. The following explanation of the sources of mortality data in India will help in understanding the sources in developing countries:

1. Vital Registration: In India the history of collecting vital data dates back to 1886. Vital Registration has been the function of the Registrar General of India. It has been reported by the Office of the Registrar that during 1941-51 the under registration of mortality rate was 31.3. In 1951-61 it was 50.4. The same source provides data for under registration of deaths in different states of India. Thus, there is a serious handicap for gathering mortality data in India.

2. National Sample Survey: Another source of mortality data in India is the National Sample Survey (MSS). It collects information on a variety of topics. It was established in 1949. It is gathering mortality data since October 1953. Its estimates are better than those of Registrar General of India. But it also suffers from certain limitations like recall lapse and mis-statements of events due to the mixing of the reference period.

3. Sample Registration Scheme: This scheme was launched by the Registrar General of India in 1964. It is also known as Sample Registration System. It aims at obtaining more reliable mortality data. It involves continuous enumeration by a part time local resident enumerator, along with a six monthly cross check survey by a supervisor, manual matching of two sets of records, verification of discrepancies of the field, preparation of a final list of verified events and calculation of birth and death rates based on them. This scheme was first introduced as a pilot scheme in 1964 in Bihar, Gujarat, Kerala, Maharashtra and Mysore; for the purposes of testing the schedules and instructions, assessment of organisational problems and orientation of officials involved at all levels. In 1966 there was full scale sample registration in all the States with a stratified one stage sample in 156 villages. In the urban areas a stratified two-stage random sample was drawn. The rural area covered had a population of 350 million, spread over 545,000 villages in sixteen States. The urban areas covered had a population of 79 million in 2,700 cities and towns. Since the introduction of this scheme, more reliable information on birth and death rates, age-specific fertility and mortality rates, infant and adult mortality, etc., have become available.

4. Indirect Methods: Besides the above mentioned direct methods of obtaining death rates, demographers also use the following indirect methods of estimation of mortality. Firstly, age data of two consecutive censuses are used and the death rates are obtained through the application of 'differencing method', 'reverse survival method' in combination with the differencing method, 'stable' and 'quasi-stable' population methods, etc.

Measures of Mortality

The following are the most important basic measures for the general understanding of the process of mortality:

1. Crude Death Rate: This is the most simple, the most commonly used and the most quickly calculated and understood measure of mortality. Crude death rate is a ratio of the total registered deaths of a specified year to the total mid-year population, multiplied by 1000. It is computed as follows:

$$\frac{\mathrm{D}}{\mathrm{P}} \times k$$

where

D is the total number of deaths registered during a calendar year (January 1 to December 31).

P is the total population at the middle of the year (July 1); *k* is 1000.

For example, the crude death rates for Greater Bombay in 1973 have been computed as follows:

Total number of deaths 1973;

(January 1 to December 31) = 61,931

Total population at the middle of the

year, (*i.e.*, mid-year population

July 1, 1973) = 6,551,000

Therefore,

the crude death rate for

Greater Bombay for 1973 $= \frac{61,931}{6,551,000} \times 100$

$= 9.45.$

The crude death rate expresses the frequency of deaths in total population as a single number. For example, if it is said that in 1973 the crude death rate in Greater Bombay was 9.45, it means that 9.45 deaths occurred per 1000 population. The crude death rate provides the basis for computing the rate of natural increase in population by comparison with the crude birth rate. It is the most widely available index of mortality. It may be compared with similar data from other countries to know the trend in mortality. However, it is not a refined measure. It suffers from severe limitations, the most glaring of which are the following:

1. Its coverage of death statistics is inadequate.
2. It hides the experience of population group with varying mortality.
3. It gives a greater weightage to the mortality experience of large group in the population.
4. It does not take cognisance of the differences in the age-sex structures of different populations.

To overcome the above mentioned limitations are used age specific death rates.

2. Average Life Expectancy: This is average expectation of life at birth. It is a useful measure of mortality because it is not influenced by the age structure. It is derived from the life-table which is constructed to summarise the mortality experience, of a single hypothetical generation. Average life expectancy means the average-number of years of life which cohort of new born babies may be expected to live. This measure is rather complicated to calculate. However, it is most easily understood by the common man. Therefore, it is widely used in different countries.

3. Infant Mortality Rate: According to George W. Barclay, "Infants are defined in demography as an exact age group, namely, age zero, or those children in the first year of life who have not yet reached age one."[1] The infant mortality rate is a measure of the risk of death between the birth of the baby and its first birth day. It is computed as follows :

$$\frac{d_o}{B} \times K$$

where:

d_o is the number of deaths below age one, registered during calendar year,

B is the number of live births, registered during the same year,

K is 1,000.

For example, infant mortality rate for Greater Bombay for 1973 was computed as follows:

Total number of registered deaths among infants during 1973 = 7,023

Total number of registered live births during 1973 = 81,642

Therefore, infant mortality rate for Greater Bombay for 1973 $= \frac{7{,}023}{81{,}642} \times 1{,}000$

$= 86.02$

The above mentioned mortality rate shows that in 1973, 86.02 infants per 1,000 live born babies died during the first year of their life in Greater Bombay. These measures of mortality will be discussed in more details in sequence.

CRUDE DEATH RATE

Data on crude death rate shows that it differs in developed and developing countries. It has gradually changed almost everywhere but particularly in developed countries. During 1840-1965 the average life for developed countries increased from 41.0 years to 72.3 years. The most striking gains were made in the decade 1940-1950 immediately after the Second World War. According to United Nations the life expectancy at birth for both sexes during 1840-1965 for six European countries including Denmark, England and Wales, France, Norway, Sweden and Massachusetts

1. *Ibid.*

(USA) was 41.0 in 1940 and 72.3 in 1965[1]. The crude death rate in Europe varied very much during the period 1906-1909. Almost all the countries of Europe together with North America, Australia, New Zealand, Argentina, Japan, and the USSR have shown declining crude death rates upto 1950 after which the decline was comparatively small. The crude death rate in 1974 was 13.3 in German Democratic Republic and the lowest 6.5 in Japan. On the other hand in developing countries one finds high crude death rate. The situation has not appreciably improved even in recent years. For example, according to Sample Registration Bulletin,[2] the crude death rate in India was 16.8 in 1968, 19.1 in 1969, 17.3 in 1973, 16.4 in 1971, 18.9 in 1972, 17.0 in 1973, 15.9 in 1974 and 16.1 in 1974-75. This shows almost no change in so many years. The death rate is lower in the urban areas and, has also fallen during the years. For example, according to the above mentioned source, during 1968-1975 in India urban death rate was 11.4 for 1969 and 9.6 for 1974-75. Broadly, it can be said that the death rate in India in 1961 was 21. It came down to 17.18 in 1965 and 14.15 in 1976. This has however shown regional variations. For example, life expectancy in the period 1951-1961 in India was 36.8 for Assam, 36.9 for Andhra Pradesh and 48.3 for Kerala, 47.5 for Orissa, etc. As a general rule death rate in urban areas is lower than the rural areas. This is particularly due to better health and medical conditions.

Causes of High Death Rate

United Nations and other agencies have tried to analyse the causes of high death rate, particularly upto the 19th century, almost throughout the world. It has been found that the most important reasons for high mortality rates were as follows:

1. Famines and Food Shortages: During the period 1000 AD to 1885 AD almost 450 localised famines were recorded in Western Europe. The situation was even worst in Asia, famine was an almost constant factor. During the period 108 BC — 1911 AD China experienced 1828 famines, almost one each year. Besides famines, food shortages were due to insufficient food supply resulting into malnutrition, diseases and deaths.

---

1. United Nations, *The Determinants and Consequences of Population Trends,* Vol. I, ST/SOA/SER. A50, Population Studies No. 50, New York: 1953, p. 111.
2. *Sample Registration Bulletin,* Vol. VII, New Delhi: Office of the Registrar General of India 1973, p. 2; *Sample Registration Bulletin.* Vol. X. No. 2,1976 p. 2.

2. Epidemics. Until two centuries back scientific knowledge about diseases did not exist and therefore communicable diseases took a heavy toll of life. These included typhoid, dysentery, smallpox, malaria, typhus, tuberculosis, pneumonia, yellow fever and plague. Child mortality was high due to communicable diseases such as enteritis, measles, whooping cough, scarlet fever, diphtheria, etc.

Table 9.1

Estimated Crude Death Rates for States and Union Territories, 1985-1989

State/Union Territory	Area	1985	1986	1987	1988	1989*
1	2	3	4	5	6	7
1. Andhra Pradesh	Combined	10.3	9.9	9.9	10.2	9.3
	Rural	11.1	10.7	19.7	10.9	10.0
	Urban	7.3	7.1	7.3	7.4	6.5
2. Arunachal Pradesh	Combined	14.3	15.0	13.2	17.2	14.1
	Rural	15.2	15.9	14.2	18.4	15.0
	Urban	2.2	4.6	2.6	5.0	4.7
3. Assam	Combined	13.2	12.6	11.6	11.8	10.3
	Rural	13.5	12.9	11.9	12.1	10.5
	Urban	8.4	7.9	8.1	7.9	7.5
4. Bihar	Combined	15.0	13.8	13.1	12.6	12.1
	Rural	15.6	14.4	13.6	13.0	12.5
	Urban	9.0	8.8	8.0	8.1	7.9
5. Goa	Combined	8.0	7.6	7.5	7.9	7.8
	Rural	8.9	7.9	8.5	8.5	8.2
	Urban	6.0	6.9	5.4	6.8	7.2
6. Gujarat	Combined	10.8	10.5	9.8	11.0	9.6
	Rural	11.8	11.3	10.8	11.8	9.9
	Urban	8.7	8.6	7.6	9.2	8.8
7. Haryana	Combined	9.1	8.7	8.8	9.8	8.4
	Rural	9.7	9.2	9.4	10.4	9.0
	Urban	7.1	6.6	6.9	7.6	6.5
8. Himachal Pradesh	Combined	10.5	8.7	8.5	9.6	8.7
	Rural	10.8	8.8	8.7	9.9	8.9
	Urban	6.5	7.2	5.3	5.0	6.1
9. Jammu & Kashmir	Combined	9.8	8.6	7.7	8.4	7.9
	Rural	10.5	9.0	8.0	9.1	8.3
	Urban	7.2	6.8	6.4	6.0	6.4
10. Karnataka	Combined	8.8	8.7	8.7	8.8	8.7
	Rural	9.8	9.4	9.7	9.5	9.5
	Urban	6.1	6.8	6.1	7.0	6.5

11. Kerala	Combined	6.5	6.1	6.1	6.4	5.9
	Rural	6.5	6.0	6.1	6.3	5.9
	Urban	6.6	6.9	6.2	6.7	6.0
12. Madhya Pradesh	Combined	14.2	13.6	13.3	14.3	12.8
	Rural	15.3	14.8	14.6	15.4	13.8
	Urban	9.4	8.8	8.0	9.8	8.3
13. Maharashtra	Combined	8.4	8.4	8.3	8.9	7.9
	Rural	9.4	9.7	9.5	10.1	8.9
	Urban	6.7	6.1	6.1	6.7	6.1
14. Manipur	Combined	7.7	6.7	5.6	6.8	6.7
	Rural	7.9	7.1	5.9	7.3	7.0
	Urban	7.1	5.2	4.5	5.3	6.0
15. Meghalaya	Combined	12.7	10.1	9.1	9.1	11.3
	Rural	14.3	11.2	10.2	10.6	12.6
	Urban	5.6	5.3	3.6	2.7	4.8
16. Nagaland	Combined	6.3	5.9	4.9	5.0	4.1
	Rural	7.0	6.6	5.5	5.7	4.7
	Urban	3.0	2.7	2.6	1.7	1.3
17. Orissa	Combined	14.0	13.0	13.1	12.3	12.6
	Rural	14.6	13.5	13.7	12.8	13.1
	Urban	8.1	8.1	7.8	7.1	8.0
18. Punjab	Combined	8.9	8.2	8.1	8.4	8.3
	Rural	9.7	8.7	8.5	8.8	8.8
	Urban	6.7	6.6	7.1	7.2	6.8
19. Rajasthan	Combined	13.2	11.7	11.6	14.0	10.6
	Rural	14.0	12.5	12.5	15.2	11.3
	Urban	9.6	8.4	7.8	8.7	7.7
20. Sikkim	Combined	10.7	11.7	10.3	10.1	9.1
	Rural	11.7	12.9	11.4	11.1	10.1
	Urban	6.2	6.1	5.4	5.5	4.3
21. Tamil Nadu	Combined	9.5	9.5	9.9	9.3	8.6
	Rural	10.9	10.7	11.1	10.3	9.7
	Urban	6.9	7.1	7.6	7.3	6.6
22. Tripura	Combined	9.9	10.3	9.2	8.1	7.7
	Rural	10.1	10.5	9.5	8.5	7.9
	Urban	8.0	9.2	6.3	4.6	5.7
23. Uttar Pradesh	Combined	15.8	14.6	14.5	13.2	12.6
	Rural	17.2	15.7	15.5	14.1	13.7
	Urban	9.6	10.0	9.9	9.4	8.2
24. West Bengal	Combined	9.6	8.8	8.8	8.4	8.6
	Rural	10.7	9.6	9.7	9.4	9.3
	Urban	6.8	6.9	6.5	5.9	6.8

Table 9.1 (Contd.)

1	2	3	4	5	6	7
UNION TERRITORIES						
1. Andaman & Nicobar	Combined	6.8	7.8	6.1	6.4	5.9
Islands	Rural	7.9	8.5	6.5	7.1	6.6
	Urban	3.4	5.5	4.5	4.2	3.4
2. Chandigarh	Combined	4.0	4.6	3.8	4.7	3.8
	Rural	6.1	4.6	5.8	6.0	6.6
	Urban	3.8	4.6	3.7	4.6	3.6
3. Dadra & Nagar						
Haveli	Rural	11.9	9.4	11.3	9.8	8.5
4. Daman & Diu	Combined	10.2	8.1	7.1	8.9	8.2
	Rural	9.1	8.9	8.6	10.5	7.7
	Urban	11.6	7.1	4.8	6.6	8.9
5. Delhi	Combined	8.1	7.3	7.5	7.6	6.7
	Rural	10.1	8.7	8.5	8.3	7.7
	Urban	7.9	7.2	7.4	7.6	6.6
6. Lakshadweep	Combined	7.2	4.9	6.3	6.6	6.0
	Rural	9.2	5.4	6.8	6.2	8.5
	Urban	5.0	4.2	5.7	7.0	3.1
7. Pondicherry	Combined	7.2	8.3	8.0	7.9	7.8
	Rural	8.3	8.7	8.9	8.7	8.2
	Urban	6.3	8.0	7.3	7.9	7.5
INDIA						
(Excluding Bihar	Combined	11.7	11.0	10.9	11.1	
& West Bengal)	Rural	12.9	12.1	12.0	12.0	
	Urban	7.8	7.7	7.5	7.9	
(Including Bihar	Combined	11.8	11.1	10.9	11.0	10.2
& West Bengal)	Rural	13.0	12.2	12.0	12.0	11.1
	Urban	7.8	7.6	7.4	7.7	7.1

*Provisional

3. Recurrent Wars: Recurrent wars in different countries have taken a heavy toll of life. For example, in the Franco-Prussian War of 1870-71, 13,000 amputations had to be performed of which 10 thousand were fatal. In 20th century the two great wars brought death of such a wide magnitude in such a broad area that war is considered to be the most important cause of deaths.

4. Poor Sanitary Conditions: Before the present century, in pre-industrial times the sanitary conditions were very poor in most of the countries. Even in industrial societies the environments were filthy. Most of the cities suffered from overcrowding and poor sanitary conditions. Upto 13th century the use of soap was almost unknown.

All the above mentioned factors have led to high mortality rates upto 19th century. However, after the agricultural and industrial revolutions mortality rates have fallen everywhere. Among the most important factors determining deduction in mortality rates in the developed countries in the past two centuries may be mentioned the following:

1. Agricultural revolution started in England around 1700 AD and spread throughout Europe and the European settlements in the world.

2. The development of the steam engine led to the growth of transport facilities due to which food could be easily sent to different areas.

3. Increase in per capita income led to availability of nutritious food resulting in decline in mortality.

4. Advances in technology and improvements in the standards of living led to decline in mortality.

5. Mortality was reduced due to improvements in sanitary conditions and public health measures particularly in developed countries.

6. Social reforms decreased industrial hazards and improved health of working population.

7. The development of asepsis (precautionary exclusion of pathogenic micro-organisms) and antisepsis (killing or inhibiting the growth of micro-organisms already present) helped in the reduction of mortality.

8. Another important cause of decline in mortality was the development of immunology. This checked chicken pox, cholera, sheep anthrax, hydrophobia and diphtheria. It also immunised against tetanus, typhoid, yellow fever, scarlet fever, poliomyelitis, influenza, measles, whooping cough, etc.

9. In late 1930 chemotherapy or use of drugs to cure or inhibit the progress of diseases was advanced. Considerable decline in mortality was noticed after the Second World War by the use of anti-tuberculosis drugs. Today, fearful diseases like smallpox and plague have almost disappeared.

10. Increase in the supply of food in almost all the countries of the world have led to decline of mortality.

The above mentioned factors are responsible for recent mortality decline particularly in the more developed countries and also to a great extent in developing countries. As compared to developed countries, the above advantages are not so much available in developing countries. Therefore, the decline in mortality in these countries is considerably low.

LIFE EXPECTANCY

Life expectancy means the average expectation of life at birth. In other words, it represents the average number of years of life which a new-born may be expected to live. The following two factors have been important variables in life expectancy.

1. Sex Distinctions: As a general rule females have higher life expectancy than males, in most of the countries. This gap is wider in the developed countries as compared to the developing countries. The extent of this gap has however changed at times and places. In developed countries the gap between female and male average life expectancy has widened over a period of 70 years. In most of the countries of the world the crude death rate as well as the age specific death rate are higher for male than for females. Evidence is available to prove that males are at a definite disadvantage in life expectancy. The causes of this gap have been studied almost everywhere. Besides the biological factors the environmental factors have also been found working for this gap. The constitutional difference has little support to be the main cause. Most of the reasons are environmental such as social and economic roles, problems of outdoor life, etc. The question still remains unsolved. According to a study in India expectation of life at birth by sex during the period 1961-1971 was 47.10 for the male and 45.60 for the female. On the other hand, the proportion was 41.89 for the male and 48.55 for the female during the period 1951-1961.

2. Age: Another important variable for life expectancy is age. Death rates vary with age. Therefore, age specific death rate has been an important measure of mortality in a country. This term means the number of deaths of persons of a given age per 1000 during a given year. It is computed similar to the crude death rate. It is found different in developed and developing countries. For example in 1970 age specific death rate was 19.1 in India for all ages while in USA it was 4.7 in 1971. The corresponding figures are for Japan 3.4; for UK 2.9; for Sweden 1.5; in 1973. Compared to underdeveloped and developing countries, it may be noted that these rates are very low. Again, the death rates differ at different ages. More deaths are reported during infant and old age.

INFANT MORTALITY

Yet another important index of mortality is infant mortality. It is particularly important due to the fact that in almost all the countries it is invariably high during the first year of life. It varies tremendously from country to country. While it was 131.0 in 1971 in India, it was only 9.9 in 1973 in Sweden. Again, while it was 116 in Egypt in 1972 it was 11.3 in 1973 in Japan. However, it has been noted that in spite of the fact that Sweden has the lowest infant mortality rate in the world. Eastern European countries show higher infant mortality, as is clear by the data that it is 44.2 in Yugoslavia, 38.1 in Romania and 33.8 in Hungary. These rates are higher even in comparison to some developing countries, such as Hong Kong (16.4 in 1973), Singapore (19.7 in 1970) and Trinidad and Tobago (23.5 in 1972). In 1971 Chile, a more developed country, had an infant mortality rate of 78.8. Some 150 years back infant mortality rates in industrialised countries were around 200. In 1870 they ranged from 100 in Norway to three hundred in Germany in Europe. In late 1950 and 1960 it was 200 in Africa. Even in the beginning of the 20th century it was more than 150 in Austria, Bulgaria, Hungary, Japan, Spain, and Portugal. The fall of infant mortality had been spectacular in 20th century. In USSR it was 269 in 1913 and only 29 in 1964. In Japan it was 110.4 in 1935-39 and only 20.4 in 1964. This is also true of developing countries. In

Singapore the infant mortality rate was 152 in 1935-39 and it was only 20 in 1973. Similar decline of almost 60% has been recorded in Sri Lanka, West Malaysia, Mauritius, etc. Thus, the infant mortality rate is declining everywhere. In India according to the Sample Registration System, the infant mortality rate in the years 1968, 1969, 1970 and 1971 was 137, 140, 133 and 131 respectively. This was in the rural areas. In the urban areas however it was a bit lower, 86 during 1970 and 81 in 1971. The total infantile mortality rate in India was 125 in 1970 and 122 in 1971.

Factors Affecting Infant Mortality

The most important factors about infant mortality are genetic. Besides there are environmental factors. The following is the explanation of the factors affecting infant mortality:

1. Biological Factors: Biological factors include age of the mother, order of birth, time interval between births, etc. These may be classified into endogenous factors. Endogenous factors are biological factors related to the formation of the foetus in the womb. These include besides the factors mentioned above, weight at birth and multiple births or premature births, etc. It has been observed that foetal and neo-natal mortality rates are higher at the younger age of the mother (below 19), at first parity and for the first birth order. Upto the age of 29 of the mother these mortality rates decline and increase after it. The maturity of an infant is an important factor. Similar is the factor of the weight of the baby at birth. In 1950 low birth weight was the cause of 2/3rds of all the neo-natal deaths in USA. Chances of survival increase with the increase of weight. Endogenous factors are also known as genetic factors.

2. Environmental or Exogenous Causes: These include social, cultural, economic and environmental factors affecting infant mortality particularly during the post-neo-natal period. One of the causes of high infant mortality in some countries is the lack of availability of medicine. Most of the post-neo-natal deaths are due to communicable diseases of digestive and respiratory system such as diarrhoea and pneumonia, etc. The adverse environmental/actors including congestion, insanitation, lack of sufficient sunshine and fresh air. Among the environmental causes an important socio-cultural cause is illegitimacy. There is high rate of mortality among the illegitimate infants.

TABLE 9.2

Estimated Infant Mortality Rates for Major States, 1988 and 1989

State	Rural		Urban		Combined	
	1988	1989*	1988	1989*	1988	1989*
India	102	98	62	58	94	91
Andhra Pradesh	89	87	63	53	83	81
Assam	101	93	66	63	99	91
Bihar	99	93	70	63	97	91
Gujarat	101	92	64	70	90	86
Haryana	94	88	72	58	90	82
Himachal Pradesh	82	77	41	33	80	74
Jammu & Kashmir	75	72	53	55	71	69
Karnataka	83	89	46	53	74	80
Kerala	29	23	22	15	28	22
Madhya Pradesh	128	124	83	78	121	117
Maharashtra	76	66	50	44	68	59
Orissa	126	126	69	76	122	122
Punjab	63	72	59	53	62	67
Rajasthan	109	103	66	59	103	96
Tamil Nadu	84	80	51	43	74	68
Uttar Pradesh	132	126	81	75	124	118
West Bengal	76	82	43	53	69	77

*Provisional.

It should be remembered that biological and environmental factors interact and do not work separately. Both the factors have their roles almost everywhere. However, in developing countries the environmental factors are more important and less favourable. On the other hand, in developed countries biological factors are more important since environmental facilities are available. In India Kerala has the lowest infant mortality rate (56.8 per thousand in 1969). Uttar Pradesh has the highest rate of infant mortality showing 178.7 per thousand in 1969. In rural India infant mortality differs in different States. While it is as low as 82 in Punjab and below 80 in Kerala and Haryana; it is 140+ in Gujarat, Rajasthan and Uttar Pradesh. It also varies in different religions with Christians and Muslims having lower mortality. Among Hindus it varies in different castes, with higher castes showing low mortality.

CAUSES OF DEATH

Mortality studies have led to the study of causes of death. For example, in India the causes of death are classified into eight categories, namely (*i*) cholera, (*ii*) plague, (*iii*) small pox, (*iv*) fevers, (*v*) dysentery and diarrhoea, (*vi*) respiratory diseases, (*vii*) injuries, and (*viii*) other causes. According to the revised Manual on the International Statistical Classification of Diseases, Injuries and Causes of Death, prepared by the World Health Organisation, one thousand groups of diseases have been identified. These have been further grouped in 150 and lastly in 50. From this list of 50 groups of causes various diseases have been grouped according to their response to various health measures. These result in the following five groups:

1. Infections and parasitic diseases and diseases of the respiratory system, II. Cancer, III. Diseases of the circulatory system, IV. Deaths by violence, V. All other causes. The following table shows percentage distribution of deaths, by different causes in India during the period 1921-1964.[1]

TABLE 9.3

Causes of Death

Cause	*1921-31*	*1931-41*	*1941-51*	*1960*	*1962*	*1964*
Malaria	59.1	58.4	58.1	58.1	38.4	37.7
Cholera	3.6	2.4	1.1	1.8	0.3	0.8
Smallpox	1.2	1.1	4.0	0.9	1.0	0.9
Plague	2.6	—	0.3	—	—	—
Dysentery and diarrhoea	3.6	4.2	4.4	0.5	5.1	4.8
Respiratory diseases	NA	8.3	8.2	4.1	8.8	8.9
Others	NA	25.8	23.9	34.6	46.4	46.9
All causes	100.0	100.0	100.0	100.0	100.0	100.0

MORTALITY DIFFERENTIALS

As is clear by the survey of mortality trends in India and elsewhere, it is not uniform. The trends are changing due to certain differential. Within the same population these differentials make for change in mortality rates at different levels. Of these the most important differentials are as follows:

1. Reports (for various years), Directorate General of Health Services; *Vital Statistics of India* for various years, Registrar General of India.

1. Rural Urban Differentials: Before the 20th century higher in the urban areas of America and USA. In America in 1830 mortality was worst in large cities than in small cities or in rural areas. Similar was the case in Europe. In 1841 the life expectancy in London, Liverpool and Manchester was 35, 25 and 24 years respectively, while the average life expectancy for England and Wales was 40. Similar examples can be given from other countries. For example, in India death rate in 1972 was 16.9 of which the rural death rate was 18.9 and the urban death rate 10.3. Similarly, in 1973 the average was 15.5 of which the rural mortality rate was 17.0 and the urban 9.6. Death rate still came down in 1974 with average 14.5, rural 15.9 and urban 9.2. As has been already pointed out, rural urban differential in death rate is active in India particularly due to the availability of medical facilities in the urban areas and their scarcity in the rural areas.

2. Occupational Differentials: It is a common knowledge that some occupations involve more health hazards. Some industries are linked with characteristic diseases. Thus while death rate in some of the occupations is high, it is lower in other occupations. For example, death rate is high in workers working in the mines and chemical industries. Occupation also influences death rate by

TABLE 9.4

Estimated Age-specific Death Rates, India, 1987

Age Group	*Rural*	*Urban*	*Combined*
0–4	39.7	18.2	35.2
5–9	3.8	1.6	3.3
10–14	1.6	1.0	1.5
15–19	2.4	1.5	2.2
20–24	3.1	1.9	2.8
25–29	3.0	1.9	2.7
30–34	3.5	2.3	3.2
35–39	4.0	2.9	3.7
40–44	5.7	4.3	5.3
45–49	7.9	6.4	7.6
50–54	12.1	10.7	11.8
55–59	18.2	16.7	17.9
60–64	31.5	27.5	30.7
65–69	42.6	41.0	42.3
70 & above	89.6	88.5	89.4
All ages	12.0	7.4	10.9

death rate by providing income and standard of living. Those occupations which give high returns show lower death rates. On the other hand death rate is always higher among poor and destitutes. Systematic studies in England and Wales since 1851 have shown that in the period 1921-23 and 1930-32 mortality rates for males aged 20-64 years rose progressively from class first to class fifth occupations. By 1950 however, the males in social class second were found to have the lowest rates, while social class fourth continued to have the highest mortality. This may be taken as the general trend about occupational distinctions in mortality in most of the countries.

3. Regions: In almost all the countries region is a differential in mortality rates. For example, in India mortality rate is highest in Uttar Pradesh and lowest in Kerala. The following table gives the estimated death rate and life expectancy at birth in different States of India during the period 1941-1961[1]:

Table 9.5

Estimate Death Rate and Life Expectancy

States	Death rate		Expectation of life at birth (in years)
	1941-51	1951-61	1951-61
Andhra Pradesh	29.5	25.2	36.9
Assam	31.8	26.9	36.8
Bihar	26.6	26.1	37.6
Gujarat	29.9	23.5	40.0
Kerala	18.0	16.1	48.3
Madhya Pradesh	38.5	23.2	40.6
Madras	22.8	22.5	39.8
Maharashtra	24.9	19.8	45.2
Mysore	18.9	22.2	40.2
Orissa	29.9	22.9	40.9
Punjab	26.3	18.9	47.5
Rajasthan	27.2	24.9	46.8
Uttar Pradesh	27.2	24.90	38.9
West Bengal	28.6	20.5	44.3
India	**27.4**	**22.8**	**41.2**

1. *Sample Registration Bulletin*, New Delhi: Office of the Registrar General of India, Vol. X, No. 2, April 1976, pp. 6-7.

4. Education Attainments of Parents: An important mortality differential is the educational attainments of the parents. It is so since the educated parents have a better living standard and more knowledge concerning health. However, in Hungary an inverse relationship was noted between the educational status of parents and the levels of infant mortality. This is an exception. According to United Nations report it was 95 for the mothers who had never attended schools while for those whose mothers had attended 13 or more years of schooling it was 27.[1] In 1966 in Greater Bombay the infant mortality was low among mothers with educational attainment. It was highest among infants of illiterate mothers and lowest for infants whose mother had higher education.

5. Marital Status: It has been established by so many studies that the general mortality rates among unmarried persons are much higher than the married males and females. One of the reasons for this phenomenon is the fact that normally healthy persons tend to marry while among unmarried persons the number of unhealthy and sick is quite high. Secondly, married persons are more secured and protected. Thirdly, they lead a more balanced and sober life. All these factors contribute to lower mortality rates among married persons.

6. Religion: Study by Vaidyanathan[2] has shown that in India the Christians and Muslims have lower mortality rates than the Hindus. Thus, one finds a distinction in mortality rates in different religious groups, though obviously this cannot be due to any religious reason but due to the economic and social factors.

7. Caste: The above mentioned study also points out that *mortality differentials exist between different castes.* Among the Hindus the upper caste groups have a lower mortality rate than the lower caste groups.

8. Socio-Economic Status: Socio-economic status has proved to be an important mortality differential in different countries. The ratio however is not in straightline. One finds inverse relationship between mortality and socio-economic status as a general rule. In other words, as socio-economic status rises, rate of mortality falls and *vice versa*. However, in some of the cases it may be noted at

---

1. United Nations, *The Determinants and Consequences of Population Trends, Vol. I, op. cit.*, p. 139.
2. Vaidyanathan, K.E., "Some Indices of Differential Mortality in India." in K.E. Vaidyanathan (Ed.), *Studies in Mortality in India, op. cit.*, p. 152.

the highest level. As a general rule a middle class socio-economic status is favourable for the lowest mortality rate. Mortality rates are generally higher at the lowest socio-economic level.

MORTALITY TRENDS

Various mortality trends have been noted in developed and developing countries, of which some important trends are as follows:

1. Crude death rate in the developing countries is higher than that of the developed countries. The later have more aged persons than the former.

2. Infant mortality rates in developing countries are higher as compared to those in the developed countries.

3. The average life expectancy at birth for both male and female in developing countries is lower than those in the developed countries. Crude death rates in developed countries have recorded fluctuations with a slight upward tendency.

4. As compared to the past, at present most of the countries are recording lower death rates. This is particularly due to the elimination of epidemics and control of famines, food shortages and insanitation.

QUESTIONS FOR EXERCISE

1. What are the sources of Mortality Data? How is it analysed? Explain causes of High Death Rate.
2. Discuss causes of Death in India. Describe mortality differentials.
3. Explain Infant Mortality and its incidence in India. Describe factors affecting infant mortality.

10

Fertility: Nature, Measures and Trends

According to United Nations, "Natural fertility is the fertility which exists in the absence of deliberate birth control."[1] According to the same source, controlled fertility is the fertility which involves a deliberate use of birth control.[2] The term birth control is used in a broad sense to include intentional abortions, sterilisation and complete abstinence from coitus.[3] Contraceptive method is sometimes taken as identical with birth control method though it is a part of it. However, most of the persons use contraception and birth control in the same sense. Contraception, as is clear by the term, is the opposite of conception. In this connection it is necessary to differentiate between fertility and fecundity. Fertility, "refers to the actual reproductive performance — applied to an individual or a group".[4] On the other hand, fecundity refers to "the capacity of a man, a woman, or a couple to participate in reproduction, (*i.e.*, the reproduction of a live child)."[5] Fertility can be measured through birth rate. Fecundity, however, cannot be measured. It refers to the maximum fertility level that can be attained. However, some writers have used the terms fecundity and fertility as synonymous. A man or a woman who has given birth to a live child is considered fertile. On the other hand, those

1. United Nations, *The Determinants and Consequences of Population Trends*, Vol. 1, ST/SOA/ SER. A/50, Population Studies No. 50, 1973; p. 78.
2. *Ibid.*, p. 78.
3. United Nations, *Multilingual Demographic Dictionary*, *op. cit.*, p. 39.
4. *Ibid.*, p. 38.
5. *Ibid.*

who have not produced a single child are considered sterile. Sterility may be also used in connection with groups, though generally it is computed only among women. The total number of children born by one couple are known as family size. The sequence of births of children is birth order. This sequence in the case of mothers is known as parity which is decided by the number of children born alive. The biological limits of child birth are known as reproductive span. The physiological limits of child bearing capacity and period are known as theoretical maximum fertility. Abortions and still births are classified as reproductive wastage. Birth control by self-control is known as voluntary abstinence. All these concepts must be clearly understood in order to understand the trends and causes of fertility.

HISTORICAL BACKGROUND

Ever since the science of demography has been developed, fertility occupies the central position in it. The growth of the population depends on fertility. It is the positive force behind the expansion as well as the dynamism of a population. Prior to the Second World War fertility was dealt with mathematically. Its dynamic character was realised only in early 1930 when the birth rates in North West Europe and North America started rising instead of declining. It was termed as the period of baby boom leading to an embarrassment to demographers. Now the role of social, psychological, cultural, economic and political factors in determining differentials of fertility was realised. It was noted that due to these factors large fluctuations occur in fertility rates. For example, in Romania legalised abortions led to decline in birth rate. However, when the abortion facilities were withdrawn the birth rate was the maximum ever witnessed in one year. In 1960 the importance of birth rate in the population growth was everywhere insisted upon. In the developing countries mortality had considerably declined with no corresponding decline of birth rate, thus leading to rapid population growth. In India for example, during the period 1941-1951 the birth rate was 39.9% while it increased to 41.7% during the period 1951-1961. In some States it was as high as 43.0 in Gujarat in 1966.

NATURE OF FERTILITY

As has been already pointed out, fertility is basically biological though it is very much governed by the social norms. While the physiological basis of fertility is almost universal, the present day distinctions in fertility in different countries and in different regions of the same country are particularly due to social norms. The following are the physiological factors determining fertility:

1. Adolescent Sterility: Raymond Pearl, in his study of 142 countries in 1938, found that the onset of the first menstrual period called menarche occurred generally during the period of 13 to 17 years of age.[1] Recent studies, however, have pointed out that menarche varies with time and place. According to another study, during the last 100 years, the menstrual age of European girls has come down settling at present at 13 years.[2] This change is due to environmental factors. In the study by Pearl mentioned above it was noted that cessation of fecundity in females occurred at an average age of 46, the range being 44 to 49 years.[3] In India Kumudini Dandekar conducted a survey and concluded that in rural India menstrual period started at the age of 13.8 years and the menopausal age was before 50 years in most of the women.[4] In another study by Kamat and Kamat the menopausal age was fixed at 42.2 years.[5] It may be concluded that the period of fertility Is on an average, from the age of 15 years to 49 years in a woman. This is known as reproductive span. In other words reproductive span is between 30 and 35 years. It is not so easily identified among males, in whom It is considerably longer.

In India the age of consummation of marriage coincides with menarche. Therefore, some studies have been conducted on adolescent sterility. According to a study of Bengali women In 1947-1949, it was found that the interval between the age of consummation of marriage and the first birth decreased with the increase of the age of consummation of marriage.[6] Therefore, it can be said that by lowering the age of cohabition the interval

1. Pearl, Raymond, *The Natural History of Population*, New York; Oxford University Press, 1939, p. 49.
2. United Nations, *The Determinants and Consequences of Population Trends*, Vol. I, *op. cit.*, p. 74.
3. Raymond Pearl, *op. cit.*, p. 51.
4. Dandekar, Kumudini, *Demographic Survey of Six Rural Communities*, Bombay: Asia Publishing House, 1959, p. 61.
5. Kamat and Kamat, as quoted in *The Determinants and Consequences of Population Trends*, Vol. I. *op. cit.*, p. 74.
6. Talwar, P.P., "Adolescent Sterility in An Indian Population". *Human Biology*, Vol. 37 No. 3, September 1965, p. 258.

between consummation of marriage and the birth of the first child was increased. This led to the interesting conclusion that early marriages do not necessarily result in large families.[1] The comparative sterility of the adolescent female has been termed adolescent sterility.

2. Post-partum Sterility: Post-partum sterility means the sterility during the period after the birth of a child, temporarily for some time. During this period the possibility of conception is very rare. Menstruation is sometimes not resumed for 2 to 3 years. This period is known as post-partum amenorrhoea period. This period is longer for Indian women than for the women in Western countries due to breast feeding. For example, according to a study 82% of rural Indian women were found to have resumed menstruation after a year or more of child birth.[2] In the case of women in Belgium, however, this period was only 6 months. Due to this prolonged period the gap between 2 births for Indian women was found to be 34 to 36 months. Another social factor influencing this tendency is the voluntary abstinence from sexual intercourse following child birth in India.

3. Primary and Secondary Sterility: Another physiological factor determining fertility is the primary and secondary fertility among women or couples. Primary fertility means the innate capacity of producing children. Complete absence of this characteristic is known as primary sterility, or childlessness. In India the percentage for this is 6 in married below 15 years and 10.5 in married above 25 years of age. Thus, primary sterility varies with the female age at marriage. This again has been found to differ a little in different areas. Primary sterility is less in India as compared to developed countries. Secondary sterility means fecundity impairment due to so many reasons, natural or otherwise. For example, it may be due to certain pathological conditions.

4. Reproductive Wastage: One of the physiological factors affecting fertility is reproductive wastage, which means abortions and still births. This has been found to be different in different countries and at different times. For example, according to Bourgeois-Pichat, about 30% of conceptions result in reproductive wastage. If this wastage may be checked, the reproduction rate could increase by

1. Chandrasekaran, C., *Physiological Factors Affecting Fertility in India, op. cit.*, p. 4.
2. Dandekar, Kumudini, *Demographic Survey of Six Rural Communities, op. cit.*, p. 62.

15%.[1] In India, Robert G. Potter collected information about 1765 pregnancies in Punjab villages and concluded the reproductive wastage at 136 per thousand pregnancies.[2]

The above discussion makes it clear that fertility is not uninhibited but checked by so many factors. Therefore, in spite of the absence of artificial birth control some limits to fertility are seen everywhere.

Social and Cultural Determinants

Besides the physiological determinants pointed out above social and cultural determinants of fertility are equally important. Kingsley Davis and Judith Blake[3] have developed a model classifying the intermediate variables through which social factors affect the stages of child bearing. This model is as follows:

I. *Factors affecting exposure to intercourse* ("Intercourse Variables"):

(A) Those governing the formation and dissolution of unions in the reproductive period.

1. Age of entry into sexual unions.
2. Permanent celibacy: proportion of women never having sexual union.
3. Part of the reproductive period spent after or between unions:
   (*a*) when unions are broken by divorce, separation or desertion;
   (*b*) when unions are broken by death of husband.

(B) Factors governing exposure to intercourse within unions.

4. Voluntary abstinence.
5. Involuntary abstinence (from impotence, illness, unavoidable but temporary separations).
6. Coital frequency (excluding periods of abstinence).

---

1. United Nations, *The Determinants and Consequences of Population Trends*, Vol. I, *op. cit*, p. 75.
2. Robert G. Potter, "Foetal Wastage in Eleven Punjab Villages," *Human Biology*, Vol. 37, No. 3, September, 1965, p. 267.
3. Kingsley Davis and Judith Blake, "Social Structure and Fertility: An Analytic Framework", *Economic Development and Social Change*, Vol. 4, No. 3, April, 1965, pp. 211-235.

II. *Factors affecting exposure to conception* ("Conception Variables"):

7. Fecundity or infecundity, as affected by involuntary causes.
8. Use or non-use of contraception:
   (*a*) by mechanical or chemical means,
   (*b*) by other means.
9. Fecundity or infecundity as affected by voluntary causes (Sterilisation, sub-incision, medical treatment, etc.).

III. *Factors affecting gestation and successful parturition* ('Gestation Variables'):

10. Foetal mortality from involuntary causes.
11. Foetal mortality from voluntary causes.

The above intermediate variables governed the influence of social and cultural factors on fertility. This influence is positive or negative. For example, the practice of contraception by a significant proportion of couples has a minus value and its absence has a plus value. In other words, the fertility level in society is determined by the combined influence of the 11 variables mentioned in the model devised by Davis and Blake. As they have pointed out, "All of these variables are present in every society — each one can operate to reduce or to enhance fertility. If abortion is not practised, the fertility value of variable 11 is plus."[1] Most of these variables function almost everywhere with local distinctions. The following discussion of the more important variables will further establish this fact:

1. Intercourse Variables: As has been shown in the model given above, sexual intercourse in a society is governed by age of marriage, celibacy, voluntary; abstinence, involuntary abstinence and coital frequency, etc. Of these, the most important is the female age at marriage. Formerly, it was generally very low encouraging prolific child bearing. In the industrial countries at present it is fairly high resulting into low fertility and narrow reproductive span. According to Kingsley Davis the postponement of marriage was utilised by Japan to bring about a reduction in her fertility rates.[2] According to S.N. Agarwala, if all the Indian women were

1. Ibid, p. 213.
2. Kingsley Davis, "The Theory of Change and Response", *Population Index*, Vol. 29, No. 4, October, 1963, p.359

married after the age of 19 there would have been a 30% reduction in the birth rate by 1991-92. In Ireland fertility is appreciably low since the proportion of females unmarried upto the age of 45 is unusually high and also high is the female age at marriage.

2. Voluntary abstinence: Among Hindus in India, since the beginning of Aryan culture, the ideal of Brahmachairya has been emphasised, according to which males and females were asked to lead a life of voluntary abstinence upto the age of 25. This resulted in higher age at the time of marriage influencing fertility considerably. Again, sexual intercourse has been forbidden on various occasions by the different religious scriptures. Among Hindus the prohibition extends upto 80 to 100 days in a year. Among Muslims, however, it is for a shorter duration. This results in higher fertility among Muslim couples as compared to the Hindus. Similar injunctions may be found in religious scriptures of Christians, Jews, etc., which considerably influence fertility patterns. Nowadays, the influence of religious scriptures is waning fast. Therefore, voluntary abstinence is no more an important variable determining fertility. It has been substituted by methods of birth control which are now being more and more popularised.

3. Sterilisation and other Methods of Birth Control: The most important single variable determining fertility today is the method of birth control including abortions and sterilizations besides practices checking conceptions known as contraceptive practices or techniques. A brief enumeration of these is necessary to understand fertility variables. In a study conducted by Royal Commission on Population in 1946-47, it was found that only 16% couples married before 1910 had been using birth control methods in UK. The percentage of users during the period 1935-39 rose to 66.[1] The second natural survey conducted by Population Investigation Committee in 1967-68 found this percentage 82.1 which further rose to 91.4 during the period 1961-65.[2] In 1975 nearly 70% women were using some kinds of contraception.[3]

1. Fanning, Lewis, *Report on the Enquiry into Family Limitations and its Influence on Human Fertility During the Last Fifty Years*, London: His Majesty's Stationery Office, 1949, p. 52.
2. Glass, D.V., *Memorandum in the First Report from Select Committee on Science and Technology*, Session 1970-71. London: Her Majesty's Stationery Office, 1971, p. 192.
3. Bruce Stokes, *Filling the Family Planning Gap*, World Watch Paper 12, May 1977, p. 6.

Among the most important contraception methods are oral pills, IUD and sterilisation. These have made tremendous progress not only in developed countries but also in developing countries like Hong Kong and Singapore. The family planning movement is progressing in India right from the start of Five Year Plans. Thus, the most important variable affecting fertility in most of the societies today is the methods of contraception.

4. Sanction to Abortions: There was a time when almost every religion severely condemned the use of abortions to check births. Even now most of the religious persons are against this practice. However, not only in the developed countries but even in the societies of developing countries the stigma on abortion is gradually being eliminated and more and more safe and scientific devices for abortions are being introduced. This has been a very important variable determining population growth anywhere.

5. Norms about Family Size: Most of the great religions have laid down norms about family size which generally favour high fertility. For example, among Hindus the blessing on marriage to a girl is "may you have eight sons". This is so since every religion wanted to multiply the number of its followers. However, notions about family size have changed drastically in recent times. Psychological researches in the West have shown that the urge to motherhood is not innate but acquired due to cultural factors. Some women have shown definite aversion to motherhood. While some women want to procreate more than half a dozen children, most of the educated women today do not want to procreate more than two to three children. The general norm about the family size today is two to three children. In China it is only one child per family. The present norm in India is two children per family. In most of the developed countries, the family size is reducing. So many males and females prefer to remain unmarried. Most of them marry sufficiently late. The number of children is generally kept to the minimum. Thus, change in the norms about family size has been the most important variable determining population today.

6. Intermediate Variables: Sexual practices and marriage customs in every society are governed by the contemporary norms. Pre-marital and extra-marital sex relationships are very much governed by the current norms. In most of the modern societies norms about these are fairly lax leading to a lot of premarital and extra-marital sexual activity without any child birth. The ages of marriages of males and females are rising everywhere. In so many countries divorce has become rather easy. The most important hurdle in divorce are the children. Therefore, most of the couples are against procreating too many children. The increasing number of divorces has an adverse affect on birth rate.

The above discussion shows the social and cultural determinants of fertility. It is clear that in modem societies these are much more important than the biological determinants. Most of the governments today are actively popularising methods of birth control. These include Coitus Interruptus, Male Sterilisation or Vasectomy for males and the Rhythm Method, the Calendar Method, the Temperature Method, Mechanical and Chemical contraceptives, the Intra-uterine Device (IUD), Oral contraception and Female sterilisation. Contraceptive technology is being improved everywhere particularly concerning abortions. In most of the countries laws have become very liberal about induced abortions. Thus, the growth of population no more depends on biological factors but may be controlled by human efforts.

MEASURES OF FERTILITY

As has been already pointed out, the main sources of data about fertility are: Census, Vital Registration System and Sample Fertility Survey. Different types of measures are adopted for computing fertility according to the sources of fertility data. The main sources of data provide the following types of information:

1. Vital Registration System: The number of registered births, usually in one calendar year.

2. Census: (*a*) The number of children ever born, (*b*) Census age distribution, (*c*) The number of births during the last twelve months.

3. Sample Fertility Survey: (*a*) The number of children ever born, (*b*) The number of births during the last twelve months.

The basic measures of fertility are of three types:

1. The first type of measure is related to a particular period and based on data peculiar to it. These are, therefore, termed as period measures. The vital registration system provides data for one

year. Therefore, the question on the number of births during the last one year is asked in a census or sample survey.

2. Another measure of fertility refers to the reproductive performance of women upto a certain time. Therefore, question on the number of children ever born is asked in census or sample surveys .

3. Yet another measure of fertility attempts to measure it indirectly on the basis of the age and sex distribution of the population.

The following are the most important measures of fertility:

1. The Crude Birth Rate: The crude birth rate is the ratio of the total registered live births in a specified year in a particular area to the total mid-year population of that area multiplied by one thousand. This is expressed by the following formula:

$$\frac{B}{P} \times K$$

where

B is the total number of live births during a year;

P is the total population in the middle of that year; and K is 1,000.

The crude birth rate for a sample area of Calcutta city for 1967-68 may

Number of live births during 1967-68 = 163

Total mid-year population during 1967-68 = 9281

Crude birth rate during 1967-68 = 9.281

$$\therefore \text{Crude birth rate during 1967-68} = \frac{163}{9{,}281} \times 1{,}000$$

$$= 17.56.$$

The crude birth rate of 17.56 indicates that in the sample area of Calcutta city, there had been 17.56 births per 1,000 population during 1967-68.

As the name suggests, crude birth rate is a crude measure of fertility. It is simple and easy to calculate since it requires the minimum data. However, it suffers from several limitations.

2. The General Fertility Rate: This is a remnant of the crude birth rate It is the ratio of total live births in some specified year in a particular area to the number of women in the child bearing age, multiplied by 1,000. This is by expressed the following formula:

$$\frac{B}{P} \times K$$

where :

B is the number of live births during a year;

P is the mid-year population of women between the ages of 15 and 44 or 49; and

K is 1,000.

The general fertility rate in the sample area of Calcutta city during 1967-68 may then be computed as follows:

Number of live births during 1967-68 = 163

Mid-year female population in the age group 15-44 during 1967-68 = 1,882

Therefore:

$$\text{General fertility rate during 1967-68} = \frac{163}{1,882} \times 1,000$$

$$= 86.61.$$

The general fertility rate of 86.61 indicates that, in 1967-68, in the sample area of Calcutta city, there were 86.61 births per 1,000 women in the child-bearing age group of women.

3. Age Specific Fertility Rates: The general fertility rate is not a very effective refinement of crude birth rate. It loses sight of the fact that the fecundity of women changes during the span of the child bearing period. Therefore, further refinement of fertility measures leads to the development of Age Specific Fertility Rate, which is computed as follows:

$$\frac{b_1}{p_1} \times i$$

where :

b_1, is the number of live births to mothers of a specified age group in the population during a year;

p_1 is the mid-year female population in the same age group; i is 1,000.

The age specific fertility rate for women in the age group 20 to 24 in the sample area of Calcutta city during 1967-68 is:

Number of live births to women in the age group 20-24 during 1967-68 = 57

Number of women in the age group
20-24 during 1967-68 = 387

Therefore:

The age specific fertility rate for the
age group 20-24 during 1967-68 $= \frac{57}{378} \times 1{,}000$
$= 147.29$

Age specific fertility rates are not affected by variations in age structure. Therefore, these are considered to be refined. Since these rates are with reference to married women they are called age specific marital fertility rates. These are further refined. However, the comparison between two population groups on the basis of age specific fertility rates is full of difficulties. Therefore, Total Fertility Rate is required for such purposes.

4. Total Fertility Rate: Total fertility rate is the sum of the age specific fertility rates of women in each five-year age group from 15 to 44 or 49. This is computed by dividing the number of births with the number of women multiplied by 1,000. For example, age specific fertility rate for the sample area in Calcutta city during 1967-68 is calculated as follows:

Sum of all the age specific fertility rates of women in each five-year age group from 15 to 44 = 467.15

Total fertility rate = (467.15) x 5 ÷ 1,000
= 2.34

The total fertility rate, according to George W. Barclay, is a hypothetical rate indicating, "the total number of children that would ever be born to a (hypothetical) group of women, if the group passed through its reproductive span of life with these birth rates in each year of age."[1] It is believed that the women in this hypothetical group would survive till the end of the reproductive period: Total fertility rate is particularly useful for comparisons between the reproductive performance of two groups of women in two countries or in the same country.

5. Gross Reproduction Rate: While the total fertility rate refers to the total number of children a group of women is expected to have, the gross reproduction rate is restricted only to the number

1. Barclay, Geoge W., *Techniques of Population Analysis,* New York: John Wiley and Sons, 1958, p. 54.

of female children. This is computed by summing up age specific fertility rates, multiplying the sum by 5 and finally dividing the product by 1,000. For example, the gross reproduction rate for the sample area in Calcutta city will be computed as follows:

Total fertility rate = 2.34

Gross production rate = 2.34 x 0.49 = 1.15

In the above calculation the digit 0.49 has been arrived by assuming that the sex ratio at birth is 105 male babies per 100 female babies. Therefore, in order to arrive at the percentage of female births in the total population, the formula is so divided by 205 which is approximately 0.49. The value of the gross reproduction rate is thus about one half of that of the total fertility rate. In it also it is assumed that the women in the reproductive age groups would survive till the end of their child bearing period. Gross reproduction rate indicates the number of daughters a group of women is expected to produce. The net reproduction rate indicates the number of daughters ever born. It measures the extent to which a group of newly born girls will replace their mothers under predetermined schedules of fertility and mortality.

6. Sex-Age Adjusted Birth Rate: According to the United Nations, the sex- age adjusted birth rate is, "the number of births per 1,000 of a weighted aggregate of numbers of women, in the various five-year age groups from 15 to 44."[1] The United Nations has recommended a standard set of weights in computing this aggregate. These are 1, 7, 7, 6, 4, 1, which correspond to the average pattern of age specific fertility rates for the five-year age groups, 15-19, 20-24, 25-29, 30-34, 35-39 and 40-44 respectively. The weights are "roughly proportional to the typical relative fertility rates of various age groups."

The sex-age adjusted birth rate may be computed as follows where:

$$\text{SAABR} = \frac{\text{Number of live births in the year}}{1\times W_1+7\times W_2+7\times W_3+6\times W_4+4\times W_5+4\times W_6}$$

where:

W_1, W_2, W_3, W_4, W_5 and W_6 are the number of women in the age groups 15-19, 20-24, 25-29, 30-34, 35-39 and 40-44 respectively.

1. Registrar-General and Census Commissioner, India, New Delhi, *Pocket Book of Population Statistics*. Census Centenary 1972, pp. 78-80.

The above formula is used due to the reason that even in countries with different levels of fertility, the relative levels of age specific rates for women are rather similar. Absolute age specific fertility rates can be neither high nor low. The percentages of births at a given age do not differ very much.

7. Measures based upon Census Age: Census age distribution is utilised to compute the child-woman ratio. This is the ratio of children under five years of age to women in the child bearing age. The formula for this computation is as follows:

$$\frac{P_{0-4}}{f_{15-44}} \times K$$

where

P_{0-1} is the number of children of both sexes under the age of 5;

f_{15-44} is the number of women between the ages of 15 and 44; K is 100.

For example, the child-woman ratio for India in 1971 was: Number of children under 5 in 1971

= 78,337,100

Number of women in the age group 15-44 in 1971

= 111,327,600

Therefore:

The child-woman ratio for India in 1971

$$= \frac{78,337,100}{111,327,600} \times 1,000$$

$$= 703.66$$

Thus, in 1971 in India, there were 703.66 children per 1,000 women in the age group 15-44. Child-woman ratio suffers from serious limitations due to under-enumeration in the Census and due to the influence of infant and child mortality. Therefore, it is not considered to be very much important, though used for several purposes.

8. Measures based on Number of Children ever Born: Census survey and fertility surveys collect information on the number of children ever born from every married woman. The same source also provides data concerning the present age of the mother. Now by cross classifying the age of the currently married women and the number of children ever born to them it is possible to compute the number of children ever born. This measure is known as completed fertility or completed family size. It is a cohort measure against current measures based on reproductive performance in one year.

LEVELS OF FERTILITY IN THE WORLD

According to United Nations population studies, the estimated birth rate of world population was 31.5 per thousand during 1970-75. It was 35.6 during 1950-55. For more developed, regions the corresponding figures were 17.4 and 22.9 respectively. On the other hand for less developed regions the corresponding figures were 37.5 and 42.1 respectively. This shows the great difference between the birth rates of the more developed and less developed countries. For example, in 1950-55 the birth rate for the Africa continent was 48.1, while the same was 25.1 for North America and 19.8 for Europe. Similarly, in 1970-75, while the birth rate fell everywhere, the distinction between more developed and less developed regions was clearly perceptible. The birth rate during this period was 46.3 in Africa, 16.5 in North America and 16.1 in Europe. During the same period the birth rate in Western Africa was 48,7 while in Western Europe it was as low as 14.6.[1]

FERTILITY TRENDS IN DEVELOPED COUNTRIES

As has been pointed out above, the birth rate in developed countries is much lower as compared to the developing countries. Some of these countries, however, were having quite a high birth rate, some time back. In 18th century the birth rate in most of the present day developed countries was between 30 to 40. It was 37 in France, between 32 and 35 in Sweden and between 29 and 33 in Norway. The decline in birth rate is a phenomena particularly of the 20th century. The process, however, started in 19th century. In 1974 the crude birth rate in the well known developed countries was as follows: Canada, 15.4, United States 14.9, Argentina 22.7, Japan 18.6, Israel 28.2, Denmark 14.1, France 15.2, German Democratic Republic 10.4, Germany Federal Republic 10.1, Ireland 22.3, Norway 15.0, Romania 20.3, Spain 19.4, Portugal 19.6,

1. United Nations, *World Population Prospects* as assessed in 1973. ST/ESA/SER.A/6D, Population Studies, No. 60, New York, pp. 110-112.

Sweden 13.5, United Kingdom 13.1, Yugoslavia 18.1, Australia 18.4, USSR 18.0.[1] Thus, the developed countries have moved from high fertility to low fertility. In Europe the Eastern and Central countries have slightly higher birth rates than the Northern and the Western countries. In 1974 almost 66% of the developed countries had birth rate below 18. During the period 1900-1904 the birth rate per thousand for some of the more developed countries was as follows: Denmark 29.9, Finland 31.3, Ireland 23.1, Norway 28.5, Sweden 26.4, UK 28.2, Austria 35.7, Belgium 27.9, Germany 34.3, France 21.2, Netherlands 31.5, Switzerland 28.2. The crude birth rates in these countries during the year 1974 were: Denmark 14.1, Finland 13.3, Ireland 22.3, Norway 15.0, Sweden 13.5, UK 13.2, Austria 12.9, Belgium 12.7, Germany 10.1, France 15.2, Netherlands 13.7, Switzerland 13.1. Of these countries while the first six were from Northern Europe, the last six were from Western Europe. These may be compared to the countries of Eastern Europe and Southern Europe to see the difference. For example, in 1974 the following countries of Eastern Europe had crude birth rates as follows: Bulgaria 17.2, Czechoslovakia 19.8, GDR 10.4, Hungary 17.8, Poland 18.4, Romania 20.3, Greece 16.0, Italy 15.7, Portugal 18.4, Spain 19.4, belong to Southern Europe. This transition from high to low birth rate was, however, not in a straightline. During the First World War, it declined only temporarily. It went up during 1920-24. It declined till 1930 and then during the period 1940-45, the period of Second World War, one finds a baby boom. It was particularly so in Switzerland and Sweden where it almost reached its peak, though it started declining thereafter. In the countries directly involved in war, particularly France, England and Wales, the birth rate went up after the Second World War. In US the birth rate during 1930-34 and 1935-39 was the lowest. It went up after the Second World War and continued upto 1957 when it was 25.0. It declined after 1957 and very rapidly after 1965. An identical pattern was noticed in Canada. In USSR the rise was not very significant. The rise in birth rate is attributed to several factors such as early marriages, remarriages, demobilization of soldiers, etc.

1. Estimates prepared by the United Nations Population Division. Source: U.N., *Demographic Year Book 1975*, pp. 488-502, 518-527.

FERTILITY TRENDS IN DEVELOPING COUNTRIES

As has been already pointed out, the fertility trend in developing countries has been always more than those of the developed countries. However, in these countries also the birth rate has come down particularly in the 20th century. In 1950 the crude birth rate in some of the selected developing countries was as follows:

Table 10.1

Fertility Rate in Developing Countries

Country	*1950*	*1974*	*Per cent change*
1. *Africa*			
Mauritius	46.2	27.5	40.5
Egypt	44.9	34.8	22.6
Tunisia	46.4	37.0	20.2
Sub-total	45.2	34.9	22.6
2. *The America*			
Costa Rica	47.6	28.0	41.1
Puerto Rico	36.6	23.3	36.3
Chile	35.2	24.4	30.6
Trinidad & Tobago	37.7	26.5	29.7
Panama	40.6	31.0	23.7
Colombia	46.4	33.0	28.9
Venezuela	46.5	37.7	18.8
Cuba	30.3	25.3	16.4
El Salvador	48.1	40.3	16.2
Paraguay	45.5	39.4	13.3
Honduras	54.6	47.8	12.5
Jamaica	34.8	30.6	12.1
Nicaragua	53.4	47.5	11.1
Guatemala	48.7	43.4	10.9
Sub-total	43.2	33.4	22.7
3. *Asia and the Pacific*			
Singapore	44.4	19.5	56.1
Taiwan	45.8	23.4	48.9
Hong Kong	33.1	19.3	41.7
Fiji	44.3	28.0	36.8
Sri Lanka	38.5	27.2	29.4

Thailand	46.9	34.0	27.5
Malaysia	45.4	33.0	27.3
Korea, Rep.	37.0	25.0	32.4
Turkey	44.9	34.0	24.3
Vietnam Dem. Rep.	41.3	30.1	29.7
Sub-total	42.8	30.1	29.7
Total	43.2	31.7	26.7

It is clear from the table given above that almost all the developing countries have shown decline in fertility rate during recent years. This will be further supported by the following table showing crude birth rate for 1950 and 1974 for the 8 largest developing countries in the world.[1]

TABLE 10.2

Crude Birth Bate in Developing Countries

Country	*Crude Birth Rate (Births per 1000 population)*		
	1950	*1974*	*Per cent change*
China	37.3	26.0	–32.2
India	42.3	36.0	–15.0
Indonesia	45.0	40.0	–11.1
Brazil	41.4	38.0	–8.3
Bangla Desh	49.2	49.2	0
Pakistan	49.6	47.0	–5.2
Nigeria	49.1	49.1	0
Mexico	46.6	41.0	12.0
Total	40.8	33.7	-17.4

DEFERENTIAL FERTILITY

It should not be deduced from the data given so far that all the sections in a society have identical fertility rate. In every country today and also formerly, one finds what is known as differential fertility which means different birth rates in different sub-groups of the same population. These sub-groups may be ecological, socio-economic, educational, occupational, religious, caste, race, sub-groups, etc. In most of the countries the fertility rates in these different sub-groups have been compared. It has been found

1. W. Parker Mauldin, "Fertility-Trends: 1950-75", *Studies in Family Planning*, Vol. 1, No. 9, September 1976, p. 244.

that ecological factors govern regional differences in fertility. It is the main cause of rural urban differential fertility. Among the most important socio-economic factors governing differential fertility are: Educational attainment, economic status, occupation, employment, religion, caste and race. Fertility differential may be also due to demographic factors such as age and sex structure. The influence of different factors governing fertility is as follows:

1. Ecological Factors: These include regional differences and the difference of rural-urban residence.

(*i*) *Regional differences:* In almost every country various regions show different rates of fertility. For example, in India the lowest fertility rates are found in South India while in North one finds high fertility rate. In the former case it is less than five children per woman while in the latter region it is seven children per woman. In the remaining country the fertility rate is between five and six children per woman. These rates were noted during the period 1971-72. The survey was conducted by Sample Registration Scheme.

(*ii*) *Rural-urban residence:* As a general rule fertility rate is much higher in the rural areas as compared to the urban areas. However, in America the difference was very insignificant after the Second World War. It was constant during the period 1920-1940. However, the distinction was always noticeable. In European countries the distinction was found narrowing after 1970. It appears that In the West the rural-urban distinction in fertility rate will be almost eliminated. However, one finds noticeable distinction in India. For example, in 1974 while the crude birth rate in rural areas was 35.9, in urban areas it was only 28.4. Similar results have been shown by the National Sample Survey and the Sample Registration Scheme.

Most of the researches have shown a negative relationship between fertility and the size of the locality. This confirms the incidence of lower birth rate in urban areas as compared to the rural areas in India. Even in the urban areas it was observed that the larger the city the lower was the fertility. For example, according to a survey conducted by Office of the Registrar General, Ministry of Home Affairs, on fertility differentials in India in 1972 it was revealed that the towns with a population of more than 1 lakh had a lower fertility rate than smaller towns. Fertility behaviour of women in metropolitan areas have shown difference according to residential background. For example, rural migrant women continue to show high fertility in metropolitan areas.

2. Socio-economic factors: These include educational attainment, economic status, occupation of the husband, employment of wife and religion, caste and race. The influence of these socio-economic factors is as follows:

(*i*) *Educational attainment*: There is an inverse relationship between educational attainment particularly of the woman and the fertility rate. The higher the educational level, the lower is the family size. However, at the highest educational level the curve has shown an upward tendency. Even in high fertility countries educational attainment shows a negative relationship with fertility. In India some sample surveys have confirmed this principle. The studies conducted in the metropolitan city of Greater Bombay in 1966 and in Panaji, Goa in 1969 have confirmed negative association between the educational attainment of married women and fertility. Another recent study by the Registrar General of India, Ministry of Home Affairs, concerning fertility differentials in India in 1972 has again confirmed inverse relationships. Therefore, one finds fertility differentials according to residence. This difference may be due to two reasons, firstly, the differential age at marriage and secondly, the differential practice of family planning. Educated women marry at a higher age. They also use more sophisticated methods of birth control and also more often.

(*ii*) *Economic status:* Economic status has an inverse relationship with fertility, this was a principle believed by early demographers. Some present studies, however, have shown that fertility rate goes down with higher economic status. Inverse relationship between economic status and fertility has been observed in India in three rounds of the National Sample Survey in 1959-60, 1960-61 and 1961-62. This was further confirmed by a survey conducted in Greater Bombay in 1966 entitled fertility and family planning study, by the Registrar General of India. It was recorded that per capita monthly household expenditure has an inverse effect upon fertility. Those below ₹ 20 showed total fertility rate of 7.5 in rural and 9.5 in urban areas. On the other hand those spending ₹ 101 and above showed total marital fertility rate of 2.4 in rural and 2.5 in urban areas.

(*iii*) *Occupation of the husband*: In most of the developed countries a significant factor influencing rate of fertility is the economic status of the husband. For example, a study conducted in Europe in 1970 revealed that the wives of the farmers and farm workers recorded a higher fertility as compared to wives of men engaged in non-agricultural occupation. Similar results have been arrived at in other countries. Everywhere manual workers were found to be having more children than non-manual workers. According to S.N. Agarwala the cultivators had on an average 7.4 children, while those *in services and professions had an average of 6.6 children.*[1] According to Edwin D. Driver, the wives of unskilled workers, agriculturists and artisans have higher fertility as compared to the wives of the clerks.[2]

(*iv*) *Employment of wives*: This also has a negative relationship with fertility, though its exact nature has not been established as yet. One does not know whether women having smaller children go out for jobs or those who have jobs produce few children. Perhaps both the reasons may be equally important. It is noticed that most of the educated ladies without children take up jobs. On the other hand, most of the women on jobs practise methods of birth control and restrict their families.

(*v*) *Religion*: In most of the countries religion has been found to be an important factor effecting fertility. For example, in West it has been noticed that the fertility of Catholics exceeds that of Non-catholics in almost every country and socio-economic group. Buddhism is a populationist religion. Therefore, Buddhists have multiplied very fast. Similar is the case with Islam. Hinduism has also supported high fertility. The reason for this emphasis on big families by most of the great religions is the importance of fertility in the period when great religions were born. However, gradually everywhere the influence of religion on fertility has declined. Again, the gap between different religious groups concerning fertility is gradually narrowing.

(*vi*) *Caste and race*: Caste is an indicator of social class and economic status. Therefore, it appears to have an influence on fertility. For example, a study conducted in Lucknow city revealed that upper

1. Agarwal, S.N., *A Demographic Survey of Six Urbanizing Villages*, Bombay; Asia Publishing House, 1970, p. 103.
2. Driver, E.D., *Fertility in Central India*, Princeton: Princeton University Press, 1963, p. 93.

caste Hindus had on an average 3.8 live births, while the lower caste Hindus had a birth rate of 4.1. Similar differences have been noted in different races. In United States, for example, the Negros have shown a high fertility rate as compared to that of the Whites. This distinction, however, has been explained on socio-economic basis, thus eliminating racial differences. However, the case has not been finally settled. It is believed that the minorities, whether religious, racial or caste, tend to procreate more, thereby compensating for their small number.

The above discussion of factors influencing differential fertility differ in the intensity of their influence, Again, a multiple number of factors influence fertility everywhere, making it difficult to single out the particular factor influencing fertility. For example, in the case of educated women, it is not only education but late marriages, urban tendencies, socio-economic status and the knowledge of methods of birth control which causes lower rate of fertility. Similarly, in India for example, the high birth rate among Muslims, as compared to the Hindu community may be due to socio-economic factors, religious factors and so many other causes. Industrialisation, Westernisation, Urbanisation and socio-economic development have everywhere lowered the rate of fertility.

CAUSES OF LOW FERTILITY IN DEVELOPED COUNTRIES

Of the above mentioned factors influencing fertility rate, the following factors have influenced the low fertility in developed countries:

1. Motivational Factors: While formerly, there used to be a strong motivation for procreating more children, at present, in most of the developed countries, the motivational factors are in favour of low fertility. Of these the most important factors are desire for small family, availability of means of birth control and emphasis on sex enjoyment without strings.

2. Economic Factors: These include industrialisation and higher standard of living. Industrialisation has compelled so many males to stay in urban areas away from their females resulting in lower birth rate. Raising of the standard of living has led to the desire for a small family to maintain the standard. Therefore, in the higher economic groups in developed societies, the rate of birth has fallen very appreciably, so much so that childlessness is an increasing phenomena.

3. Social Factors: Social factors today are closely linked with economic factors. In fact social factors are the most important determinants of the present fall in fertility rate. The most important social factors determining fertility are as follows:

(*i*) *Urban society*: Urban society, as compared to the rural society, lays more emphasis upon enjoyment, individualism, small family, high standard of living, social change, etc. Almost all the characteristics of modern society favour low fertility.

(*ii*) *Modern family*: Modern family, with all its characteristics, has led to lower birth rate. The ideal of high standard of living, more education for children, more health care of the female and the children, etc., have motivated to two children and even to one. For the same reasons the tendency of not marrying, marrying at a late age, marrying temporarily and sex enjoyment as the main purpose of marriage have resulted in low fertility.

(*iii*) *Higher standard of living*: Unprecedented improvement in the standard of living and the high cost of the modern gadgets have considerably inflated family budgets. Therefore, efforts have to be made to keep the family strictly limited to meet the high costs of living and bring up children.

(*iv*) *Social mobility*: High social mobility is characteristic of developed societies both within the country as well as outside the country. Some of the people are constantly transferred on their jobs. Many others have to migrate from one place to another. This social mobility requires small families. Today it is possible to rise in social status vertically. Therefore, in the race for vertical progress in social status the people are severely limiting their families.

(*v*) *Education*: The most important social factor determining low fertility in developed countries is education, bringing a rational outlook, knowledge of means of birth control, individuality, health care, economic ambitions and realisation of personal ends. Of these the last is the most important. In the words of Frank W. Notestein, large families became, "A progressively difficult undertaking; expensive and difficult for a population ever increasingly freed from old taboos and increasingly willing to solve its problems rather than accept them."[1] The famous demographer pointed out that the decline in fertility in the West is a result of the growth of urban industrial society and the development of technology. In his own words, industrialisation and urbanisation resulted in, "The development of a rational and secular point of view; the growing awareness of the world and modern techniques through popular education; improved health; and the appearance of alternatives to early marriage and child bearing as a means of livelihood and prestige of woman."[2]

CAUSES OF HIGH FERTILITY IN DEVELOPING COUNTRIES

In contrast to the above mentioned factors resulting in low fertility, the following factors have resulted in high fertility in developing countries:

1. Motivational Factors: According to Ronald Freedman, high fertility is an adjustment, "to the central importance in community life of familial and kinship ties"[3] In pre-industrial societies and in agricultural social group there is emphasis upon corporate activities. Joint family, joint cultivation, joint occupations and community living motivate in favour of high fertility and against low fertility. In agricultural societies children are valued due to economic, social, religious and cultural factors. Economically they start earning and helping the parents in a very young age. Several females with dozens of children are assets to a male in backward societies particularly in Africa. Most of the great religions have eulogised the birth of a son. In society again, bigger family leads to higher social status in most of the primitive societies. In many primitive societies the socio-economic status of a person is measured by the number of his wives. This has encouraged polygamy and reckless procreation. Wars have also been motivating higher birth rate. Another significant motivating factor has been the fatalistic attitude such as the theory of Karma

1. Frank W. Notestein, "Population: The Long View" in Theodore W. Schultz's *Food for the World*, Chicago: University of Chicago Press, 1945, p. 39.
2. Frank W. Notestein, "Economic Problems of Population", Chicago, *Eighth International Conference of Agricultural Economists*, 1953, London: Oxford University Press, 1953, pp. 15-18.
3. Ronald Freedman, "Norms for Family Size" as quoted in the United Nation's *Determinants and Consequences of Population Trends*, Vol. 1, *op. cit.*, p. 92.

in India, according to which, 6"children are the gifts of God". Similar views have been expressed by most of the great religions thus motivating high fertility. It may be remembered here that along with Hinduism, Islam, Judaism, Christianity has also motivated high fertility, but this has been counteracted by other factors in developed countries. On the other hand, among the countries professing Hinduism, Islam and Judaism, religion has motivated high fertility.

2. Economic Factors: Widespread poverty leads to illiteracy, lower standard of living and corresponding high fertility. The children in lower economic group very soon start helping their parents in earning their living. Therefore the number of children is rather a welcome factor. Again, lower economic j status leads to fatalism motivating high fertility.

3. Social Factors: Social factors such as joint family, caste system, lack of social mobility, lower status of women, community life and joint occupations encourage fertility.

Due to the above mentioned factors one finds a high rate of birth in developing countries. Therefore, the governments in these countries have launched family planning movements to curb birth rates. As it is a well known principle these days that peace and prosperity anywhere requires peace and prosperity everywhere, most of the developed countries are giving aids to developing countries to check population growth. Similar campaigns have been organised by subsidiaries of United Nations to curb population growth in developing countries. These efforts have shown some results in some countries particularly in big countries like China and India. However, most of the developing countries, particularly the Islamic countries, are still showing high fertility rate. In fact unless social, cultural, economic and religious changes occur in these countries, the efforts of United Nations or those of the developed countries will not bear fruits.

THEORIES OF FERTILITY

Theories of fertility have been advanced to explain population growth in particular circumstances. They analyse cause effect relationships and point out the factors determining fertility. The various theories have been classified into 4 categories: Biological, Social, Economic and Socio-economic theories.

1. Biological Theories: These theories, as is clear by the terms used, lay emphasis upon biological factors influencing fertility. The most important theories in this category are: The Density Principle propounded by Michael Thomas Sadler in his work entitled. *The Law of Population*. Another significant biological theory is the Diet Principle propounded by Thomas Doubleday in 1841. In 1952 Josue de Castro, in his book *Geography of Hunger* emphasised biological factors. In 1880 Herbert Spencer advanced biological theory of fertility. Another biological theory has been advanced recently by the Italian biologist Corrado Gini.

2. Social Theories of Fertility: Sociologists have advanced social theories of fertility. Different social theories emphasized different factors determining fertility. One of the most important social theory of fertility is known as the theory of social capillarity. According to Arsena Dumont, a French Philosopher, the urge to rise in social status influences fertility. Kingsley Davis advanced a fertility theory of Change and Response based on the theme of social capillarity, *i.e.*, the desire to rise in the social scale.

Another important social theory of fertility is known as theory of Diffusion or Cultural Lag. It explains the spread of the concept of birth control all over the world. "According to the cultural lag theory of fertility differentials in countries where fertility has been declining, attitudes and practices conducive to diminishing fertility have been adopted first by the better educated, wealthier, and socially more favoured groups of the city population and transmitted in the course of time to intermediate and lower status groups and to the rural areas."[1] This theory has been supported by James Beshers in his study in Prussia. Amos Hawley supported the theory of diffusion influencing differential fertility. This theory has been criticised by Carlsson on the following two grounds[2]:

(*i*) Did birth control within marriage exist on a considerable scale before the secular decline of fertility begin, or did the decline end a phase in which control was not practised by married couples at all or very rarely at most?

(*ii*) Does the pattern of the spread of fertility decline, in fact, conform to the assumptions so prominent in current theory?

1. United Nations, *Population Bulletin of the United Nations* No. 7,1965, New York: 1965, p. 123.
2. Gosta Carlsson, "Decline of Fertility: Innovation or Adjustments Process?" *op. cit.*, p. 150.

Carlsson maintained that the theory of cultural lag is not a sufficient explanation. It does not explain as to why birth rates decline in the West. However, the theory does provide a partial explanation of fertility differentials in low fertility countries.

(*iii*) *Theory of Change and Response:* In 1963 Kingsley Davis pointed out that social changes and responses to them have widely influenced fertility. Multiphasic deliberate response in Western countries to social changes have led to decline in fertility. For example, response to methods of contraception has been an important factor in lowering fertility rate. Thus, demographic behaviour can be explained in terms of change and response. David Glass accepted in 1965 that the theory of change and response is more comprehensive, sophisticated and documents multiphasic responses particularly in Ireland and Japan. He, however, points out that historical facts in some countries in Europe do not fit in well with this theory. Similarly, it cannot be applied to the developing countries since they cannot wait for spontaneous response.

3. Economic Theories of Fertility: Among the economic theories of fertility, laying emphasis upon economic factors, the following two theories have been important contributions to the economic interpretation of fertility during 1960-1970:

(*i*) *Liebensteins' Theory.* In his book 'Economic Backwardness and Economic Growth' (1957), Harvey Liebenstein formulated a theory which explained the factors determining the number of children desired by each couple. It was based upon the assumption that people calculate the number of children they should have on the basis of satisfactions or utilities and cost both monetary and psychological. The types of utilities derived are: (*a*) The utility of the child as a consumption good or a source of pleasure, (*b*) The utility as a productive unit, and (*c*) The utility as a source of security in the old age. The two types of costs involved are direct costs and indirect costs. The former include conventional current expenses while the latter include opportunities foregone due to the additional child. According to Liebenstein, the following three changes occur due to the effect of utilities and costs : income effect, survival effect and occupational distribution effect. Liebenstein pointed out that this framework can be used, "To draw the relationship in such a way that, in general, the outcome is such that as the per capita income grows, the number of high parity children for the representative family falls"[1] This theory has been accepted to be explanatory rather than predictive.

(*ii*) *Theory of Backer*: In 1960 Backer presented his economic theory of fertility in his article entitled 'An Economic Analysis of Fertility'. He applied micro-consumption theory to fertility. He argued that fertility behaviour is the result of household choice. The choice of purchase of durable goods is made after a careful evaluation of the utilities derived and the costs incurred. Treating children as household commodities, Backer argued that a couple's decision in this respect depends on the balance of preferences, the constraints of income and the costs of the child. If knowledge of birth control were widespread, fertility would be directly related to the income. This theory has been criticised by Liebenstein, Richard Esterlin and Judith Blake. According to Liebenstein it presented the economist with a puzzle. According to Richard Sterlin tastes cannot be taken as immutable facts. Judith Blake has criticised Backer's attitude of viewing fertility performance as economic behaviour.

(*iii*) *Socio-economic*: Theories. An example of socio-economic theory of fertility is what is known as the Threshold Hypothesis. This has been presented by demographers at the United Nations. In It an attempt has been made to study the relationship between the level of fertility and various indicators of the socio economic level. It is based on the data collected from various countries. It uses the following 12 indicators: per capita income, energy consumption, degree of urbanisation, proportion of economically active male employed in non-agricultural activities, hospital beds per thousand population, life expectancy, infant mortality rate, proportion of married women in the 15-19 age group, female literacy rate, newspaper circulation, number of radio sets and the cinema attendance. The value of each of these indicators differs in countries showing high and low fertility. It may be inferred, "That the countries of the highest fertility are on that account at a disadvantage in development, or that a very low level of development is conducive to exceptionally high fertility."[2] These findings of the United Nations are consistent with the threshold hypothesis "which dwells on the role of social and economic

1. Harvey Liebenstein, "An Interpretation of the Economic Theory of Fertility: Promising Path or Blind Alley?" in *Journal of Economic Literature*, Vol. 12,1974, p. 460.
2. United Nations, *Population Bulletin of the United Nations*, No. 7, 1965, *op. cit*, p. 142.

development in bringing about the transition from high to low fertility." According to this hypothesis, "in a developing country where fertility is initially high, improving economic and social conditions are likely to have little, if any, effect on fertility until a certain economic and social level is reached; but once that level is achieved, fertility is likely to enter a decided decline and to continue downward until it is again stabilized on a much lower plain."[1] The findings have not supported the threshold hypothesis. It has been criticised on several grounds. Recent findings have shown that this theory is open to all the criticisms applicable to the demographic transition theory. It has initiated the controversy about the role of socio-economic development in fertility reduction. While some social thinkers believe that fertility cannot be reduced without an increase in socio-economic development, others hope that it may be realised by family planning programmes. In fact, both the alternatives are equally valuable. Therefore, at present, agencies of the United Nations are making efforts in both directions.

QUESTIONS FOR EXERCISE

1. Define fertility and discuss its nature.
2. Describe determinants and measures of fertility.
3. Discuss fertility trends in developed and developing countries of the world.
4. Describe the influence of different factors on fertility differentials.
5. Explain the causes of low fertility in developed countries.
6. Discuss the causes of high fertility in developing countries.
7. Discuss important theories of fertility.

1. *Ibid.*, p. 143.

11
Fertility in India

Among developing countries, India occupies an important place as the second biggest country after China. Before independence there were almost no efforts for checking the population growth. Due to illiteracy the census data in the beginning was hardly reliable. Several attempts were made to assess the rate of fertility in the country. In 1911, Marten, the Superintendent of Census Operations of C.P. and Berar attempted to obtain data concerning, "The size and sex constitution of the family in the Central Provinces, and related fecundity in different castes and different parts in the Central Provinces."[1] In 1921 census information was collected in Bengal, Bihar, Orissa, C.P., Punjab, Baroda and Travancore States about the size and sex compositions of families and fertility in married life. The information was however hardly reliable. In 1931 statistics were collected about age at marriage, sex composition, size of the family, etc., in census operation, from all sections of society, in each part of India except U.P. The Indian Fertility Enquiry, as this data collection was known, showed that the data was badly collected and inefficiently handled, in 1951 Census, the item concerning fertility was optional. Therefore, Madhya Pradesh, Travancore, Cochin and Bihar alone collected statistics on Child birth, child survival and other maternity data. However, the process was marred by severe defects. After 1961 census, post-census fertility surveys were conducted in various states in India. These usually covered only 1% of the rural blocks and 2% of the urban blocks. Data were available from 5 states — Andhra Pradesh, Assam, Gujarat, Kerala and Orissa. In 1971

1. Marten, J.T., *Census of India, 1911*, Vol. 10, *Central Provinces and Berar*, Calcutta: Superintendent, Government Printing Press, Appendix to Chapter VI, p. 125.

Census information was gathered on child births in the household during the reference period of 12 months.

The following persons and agencies collected data about birth rates in India from 1901 to 1974:

1. *K. Davis*, Davis collected the following year-wise data about birth rate in India per 1000 population 1901-1911 (49.2); 1911-1921 (48.1); 1921-1931 (46.4); 1931-1941 (45.2).
2. *Official data*: 1951-1961 (41.7).
3. *P.M. Visaria, G.B Saxena, Rele and Sinha*. The birth rate according to these during the period 1951-1961 was 44.9, 46.0, 45.0 respectively.
4. *United Nations Manual IV*. 1951-1961 (45.1).
5. *Adlakha and Kark* 1961-1971 (40.5-42.0)
6. *Rele and Sinha*. 1961-1971 (40.0).
7. *S. Raghavachari* By reverse survival method the following age-wise birth rate was discovered during the period 1961-1971: Age 0-4 (40.2); Age 5-9 (41.6); and Age 0-9 (41.1).
8. *Sample Registration System*: According to this system the following year-wise data concerning birth rate was gathered: 1970 (35.8); 1971 (36.9); 1973 (34.6); 1974 (34.5).

Besides, survey was conducted by Registrar General of India in 1961 providing the following birth rate per 1000 population:

TABLE 11.1

Birth Rate for Thousand Population, 1961

State	*Rural Birth Rate*	*Urban Birth Rate*
Assam	44.9	42.3
Jammu and Kashmir	33.5	25.5
Kerala	36.2	31.3
Mysore	34.2	32.1
Orissa	36.5	31.9
Punjab	39.2	34.5
Rajasthan	40.4	41.1
Uttar Pradesh	36.8	32.7

Notable among the various agencies are the following which conducted survey of average number of children born alive per woman of unbroken marriage till she passes the reproductive age, in rural and urban areas:[1]

1. Bhende, A. A., Kaitkar T., *Principles of Population Studies*, Himalaya Publishing House (1973), Bombay, p. 340.

1. *Bengal Survey*: 1946-49.

2. *Gokhale Institute of Politics and Economic Surveys*: Poona (1951-52), Poona (1956), Nasik (1954), Kolaba (1953-54) and Satara North (1952-54).

3. *UN. and Government of India Mysore Study*: Bangalore City 1952, Rural areas 1952. The survey of Bangalore city provided data about fertility by caste and religion which was: Hindus 5.4, Muslims 5.7, Christians 4.7.

Table 11.2

State-wise Growth of Population 1991

State	*Population*	*% Growth*	*Density*
1. Andhra Pradesh	66,304,854	23.82	241
2. Arunachal Pradesh	858,392	35.86	10
3. Assam	22,294,562	23.58	284
4. Bihar	86,338,853	23.49	17
5. Goa	1,168,622	15.96	316
6. Gujarat	41,174,060	20.80	210
7. Haryana	16,317,715	26.28	369
8. Himachal Pradesh	5,111,079	19.39	92
9. Jammu & Kashmir	7,718,700	28.92	76
10. Karnataka	44,817,398	20.69	234
11. Kerala	29,011,237	13.98	747
12. Madhya Pradesh	66,135,862	26.75	149
13. Maharashtra	78,706,719	25.36	256
14. Manipur	1,826,714	28.56	82
15. Meghalaya	1,760,626	31.80	78
16. Mizoram	686,217	38.98	33
17. Nagaland	1,215,573	56.86	73
18. Orissa	31,512,070	19.50	202
19. Punjab	20,190,795	20.26	401
20. Rajasthan	43,880,640	28.07	128
21. Sikkim	403,612	27.57	57
22. Tamil Nadu	55,638,318	14.94	428
23. Tripura	2,744,827	33.69	262
24. Uttar Pradesh	138,760,417	25.16	471
25. West Bengal	67,982,732	24.55	766
UNION TERRITORIES			
1. A & N Islands	277,989	47.29	34
2. Chandigarh	640,725	41.88	5,620
3. Dadra & Nagar Haveli	138,542	33.63	282
4. Daman & Diu	101,439	28.43	906
5. Delhi	9,370,475	50.64	6,319
6. Lakshadweep	51,681	28.40	1,615
7. Pondicherry	789,416	30.60	1,605

TABLE 11.3

Decadal Growth of Population: 1971-81 and 1981-91

India/State/ Union Territory	*Decadal growth of population*		*per cent to total growth of India*	
	1971-81	*1981-91*	*1971-81*	*1981-91*
India	135,169,445	160,601,764	100.00	100.00
States				
1. Andhra Pradesh	10,046,965	12,75,181	7.43	7.94
2. Arunachal Pradesh	164,328	226,553	0.12	0.14
3. Assam	3,416,096	4,253,314	2.53	2.65
4. Bihar	13,561,365	16,424,119	10.03	10.23
5. Goa	212,629	160,873	0.16	0.10
6. Gujarat	7,388,324	708,261	5.47	4.41
7. Haryana	2,885,311	3,395,596	2.13	2.11
8. Himachal Pradesh	820,384	830,261	0.61	0.52
9. Jammu & Kashmir	1,370,757	1,731,311	1.01	1.08
10. Karnataka	7,836,700	7,681,684	5.80	4.78
11. Kerala	4,106,305	3,557,557	3.04	2.22
12. Madhya Pradesh	10,524,725	13,957,018	7.79	8.69
13. Maharashtra	12,371,936	15,922,548	9.15	9.91
14. Manipur	348,200	405,761	0.26	0.25
15. Meghalaya	324,120	424,807	0.24	0.27
16. Mizoram	161,367	192,460	0.12	0.12
17. Nagaland	258,481	440,643	0.19	0.27
18. Orissa	3,425,656	5,141,799	3.27	3.20
19. Punjab	3,237,855	3,401,799	2.40	2.12
20. Rajasthan	8,496,056	9,618,778	6.29	5.99
21. Sikkim	106,542	87,227	0.08	0.05
22. Tamil Nadu	7,208,909	7,230,241	5.33	4.50
23. Tripura	496,716	691,769	0.37	0.43
24. Uttar Pradesh	22,521,368	27,897,905	16.66	17.37
25. West Bengal	10,268,636	13,402,085	7.60	8.35
UNION TERRITORIES				
1. A. & N. Islands	73,608	89,248	0.05	0.06
2. Chandigarh	194,359	189,115	0.14	0.12
3. Dadra & Nagar Haveli	29,506	34,866	0.02	0.02
4. Daman & Diu	16,330	22,458	0.01	0.01
5. Delhi	254,708	3,150,069	1.59	1.96
6. Lakshadweep	8,439	11,432	0.01	0.01
7. Pondicherry	132,764	184,945	0.10	0.12

Table 11.4

Ranking of States and Union Territories by Population Size, 1991

Rank (1991)	State/Union Territory	Population 1991	Per cent to total Population of India 1991	Per cent to total Population of India 1981
1.	Uttar Pradesh	138,760,417	16.44	16.22
2.	Bihar	86,338,853	10.23	10.23
3.	Maharashtra	78,706,719	9.33	9.19
4.	West Bengal	67,982,732	8.06	7.99
5.	Andhra Pradesh	66,304,854	7.86	7.64
6.	Madhya Pradesh	66,135,862	7.84	7.64
7.	Tamil Nadu	55,638,318	6.59	7.08
8.	Karnataka	44,817,398	5.31	5.43
9.	Rajasthan	43,880,640	5.20	5.01
10.	Gujarat	41,174,060	4.88	4.99
11.	Orissa	31,512,070	3.73	3.86
12.	Kerala	29,011,237	3.44	3.72
13.	Assam	22,294,562	2.64	2.64
14.	Punjab	20,190,795	2.39	2.46
15.	Haryana	16,317,715	1.93	1.89
16.	Delhi	9,370,475	1.11	0.91
17.	Jammu & Kashmir	7,718,700	0.91	0.88
18.	Himachal Pradesh	5,111,079	0.61	0.63
19.	Tripura	2,744,827	0.32	0.30
20.	Manipur	1,826,714	0.22	0.21
21.	Meghalaya	1,760,626	0.21	0.19
22.	Nagaland	1,215,573	0.14	0.11
23.	Goa	1,168,622	0.14	0.15
24.	Arunachal Pradesh	858,392	0.10	0.09
25.	Pondicherry	789,416	0.09	0.09
26.	Mizoram	686,217	0.08	0.07
27.	Chandigarh	640,725	0.08	0.07
28.	Sikkim	403,612	0.05	0.05
29.	Andaman & Nicobar Islands	277,989	0.03	0.03
30.	Dadra & Nagar Haveli	138,542	0.01	0.01
31.	Damon & Diu	101,439	0.01	0.01
32.	Lakshadweep	51,681	0.01	0.01

Table 11.5

States and Union Territories Arranged in Descending Order of Density in 1991

Rank in 1992	State/ Union Territory	Density (per sq. km.) 1981	1991
1.	Delhi	4,194	6,319
2.	Chandigarh	3,961	5,620
3.	Lakshadweep	1,258	1,615
4.	Pondicherry	1,229	1,605
5.	Daman & Diu	705	906
6.	West Bengal	615	766
7.	Kerala	655	747
8.	Bihar	402	497
9.	Uttar Pradesh	377	471
10.	Tamil Nadu	372	428
11.	Punjab	333	401
12.	Haryana	292	369
13.	Goa	272	316
14.	Assam	230	284
15.	Dadra & Nagar Haveli	211	282
16.	Tripura	196	262
17.	Maharashtra	204	256
18.	Andhra Pradesh	195	241
19.	Karnataka	194	234
20.	Gujarat	174	210
21.	Orissa	169	202
22.	Madhya Pradesh	118	149
23.	Rajasthan	100	128
24.	Himachal Pradesh	77	92
25.	Manipur	64	82
26.	Meghalaya	60	78
27.	Jammu & Kashmir	59	76
28.	Nagaland	47	73
29.	Sikkim	45	57
30.	Andaman & Nicobar Islands	23	34
31.	Mizoram	23	33
32.	Arunachal Pradesh	8	10

4. *National Sample Surveys*, 1951-52, 1960-61, 1961-62.

5. *Office of the Registrar General Surveys:* 1951 Census, 1961 Census, Post-Census Survey 1961.

6. *Kanpur and Lucknow Surveys,* 1951.
7. Patna Survey, 1956.
8. Delhi Survey, 1958-60.
9. Greater Bombay Fertility Survey, 1966.

BIRTH RATE IN INDIA

The following table shows estimates of birth rate in India since 1881 to 1971 based based upon indirect method of estimation :

TABLE 11.6

Estimate of Birth Rate in India, 1881-1971[1]

Period	Reserve survival ratio method	Quasi-stable population method (S.P. Jain	Vig's estimate based on quasi-stable techniques
	1	2	3
1881-1891	48.9		
1891-1901	45.8		
1901-1911	49.2	52.4	51.6
1911-1921	48.1	—	50.8
1921-1931	46.4	50.8	48.4
1931-1941	45.2	46.2	46.6
1941-1951	39.9	43.1	45.0
1951-1961	41.7	40.0	45.0
1961-1971	41.1	—	—

According to Sample Registration System the following data were obtained during the period 1968-1974:

Table 11.7

Birth Rate in India : SRS Estimates, 1968-74[2]

Year	Rural	Urban	Total
1968	38.0	—	—
1969	38.8	32.6	37.6
1970	38.9	29.7	36.8
1971	38.9	30.1	36.9
1972	38.4	30.5	36.6
1973	35.9	28.9	34.6
1974	35.9	28.4	34.5

1. *Vital Statistics of India for* 1971, New Delhi: Office of the Registrar General of India, pp. xi and xiii.
2. Agarwal, S.N., *India`s Population Problems,* Tata McGraw Hill, New Delhi, (1977), p. 139.

Different surveys were conducted during the period 1961-1968 in different areas of the country by different agencies. The following are the results of these surveys:[1]

1. *Gandhi Gram Project, Madurai* — 1962 (40.0); 1965 (36.3).
2. *Singur Rural Area* — 1962 (39.3); 1966 (34.2).
3. *Tea Estates of Assam* — 1960 (43.4); 1966 (31.2).
4. *Doona Dooma Area, Assam Valley* — 1963 (35.1); 1965 (27.8).
5. *Najafgarh Block, New Delhi* — 1966 (37.5); 1968 (31.9).
6. *Haryana Study* — 1961 (36.0); 1968 (32.4).
7. *Gujarat Study* — 1966 (43.0); 1968 (40.6).
8. *Dooar's Plantation, West Bengal* — 1963 (35.1); 1965 (27.8).

It may be noted from the data given so far that one finds regional variations in birth rate in India. Birth rate is high in the states of Rajasthan, Uttar Pradesh, Madhya Pradesh, Gujarat and Assam.

AGE SPECIFIC FERTILITY RATE

Crude birth rate does not give any idea of the age structure of the population in connection with fertility. Therefore, attempts have been made to find out age specific fertility rate. This means ratio of births in a year to females of a given age or age group. The following table gives information about age specific fertility rate per thousand females in India conducted in different years in rural and urban areas, by National Sample Survey and Sample Registration System:

Table 11.8

Estimated Crude Birth Rates for States and Union Territories, 1985-1989

(per thousand)

State/Union Territory	*Area*	*1985*	*1986*	*1987*	*1988*	*1989*
1	2	3	4	5	6	7
1. Andhra Pradesh	Combined	29.9	31.6	30.3	27.4	25.6
	Rural	29.8	32.4	30.9	27.6	26.0
	Urban	30.2	28.7	28.2	26.3	24.1
2. Arunachal Pradesh	Combined	35.5	40.2	36.3	40.0	35.2
	Rural	35.9	40.7	37.0	40.9	35.8
	Urban	30.5	33.9	29.0	30.3	28.8
3. Assam	Combined	34.3	34.7	34.2	32.9	29.1
	Rural	35.0	35.5	34.9	33.6	29.7
	Urban	25.0	24.8	25.7	24.6	21.6

1. *Family Planning in India, Programme of Information*, 1971-72, New Delhi: Department of Family Planning, Government of India, 1972, p. 55.

4.	Bihar	Combined	37.8	36.5	36.6	37.3	34.4
		Rural	38.5	37.2	37.3	38.1	35.1
		Urban	31.1	29.8	30.1	30.4	27.6
5.	Goa	Combined	18.5	20.2	18.9	17.7	15.5
		Rural	18.0	19.9	19.4	17.9	15.1
		Urban	19.3	20.8	18.0	17.4	16.2
6.	Gujarat	Combined	33.0	32.2	30.8	29.5	28.7
		Rural	33.8	32.9	31.6	30.1	29.6
		Urban	31.2	30.8	29.0	28.1	26.5
7.	Haryana	Combined	35.7	35.3	34.5	33.8	34.8
		Rural	36.5	36.9	35.4	35.0	36.3
		Urban	32.9	29.6	31.3	29.9	29.9
8.	Himachal Pradesh	Combined	30.2	30.6	30.8	32.2	27.7
		Rural	30.7	31.3	31.4	32.9	28.3
		Urban	23.8	20.0	22.7	22.8	20.3
9.	Jammu & Kashmir	Combined	33.6	33.4	31.0	33.1	30.7
		Rural	35.9	35.6	32.6	35.5	32.6
		Urban	25.4	25.4	25.1	24.0	23.3
10.	Karnataka	Combined	29.6	29.0	28.9	28.7	27.9
		Rural	30.9	29.9	29.9	30.1	28.9
		Urban	26.2	26.8	26.3	24.9	25.0
11.	Kerala	Combined	23.3	22.5	21.7	20.3	19.8
		Rural	23.1	22.4	21.5	20.0	19.7
		Urban	24.1	23.0	22.3	21.4	20.2
12.	Madhya Pradesh	Combined	39.4	37.2	36.4	37.0	35.1
		Rural	41.0	39.0	37.5	38.4	36.4
		Urban	33.0	30.1	31.9	31.2	29.8
13.	Maharashtra	Combined	29.0	30.1	28.9	29.4	28.3
		Rural	29.8	31.7	30.2	31.4	30.4
		Urban	27.7	27.4	26.6	25.8	24.4
14.	Manipur	Combined	28.5	25.7	25.9	25.8	22.4
		Rural	29.8	27.4	27.7	27.7	24.3
		Urban	24.4	20.2	19.9	19.6	16.0
15.	Meghalaya	Combined	39.1	35.4	34.9	36.4	31.1
		Rural	42.4	38.3	38.6	40.5	33.6
		Urban	24.1	21.7	17.6	17.7	19.0
16.	Nagaland	Combined	25.3	25.2	21.7	22.3	19.8
		Rural	28.4	26.6	23.7	23.8	20.8
		Urban	11.2	18.6	13.0	15.5	14.9
17.	Orissa	Combined	30.7	32.5	31.0	31.9	30.2
		Rural	30.9	33.2	31.6	32.5	30.7
		Urban	28.3	26.8	25.7	26.5	24.9
18.	Punjab	Combined	28.5	28.7	28.7	28.5	28.4
		Rural	28.8	29.0	28.9	28.9	28.7
		Urban	27.6	27.6	27.9	27.5	27.5
19.	Rajasthan	Combined	39.7	36.4	35.1	33.3	33.9
		Rural	41.1	37.9	36.3	34.4	35.0
		Urban	33.6	29.8	29.8	28.4	28.5

20. Sikkim	Combined	33.1	32.1	33.3	33.8	31.4
	Rural	35.1	33.8	34.6	35.8	32.8
	Urban	24.2	24.4	27.2	25.0	24.5
21. Tamil Nadu	Combined	24.7	23.8	24.0	22.7	23.1
	Rural	25.2	24.1	24.1	23.4	23.5
	Urban	23.8	23.1	23.7	21.4	22.2
22. Tripura	Combined	27.3	28.5	28,2	26.6	25.7
	Rural	27.6	29.1	29.1	27.5	26.6
	Urban	24.5	22.4	19.5	17.8	16.8

Table 11.9

Age Specific Fertility Rate[1] 1959-69

	National Sample Survey				*Sample Registration System (Rural)*	
	(Rural)		*Urban*			
Age group	*1959-60*	*1964-65*	*1959-60*	*1964-65*	*1968*	*1969*
10–15	1.0	2.5	0.9	—	—	—
15–20	143.9	83.2	99.6	67.5	109.4	97.9
20–25	263.6	247.2	226.9	251.9	251.4	261.9
25–30	244.3	241.3	208.2	271.5	272.6	266.9
30–35	188.3	195.4	160.4	195.1	224.3	226.0
35–40	127.9	177.5	102.4	130.9	172.3	158.3
40–45	49.6	79.1	41.8	12.1	81.6	77.1
45–49	17.6	33.4	9.9	8.5	39.7	35.5
50–54	2.3	3.6	—	—	—	—

The above data about age-specific fertility rate shows a broad peak type fertility curve. While the National Sample Survey shows early peak type fertility in the age group 20-25, the Sample Registration System shows late peak type fertility reaching in the age group 25-30. Therefore it is more sensible to conclude that the fertility of Indian women reaches its peak in age group 20-25 and remains constant during the age group 25-30.

Table 11.10

Estimated Age-specific Fertility Rates and Other Fertility Indicators, India, 1987

Age group	*Rural*	*Urban*	*Combined*
15–19	97.5	58.7	88.3
20–24	262.8	221.3	252.3
25–29	223.3	184.6	213.5

1. National Sample Survey, *Fertility and Mortality Rates in India*, New Delhi, Manager of Publications, 1963, p. 12.

30–34	148.4	96.4	135.9
35–39	88.1	49.6	78.8
40–44	40.2	18.8	35.5
45–49	17.9	5.3	15.1
Crude birth rate	33.7	27.4	32.2
General fertility rate	141.8	108.5	133.8
Total fertility rate	4.4	3.2	4.1
Gross reproduction rate	2.1	1.5	2.0

BIRTH BY DURATION OF MARRIED LIFE

The following table shows distribution of births by duration of married life in India:

Table 11.11

Distribution of Births by Duration of Married Life[1] Percentage of Total Births 1965

		Duration of Married Life (in Years)						
States		1-5	5-10	10-15	15-20	20-25	25-30	30+
Bihar	R	10	26	27	18	11	5	3
	U	19	32	22	13	7	4	3
Gujarat	R	20	27	26	15	8	3	1
	U	21	30	26	12	8	2	1
Jammu and	R	16	26	27	17	12	—	2
Kashmir	U	19	26	27	16	11		1
Kerala	R	25	27	24	15	7	2	0
	U	27	28	24	15	7	2	0
Madhya	R	15	28	26	17	9	4	1
Pradesh	U	17	28	26	17	9	3	1
Tamil Nadu	R	25	30	21	13	7	2	2
	U	27	28	21	15	6	2	1
Maharashtra	R	15	26	26	17	10	4	2
	U	18	28	26	16	8	3	1
Karnataka	R	18	24	28	17	9	3	1
	U	19	27	28	15	8	2	1
Orissa	R	21	27	25	14	9	2	2
	U	20	29	25	14	8	2	2
Rajasthan	R	12	26	25	19	11	5	2
	U	15	29	22	17	10	4	3
Delhi	U	25	27	25	15	6	2	0

1. Mahrotra, G.K., "Birth Order Distribution and its Implications on the Fertility of Indian Women", *Journal of Family Welfare*, Vol. XI, No. 3, March 1965, p. 28.

The above table shows that most of the births take place within 5 to 15 years of married life. In some rural areas 10% of the total births occur within 1-5 years of married life. Very few births occur after 25 years of married life. This shows that if married couples may be persuaded to use contraceptives for the first few years of their married life, the birth rate may be considerably reduced in India.

BIRTH ORDER

Birth order means the sequence of time and duration in the births of different children of a couple. The following table shows percentage distribution of birth order in India in different States, in different age groups, in rural and urban areas.

TABLE 11.12

Percentage Distribution of Birth Order[1] 1965

States	*Rural Order of Birth*			*Urban Order of Birth*		
	1-3	*4-5*	*6+*	*1-3*	*4-5*	*6+*
Bihar	65	24	11	62	24	14
Gujarat	53	26	21	52	25	23
J&K	58	26	16	53	29	18
Kerala	53	25	22	54	24	22
Madhya Pradesh	54	25	21	53	26	21
Madras	63	23	14	63	23	14
Maharashtra	58	25	17	55	25	20
Mysore	55	24	21	53	24	23
Orissa	64	23	13	63	23	14
Rajasthan	58	25	17	56	23	21
Delhi	—	—	—	55	26	19

According to S.P. Jain in India in 1951 the percentage of births of different order was first 20.1, second 17.6, third 15.5, fourth 13.1, fifth 10.9 and sixth 22.1[2]. Roughly speaking 1/4th of all the births in urban and rural areas are of the fourth and the fifth orders. The first three births are lower in the urban areas and higher in the rural areas. Sixth and higher order births are more or less same in both urban and rural areas. Thus, the fertility in urban areas is a little lower than in rural areas.

---

1. *Ibid.*, p. 32.
2. Jain, S.P., "Indian Fertility — Our Knowledge and Gaps", *Journal of Family Welfare*, Vol. X, No. 4, June, 1964, p. 25.

FERTILITY BY RESIDENCE

As is clear by the tables given so far one finds a difference in fertility in rural and urban areas in India. As a general rule the birth rate in urban areas is lower than in the rural areas. Even within the urban areas metropolitan cities exhibit relatively lower fertility than smaller cities. For example, the birth rate in Greater Bombay, Delhi and Calcutta is lower than the national average. This is partly due to the low proportion of females in the population of these cities.

FERTILITY BY CASTE AND RELIGION

Different surveys have revealed different rate of fertility in different religions and castes in India. The fertility among Muslims is much more than the fertility among Hindus. Different surveys have revealed this distinction. According to the Mysore Population Study, sponsored by United Nations the fertility of different religions in Bangalore city was : Hindus 5.4, Muslims 5.7, Christians 4.7. The average fertility in different religions in urban areas was found to be Hindus 5.2, Muslims 6.7, Christians 5.5. This was further confirmed by the rural percentage of Hindus 4.8 and Muslims 5.0. These data were confirmed by other studies. According to the Social Survey of Kanpur in 1954-55 by D.N. Majumdar the fertility rate among Muslims and Hindus was 8.021 and 7.037 respectively.[1] According to another study by G.B. Saxena about fertility in 3 villages of Uttar Pradesh the fertility rate among different sections of society by caste and religion was found as follows: Muslims 6.24, Hindus 6.16, Rajputs 6.77, Artisan Castes 5.50 and Bhangis and Chamars 5.43.[2] According to S.N, Agarwal's study of fertility in 6 urbanising villages, the fertility rate among different castes was: Brahmin 7.19, Jat 7.11, Gujar and Aheer 6.97, Artisan Castes 7.16, Bhangi and Chamar 7.24. The average fertility rate for all castes was found to be 7.08.[3] According to another study of fertility in central India the differential fertility was found as follows:

---

1. Majumdar, D.N., *Social Contours of an Industrial City*, Bombay, Asia Publishing House, 1960, p. 174.
2. Saxena, G.B., *A Study of Fertility and Family Planning in 3 Villages of Uttar Pradesh*, New Delhi, Institute of Economic Growth, 1969.
3. Agarwal, S.N., *A Demographic Study of 6 Urbanising Villages*, Bombay, Asia Publishing House, 1970, p. 101.

Muslims 4.6, Hindus 4.5, Buddhists 4.9, other religions 4.1, and average for all castes 4.5.[1] According to the study entitled, *Social Profiles of a Metropolis* the differential fertility was: Muslims 3.7, Hindus 3.4, Christians 2.7, Sikhs 2.8 and other religions 2.7.[2]

The above studies reveal the influence of castes and religions on fertility rate. The reasons for this differential fertility, however, are not as much definite. It may be noted that Bhangis and Chamars and artisan castes have a higher fertility rate than other castes among Hindus. However, this difference may not be so, much due to caste but due to socio-economic status and illiteracy. Similar arguments may be given about the lower fertility rate among high caste Hindus. It may be more due to education and higher socio-economic status. Again, as has been already pointed out, minorities everywhere tend to breed fast.

FERTILITY AND EDUCATION

Several studies have pointed out an inverse correlation between education and fertility. The Mysore study pointed out above has shown that in Bangalore city the average number of children born to females of the age of 50 and who were illiterate was between 5.3 and 5.5. No significant difference was found in the fertility of illiterates and women educated upto middle school standard. However, the fertility rate of woman educated upto High School or more was only 3.9. This is not only due to a better knowledge of birth control methods by educated females but also due to late marriages after education. Generally, the husbands of educated females were also more educated and therefore having more knowledge of methods of birth control and also more desire for family planning to maintain a higher standard of living. The 16th round of the National Sample Survey 1960-61 also showed similar results. The studies by Mukerjee and Driver have also confirmed differential fertility on different educational levels. This is shown in the table given below:

1. Driver, E.D., *Differential Fertility in Central India,* Princeton University Press, New Jersey, USA 1963, p. 88.
2. Mukerjee, R.K. and Baljit Singh, *Social Profiles of a Metropolis,* Bombay Asia Publishing House, 1961, p. 166,

TABLE 11.13

Average Number of Children Born Alive to Couples Classified by Educational Level of Husband and Wife, 1965

Mukerjee[1]				*Driver*[2]			
Wife		*Husband*		*Wife*		*Husband*	
Illiterate	3.5	Illiterate	3.5	Illiterate	4.7	Illiterate	5.0
Primary	3.4	Primary	3.3	Primary	4.3	Primary	4.3
Secondary	3.1	Secondary	3.2	Above		Middle	
Technical	3.0	Technical	3.2	Primary	3.4	School	4.1
College	3.0	College	3.4	Total	4.5	High School	3.9
Post-graduate	2.5	Post-graduate	3.3			Matriculation	4.3
Private	3.7	Private	4.0			College	3.9
						Total	4.5

ECONOMIC STATUS AND FERTILITY

According to the Seventeenth Round of National Sample Survey the birth rate by per capita monthly household expenditure and urban rural residence was as follows:[3]

TABLE 11.14

Birth Rate by Per Capita Monthly Household Expenditure and Urban-Rural Residence, 1965

Per Capita Monthly Expenditure in Rupees	*Urban*	*Rural*	*Per Capita Monthly Expenditure in Rupees*	*Urban*	*Rural*
0-5	42.9	42.1	55-60	31.6	33.6
5-10	40.2	41.9	60-65	35.8	31.9
10-15	41.6	42.0	65-70	30.6	36.1
15-20	41.2	43.0	70-75	31.1	31.5
25-30	37.9	40.7	75-80	25.8	33.9
30-35	25.7	39.7	80-85	26.5	28.8
35-40	36.0	32.0	85-90	23.0	31.3
40-45	36.2	35.4	90-95	19.2	21.6
45-50	39.3	36.1	95-100	15.0	20.4
50-55	33.1	35.8			

1. *Ibid.*, pp. 163-164.
2. Driver, E.D., *Differential Fertility in Central India*, pp. 99-101.
3. National Sample Survey, Seventeenth Round, Delhi: Manager of Publications, 1965, pp. 22-23.

The above table shows that fertility rate in urban areas is almost everywhere lower than that of the rural areas. The influence of economic status however, working in favour of lower fertility, crosses this tendency to show that even in rural areas fertility is lower in higher economic level groups as compared to fertility in urban areas in lower economic groups. However, other studies have not shown so much specific influence of economic status upon fertility. For example, Driver's study has shown fertility rate of 4.5 for all income groups while it was 4.6 both for monthly income below 500 and above 2000.[1] It may be noted that similar results were obtained by Mukerjee when he showed that the fertility rate in 500-1000 monthly income groups was 3.3 uniformly.[2]

OCCUPATION AND FERTILITY

Studies by several Sociologists have shown that occupation is a fertility differential in India. In some cases however, this has not been clearly confirmed. For example, according to Mysore Study the average number of children born alive to couples in high professional and managerial workers as well as among domestic and other services workers was uniformly 5.0. However, other studies have shown some distinction. For example, G.B. Saxena in his study of differential fertility, in rural Uttar Pradesh, shows that while the fertility for service class was 6.4 and business and artisans 6.6, the fertility among agriculturists was 7.1 and among labourers as much as 7.8. The general tendency of higher fertility among occupations of cultivation and manual labour has been confirmed by so many other studies in India. The fertility rate of clerical workers was found to be lowest in his study by E.D. Driver.[3] All these studies show that there is some influence of occupation upon fertility. However, occupation is not the only cause of higher fertility among cultivators and labourers. Equal importance must be given to illiteracy and lower economic and educational status.

MARRIAGE AGE AND FERTILITY

Different studies have clearly shown an inverse correlation between marriage age and fertility. As a general rule, the higher

1. Driver, E.D., *Differential Fertility in Central India*, p. 88.
2. Mukerjee, R.K., and Baljit Singh, *Social Profiles of a Metropolis*, p. 167.
3. Driver, E.D., *Differential Fertility in Central India*, p. 93.

the marriage age the lower is the fertility rate. This is clear by the following table :[1]

TABLE 11.15

Average Number of Children per Woman of Completed Maternity, 1964

States		*Marriage Age*		
		Below 18	*18-23*	*23 and above*
Jammu & Kashmir	Rural	5.1	4.2	3.2
	Urban	5.2	4.2	3.7
Punjab	Rural	5.7	5.2	4.4
	Urban	6.0	5.5	4.7
Kerala	Rural	6.2	5.5	3.9
	Urban	6.2	5.5	4.0
Uttar Pradesh	Rural	4.2	4.0	3.7
	Urban	4.5	4.0	3.7

As is clear by the data in the above mentioned table for States in India, while the fertility below 18 is almost the maximum, it Is minimum above 23 and average in the age group 18-23 years. Similar results have been obtained by studies of average number of children born alive by effective marriage age in other States in India. For the total country, according to Sample Registration Bulletin, 1976[2] fertility rate was: 5.7 below 18; 4.8 in the age group 18-20 years; 4.2 above 21 years of age in rural areas. In urban areas the corresponding fertility rate was 5.6, 4.8 and 4.3 respectively. Similar results were found in almost every State in India. This shows that fertility Is definitely maximum below 18 years everywhere and minimum above 23 years. According to the data collected by *The Mysore Population Study* females marrying between the ages of 14 and 17 give birth to 5.9 children while those marrying between 18 and 21 give birth to 4.7 children.[3] In his study *Social Contours of an Industrial City*, D.N. Majumdar pointed out that in Kanpur the females marrying upto the age of 15 gave birth to 6.9 children while those marrying after 19 procreated only 6.0 children.[4] Similar studies in other metropolitan cities like Calcutta, Madras, Delhi and Lucknow have registered a difference of 0.5 and 1.0 child in different ages of marriage. According to

1. Jain, S.P., *Certain Statistics on Fertility of Indian Women*, New Delhi: Office of the Registrar General, 1964, p. 3.
2. *Sample Registration Bulletin*, Vol. X, No. 1, New Delhi: Office of the Registrar General of India, 1976, pp. 3-3.
3. *Op. cit.*, p. 119.
4. *Op. cit.*, p. 161.

the report of S.P. Jain, the fertility rate in India among females marrying between the ages of 18 and 22 is lower as compared to those marrying by the age of 18.[1] According to S.N. Agarwala females marrying between the ages of 16 and 19 give birth to nearly the same number of children but females marrying at the age of 19 and above procreate fewer children.[2]

TABLE 11.16

Estimated Age-specific Marital Fertility Rates and other Fertility Indicators, India, 1987

Age group	*Rural*	*Urban*	*Combined*
15–19	248.5	299.2	255.3
20–24	31 8.4	325.1	319.8
25–29	239.5	208.6	231.9
30–34	157.2	103.2	144.3
35–39	95.2	53.7	85.1
40–44	40.2	21.4	40.0
45–49	21.5	6.5	15.1
General Marital Fertility Rate	179.6	152.5	173.6
Total Marital Fertility Rate	5.6	5.1	5.5

FUTURE OF FERTILITY IN INDIA

The future growth in India's population will be largely determined by the trend in birth rate which, unfortunately, goes on quite high in spite of all efforts in the family planning movement. Undoubtedly, the movement has made some headway, but in the context of the total country and its rate of fertility the progress is not significant. This is confirmed by the Census data of 1981 which has been given elsewhere in this book. The main hurdles in the way of control are illiteracy, communalism, lower economic status and lack of sufficient efforts and co-ordination.

STERILITY IN INDIA

According to Multilingual Demographic Dictionary, sterility may be defined as the lack of capacity of a man or a woman or a couple to participate in reproduction.[3] Sterility is the opposite of

1. Jain, S.P., *Certain Statistics on Fertility of Indian Woman to Show the Effect of Age at Marriage*, New Delhi: Office of the Registrar General, India, 1964, p. 3.
2. Agarwala, S.N., *A Demographic Study of Six Urbanising Villages*, pp. 107-111.
3. *Multilingual Demographic Dictionary*, English Section, New York: United Nations Department of Economic and Social Affairs, 1958, p. 38.

fecundity. It is different from childlessness since it is inborn while the latter may be voluntary. A childless woman may be sterile while a sterile woman must be childless.

Types of Sterility

Demographers have distinguished between two types of sterility: Primary and Secondary. The primary sterility is the case where the woman has never been able to procreate. Secondary sterility arises after the birth of one or more children. Another significant distinction between types of sterility has been made on the basis of periodicity. A woman who cannot procreate has permanent sterility. On the other hand normally a woman is sterile throughout an anovular cycle, in which ovulation does not occur. She is also sterile from the end of one 5 pregnancy to the beginning of other. In India among the illiterate and poor women temporary sterility is the only check on the periodicity of birth. Temporary and secondary sterility hardly needs any cure. On the other hand permanent and primary sterility is always a source of so much trouble and frustration to the woman everywhere. The following is the description of the extent of the above types of sterility in India as found out by several surveys.

1. Primary Sterility in India: In the Census in 1921, 1931 and 1951 in India, data on primary sterility were collected in some selected areas of the country. Relevant information is available by age and marriage duration during the period 1931 and 1951. Besides, localised surveys have also collected important information. According to the Census 1921 report, the information on sterility in Punjab relating to 166, 149 families showed that 6% couples were sterile on an average, the highest percentage being 7.7 among menials and the lowest 4.7 among the traders.[1] The Census 1931 report defined sterility as childlessness for 15 years and over after marriage. The average of sterility according to Census report was 6% of married couples. The data for sterility according to 1951 census are given in the following table:

The National Sample Survey in its second round in 1951 collected information on sterility which was defined as the proportion of the childless couple married for 22 years or more to the total couples with a marriage duration of at least 22 years. The incidence of fertility was worked out to be 7.5%. The number

1. *Census of India*, 1951, Paper No. 5 of 1953, Maternity Data 1951 Census, Appendix II, Delhi: Manager of Government Publications, 1953, p. 91.

TABLE 11.17

Proportion of Sterile Marriages by Marriage Duration,[1] 1951

Age of Wife at Marriage	*Duration of Marriage (in Years)*				
	0-5	*5-10*	*10-15*	*15+*	*All Durations*
0–12	0.5006	0.1668	0.0519	0.0221	0.0804
13–14	0.3094	0.1534	0.0991	0.0447	0.1259
15–19	0.2967	0.1733	0.1332	0.0724	0.1581
20–29	0.2787	0.1609	0.1164	0.0655	0.1358
30 & above	0.3172	0.2325	0.1607	0.0746	0.1637
All Ages	0.3030	0.1640	0.1134	0.0563	0.1390

of couples surveyed was 6,060. Among these couples of all ages the rate of sterility for different periods in India was: 1910 (7.4); 1920 (7.6); 1930 (7.5). The sterility rate for 3,723 couples below 15 years of age for the above mentioned periods was 7.3, 8.1 and 7.5. Among 2,341 couples of ages 15 and above the rate of sterility for the above mentioned periods was 7.6, 6.6 and 7.6 respectively. The above data are concerning rural sample couples.[2] The conclusion of this study has been supported by several other studies. For example, the study of 1,904 married females in a cluster of villages near Lucknow by Baljit Singh has given the incidence of sterility as 7.7%[3]. Defining sterility as childlessness among women married for 15 years or more, G.B. Saxena gave a low figure of 4.9 for a sample of 1,336 women of rural Uttar Pradesh. The following table exhibits the condition of sterility in some Indian States in 1961, according to the fertility survey and sample census carried out by the Registrar General of India:

The above data clearly show that the incidence of sterility in India is between 6 and 7.5% of the married couple. It appears to increase with a rise in female marriage age. It is 6% among women married before the age of 15. On the other hand, it is 10.5% among women whose marriage age is between 20 and 30. According to

1. *Census of India*, 1951, Paper No. 5 of 1953, Maternity Data 1951 Census, Appendix 11, New Delhi: Manager of Government Publications, 1953, p. 93.
2. Das Gupta, Ajit *et al*, *Couple Fertility*, NSS No. 7, 1955, p. 45.
3. Singh, Baljit, *Five Years of Family Planning in the Countryside*, Lucknow: J.K. Institute of Sociology and Human Relations, 1957, p. 22.

TABLE 11.18

Percentage of Childless Couples in Some Selected States, 1961[1]

States	*Rural*	*Urban*
Assam	5.6	4.4
Jammu & Kashmir	6.0	4.9
Kerala	2.6	2.4
Madhya Pradesh	5.9	6.8
Punjab	3.4	3.6
Rajasthan	6.0	6.4
Delhi	1.0	3.2
Uttar Pradesh	6.4	7.1

the Registrar General of India, Sample Survey of Percentage of Childless Women by age at marriage and residence in 1961 the following was the incidence of sterility.[2]

TABLE 11.19

Percentage of Childless Women by Age at Marriage and Residence, 1961

States	*Age at Marriage*							
	Below 18		*18-22*		*23 and over*		*All ages*	
	Rural	*Urban*	*Rural*	*Urban*	*Rural*	*Urban*	*Rural*	*Urban*
Jammu & Kashmir	4.6	4.5	8.1	5.6	11.1	6.8	6.0	4.9
Punjab	2.9	2.6	4.0	5.7	7.6	9.6	3.4	3.6
Kerala	1.3	1.9	4.3	2.9	8.9	5.3	2.6	2.4
Uttar Pradesh	6.1	6.2	7.3	9.2	6.4	10.7	6.4	7.1
Madhya Pradesh	4.6	5.2	8.6	11.2	32.5	23.9	5.9	6.8

A comparison of the above mentioned data with the corresponding data available in some Western countries shows a higher percentage of sterility in the West. For example, the incidence of sterility in some of the prominent Western countries during the period 1931-36 was: USA 10.2, Sweden 10.0, Norway 6.5, Italy 7.4, South Africa 7.2. This shows an average much more than that in India. The lower sterility percentage in India may be due to several reasons such as under-reporting, low average age of female marriage, etc.

1. Jain, S.P., "Indian Fertility: Our Knowledge and Gaps", *Journal of Family Welfare*, June, 1964, pp. 24-25.
2. *Ibid.*

2. Secondary Sterility in India: In European countries the proportion of sterility rises with increases in the age of maternity. The age of maternity in India, however, is considerably low. Delhi Demographic Centre carried out a survey of 6 villages for the study of secondary sterility. The rate of sterility for different age groups was: 20-25 2; 25-30 9; 30-35 20; 35-40 42; 40-45 77; 45-50 86. The percentage of couples unable to conceive after the given birth according to this report was as follows:[1]

Table 11.20

Percentage of Couples Unable to Conceive after the Given Birth, 1970

Number of Births	Percentage	Cumulative Percentage
1	1.8	1.8
2	2.1	3.9
3	3.1	7.0
4	4.9	11.9
5	6.7	16.8
6	9.8	28.4
7	14.7	43.1
8	16.0	59.1
9	13.3	72.4
10	11.2	83.6
11 and over	16.4	100.0

An important cause of secondary fertility is the age of menarche and menopause. Several local surveys carried out in India have put the age of menarche between 13 and 14 years in India. The age of menopause according to several surveys has been reported between 42 and 45 years. As a rule there is complete sterility in a woman after menopause. Therefore the incidence of sterility should be checked during the period of menarche and menopause.

QUESTIONS FOR EXERCISE

1. Describe Fertility in India. Point out its various differentials.
2. Write short note on Sterility in India.

1. Agarwala, S.N., *A Demographic Study of Six Urbanising Villages*, Bombay, Asia Publishing House, 1970, p. 109.

12

Migration: Types, Measurement, Theories and Trends

The most important component of population change, besides mortality and fertility, is migration. According to the Concise Oxford Dictionary, to migrate means to move from one place, country or town to another. The migration is the movement from one place to another within the country or outside it. Migration among human beings however, is not biological. It is social, economic, political or cultural. The most important causes of migration are economic and political. The rush of immigrants in India from Bangladesh and Pakistan from time to time is mainly due to political reasons. Most of the emigration and immigration is due to political reasons. In 1947 in Indian continent a large number of people migrated from India to Pakistan and *vice versa* due to political reasons. Thus, though migration is generally voluntary it is also sometimes compulsory due to political reasons. Within the country generally there is a migration from rural to urban areas. In some Western countries in some cases one may also find migration from urban to rural areas. All these different types of migration make important changes in population. In contrast to migration among animals, migration among human beings has been defined by Donald J. Bogue thus: "It is thus a response of Human organisms to economic, social and demographic forces in the environment."[1]

---

1. Donald J. Bogue, *Principles of Demography*, New York: John Wiley and Sons, 1969, p. 753.

The study of migration is important due to following reasons:

1. It decreases or increases the size and structure of any population drastically.

2. It determines the size and the rate of population growth as well as its structure and characteristics.

3. It plays an important role in the distribution of the population of any country. Thus, it is useful in preparing regional population projections.

4. It determines the growth of labour force in any area.

5. It is the symptom of basic social change in any country.

6. It is related to business cycle, supply of skilled and unskilled workers, growth of industries and the employment.

7. It is the basis for the analysis and solution of the social and psychological problems arising out of population changes, particularly large scale migration.

According to the United Nations Multilingual Demographic Dictionary, "Migration is a form of geographical mobility or spatial mobility between one geographical unit and another, generally involving a change in residence from the place of origin or place of departure to the place of destination or place of arrival."[1] The migration defined here is permanent migration as distinguished from other forms of movement.

Types of Migration

The following types of migration have been distinguished by the sociologists and demographers :

1. Immigration and Emigration: These terms are used in the context of international migration from one country to another, for example, immigration of Hindus from Bangladesh to India and emigration of Indians to United States.

2. In-migration and Out-migration: In-migration, as the term suggests, refers to movement in a particular area. On the other hand, out-migration, as is clear by the term, means movement out of a particular area. However, both these terms are applicable to internal or within the country migration only, for example the migration of rural people to urban areas in India everywhere.

1. United Nations, *Multilingual Demographic Dictionary, op. cit*, p. 46.

3. Gross and Net Migration: Gross migration is the volume of migration. It is the total of the arrivals of immigrants and in-migrants and departures of emigrants and out-migrants. On the other hand, net migration is the difference between the total number of persons coming in and the total number of persons living out. Thus, net migration is the balance of migration.

The term Migratory Movement is used for the section of population movement due to migration. The total number of moves made during a given migration interval which have a common area of origin and a common area of destination, are known as Migration Streams. The most general types of migration, however, are internal migration and external or international migration.

INTERNAL MIGRATION

Internal migration is the movement of people within the country. It varies considerably from a few kilometres to several thousand kilometres, for example, migration to Bombay, Calcutta, Madras and Delhi from every corner of the country. On the other hand, people are constantly changing residence from one town to another town or one village to another village due to matrimony, occupation or several other reasons. The operational definition of migration as change of residence from one civil division to another is generally applicable to internal migration, A person who has changed his usual place of residence from one area to another is known as a migrant and his activity is known as migration.

Sources of Data Concerning Internal Migration

The principal sources of data concerning internal migration are as follows:

1. Census: National Census is the most important source of data concerning internal migration in a country. Such Censuses are taken everywhere in almost all the countries. A Census report directly asks the place of birth, the place of last residence, the duration of residence in the place of enumeration and the place of residence on a specified date before the Census. These questions have been recommended to be given top priority in Census operations by the United Nations. In India in 1971 the question concerning the place of the last usual residence was asked to obtain information on migration.

2. Sample Surveys: Sample Surveys are the sources of direct information on internal migration. They provide information on the characteristics of the migrants, their motives for migration and their attitudes towards migration. These data are useful in studying the question of internal migration in depth. These techniques have been widely used in India.

3. Population Registers: Population registers record residential changes. Therefore, they supply valuable data concerning internal migration.

METHODS OF MEASUREMENT

The methods of measuring internal migration have been classified as direct and indirect.

1. Direct Measures for Estimating Migration: These include place of birth, duration of residence, place of last residence and place of residence at a fixed prior date.

(*i*) *Place of Birth:* Place of birth gives information about Migrants and Non-migrants. Migrants are the persons enumerated in a place which is not their place of birth. Non-migrants are the persons enumerated in the place where they are born. These terms are generally applicable to States. For example in India Census data show place of birth. It shows population classified by state of birth and state of enumeration. It gives data concerning life-time in-migrants by state of origin, out-migrants by state of destination and net life-streams of migration, in different States of India. The place of birth provides data concerning rural-urban migration. For example, according to 1971 Census of India life-time rural-urban migration was of about 23.8 million persons. Urban-rural migration was of about 7.8 million persons and the net migration to the urban areas was of about 16 million persons. The following are the advantages of using place of birth for measurement of life-time internal migration in a country:

1. The question on the place of birth is simple and easy to ask. It is also easily understood.

2. The information obtained through this question is generally correct and complete since it is expected that a normal person would easily remember his or her place of birth.

However, the place of birth as a measure of life-time internal migration suffers from the following disadvantages:

1. Since answers to the Census questionnaires are generally given by the tread of the family or some important members of the household, the possibilities of errors are there.

2. There may be deliberate misreporting for some political reasons.

3. There may be a tendency to report a better known place as the place of birth instead of the actual place of birth.

4. Another source of error is the frequently changing boundaries of a State lue to political reasons of which the respondent may be unaware.

5. Sometimes some social practice may introduce artificial bias about the information on the place of birth. For example, in India, girls go to their parental homes for their first delivery due to which the child born becomes a life-time migrant though actually he or she is a non-migrant for every other purpose.

Due to the above mentioned limitations about birth place, it is suggested hat the usual place of residence of the parents should be taken as the place of birth of a child.

6. This practice is based upon the assumption of a single movement directly from the place of birth to that of enumeration. Actually some persons might rave moved into the place of enumeration from some place other than the place of birth.

7. It assumes that all persons enumerated at their places of birth are non-migrants. This, however, may not be true for some of these persons may be returned migrants.

8. The birth place data do not convey any idea about the time of movement which may be from 4 days to 50 years, before the date of enumeration.

Comparing the advantages and disadvantages of using birth place data as in index of migration, it is suggested that in spite of its simplicity and facility it should be used with caution.

2. Duration of Residence: Along with the question concerning place of birth and place of enumeration, sometimes a question about duration of residence s asked in a Census. On the basis of the answers to this question are distinguished: All who have ever migrated, those born outside the areas of enumeration and those born in the area of enumeration. These data fill a serious gap in the place of birth approach. It is the basis of distinction between migrants and non-migrants. It gives information on the timing of the last move of life-time migrants. In 1961 Census tabulisation for India, migrants were classified into the following categories: (A) Less than one year, (B) one to five years, (C) 6 to 10 years, (D) 11 to 15 years, (E) 16 and over and, (F) period not stated. The advantages of duration of residence as a direct measure for estimating migration are as follows:

1. It takes into account the number of return migrants. Return migrants are those persons who were born in a given area but who subsequently moved out of it but later returned to it.

2. It gives an idea about the category of migrants according to the trends in past migration.

This measurement, however, suffers from the following problems or limitations:

1. Usually the head of the family gives the information. He may not know exactly the duration of residence of each person in the family.

2. The percentages of those for whom information on duration of residence is not available are higher for females.

3. The data on duration of residence are affected by the digit preference tendency of the respondents. For example while some persons have a tendency to report duration as 3, 7, 11, 13, 17, etc., while others may report as 10, 15, 20, 25, etc., this recall lapse on the part of respondents results in a large measure of inaccuracy of the data.

3. Place of Last Residence: The question concerning the place of last residence fills up the gaps of place of birth data. This information may be classified into two categories: (*i*) Migrants whose place of last residence and the place of present residence are different, and (*ii*) non-migrants who have never moved outside the area of their place of birth These data may be used to measure migration in exactly the same way as data on the place of birth are used. These data, however, are more useful for an analysis of migration when cross-classified with the data on the duration of residence. It reflects a direct movement from the place of origin to the place of destination.

4. Place of Residence at a Fixed Prior Date: In some Census questionnaires a question is asked about the place of residence at a fixed prior date. The answers to these questions are important since migration interval in it is given by a comparison of residence at two definite points at time. A migrant is defined as a person whose residence at the Census date differs from his residence at the specified prior date. This data is utilised for computation of "prior migration rate". For example, in a study of Rural Migration Patterns in South Maharashtra, conducted by International Institute for Population Studies, Bombay, in 1965, a question was asked about the place of residence five years earlier, *i.e.*, between 1961 and 1966. The data gathered showed that the migration rate was 8.7% for females and only 3.5% for males.[1] The measurement of migration on the basis of residence at a fixed prior date is simple and therefore useful and satisfactory. However, the possibility of inaccuracy due to recall lapse cannot he ruled out. The data cannot be used properly if the reference period for the question is not the same as the inter-censual period.

INDIRECT MEASURES FOR NET INTERNAL MIGRATION

The measures of migration discussed so far are direct. However, more indirect measures are used for estimating net internal migration particularly during the two successive census operations. The population may grow due to increase or due to migration. The difference between the actual population count at the end of the period and the expected population growth gives the estimates of the net change due to migration. The most important methods for arriving at such estimation are — the Vital Statistics Method, the Survival Ratio Method and the Migration Rate.

1. The Vital Statistics Method: Vital Statistics means the data concerning population based upon birth and death. It is obtained on the basis of the data on the birth and death of the inhabitants. It gives an estimate of a natural increase between two census operations. By subtracting the natural increase from the total population change, the estimate of net migration can be achieved. This method is used not only in the estimation of national but also international migration. The formula for estimation of net migration is as follows:

1. Vatsala Narain, A. Sebastian and P. Hanumantharayappa, *Rural Migration Patterns in Southern Maharashtra, op. cit.*t p. 43.

$$\text{Net M} = (P_1 - P_0) - (B - D)$$

where, for any given area,

Net M is the net migration

P_0 is the population at the earlier census

P_1 is the population at the later census

B is the number of births in that area during the inter-censal period.

D is the number of deaths which occurred in that area during the same period.

The following is an example of the use of the Vital Statistics Method for the estimates of net migration:

Table 12.1

Estimates of Net Migration to Madras City by the Vital Statistics Methods, 1951-1961[1]

1.	Population of Madras	1951=P_0=14,16,056
2.	Population of Madras	1961=P1+1=17,29,141
3.	Increase in Population	1961-1951=(2) – (1)=3,13,085
4.	Number of Births in Madras	1951-1961=B=6,53,190
5.	Number of Deaths in Madras	1951-1961=D=3,71,286
6.	Natural Increase in Madras	1951-1961=(4) – (5)=2,81,904
7.	Net Migration to Madras	1951-1961 =(3) – (6)=31,181

Vital statistics method, however, cannot be much useful in developing countries. The data obtained in these countries are not adequate due to errors in the reporting of births and deaths.

2. The Survival Ratio Method: This method, as is clear by the name, is based upon the use of estimates of probability of survival. It requires information about age distribution by sex, as enumerated in each area in two successive Census operations. The differences between the enumerated population at the end of the 2nd Census and the expected survival of the population at the time gives an estimate of net internal migration. Sometimes net migration may be estimated by computing the survival ratios of two consecutive Census operations. This is particularly in the case where appropriate life-tables are not available, and also where the use of available life-tables is forbidden due to one reason or

1. United Nations, Manual VI, Methods of Measuring Internal Migration ST/SOA/ SER, A/47, *Population Studies* No. 47, New York : 1970, p. 24.

another. This method cannot be used for the estimation of net migration for persons born during the inter-censal period. The data obtained by it about migration are better than those achieved by computing life-table survivorship probabilities.

3. The Migration Rate Method: The computation of migration rate shows the number of migrants in a given population during a given interval period. The formula for this computation is given below:

$$m = \frac{M}{P} \times k$$

where:

m is the rate of migration for the specified migration interval;

M is the number of migrations or the number of persons migrating during the interval;

P is the population exposed to the likelihood of migration during the interval (mid-year population);

k is 100 or 1000.

THEORIES OF INTERNAL MIGRATION

Theories of internal migration discuss the different factors governing migratory movements. Such factors may be social, economic, political and even psychological. Therefore an internal migration is studied not only by sociologists but also by social psychologists, economists and political scientists. Researches in the field of migration are generally empirical. They contain a factual description of migratory movement. Majority of the studies lack generalisation. Demographers have devoted their attention particularly to methodological problems of the measurement of internal migration. Therefore, the present knowledge of the phenomena of migration is quite elementary. The study of motivational factors of migration is more complex than the study of factors of fertility and mortality. Therefore, two distinctly different approaches are made towards this study.

1. Theory of Push and Pull Factors: This approach is situation-oriented. It attempts to study the factors which impel persons to move out of their place of origin. It also studies the conditions and situations that attract persons from outside to migrate. This is the traditional approach to the study of motivation for migration. Comparative studies have been made to find out the relative importance of push and pull factors. Push factors are those which motivate going outside from within. These include high natural rate of population growth creating population pressure on the existing resources, exhaustion of natural resources, droughts, floods, natural calamities such as earthquakes and famines, acute social, religious or political conflicts, etc. The pull factors, on the other hand, include those which pull migratory population from outside. These factors include establishment of new industries, provision of new opportunities of employment, facilities of higher education, better climatic conditions etc. The variable of technological change which results in the establishment of a number of attractive factors in urban areas is a very strong pull migration from rural to urban areas. The modern agricultural machinery frees so many persons from the bondage to agriculture and pushes their migration to urban areas. The theory of push and pull factors is useful in the study of factors affecting migratory movements. It often offers sufficient explanations of migration. It, however does not lead to any theory. According to William Peterson, "It implies that man is everywhere sedentary remaining fixed until he is induced to move by some force."[1] In most of the cases it has been observed that migration is not the result of push or pull factors alone or singly but of the combination of both. The motivational aspects of migration are highly subjective. The push and pull theory does not explain why some people migrate while others do not under the same circumstances.

2. Empirical Generalization in the Form of Mathematical Models: According to United Nations, *The Determinants and Consequences of Population Trends*, Vol. I, another approach to the study of internal migration is the formulation of empirical generalizations and description of the patterns of migration in the form of mathematical models which are valid as universal laws.

3. Theory of Everett Lee:[2] According to Everett Lee the decision to migrate and the process of migration is determined by the following four factors:

(*i*) *Factors Associated with the Area of Origin:* In each area there are several factors which motivate migration outside the area.

---

1. William Peterson, *Population*, London, MacMillan Company, 1969, p. 289.
2. Everett S. Lee, "A Theory of Migration", in J.A. Jackson (Ed.), Migration, Cambridge: University Press of Cambridge, 1969.

(*ii*) *Factors Associated with the Area of Destination:* These factors are more important as pull factors while the former work as push factors. It is not necessary that the pull factors are always real. Sometimes they are based upon inadequate information. For example, the lure of the city for a villager is often based upon false and exaggerated estimates.

(*iii*) *Intervening Obstacles:* These obstacles intervene migration. Therefore they must be overcome before migration takes place. The most important intervening obstacles are distance and transportation. These have been considerably reduced in modern time due to technological advance.

(*iv*) *Personal Factors:* These are the most important factors determining migration. Since they determine internal motivation. In fact it is not the factors associated with the place of origin or destination but rather the individual's perception of them which determine actual migration. Personal factors change according to individual differences. While some persons are more resistant to the change of residence, others are eager for such a change. Therefore, migration is not rational and any generalization concerning it must allow exceptions. Sometimes migration may not be the result of one's own decision. For example, wives accompany their husbands, children accompany their parents. Since migration in such cases is a result of other person's migration and a process in sequence, therefore it is known as sequential migration.

Conceptual Framework for Migration Analysis

Lee has formulated several hypotheses within the conceptual framework of the above mentioned 4 types of factors. These hypotheses are as follows:

1. Volume of Migration: (1) The volume of migration within a given territory varies with the degree of areas included in that territory; (2) The volume of migration varies with the diversity of the people; (3) The volume of migration is related to the difficulty of surmounting the intervening variables; (4) The volume of migration varies with fluctuations in the economy; (5) Unless severe checks are imposed, both the volume and rate of migration vary with the state of progress in a country or area.

2. Streams and Counter-streams of Migration: (1) Migration tends to take place largely within well-defined streams; (2) For every major migration stream, a counter-stream also develops; (3) The efficiency of the stream (ratio of stream to counter-stream or the net redistribution of population affected by the opposite flow) is high if the major factors in the development of a migration stream are minus factors at origin; (4) The efficiency of the stream and the counter-stream of migration tends to be low if the place of origin and the place of destination are similar; (5) The efficiency of migration streams will be high if the intervening obstacles are great; (6) The efficiency of a migration stream varies with economic conditions, being high in prosperous times and low in times of depression.

3. Characteristics of Migrants: (1) Migration is selective; (2) Migrants responding primarily to plus factors at destination tend to be positively selective; (3) Migrants responding primarily to minus factors at origin tend to be negatively selective, or where the minus factors are overwhelming for the entire population group, they may not be selected at all for migration; (4) When all migrants are considered together, selection for migration fends to be bimodal; (5) The degree of positive selection increases with the difficulties posed by the intervening obstacles; (6) The heightened propensity to migrate at certain stages of the life-cycle is important in the selection of migrants; (7) The characteristics of migrants tend to be intermediate between the characteristics of the population of the place of origin and of the population of the place of destination.

MIGRATION DIFFERENTIALS

Migration is differential as is the case with mortality and fertility. These migration differentials have been studied by sociologists and demographers for various purposes. Migration differentials include so many factors such as age, sex, marital status, educational attainments and occupation. Their study shows why some persons migrate and others do not. They form a basis for a suitable migration theory. They provide data for the discovery of migration laws. Migration is selective. It depends on different attributes of persons. For example, the migration from village to city is mostly found in rural males. A study of migration differentials is therefore necessary to understand the factors determining migration. The most important migration differentials are as follows:

1. Age: It has been found by many studies that age is an important migration differential. Most of the migrants are adolescents and young adults. This is true both in internal and international migration. According to Zachariah, among the migrants to Greater Bombay in 1961 there was an excess of adolescents and young adults. 81.05% were in the age group 15-59 years. Less than 10% of the migrants were below the age of 10. According to the study conducted by Dorothy Thomas in 1938 it was found that persons in teens, twenties and early thirtees are more migratory than other groups.

2. Sex: Revenstein laid down a law of migration in 1885 by saying, "females appear to dominate among short journey migrants." However, most of the studies, particularly in Asia and Africa, have contradicted this statement. According to these studies sex is an important migration differential but it is in favour of the male. The studies conducted in Greater Bombay in 1961 revealed that males pre-dominated among the migrants, This is true about most of the cosmopolitan cities of the world. Among manual workers particularly, the migrants to the cities are males with the result that the proportion of males in the population becomes higher. This has led to the institution of prostitution in the cities. However, there may be certain exceptions to this rule. It has been found that rural migration is dominated by females due to marriage. It should be remembered here that a major factor in migration within the country is the marriage custom that the bride has to migrate to the place of the husband. The migration due to occupation is generally male dominated, particularly in India and other developing countries where working males very much outnumber working females. In the developed countries however, the female migrants may not be lagging behind male migrants in search of occupation. These two factors, the occupation and marriage, make the sex differential in migration a complex affair making it different in different cases.

3. Marital Status: An important migration differential is the marital status. It is known that most of the rural migrants to the city are males who leave their families behind in the rural areas. The number of females who migrate to cities because of marriage is almost 50% of the female migrants. In those countries where married women also seek employment the situation might be different. For example, in Latin America, a large number of urban migrants in search of employment are females. In fact not much data are available to determine the influence of marital status as a differential in migration within the country as well as out of it.

4. Educational Attainment: Most of the studies have established that people with higher educational attainments in the rural areas tend to migrate to the city in search of better job opportunities. This is particularly so in the case of developing countries. The situation, however, is not so simple. As unemployment grows in cosmopolitan cities, men with educational qualifications migrate to other areas. Again, among the urban migrants the uneducated labourers far outnumber those with educational qualifications. It is generally seen that in cities educated unemployment is more rampant while uneducated persons easily get employment as labourers. Studies have been conducted in Greater Bombay about the educational attainment of the migrants. In the United States during the period 1940-1950 among the net out-migrants from rural areas were very highly educated persons as well as persons with low educational attainments. In England and Wales the educational attainment was a positive factor in migration. Similar reports have been achieved from other countries.

Besides the above mentioned migration differentials there might be some other minor factors determining migration within the country and also outside it. For example, wealth and money is one such factor due to which people migrate from small towns to big cities in search of big business. For example, most of the Marwaries have migrated to cosmopolitan cities like Calcutta from rural Rajasthan in search of big business. Similarly, in Bombay people flock from so many rural areas to try their luck in big business. This is particularly so since in rural areas big money cannot be easily used for further multiplication. Very high educational attainment is one of the causes of international migration. However, equally important causes of such migration are the lure of Western culture, the freedom, the opportunities of progress and the sense of adventure in international migration. However, the above mentioned migration differentials are the most important determinants of migration within the country as well as out of it.

INTERNATIONAL MIGRATION

International migration has created big nations and important events in the history of the world. An example of this phenomena is USA and other American countries where migrants from different European countries have created new nations. Therefore, international migration is an important subject of study among, sociologists and demographers all over the world.

MIGRATION IN INDIA

The most important source of data concerning migration in India are the decennial population Census reports. In the Census 1881 a question was asked from the respondent about his or her place of birth and the period of residence at present place. This has provided data concerning internal migration in India. Since then this question was repeated in every Census operation. The scope of Census operation widened in every decade. In 1961 Census information was collected on the duration of residence at the place of enumeration. In 1971 Census a question was asked about the place of last residence. Information was also collected about the district and State of the birth place. Another important source of data concerning migration in India are the National Sample Surveys. The first National Sample Survey was concluded in 1951 providing data about migration. Since then so many surveys have provided important data about inter-State migration, rural-urban migration and international migration in the Indian context.

Trends of Migration in India

In the Census 1931 the number of persons born outside India were enumerated as 7,30,546. It was estimated that roughly 2.5 million Indians were living outside the country. This gives a lifetime migration balance of 1.75 million persons. According to Census 1961, 9.5 million persons living in India were born outside the country. Of these 8.3 million came from Pakistan and Bangladesh. Thus, 1.2 million foreigners were living in India. According to 1971. Census, the persons born out of India numbered 0.9 million including 0.81 million immigrants from Pakistan and Bangladesh. The number of foreigners was therefore 0.9 million in 1971, 0.4 million males and 0.5 million females; 0.6 million urban and 0.3 million rural. According to 1971 Census and most of the Census reports in India it has been established that Indian population is virtually immobile. In 1961 Census, 68.6% of the population was enumerated at the place of birth. In 1971 this percentage was 68.8. This shows that the percentage of the immobiles was almost double to that of the migrants, though the percentage of lifetime migrants decreased in 1971 Census. Another important trend in migration in India is that most of the migrants move only short distances. According to 1971 Census, 65.84% of migrant population was born outside the district of enumeration. The Census operation from 1891 to 1931 indicated that the percentage of persons enumerated in the province of their birth was almost static. Thus, the tendency of inter-State migration has not changed in India. According to Kingsley Davis, the most important factors determining the immobility of Indian population are predominance of agriculture, the caste system, early marriage, joint family, diversity of languages, variety of culture and lack of education, etc.[1]

A third important trend in internal migration in India is the predominance of females among the migrants. It is due to the custom of married women migrating to the place of their husbands. However, female migration is generally at short distances. Village exogamy has been an important factor in female migration in India.

In the history of Indian Demography, the problem of migration became complicated in 1947 due to the influx of refugees from both .the 'wings of Pakistan. Another important factor was the reorganization of States, Union Territories and delimitation of district boundaries. The economic development and industrialisation of several areas in the country was another important factor in the increase in migration. Migration in India can be studied as Cumulative Lifetime Migration, Net Migration, Rural Urban Migration, Marriage Migration, Lifetime Migration and Migration by Age. This will be now discussed in more details.

CUMULATIVE LIFETIME MIGRATION

The following table gives an idea about the Cumulative Lifetime Migration in India as found by different Census reports:

1. Kingsley Davis, *The Population of India and Pakistan*, New York: Russell and Russell, 1968, p. 108.

TABLE 12.2

Persons Enumerated in a State Different from the One in which they were Born

Year	Enumerated Outside the State of Birth	Percentage of the total Population
1891	1,06,52,359	3.8
1901	93,60,026	3.3
1911	1,08,11,678	3.6
1921	1,11,97,376	3.7
1931	1,20,79,576	3.6
1951	1,05,02,903	3.1
1961	1,45,24,434	3.3
1971	1,68,85,000	3.1

As a result of inter-state migration during 1951-1971 the following States gained in population: West Bengal, Maharashtra, Delhi, Madhya Pradesh, Assam, Punjab, Mysore (Karnataka) and Gujarat. The following States were the losers: Uttar Pradesh, Bihar, Kerala, Rajasthan, Andhra Pradesh, Tamil Nadu, Orissa, Jammu and Kashmir. According to the estimates of net migration during 1961-1971, however, Tamil Nadu, Jammu and Kashmir, Bihar, Orissa gained in population. On the other hand, Karnataka and Punjab lost In population. The States of Uttar Pradesh Kerala and Andhra Pradesh remained among the losing States. In nearly all the States the net migration of males has been greater than that of the females. The overall direction of population redistribution through internal migration during the period 1951-1961 has been from the South and South-East to the North-East and North-West of India. In other words, population migrated from areas of comparatively low economic development to areas of higher economic development.

Cumulative lifetime migration is not a satisfactory index of migration. Therefore, internal migration has been estimated by the Census survival method. United Provinces, Bihar and Orissa, Rajputana, Madras, Hyderabad, Punjab, Bengal and Jammu and Kashmir lost their population due to out-migration whereas Assam, Bombay, Central Provinces, Central India, Travancore-Cochin and Mysore gained. United Provinces, which in 1931 had 14 per cent of the population of the country and 6 per cent of the total land areas lost 760 thousand people during 1901-31. During 1901-11, 1,57,000 males moved out of United Provinces and 40,000 moved in. Thus, the net loss was 1,17,000 males. But 64,000 females moved out and 67,000 moved in so that there was a net gain of 3,000 females. The combined net loss, however, was 1,14,000. Likewise in the 1921-1931 decade 274,000 males and 1,65,000 females moved out, while 68,000 males and 87,000 females moved in. The net loss was of 2,06,000 males and 78,000 females the total being 2,84,000. Out-migration from United Provinces has been mostly to Bengal, Bombay and Punjab.

Bihar and Orissa lost about 88,000 persons to Bengal and 14,000 to Assam during 1921-1931. But Bengal, in turn, lost 2,66,000 persons to Assam during the same period. 1911-1921, Bengal gained 2,98,000 persons from Bihar and Orissa and lost 2,12,000 to Assam. Assam gained 5,75,000 persons during 1911-1921 and 328,000 during 1921-1931.

Analysing the data of inter-State net migration in India as given by different Census reports, S.N. Agarwala has pointed out, "It is indeed surprising that barring Bombay (Maharashtra), Mysore (Karnataka) and Travancore-Cochin (Kerala) all other States should have lost due to out-migration during the 1941-1951 decade. Assam, which has always been a gainer, also shows net outmigration during the decade. It appears that the assumptions which have been made for estimating internal migration by States may not be wholly appropriate."[1]

RURAL-URBAN MIGRATION IN INDIA

Most of the studies of migration in India have revealed that the migration from rural to urban areas is very small in comparison to migration from one rural area to another. Migration by marriage is generally from one rural area to another. It is only in the search of occupation that migrants go to urban areas from the village. The speed, however, is very slow. According to the Census 1971 among the migrants in India 70.66% were from one rural area to another. The rural-urban migration was 14.88%, the urban-rural migration was barely 4.88%. In the study of rural-urban migration, four aspects have to be particularly studied. These

1. Agarwala, S.N., *India's Population Problem*, Tata McGraw Hill, 1977, New Delhi, p. 171.

are: 1. rural to rural migration or rural turnover; 2. rural to urban migration or push-pull activity; 3. urban to urban migration or urban turnover; and 4. urban to rural migration or reverse push back. According to the estimate by Zachariah, the rural-urban migration in India during the period 1951-1961 was 5.2 million. This is 8.4% of the 1951 urban population. According to a recent report India continues to be predominantly rural although its urban population increased by more than 49 million during the 1971-1981 decade. The rural-urban distribution of the population obtained from the quick tabulation of provisional totals of the 1981 Census shows that 76.27 per cent of the population is rural.

The Census Commissioner recently released figures putting the urban population in 1981 at 15,61,88,507 The balance of the total population 65,81,40,676 is considered rural. These figures exclude Assam where the Census has not so far been held and Jammu and Kashmir where the Census was taken two months after the February-March enumeration in the rest of the nation.

The 1981 urban population of 23.73 per cent compared to 20.22 in 1971, 18.26 in 1961, and 17.62 in 1951 when the first post-independence Census was taken. The urban population was a mere 10.40 per cent in 1911. Dadra and Nagar Haveli as well as Lakshadweep entered the stream of urbanisation for the first time during the 1971-1981 decade. Maharashtra is the most urbanised State with 35.05 per cent of its population in urban areas. Tamil Nadu, Gujarat, Karnataka, Punjab and West Bengal follow in descending order. These States have a higher urban population than the national average of 23.73 per cent. At the other end, Himachal Pradesh, Dadra and Nagar Haveli and Arunachal Pradesh have more than 90 per cent of their population in rural areas.

Kerala, Meghalaya, Uttar Pradesh, Sikkim, Nagaland, Bihar, Orissa and Tripura have more than 80 per cent rural population, Nagpur, Lucknow and Jaipur crossed the one million mark at the 1981 Census. They joined the group of Calcutta, Greater Bombay, Delhi, Madras, Hyderabad, Ahmedabad, Bangalore, Kanpur and Pune as big cities or urban agglomerations. Together the 12 cities and urban agglomerations account for 44.56 per cent of the urban population.

Trichur in Kerala has the highest literacy rate of 81.09 per cent. Sambhal in Uttar Pradesh is the least literate city (24.84 per cent).

According to the 1971 Census, of the 548 million population in 1971, 376 million remained at their place of birth, 310 million in the rural areas, and 66 million in the urban areas. Among the remaining 172 million persons, 108 million were enumerated within the district of enumeration and another 36 million within the State. Only 19 million persons were enumerated in a State outside their place of birth and 0.9 million persons born in countries other than India. Most of the 19 million persons who migrated outside the State of their birth moved short distances and to border districts.

Table 12.3

Rural and Urban Population: 1901 — 1991, India

Census Year	*Population (million)*		*Percentage of total Population*	
	Rural	*Urban*	*Rural*	*Urban*
1901	213	26	89.2	10.8
1911	226	26	89.7	10.3
1921	223	28	88.8	11.2
1931	246	33	88.0	12.0
1941	275	44	86.1	13.9
1951	299	62	82.7	17.3
1961	360	79	82.0	18.0
1971	439	109	80.1	19.9
1981[1]	524	159	76.7	23.3
19912[2]	629	218	74.3	25.7

Source: Census of India 1991, Final Population Totals

1. The 1991 Census could not be held in Assam. The figures for 1981 for Assam have been worked out by interpolation.
2. Includes projected population of Jammu and Kashmir.

MARRIAGE MIGRATION

A sex-wise break-up of the data concerning migration in India shows that more females than males migrated. In 1961 the break-up of migration from rural to rural was 23.73% males and 76.27% females. The number of females was higher even in urban to rural migration. In 1961, this was 39.15% males and 60.85% females. On the other hand, as has been pointed out earlier, among rural to urban migrants the number of males was higher being 54.03% while the percentage of female migrants was 45.97. According to 1971 migration data in India, 22.42% males and 77.58% females migrated from rural to rural; 37.13% males and 62.87% females migrated from urban to rural areas. The percentage of migrants from rural to urban areas in 1971 was 52.07 and 47.93 respectively. These data show that among migrants from rural to rural and urban to rural the percentage of females is higher in India. This is due to marriage migration. The chief causes of migration in urban areas are marriage, transfer of the earning member, search of employment and search of better employment. Of the total rural urban migration roughly 1/2 of the female migration is marriage migration. The percentage of women migrating from rural areas to urban areas in search of employment is very limited in India. Marriage migration accounts for migration of 0.6% males and 46.2% females in all the urban areas. The most important cause of female migration is marriage, followed by transfer of the earning member. The most important cause of migration for males, however, is search for employment followed by transfer of the earning member.

MIGRATION BY AGE

Several studies of migration in India have established that the heaviest migration in both the sexes is found in the age groups 15-34 and 35-39. Among males 16.6% belong to the age group 0-14; 48% to age group 15-34; 30.7% to the age group 35-39 and 4.7% to the age group 60 and above. The corresponding percentage for females according to 1971 Census were 20.5; 47.3; 26.0 and 6.2. The higher number of migrants in younger age is due to the easy mobility of youths marriage, search for better employment, etc. It is due to the absence of all these causes that migration is very low in upper age groups.

LIFETIME MIGRATION

Lifetime migration is studied by the distance of migration. Migration within the district is called short distance migration. Migration within the state is known as medium distance migration. Migration between states is known as long distance migration. All these types of lifetime migration may be rural to rural, rural to urban, urban to rural and urban to urban. In

India, it has been found by the migration data during the period 1961-1971 that lifetime migration was as follows: Short distance migration was 70% of the female and 50% male migration. Long distance migration accounted for 20% of the male and 10% of the female migration. Medium distance migration accounted for 27.44% male migration and 19.88% female migration. There is not much significant difference in the percentages of short distance, medium distance and long distance lifetime migration during the Census 1961 and 1971. The most important lifetime migration both among males and females in India is short distance and that too rural to rural. This is followed by medium distance lifetime migration with the same tendency of maximum rural to rural migration. Long distance migration, however, is a bit distant. While among females it is maximum from rural to rural, among males it is maximum from rural to urban.

DURATION OF RESIDENCE

The question concerning duration of residence was asked in the last three Censuses in India. The table 12.4 provides data in this connection:

The data of table 12.4 show that in India the most important area of migration is rural to rural. This is not so in developed countries where the rural-urban migration tendency is dominant. In India also, with the growth of industries the rural-urban migration is increasing. The pace of urbanisation, however, is very slow in India due to insufficient and small industrial growth and lack of sufficient employment opportunities in urban areas. It is well-known that educated unemployment is the most serious and biggest part of unemployment and this is particularly found in the urban areas. In the more developed countries however, the process of rural-urban migration has been accelerated not by the push factors as in less developed countries but by the pull factors such as employment opportunities, economic opportunities, educational opportunities, health services, better services, better public service facilities, better cultural and recreational opportunities and better implementation of social legislations conaming working conditions, social welfare and relief programmes. The most important single factor influencing rural urban migration is and has been Industrial Revolution in European countries and other developed countries like Japan.

TABLE 12.4

Migrants Classified by Sex and Duration of Residence, 1961 and 1971

Duration of Residence	*Percentage of total Migration in each Category*	*Percentage Distribution by Sex*	
		Male	*Female*
1961			
Less than 1 year	9.88	48.37	51.63
1-5 year	22.94	40.36	59.64
6-10 years	16.23	30.51	69.49
11-15 years	12.91	27.69	72.31
16 years and over	35.21	20.63	79.37
Period not stated	2.82	35.40	64.60
1971			
Less than 1 year	4.36	51.03	48.97
1-4 years	18.33	41.36	58.64
5-9 years	13.84	33.01	66.99
10-19 years	21.36	25.99	74.01
20 years and over	27.26	20.59	79.41
Period not stated	14.85	36.65	63.35

QUESTIONS FOR EXERCISE

1. What is Migration? Describe its types.
2. Describe the nature, sources and methods of measurement of Internal Migration.
3. Describe important theories of Migration.
4. What are Migration Differentials? What is International Migration?
5. Write an essay on Migration in India.

13

Urbanisation: Measurement and Trends

One of the most important subjects for demographical studies today is urbanisation. Several terms and concepts have been prevalent in this connection. The most important of these are urban place, locality, urban agglomeration, urban population, urban growth, urbanisation and urbanism. These will now be more accurately defined in order to understand the phenomena of urbanization.

1. Urban Locality: According to United Nations, localities are of three types: administrative, economic and ecological. Of these three types the last covers the internationally recommended definition of locality as "A distinct population cluster (inhabited place, settlement, population nucleus, etc.), of which the inhabitants live in closely adjacent structures. The locality usually has a commonly recognised name, but it may be named or delineated for purposes of the Census. Localities are not necessarily the same as the smallest civil division of a country."[1] The United Nations has identified three main types of localities in order to classify urban areas: (1) Agglomerations or clusters of population without regard to official boundaries or administrative functions; (2) Localities with fixed boundaries, having a legally recognised 'town' status, some form of local government and an official designation as 'city', 'borough', 'urban district' or 'municipality', and (3) Minor civil divisions, such as communes with fixed boundaries, which

1. Henry S. Shryock, *et al*. *The Methods and Materials of Demography*, Vol. 1, Washington D.C.: U.S. Bureau of the Census, 1973, p. 21.

actually comprise the entire country and may or may not have local government or 'town status'.[1]

2. Urban Place: Urban Place means the area demarcated as urban regardless of boundary. It is determined more by certain characteristics of urban population. In India the criteria was established in 1961 Census according to which urban areas should have (*i*) a density of population of not less than 1,000 per square mile; (*ii*) population of 5,000; (*iii*) at least three-fourths of the working population not dependent on agriculture; and (*iv*) a few pronounced urban characteristics. The criteria in other countries, however, are very much different. Therefore, the United Nations has suggested that each country should decide for itself which areas are urban and which are rural. However, most of the countries accept the criterion that an urban place should have a population of 20,000 or more, as suggested by the International Urban Research Centre at the University of California, Berkeley.

3. Urban Agglomeration: According to the United Nations, "A large locality of a country, (*i.e.*, city or a town) is often a part of an urban agglomeration, which comprises the city or town proper and also the sub-urban fringe or thickly-settled territory lying outside of, but adjacent to, its boundaries. The urban agglomeration is, therefore, not identical with the locality, but is an additional geographical unit, which includes more than one locality."[2]

4. Urban Population: This term means the population which lives in urban areas, whatever may be the criteria for urban.

5. Urban Growth: Urban growth, as is clear by the term, is the growth in urban place. In other words, it is the growth in urban population.

6. Urbanism: This term is used for the way of life associated with living in urban areas. The characteristics of urban life, however, cannot be described exhaustively. Some of the more important characteristics are individualism, rationalism, impersonal relations, secondary institutions and associations, speed pollution, variety multiplicity, fast transport and communication,

---

1. Hilde Wander, "Basic Data Needed for the Study of Urbanisation: An Examination of Data on the Urban Population in the Censuses of Selected Countries." In Sidney Goldstein and David Sly (Eds.), *Basic Data Needed for the Study of Urbanisation*, p. 43.
2. United Nations, *Principles and Recommendations for the 1970 Population Censuses*, p. 51.

complex life, better technological facilities, etc. All these are also characteristic of urbanisation.

7. Urbanisation: Urbanisation has been often used to denote the level of population concentration in an urban area. Hope Tisdale Eldridge treats urbanisation as a process of population concentration and identifies two elements in the process: (1) The multiplication of points of concentration, and (2) the increase in the size of individual concentrations.[1] Urbanisation can occur only when the rate of growth of the urban population is greater than the rate of growth of the non-urban population in a country.

MEASURES OF URBANISATION

The most important source of data concerning urbanisation is the population census. The process of urbanisation can be measured in terms of four demographic aspects or dimensions: (1) The degree of urbanisation; (2) The tempo of urbanisation; (3) The concentration and dispersion of population; and (4) The components of urban growth. The most important measures of urbanisation are: (1) Percentage of population in urban areas; (2) Ratio of urban rural population; (3) Size of locality of residence of the medium inhabitant; (4) Tempo of urbanisation. These will now be discussed in more details.

1. Percentage of Population in Urban Areas: This is the simplest and the most common measure of urbanisation. It is calculated as follows:

$$PU = \frac{U}{P} \times 100$$

where:

PU is the percentage of urban population;

U is the urban population; and

P is the total population.

According to 1971 Census of India:

The urban population	= 109,094,309
Total population	= 548,159,652

Therefore,

1. Hope Tisdale Eldridge, "The Process of Urbanisation" in J.J. Spendler and O.D. Duncan (Eds.), *Demographic Analysis*, Glencoe Illinois: Free Press, 1956, pp. 338-343.

the percentage of urban population in India

$$= \frac{109,094,309}{548,159,652} \times 100$$

$$= 19.90$$

Thus, this measure is easy to calculate and interpret. The data for it are also easily available. However, it suffers from several weaknesses. Firstly, the definition of an urban area differs from country to country, and also within the same country at different times. Secondly, it does not give us any indication of the percentage of population living in different type of towns.

2. Ratio of Urban-rural Population: This is also a popular measure adopted in census surveys in India. It is calculated as follows:

$$UR = \frac{U}{P} \times 100$$

where:

UR is the urban-rural ratio;

U is the urban population; and R is the rural population.

Ratio of urban-rural population indicates the tempo of urbanisation.

Therefore, it is useful for historical comparisons.

3. Size of Locality or Residence of the Median Inhabitant: This measure follows the principles of median age. It is calculated by the following formula:

$$MI = Q_1 + (Q_1 +_1 - Q_1) \frac{50 - PP_1}{PP_{1+1} - PP_1}$$

where :

MI is the median inhabitant;

PP_1 is the cumulative per cent of the population for the locality under 50 per cent;

PP_{1+1} is the cumulative per cent of the next locality size category;

Q_1 is the upper limit of the locality size i; and

Q_{1+1} is the upper limit of locality size i_{+1}.

For example in 1960 in Mexico the five categories of locality had the population shown below:

Total	3,49,23,129
Less than 1,000	1,22,22,347
1,000-2,499	49,95,644
2,500-4,999	29,59,460
5,000-99,999	82,33,426
10,00,000 and over	65,12,232

On the basis of the above data the following calculation is made: Size of locality or residence of the median inhabitant:

$$MI = Q_1 + (Q_1+_1 - Q_1)\frac{50 - PP_1}{PP_{1+1} - PP_1}$$

$$= 2{,}499 + (4{,}999 - 2{,}499)\ \frac{50.00 - 49.30}{57.78 - 49.30}$$

$$= 2{,}705.$$

4. Tempo of Urbanisation. Tempo of urbanisation shows the rate of change brought about by urbanization. It is calculated on the basis of annual population growth rates. In it the demographer tries to find out how the urban change had occurred and whether it was linear, geometric, exponential or hyperbolic.

Besides the above mentioned measures of urbanisation certain other aspects have been of interest to the researchers in this field. For example, researches have been made in urban population growth in terms of the various components such as the different localities or the demographic components within these localities.

TRENDS OF WORLD URBANISATION

The United Nations has gathered data about trends of world urbanisation. In 1965, approximately 35% of the world's population lived in urban areas. Within this the percentage of the developed regions was 61 and for the developing countries it was only 23. The lowest level of urbanisation is found in Africa. While for the total continent it is 20%, the break-up for different regions is as follows: Eastern Africa 8, Middle Africa 14, Western Africa 18, Northern Africa 32, and Southern Africa 44%. The next in line is Asia with 22% urban population. On the other hand, the urban population in developed countries is very high such as, Northern America 72, Oceania 67, Europe 61, USSR 53 and Latin America 52. The highest level of urbanization in 1965 was in Australia and New Zealand, 82%. It was followed by Northern Europe 75%, Temperate South America 73% and Western Europe

72%. It may be noted here that though the level of urbanisation in Asia is very low, it being the largest continent, with China and India covering 2/3 of the total world population, it constitutes a little more than 1/3 of the urban population of the world. Most of the less developed countries have a very low percentage of urban population. For example the urban population percentage in the following countries: Chile 76.0, Egypt 41.2, India 19.9, Indonesia 17.4, Kenya 9.9, Mexico 58.7, the Philippines 31.7, Sri Lanka 22.4, Thailand 13.2 and Uganda 7.7. The number of cities over 1,00,000, in these countries is very small and yet a very high percentage of urban population lives in these cities. For example, the percentage of urban population living in cities with 1,00,000 population in some developing countries is: Egypt, 72.9, Kenya 70.04, Indonesia 65.98 and Mexico 62.68, India 48.47.

Large Cities

The existence of large cities is found in the world since ancient times. Babylon had a population of 3,50,000 in 6th century BC. Some other big cities in ancient times were Patliputra 5,00,000 in 400 BC, Alexandria 7,00,000 in 100 BC, Rome 11,00,000 in 200 AD, Baghdad 7,50,000 in 900 AD and Angkor 15,00,000 in 10th or 11th century. Up to the 18th century Asia had more urbanisation than Europe. However, Europe gradually led in urbanisation due to economical reasons. The Western urban centres were mainly commercial. Other factors which led to the emergence of urban centres are sea and river mercantile trade and industrial revolution. During the period 1800-1950 the percentage of urban population rose from 3.0 to 29.8. The percentage of inhabitants in urban centres with more than 1,00,000 rose from 1.7 to 13.1. In 1920 the world total population of agglomerations of 20,000 or more inhabitants for major areas of the world was 266.4 million. This population developed in succeeding decades as follows: 1930 — 338.2, 1940 — 431.5, 1950 — 533.0, 1960 — 760.3. The percentage of this urban population to the total population of the world was: 14.3 in 1920, 16.3 in 1930, 18.8 in 1940, 21.2 in 1950, 25.4 in 1960. The percentage of urban population in developing regions was 15.4 in 1960, while in more developed regions it was 46.0. The average annual rates of growth of urban population for the world, developing regions and more developed regions during the period 1920-1960 will be clear from the following table :[1]

1. United Nations, *Growth of the World's Urban and Rural Population*, 1920-2000, New York: 1969, p. 24, Table 8 and p. 118, Table 50.

Table 13.1

Annual Growth of Urban Population

	Agglomerations of 20,000 or more inhabitants		*Cities of 1,00,000 or more inhabitant*	
	1920-1960	*1950-1960*	*1920-1960*	*1950-60*
World	2.6	3.6	2.9	3.9
Developing Regions	3.7	4.9	4.7	5.7
More Developed Regions	2.1	2.7	2.2	2.9

URBANISATION IN INDIA

Some urban centres in India flourished from time to time though the country has always been predominantly rural in character. For example, Varanasi and Prayag were great centres of learning for so many centuries. In 19th and early 20th century Bombay and Calcutta were famous industrial centres. The process of urbanisation however has particularly grown in the twentieth century. The definition of an urban unit was fixed first of all in 1961, according to which the term included all municipalities with 5,000 or more inhabitants. A place with less than 5,000 inhabitants could also be considered urban if the Census Superintendent believed to be so. Since the 1961 Census the criteria for urban localities are: (*i*) Urban density of not less than 1,000 per square mile, (*ii*) at least three-fourth of the working population should be engaged in non-agricultural activities. However, all the localities with the municipal local self-government were included in urban class irrespective of the fact whether they fulfilled the above criteria or not.

Growth of Urban Population in India

Table 13.2 shows the growth of urban population in India since 1901 to 1971.

Indian censuses have classified the towns in 6 classes on the basis of population sizes as follows: I — 1,00,000 and over, II — 50,000 to 99,999, III — 20,000 to 49,999, IV — 10,000 to 19,999, V — 5,000 to 9,999, VI — below 5,000. Table 13.3 shows the growth of percentage of urban population in India in different classes of towns.

Table 13.2

Growth of Urban Population in India, 1901-1971[1]

Year	*Number of towns*	*Total urban population (in millions)*	*Percentage of urban population to total population*	*Percentage growth of urban population during the decade*
1901	1881	25.85	10.84	—
1911	1875	25.94	10.29	0.3
1921	2012	28.09	11.17	8.3
1931	2145	33.46	11.99	19.1
1941	2329	44.15	13.85	32.0
1951	2924	62.44	17.29	41.4
1961	2462	78.94	17.97	26.4
1971	2641	109.10	19.90	38.2

Table 13.3

Percentage of Urban Population in India by Class of Town, 1901-1971[2]

Size Class	*1901*	*1911*	*1921*	*1931*	*1941*	*1951*	*1961*	*1971*
I	22.9	24.2	25.3	27.4	35.4	41.8	48.4	52.4
II	11.8	10.9	12.4	12.0	11.8	11.1	11.9	12.2
III	16.6	17.7	16.9	18.8	17.7	16.7	18.5	17.4
IV	22.1	20.5	18.9	19.0	16.3	14.0	13.0	12.0
V	20.4	19.8	19.0	17.3	15.4	13.2	7.7	5.2
VI	6.3	7.0	7.4	5.6	3.5	3.2	1.0	0.8

This population growth has not been identical in different states. The following table shows the percentage of urban population growth in different states of India in 1961-1971:

Table 13.4

Growth of Urbanisation by Class of Towns

Class of town	Population in '000s					
	1901	1951	1961	1971	1981	1991[3]
I. 1,00,000 and above	6,661	27,507	39,883	61,226	94,504	1,38,802
	(26.00)	(44.63)	(51.42)	(57.24)	(60.42)	(65.20)
II. 50,000 - 99,999	2,892	6,137	8,713	11,680	18,190	23,309
	(11.29)	(6.96)	(11.23)	(10.92)	(11.63)	(10.95)
III. 20,000 - 49,999	4,007	9,688	13,139	17,126	22,409	28,079
	(15.64)	(15.72)	(16.94)	(16.01)	(14.33)	(13.19)

1. Government of India, *Country Statement of India*, November 1972, pp. 1-13.
2. C.I.C.R.E.D., *The Population of India*, 1974, *World Population Year Series*, p. 79.
3. Provisional.

IV. 10,000 - 19,999	5,335	8,399	9,902	11,706	14,930	16,531
	(20.83)	(13.63)	(12.77)	(10.94)	(9.54)	(7.77)
5,000 - 9,999	5,159	7,993	5,329	4,756	5,603	5,532
	(20.14)	(12.97)	(6.87)	(4.45)	(3.58)	(2.60)
VI. Less than 5,000	1,562	1,906	597	473	784	614
	(6.10)	(3.09)	(0.77)	(0.44)	(0.50)	(0.29)
All classes	25,616	61,630	77,562	1,06,967	1,56,420	2.12.867
	(100.00)	(100.00)	(100.00)	(100.00)	(100.00)	(100.00)
Urban population as percentage to total Population	10.84	17.29	17.97	19.91	23.34	25.72

Source: Part II-A (*i*) & (*ii*) 1981

Note: Excludes Assam and Jammu and Kashmir.

Figures within brackets are percentage total urban population for the census year.

Table 13.5

Percentage of Urban Population in India and the Different States of India, 1961 and 1971[1]

States	*1961*	*1971*
Andhra Pradesh	17.44	19.35
Assam	7.37	8.39
Bihar	8.43	10.04
Gujarat	25.77	28.13
Haryana	17.23	17.28
Himachal Pradesh	6.34	7.06
Jammu and Kashmir	16.66	18.26
Kerala	15.11	16.28
Madhya Pradesh	14.29	16.26
Maharashtra	28.22	31.20
Karnataka	22.33	24.31
Orissa	6.32	8.27
Punjab	23.06	23.80
Rajasthan	16.28	16.61
Tamil Nadu	26.69	30.28
Uttar Pradesh	12.85	14.00
West Bengal	24.45	24.59
Total — India	17.98	19.89

1. Ashish Bose, *Studies in India's Urbanisation*, 1901-1971, New Delhi: Tata McGraw-Hill Publishing Co. Ltd. (First revised edition), 1974, p. 118.

Table 13.6

Growth of Urban Population in India, 1872-1991

Year	*Urban Population (% of Total)*	*Increase*
1872	8.8	—
1881	9.3	+ 0.5
1891	9.4	+ 0.1
1901	10.00	+ 0.6
1911	9.4	- 0.6
1921	11.3	+ 1.9
1931	12.1	+ 0.8
1941	13.9	+ 1.8
1951	17.3	+ 3.4
1961	18.0	+ 0.7
1971	19.0	+ 1
1978	21.0	+ 2
1981	23.31	+ 2.31
1991	26.0	+ 2.69

According to Census 1981, Maharashtra had the maximum urban components of 35.03%, while Himachal Pradesh had the urban component at 7.71. Uttar Pradesh had an urban component of 18.01, a growth of 4.02% on 1971 Census.

Urban Population Growth in U.P.

According to 1981 Census, U.P. has a population of 111 million, constituting one-sixth of India's population, about 91 million are in rural areas and 20 million in urban areas comprising 82 per cent and 18 per cent respectively.

Five districts of Lucknow, Dehradun Kanpur, Agra and Jhansi are on the top. They have maintained their order in urbanisation during the decade. On the lowest rung stand Sultanpur, Tehri-Garhwal, Basti, Pratapgarh, and Pithoragarh. In absolute terms the district of Basti has the largest rural population component (34,04,916) followed by Gorakhpur (33,94,809), Deoria (32,55,923), Azamgarh (32,15,334) and Allahabad (30,10,921). On the other hand Kanpur district has the largest urban population (17,82,665) followed by Agra (11,10,364) and Lucknow (10,51,633).

Uttar Pradesh and Karnataka are the two states which have a higher growth rate of population than the all-India average though from 1901 to 1971 they had a lower growth rate than the all India average. Since 1901 the population of Uttar Pradesh had more than doubled from mere 48.6 million to 111 million. The rural population of the state had also more than doubled from a mere 43.2 million to 91 million.

On the other hand, the urban population quadrupled from a mere 5.4 million today during the last decade. While the rural population has gone up by 19.7 per cent, the urban population increased by 61.2 per cent.

In all there are 704 towns in Uttar Pradesh which together comprise the urban area. They consist of five municipal corporations, 187 municipal boards, 22 cantonment boards, 47 notified areas, 418 town areas and 25 census towns. In 1981 Uttar Pradesh equals Punjab and is higher than Haryana, Arunachal Pradesh, Nagaland and Sikkim in the sex ratio. The districts where the females outnumber males are Tehri-Garhwal, Almora, Pithoragarh, Chamoli, Azamgarh, Pratapgarh and Jaunpur.

Characteristics of Urban Population

The following table shows sex ratio in different classes of towns during the period 1901-1971:

Table 13.7

Sex Ratio of Urban Population by Class of Towns 1901-1971[1]

	Class of Towns					
	I	*II*	*III*	*IV*	*V*	*VI*
1901	785	935	940	967	968	927
1911	730	878	907	945	952	912
1921	709	836	874	930	941	905
1931	724	836	865	909	928	888
1941	721	867	873	923	934	894
1951	789	884	899	935	946	902
1961	799	868	885	914	902	854
1971	827	887	899	911	897	858

The rate of literacy in urban areas is more than the rural areas in the country.

1. Mehrotra, G.K., *Birth Place Migration in India*, New Delhi, Office of the Registrar General of India, 1974, pp. 97-104.

Table 13.8

Literacy Rate by Size of Towns and by Sex, India, 1961 and 1971[1]

Size of Cities/Towns	1961 Persons	1961 Male	1961 Female	1971 Persons	1971 Male	1971 Female
Over 1 million	56.4	63.9	46.4	59.2	66.0	50.4
Between 0.5-1 M	49.6	58.4	38.4	53.9	62.6	43.6
Between 0.1-0.5 M	48.5	58.5	36.8	53.7	62.6	43.7
Cities below 0.1 M	51.8	60.7	40.7	56.2	64.0	46.6
Non-City Urban	43.0	54.7	29.7	48.2	58.7	37.0
Urban (India)	46.9	57.5	34.5	52.5	16.6	41.9
All India	24.0	34.4	13.0	29.3	39.5	18.4

Overcrowding is a universal feature of urban localities. The following table shows the percentage distribution of household by number of rooms in selected Indian cities in 1971:

Table 13.9

Percentage Distribution of Households by Number of Rooms, Selected Indian Cities, 1971[2]

	One room	Two rooms	Three rooms	Four rooms	Five and above	Unspecified
Greater Bombay	77.4	14.2	5.3	1.9	1.1	0.1
Calcutta	67.6	17.3	8.1	3.8	3.3	0.02
Pune	65.1	20.9	7.3	3.6	3.1	0.2
Kanpur	59.6	27.0	7.1	3.3	3.0	0.01
Ahmedabad	57.5	27.5	7.8	3.9	3.2	0.1
Delhi	57.4	25.4	9.4	4.3	3.1	0.5
Madras	53.6	24.4	11.0	5.2	5.4	0.5
Total Urban	50.1	26.9	11.4	5.7	5.6	0.2
Total Rural	47.3	28.5	12.1	6.0	6.0	0.2

The above table shows that in major cities in India like Greater Bombay, Calcutta, Pune, Kanpur, and Ahmedabad the population between 85 and 90 per cent of the household lives in one or two rooms. This shows an acute shortage of housing in urban areas.

1. *The Population of India,* CICRED Series, New Delhi: Office of the Registrar General of India, 1974, p 85.
2. *The Population of India,* CICRED Series, New Delhi: Office of the Registrar General of India, 1974, p. 86.

This will be further clear by our report of overcrowding in Greater Bombay. In 1971 the sequence of the first 10 largest cities in India was as follows: Calcutta, Greater Bombay, Delhi, Madras, Hyderabad, Ahmedabad, Bangalore, Kanpur, Pune, Nagpur. According to Registrar General of India the urban population is likely to increase to 205.1 million by 1991 and to 278.3 million by 2001.

OVER-CROWDING IN INDIAN METROPOLITAN CITIES

Life in Indian metropolitan cities like Calcutta, Bombay, Delhi and Madras is becoming a nightmare for a majority of the people and if the present trends continue, there will be a total failure of the urban system by the end of the century, according to environmentalist Rashmi Mayur. Dr. Mayur points out that while there is an appreciable decline or stabilisation of large cities in industrialised countries, the pace of urbanisation is increasing significantly in the less developed nations, Mexico, India and Egypt being prime examples. Dr. Mayur lists the present urban growth rate at four per cent yearly, approximately twice the rate of population growth, half the growth being natural and, the rest due to migration from rural areas. The present rate of urbanisation, he says, will be accelerated after 1985 and by the end of the century, the approximate number in various urban centres all over India will reach 335 to 350 million people.

According to Press Trust of India, Bombay's population is expected to almost double during the next 20 years, making it the second most populous city in the world after Tokyo, according to projections by the United Nations.

Bombay is at present the sixth largest urban agglomeration with a population of 14.5 million. It is expected to gain 12.9 million residents to tally a population of 27.4 million by 2015.

Calcutta with 11.5 million people is also among the top 15 urban agglomerations.

Tokyo is currently the largest agglomeration with 26.5 million people, more than one and a half times as large as the second largest agglomeration, New York with 16.3 million inhabitants.

Bombay: A Profile of Present Over-crowding

1. Area, Population, etc: Area 437.71 sq km, Population 8.2 million (1981 Census), Density of population per sq. km. 18,733.86, Sex ratio 775 females per 1000 males, Percentage of literacy 68.2, Slum-dwellers 35 lakhs, Birth rate per 1000, 81.6, Death rate per 1000, 26.9.

2. Education and Health: Pre-primary and primary schools 1,859, Secondary schools 650, Higher secondary schools 115, Number of higher and special education institutions 437, Pre-primary and primary students 7.55 lakhs, Secondary school students 4.25 lakhs, Higher secondary school students 1.52 lakhs, Number of hospital beds 25,000.

3. Entertainment, Hotels, Restaurants: Cinema house 142, Total number of seats, 95,000, Radio licences issued 3,92,307, T.V. licences issued 2,05,274, Residential hotels 635, Number of rooms 25,000, Eating houses and restaurants 11,520.

4. Transport. Total railway length 197 km No. of commuters carried per day 5.5 million. Total road length 1,410.60 km. Buses 2,052 (93% operational efficiency), No. of passengers carried per day (BEST) 4.5 million, Contract carriers 250, Lorries 65,000, Taxis 50,000, Private cars 30,000, Slow moving vehicles (including handcarts and bullock-carts) 15,000. Petrol Stations 257, Motor spirit used 18,374 kilolitres, High speed diesel used 14,710 kilolitres, Daily vehicle coverage of cars 5,10,000 km., Daily coverage of diesel vehicles 2,45,000 km.

5. Communications: Total number of assorted mail pieces daily 2.5 million (10% of the country's total), Number of postmen 4,500, Marriage invitation cards 20,000, parties cards 28,000, Function cards 3,200, Greeting cards 19,140, Airmail sent to 140 countries, Telephone connections 2,80,366, Telephone revenue ₹ 95.69 crores, Telephone waiting list 1,23,156, Telex connections 4,616, Telex revenue ₹ 23.18 crore, Telex waiting list 1,800. Street-side hoardings 6,000, Pole Ads. 15,000, Kiosks Ads. 6,000, Bus fleet Ads. 2000.

6. Immigration: In 1980: 2,00,000, influx per day 3,000 families, rate of growth due to immigration 50% (Mexico, Cairo and Jakarta 5%), Initial area 26 sq. mile, Megalopolis area 169 sq. miles.

7. Housing: Dharavi the biggest slum in Asia, population .5 million, footpath dwellers .5 million, persons living in buildings likely to collapse 15%, number of buildings likely to collapse 11,000, cost of apartment rupees 2,000 per sq. foot, shortfall of public housing 5,000 units per year, private housing construction 20,000 units per year, backlog of housing units 8,00,000, yearly shortage of housing units 55,000.

8. Social Problems: Average income of 75% families Rs. 600 per month, income of 10% persons ₹ 250 per months, beggars 2,00,000, unemployed 5,00,000 partially employed 1 million, water available to slum dwellers, 10 gallons per person, daily garbage generation 3,200 tons, road accidents (in 1980) 23,000, accidental deaths 706, daily pollutants discharged in the air 1,500 tons, incidence of lungs diseases 9 to 20%, noise pollution 72 decibels in busy areas, rats 9 million, sick and hungry dogs 2. million, amount of pollution in slum areas equal to smoking of 30 cigarettes per day.

9. Industrial Units: Large and medium units 798, small scale units 14,531, per capita income ₹ 1,800, textile mills 54, industrial daily employment, 164,187, wholesale merchants 8,000, paid up capital ₹ 67 crore, city mills consumption 1,11 million cotton bales, chemical industries 45% of the national production, dyestuff units 70% of national output, Film industry biggest in Asia. Total industrial investment ₹ 10,000 crores, major trade unions : CITU, AITUC, 1NTUC, HMS, BMS, etc.

10. Banking: Banking offices 940, Banking offices (cooperative) 210, Registered money-lenders 2,140.

11. Revenue and Finance (1980-81: Amount In Crores): Income Tax 900.0, Corporation Tax 376.95, Non-Corporation Tax 458.37, Wealth Tax 20.32, Gift Tax 1.36, Estate Duty 4.32, Interest Tax 23.09, Sales Tax 600.00.

12. Miscellaneous: Influx per day 300 families, cement consumed per quarter 2 lakh tons, rice sold per day (100 kg bags) 45,000, wheat sold per day (100 kg bags) 42,000, meat sold per day 45,000 kg, vegetables arriving daily 700 tonnes, annual rainfall 19.2 mm, registered shops 1,28,430, commercial establishments 17,626, daily average water supply 430 million gallons, share of Bombay Port in India's total foreign trade 21.1%, total value of foreign trade carried by foreign traders 5,637 crore, private markets 19, milk consumed-daily 1.9 million litres, Newspapers dailies

42, magazines 764, Municipal markets 74, income of Municipal Corporation in 1981-82 Rs. 263.86 crore (more than the income of H.P. state ₹ 218 crore).

13. Future Predictions for 2001 AD. Slums population 75%, shortage of housing units 2.4 million, growth of suburbs 50%, sex ratio 1,000 to 900 females, number of people aged 60 and above will be 1 million, increase of railway travel will be 300 per cent, demand for bus services 150%, total demand of bus trips per year 1.5 billion, number of vehicles 6,50,000, water shortage 350 million gallon per day, garbage collected per day 6,500 tonnes. It will be difficult to quantify the institutional breakdown, crime, corruption, alienation, etc., arising out of the giganticism of the city.

Alternative to doom—(1) Available resources must be judiciously and selectively used. Efforts should be made to create new and indigenous resources. (2) The benefits of resources must be distributed equitably and for the total development of society. (3) A fair system of sharing and contribution of resources as between the Centre and the State Government must be created.

However, Dr. Mayur cautions, there are two points concerning these assumptions, one that possibly by 1985 some dramatic technology for population control may deter the growth considerably, mostly in urban areas, and secondly, a revolutionary upsurge may influence urban-rural division of the population in an unforeseen direction.

The over-urbanisation is evident in various ways. One is underdevelopment by which certain types of urban technology necessary for modernisation is scarce, unavailable or not used. Secondly, urban forms, city governments and economic planning are archaic, with little relevance to the Indian setting.

Dr. Mayur argues that the urban social structure reflects institutions, attitudes, values and rituals of rural India, determining policies and influencing development which conflict with the building of a healthy and progressive urban society.

Finally, the continuous accentuation of the urban-rural dichotomy has led to the parasitic relationship between the city and the hinterland, by which, because, of the disadvantageous relationship of the latter, much of its vitality is drained away and is concentrated in the urban areas for the benefit of a limited number of people.

At the outset it seems that if the trends continue as projected, the future of urbanisation in India will be disastrous if not catastrophic. Broadly speaking, there will be 20 cities with a population of about one million each and at least 600 cities with a population between 50,000 and 5,00,000, small towns will decline in number.

The spectacular population growth, specially in urban areas, will strain all resources and social institutions beyond any Malthusian calculation. Even if the food production is doubled by the end of the century to 220 million tonnes per year (which is likely), there will still be a deficit of at least 30 million tonnes per year.

He says that if the economic growth picks up again and the per capita GNP increases at the rate of two per cent yearly on an average over the ₹ 950 GNP per capita today, by the end of the year 2000, it will hardly be ₹ 1800 GNP per capita, which will not take the masses above the poverty line. On the contrary, since much of the surplus will be absorbed by the increasing population, at least 65 per cent of the urban population will be living below the desired minimum.

Dr. Mayur says that for the projected population 70 million dwellings will be required. Water needs will touch 8.75 billion gallons daily. Transportation will shockingly halt due to enormous disruption and dislocations generated by continuously inadequate facilities.

Probably the most gruesome problem will be that of energy shortage. The problem of environmental pollution will plague Indian cities and towns even more seriously.

The literacy rate, which is 32 per cent today in the urban areas, will reach 60 per cent in the next 22 years. The relevance of the present education system to the future development will be increasingly questioned but the present entrenched system will hardly go through any major changes. The manufacturing sector will remain the main employer.

The cost of health will grow in geometrical progression yet for a large number of people ill-health will be the way of life. The joint family system, the backbone of Indian society for centuries, will experience the strain of modernisation.

Urban development, Dr. Mayur says, should be made part of the regional planning based on resources requirements, economic viability, optimum productivity, cultural growth and integrated development, halting any further growth in major metropolitan areas.

Every region, city and town should have a data bank, he feels, supplying scientific, up-to-date information for planning, integrated, long-range development and proper resources allocation.

Dr. Mayur says it is not necessary for urban society to suffer from various social ills such as loneliness, crime, breakdown of social relations or alcoholism as many aspects of family relations can be restructured to accomplish the goal of building a new and happy society.

However, the more pervasive picture he paints of urban life in India today is pockets of glistening modern skyscrapers, surrounded by squalid slums, stretching far into the suburbs with all the concommitant problems of poverty, unemployment, pollution, traffic, congestion, crime, filth and misery.

SLOW URBANIZATION IN INDIA, 1991

The growth of urban population in the country during the last decade (1981-1991) has surprisingly slowed down by about ten per cent, as compared to the earlier decade of 1971-1981. This is also an index of the new trend of a comparative slowed down migration of people from rural to urban areas in the country during the last decade.

This interesting aspect has been brought out in the latest report of the Registrar-General and Census Commissioner on "Rural-Urban Distribution" of the country's population (Paper-2) on the basis of the 1991 census. During 1971-1981, the growth of urban population was recorded as 46.14 per cent, and between 1981-1991, it went down to 36.19 per cent

This is notwithstanding the fact that the number of cities and towns has been consistently increasing there were 3,126 cities and towns in 1971, and the figure went up to 4,029 in 1981 and it now stood at 4,689. The urban population in the country was now 25.72 per cent of the country's more than 84.43 crore population.

With the change of growth pattern, the big four cities, which were earlier classified as metropolitan cities, are no longer metros; they have"graduated" into "megacities" now. The four megacities, with a population of more than five million are Bombay, Calcutta, Delhi and Madras. Then comes metros, which are now 23, with each having a population of between one and five million. These included Hyderabad, Bangalore, Ahmedabad, Pune, Kanpur, Ludhiana, Baroda, Patna, Varanasi and Nagpur.

The growth of urban population has, however, been uneven. If on one extreme is Haldia, where the population growth recorded during the last decade was about 374 per cent, Vanparai in Tamil Nadu represented the other extreme with a minus eight per cent in growth.

Big cities (Class I) in 15 States like West Bengal, Andhra Pradesh Maharashtra, Madhya Pradesh, Uttar Pradesh and Tamil Nadu had more than 50 per cent of urban population. Again, in the two States of Maharashtra and West Bengal, the share of population was very high, *viz.* 77,85 per cent and 81.71 per cent, respectively. About two-thirds of the urban population in Gujarat, Karnataka and a few other States lived in class one cities.

In terms of levels of urbanisation in various States, the position is rather perplexing. In several States like Gujarat, Tamil Nadu, Karnataka and Punjab, the level of urbanisation has been higher than the national average of 25.72 — varying between 26 and 34 per cent.

Another interesting point brought out in the just released census report (which is follow-up of the one on population released a few months ago) is that the "tempo" of urbanisation has slowed down. The annual growth has declined from 3.09 per cent during the next decade (1981-1991).

Among the States, Mizoram has recorded a growth rate in urban population of 160.27 per cent

Delhi has, however, shown a rapid increase in its population over the years. In 1911, its population was about 2.38 lakh, the year when Delhi became the national Capital. By 1951, it recorded a very large growth of 106.58 per cent. But later the tempo of the growth rate started slowing down from 1961 onwards — from 54.57 per cent during 1961-1971 to 46.18 per cent during 1981-1991.

QUESTIONS FOR EXERCISE

1. Distinguish urbanisation from other concepts used in this connection.
2. How will you measure urbanisation? Trace urban population growth in India. Account for the slow rate of urbanisation.
3. Write short note on overcrowding in cities.

14

Labour Force: Sources, Measures and Trends

An important characteristic of the population of a country is the size and quality of labour force. Labour force is influenced by mortality, fertility and migration. All these factors determine labour force in a country.

Definition of Labour Force

According to the United Nations, labour force has been defined as, "An economically active population." According to S.N. Agarwala, "Labour force is defined to include persons who actually work for wages and salaries, own-account workers, employers and unpaid family workers and also those who are unemployed but seeking work. It does not include persons employed in activities which are economically unproductive like renters, pensioners, beggars and dependents."[1] In the words used by Multilingual Demographic Dictionary, "For a statistical measurement of the working population, the gainful worker concept or the labour force concept may be used. According to this concept, the working population is defined as being composed of those persons who have a gainful occupation which they normally engage in. According to the labour force concept, the working population is defined as a group of persons who are working at a gainful occupation or wanting or seeking such work during a specified period preceding the inquiry."[2]

Labour force has been equated to economically active population or working population which has been defined by

1. Agarwala, S.N., *India's Population Problem.*, p. 186,
2. United Nations, Multilingual Demographic Dictionary, *op. cit.*p. 23.

the Multilingual Demographic Dictionary as follows: "Generally speaking, the working population consists of those individuals who take part in the production of economic goods and services, including unpaid family workers in an economic enterprise as well as persons who work for pay or profit."[1]

Economically active population has been defined by the United Nations as follows: "An economically active population comprises all persons of either sex, who furnish the supply of labour available for the production of economic goods and services during the time reference period chosen for the investigation. It includes both persons in the civilian labour force and those serving in the armed forces."[2] Economically active population again has been classified as (*a*) Employed, (*b*) Unemployed. The population other than economically active comprises the following four groups: (*a*) Home makers, (*b*) Students, (*c*) Income recipients, (*d*) Others. The size of employed and unemployed population is calculated in a certain reference period which, according to the United Nations, has been recommended as one week. Statistical measurement of the working population is measured in terms of the gainful workers concept or the labour force.

Sources of Data

The most important source of data concerning labour force is the population Census. In India information on employment has been collected in all the Censuses beginning from 1881. However, each Census has defined the term worker differently. In the 1951 Census the classification of worker and non-worker was based on the dependency approach in which persons were classified as earners, earning dependents and non-earning dependents on the basis of their gainful occupation. In the Censuses 1961 and 1971 however, a dual approach was adopted. In this approach for those employed in traditional activities like agriculture, their activity during the last season was recorded, on the other hand in the case of those in regular employment, a reference period was adopted and the activity during the period recorded. The data concerning developed and developing countries is compiled by Demographic Year Book published by the United Nations, particularly in the year 1972-73. Besides, data concerning labour

1. *Ibid.*, p. 23.
2. *United Nations, Principles and Recommendations for 1970.*

force is also collected by special Manpower Surveys or Labour Force Surveys. For example, in India the various rounds of the National Sample Survey (NSS) estimates of the labour force are collected in terms of sex, age, marital status, rural or urban region and educational attainment, etc.

Analysis of Labour Force Data

Analysis of labour force data is generally conducted by labour force participation rates or economic activity rates. Crude as well as refined measures are used for the study of the labour force. The Crude Labour Force Participation Rate or Crude Activity Rate indicates the size of the labour force in proportion to the size of the total population. Besides there are other measures such as the General Labour Force Participation Rate and the Age Sex Specific Labour are as follows:

1. Crude Labour Force Participation Rate or Crude Activity Rate: This is calculated by computing the total number of persons in the labour force in the numerator and the total population in the denominator and then multiplying the quotient by 100. For example, the male labour force participation rate in 1971 in India was 52.50. This was computed as follows:

The total number of male workers

$$= 14{,}90{,}75{,}136$$

The total male population $= 28{,}39{,}36{,}614$

The male labour force participation rate

$$= \frac{14{,}90{,}75{,}136}{28{,}39{,}36{,}614} \times 100$$

$$= 52.50.$$

This measurement suffers, from the following limitations:

(*i*) The data are affected by the age distribution of the population.

(*ii*) The data suffer from all the weaknesses from all the crude rate used in demographic analysis in any country.

(*iii*) Very young persons and very old persons are not exposed to the risk of labour force participation.

2. The General Labour Force Participation Rate: This measurement is useful to calculate the refined labour force participation rate. It is calculated by relating the total labour force only to the population above the specified minimum age. Thus, it is computed only in the working age groups. It often specifies minimum as well as maximum age. For example, in 1971 the general labour force participation rate in India was 86.89 which was computed as follows:

Number of male workers in the age group

15-59 = 12,87,23,291

Number of males in the age group 15-59

= 14,81,40,059

General labour force participation rate males

$$= \frac{12,87,23,291}{14,81,40,059} \times 100$$

$$= 86.89$$

3. The Age-Sex Specific Labour Participation Rates: This measurement is useful for comparisons between the various regions of a country or between various countries. The data are not affected by the age composition of the population. All the three above mentioned measures may be computed separately. In 1971 in India the labour force participation rate in 20-24 age group was 81.30 for males and 17.85 for females. In the case of males it was computed as follows:

Total population = 2,15,62,684

Males engaged in labour force = 1,75,29,831

Labour force participation rate = 81.30.

This was calculated by dividing the number of males engaged in labour force from the total number of population and multiplying it by 100. For example, the labour force participation rate in the case of formates for the same age group was calculated as follows:

$$= \frac{2,15,19,694}{34,40,492} \times 100 = 17.85$$

Similar rates may be calculated for other age groups such as 15-19, 25-29, 30-39, 40-49 and so on upto 60 years of age after which generally people do not work. It has been found by comparisons of specific labour force participation rate in different ages that before age 25 it increases with each successive age group but after 45 years of age it declines with each successive age group and very sharply after 65 years of age. No significant variations are observed in the average activity rates between the ages 20 and 55, at different levels of development in different countries. However, differences are observed in the higher ages. For example, in the least developed countries the average male participation rates in the age group 55-65 are highest. In agricultural countries economic necessity compels men to continue to work as long as they are physically fit. Therefore, one finds a more pronounced participation rate in higher ages in these countries. Similarly, in agricultural and developing countries children start working at a very young age. On the other hand in economically advanced countries the participation of children in the activity group is very limited due to enforcement of compulsory education and the labour laws. It may be understood why in India the labour force participation rate is higher among children and old persons due to the above mentioned reasons concerning agricultural and developing countries.

4. Standardized Labour Force Participation Rate: This fulfils the need for a summary measure which will not suffer from the weakness of the crude participation rate. It is useful for comparing the degree of participation of persons in the labour force in various countries. It is calculated for all age groups whose total is divided by the total number of persons working in all ages and multiplied by 100. In India it was 61.32 in 1971. This indicates that 61.32 would have been participation rate for males in India if the Indian age distribution of males had been like that of United States.

Levels of Labour Force Participation

According to the United Nations Publication *The Determinants and Consequences of Population Trends*, Vol. I, the following are the important points of variations in the Census operations of various countries, making it difficult to compare labour force participation:[1]

(*a*) The time reference period of the Census question on economic activities. This may from a single day to one 'year, or may vaguely refer to an individual's "usual" status;

(*b*) The treatment of persons engaged both in economic and non-economic activities;

(*c*) The criteria for identifying unemployed persons; and

1. *Op cit., Population Studies,* No. 50, New York, 1973, pp. 294-295.

(*d*) The distinction in farm households between members to be classified as being in the labour force and those not economically active. The measurement of the labour force is extremely difficult under conditions prevailing in the rural areas of many less developed countries, where a marked labour scarcely exists.

Besides the above mentioned variations, different types of errors and biases make comparisons difficult. However, such comparisons have been made. It has been found that the age-specific participation rate for those below 15 years of age is the highest in Thailand where it is 43.7%. This rate for this age group is zero in developed countries like United Kingdom and Japan. Similarly, for the age groups 65-70 the participation rate in Thailand was 44.6 whereas it was only 2.5 in Sweden. This shows that very few people work in developed countries while almost half of the population in developing countries goes on working in this age. The labour force participation rate for male in India in 1971 was 55.24 in the age group 15-19 and 73.79 in the age group above 60 which shows the poverty of the country. Similar results may be observed about crude labour force participation rates for females. However, in developed countries more females join the working force. And yet the situation is almost similar to that of the male labour force. For example, in Thailand in 1970 the crude labour force participation rate among females was 46.0 while it was only 33.2 in UK and 29.5 in USA. However, it was 45.5 in USSR since the communist countries insist upon equality of sexes in labour force. Again, in Muslim countries the females do not participate in labour force, therefore, the percentage of female population in labour force has been very low in these countries. For example in 1971 it was 8.0 in Morocco. In 1970 it was 5.2 in Kuwait. In India also the situation is very much similar since the percentage was 11.9 in 1971. This shows that female labour force participation rates tremendously vary from one country to another due to different reasons. It should be remembered here that in most countries housewives are not counted in active working force despite the fact that their working hours are sufficiently long within the home. Cultural influences have been very important in this respect. For example, one finds a very high female labour force participation rate in African countries while among Muslims it is very low. Similarly it is very high in Socialist countries while it is low in Capitalist societies.

LABOUR FORCE IN INDIA

In India information on labour has been collected since the beginning of the Census in 1981. The data for the 1911, 1921 and 1961 Censuses were found quite comparable. The data for the Censuses 1931 and 1951 were not strictly comparable, due to undercounting. In 1971 Census the data for females had become entirely incomparable due to very large undercounting. According to S.N. Agarwala, "The 1971 Census departed from the previous Censuses to such an extent that the data for females have become entirely incomparable with those of the earlier Censuses. It has been estimated that if the 1971 Census had not so departed from the 1961 Census, the working force in 1971 would have been 156 million males and 71 million females instead of 149 million males and 31 million females. The very large undercount of females is spread over agricultural as well as unorganized non-agricultural activities. The view that definitional changes have resulted in a difference of 47 million in the working force is not borne out by the sample survey carried out after the 1971 Census to test such a thesis."[1]

Level of Labour Force

In 1971 the total labour force in the country was 180.4 million. Thus, 52.5% males and 11.9% females were engaged in work, making the total of 32.9%. The activity rate was higher in rural areas as compared to the urban areas. There was a striking difference in the activity rates of females in the urban and rural areas. The following table shows the labour force by sex and residence in 1971:

Table 14.1

Labour Force by Sex and Rural-Urban Residence, 1971[2]

Sex	Number of Workers (in millions)			Percentage of Workers		
	Rural	Urban	Total	Rural	Urban	Total
Male	120.4	28.7	149.1	53.5	48.8	52.5
Female	28.0	3.3	31.3	13.1	6.6	11.9
Total	148.4	32.0	180.4	33.8	29.3	31.9

1. Agarwala, S.N., *India's Population Problem*, p. 187.
2. *Census of India*, 1971, Economic Characteristics of Population, Series 1, Paper No. 3, pp. 1-73.

Age Specific Activity Rate

In 1971 out of the 180.4 million workers, 10.7 million were children below the age of 15. Again, 14.1 million were old persons above the age of 60 years and more. The majority of the labour was from rural areas, since 80% of Indian population lives in villages. A high activity rate was found in the age group 20-60. The males aged 60 and above were working 52% in urban and 77% in rural areas. A Short difference was noticeable in the activity rates of males and females. This is partly due to distinctions among rural and urban social mores and economic status. This may be visualised by Table 14.2.

Activity Rate by Educational Level

There is hardly any question of activity rate according to educational attainment in rural areas due to widespread illiteracy in rural India. Therefore, such rates have been computed only about the urban areas. Table 14.3 shows activity rate by educational level in urban areas, in India in 1971.

Table 14.2

Activity Rate by Age, Sex and Rural-Urban Residence, 1971[1]

Age	*Rural*		*Urban*		*Total*	
	Male	*Female*	*Male*	*Female*	*Male*	*Female*
1–15	7.5	3.0	2.8	0.8	6.6	2.6
15–20	62.1	18.4	33.1	5.5	55.2	15.5
20–25	86.3	20.2	67.4	9.5	81.3	17.9
25–30	95.3	21.8	90.5	11.6	94.2	19.7
30–40	97.6	23.4	95.5	13.1	97.1	21.4
40–50	97.6	24.1	95.2	14.5	97.1	22.4
50–60	95.5	20.8	87.9	12.7	94.0	19.4
60+	77.4	11.3	55.4	6.4	73.8	10.5

1. *Ibid.*

Table 14.3

Labour Force Participation Rate for Males and Females by Educational Attainment, India, 1971[1]

Educational Attainment	*Labour Force Participation Rate (per 100 persons)*	
	Males	*Females*
1. Matriculation or Higher Secondary	63.49	13.34
2. Non-technical diploma or certificate not equal to degree	64.12	22.22
3. Technical diploma of certificate not equal to degree	79.31	60.85
4. Graduate degree other than technical degree	73.48	21.58
5. Post-graduate degree other than technical degree	84.67	42.89
6. Technical degree or diploma equal to degree or P.G. degree	81.13	63.17
7. (*a*) Engineering and Technology	81.95	32.55
(*b*) Medicine	76.12	71.23
(*c*) Agriculture, Veterinary and Dairying	89.47	16.67
(*d*) Teaching	84.82	63.71
(*e*) Others	77.50	56.62

Activity Pattern of Workers

Indian Censuses divide activity pattern of workers by sector of employment. These sectors are three — Primary, Secondary and Tertiary. In 1961 the percentages of workers in these sectors of employment were 69.18, 11.48 and 19.34. In 1971 the corresponding percentages were 70.38, 11.33 and 18.29. This shows that there has been no appreciable change in the activity pattern of workers during the period 1961-1971. The distribution of female workers also shows the same pattern. In 1971 their percentage in the above mentioned sectors was 82.97, 7.67 and 9.36 respectively. This percentage will gradually change with the rise of industrialisation and economic development. Today the primary sector continues to be the most important field of worker's activity. This is clear by the above 70% total average secured by it since 1901 to 1971. The lowest position has been occupied by secondary sector which has occupied only slightly more than 10% of the total percentage of workers during the period 1901-1971. The total average for

1. *Pocket Book of Population Statistics*, New Delhi: Office of Registrar-General of India, 1922, pp. 88-89.

tertiary sector of employment has varied from 14 to 17% during the above mentioned period. This is equally applicable to the activity pattern of the female workers.

Workers by Industrial Categories

It is well known that most of the Indian males are employed in agriculture either as cultivators or agricultural labourers. While among the males the number of cultivators has been larger, among females the number of agricultural labourers has been larger. It is particularly so since most of the land is owned by males in rural areas. One finds a significant difference between rural and urban people in this respect since the majority of the urban people are engaged in various industries. This also makes significant difference in the pattern of female employment in rural and urban areas. This will be clear by the following table:

Table 14.4

Workers by Industrial Categories, Sex and Rural-Urban Residence, 1971[1]

	Rural		*Urban*		*Total*	
Industrial Category	*Male*	*Female*	*Male*	*Female*	*Male*	*Female*
1	2	3	4	5	6	7
1. Cultivators	67.4	9.1	1.5	0.2	68.9	9.3
2. Agricultural labourers	30.4	15.2	1.3	0.6	31.7	15.8
3. Livestock, forestry, fishing, hunting etc.	3.0	0.7	0.5	0.1	3.5	0.8
4. Mining and quarrying	0.5	0.1	0.3	—	0.8	0.1
5. Manufacturing, processing, servicing etc:						
(*a*) Household industry	3.8	1.0	1.2	0.4	5.0	1.4
(*b*) Other than household industry	2.9	0.5	6.9	0.4	9.8	0.9
6. Construction	1.0	0.1	1.01	0.1	2.0	0.2
7. Trade and commerce	3.3	0.3	6.2	0.2	9.5	0.5
8. Transport, storage and communication	1.2		3.1	0.1	4.3	0.1
9. Other services	6.9	1.0	6.7	1.2	13.6	2.2
Total Workers	120.4	28.0	28.7	3.3	149.1	31.3

1. *Census of India*, 1971, Economic Characteristics of Population Series I, Paper No. 3, pp. 1-73.

Workers by Employment Status

The data gathered by the 1971 Census were classified into four categories: Employer, Employee, Single worker and Family worker. As is clear by the table given below the proportion of single workers and family workers was found to be higher in the rural areas. In the urban areas, on the other hand, there was a predominance of employer and the employee categories. As is clear by the following table, the proportion of the female workers was high both in urban and rural areas:

Table 14.5

Percentage of Workers by Employment Status, Rural-Urban Residence and Sex, 1971

	Rural		*Urban*		*Total*	
Employment	*Male*	*Female*	*Male*	*Female*	*Male*	*Female*
Employer	3.4	1.1	6.1	1.4	5.2	1.2
Employer	55.1	57.1	66.6	73.5	61.7	64.7
Single worker	34.5	29.6	24.5	21.6	28.8	25.9
Family worker	7.0	12.2	2.8	3.5	4.5	8.2

According to Instructions to Enumerators for filling up the individual slip, issued by Census of India 1971, "A Single worker is a person who works by himself but not as head of household in a household industry. He is not employed by anyone else and in his turn does not employ anybody else, not even members of his household, except casually."[1]

Workers by Occupational Divisions

Total workers including the female workers in Census 1971 data were classified in ten major divisions of the national classification of occupations, excluding the categories of cultivators and agricultural workers. The term farmer was used for planters, livestock farmers, dairy farmers, poultry farmers, etc., and not cultivators. The following table shows percentage of occupational distribution of workers by rural-urban residence in 1971:

1. Census of India, 1971, pp. 32-33.

Table 14.6

Percentage of Occupational Distribution of Workers by Rural-Urban Residence, 1971[1]

	Divisional Description	*Male workers*			*Female workers*		
		Total	*Rural*	*Urban*	*Total*	*Rural*	*Urban*
0-1.	Professional, technical and related workers	8.88	9.61	8.23	13.73	8.60	20.83
2.	Administrative, executive and managerial workers	2.26	1.22	3.19	0.34	0.16	0.59
3.	Clerical and related workers	9.87	6.36	13.03	3.46	0.91	6.97
4.	Sales workers	14.01	11.75	16.04	7.53	7.16	8.05
5.	Service workers	10.54	10.19	10.86	15.35	12.53	19.23
6.	Farmers, fishermen, hunters, loggers and other workers	7.72	14.07	2.01	12.31	19.17	2.85
7,8 & 9	Production and related workers, transport equipment operators and labourers	44.19	44.17	44.21	44.99	48.81	39.70
10.	Workers not classified by occupations	2.53	2.63	2.43	2.28	2.64	1.78
All Workers		100.00	100.00	100.00	100.00	100.00	100.00

Workers by Occupation and Industry

Further, workers data in 1971 Census were further classified by occupation and industry. The occupational divisions included: 1. Professional, technical and related workers, 2. Administrative, executive and managerial workers, 3. Clerical and related workers, 4. Sales workers, 5. Service workers, 6. Farmers, fishermen, hunters and loggers, etc. 7, 8 and 9. Production and related workers, transport equipment operators and labourers. These were further divided into industrial categories, III to IX. It was found that 88% of the professional, technical and related workers were concentrated in other services. 95% of the sales workers were employed in trade and commerce. The rural and urban areas did not show much difference except in the case of 7, 8 and 9 categories.

Secondary Work Workers

In the Census 1971, every worker and non-worker was asked to tell his secondary activity. This secondary activity was undertaken in addition to the main activity. If any person participated in some

1. *Ibid.*

economic activity other than his main work that type of activity was identified as secondary work. However, most of the females who reported secondary work were non-workers. On the other hand, most of the males who reported a secondary activity were workers. While the former were mainly engaged in agricultural labour as secondary activity, the secondary activity of the males was in non-household industry, trade, business or service, etc. Of the total number of persons reporting secondary activity (51.37 million), about 92.5% or 4.94 million were from rural areas. The percentage of non-workers among males was only 4,6% while for the females it was as much as 86.8.

Non-Workers

According to the 1971 Census, the term non-workers included : full-time students as well as persons engaged in unpaid household duties, such as house-wives, other adult females, dependents, including children not attending school, disabled persons including the aged, renters, persons living on agricultural or non-agricultural royalties, beggars, vagrants, inmates of jails, mental hospitals and charitable institutions, persons not employed earlier but currently seeking employment for the first time, persons employed earlier but currently out of employment and seeking employment. The data furnished by Census gave a total of 366 million persons as non-workers. These included 232 million females and 134 million males. They were further classified into 7 categories. The maximum number included full time students, dependents and infants. The number of beggars was 7 lakh, including 4.6 lakh males and 2.8 lakh females. The percentage of illiterate males among non-workers was about, 50.8% both in the rural and urban areas. The percentage of illiterate non-workers female was 50 in the urban areas and 71.4 in rural areas. A striking fact was the differentials evident in the type of activity according to rural-urban residence as well as sex. It was found that in urban areas there were more full-time students both among male and female non-workers than in rural areas.

Trends in Labour Force Participation Rate 1901-1971

According to the 1971 Census there had been a decline in the labour force participation rates both for males and females as compared to Census 1961. This decline was sharper in the case of females. However, it has been pointed out by some scholars that this is not so much due to a real decline but a change in the definition of workers. Yet generally the decline was evident. The explanations put forward for this decline included rapid increase of population, war with China and Pakistan, severe draughts, etc. The following table shows workers' participation rate by sex during the period 1901-1971:

TABLE 14.7

Workers Participation Rate by Sex, 1901-1971[1]

Year	*Male*	*Female*	*Total*
1901	61.11	31.70	46.61
1911	61.90	33.73	48.07
1921	60.52	32.67	46.92
1931	58.27	27.63	43.30
1951	54.05	23.30	39.10
1961	57.12	27.96	42.98
1971	52.50	11.85	32.92

The above table shows a clear decline in workers participation, part of which may be attributed to definitional-change. However, it was clearly established by a sample survey carried out in March 72 that 1961-1971 decade did not keep pace with the rate of population growth due to the two wars and the two severe draughts, which haulted the five year plan and adversely affected employment opportunities within the country.

Table 14.8

Population by Category of Workers 1991

(In crore)

	Rural	*Urban*	*Total*
1991 Census			
Total Population	63.13	21.53	83.66
Total workers[1]	24.93	6.56	31.49
Marginal workers[2]	2.77	0.17	2.95
Main workers	22.16	6.38	28.54
(*i*) Cultivators	10.74	0.32	11.06
(*ii*) Agricultural labourers	7.04	0.42	7.46
(*iii*) Household industry workers	0.68	0.36	1.04
(*iv*) Other workers	3.70	5.28	8.98

Notes : 1. The figures exclude Jammu and Kashmir where the 1991 census has not been held.

2. Figures may not tally due to rounding off.

1. *The Population of India*, CICRED Series, New Delhi: Office of the Registrar-General of India, 1974, p. 110.

QUESTIONS FOR EXERCISE

1. Define labour force. Explain the sources and analysis of labour force data.
2. Write an essay on labour force in India.

15

Unemployment in India

Defining unemployment, Karl Pribram has written that "Unemployment is a condition of the labour market in which the supply of labour is greater than the number of available openings."[1] According to Fairchild, "Unemployment is forced and involuntary separation from remunerative work on the part of the normal working force during normal working time, at normal wages and under normal conditions." Generally speaking, unemployment means the non-availability of work even though there is a desire to do it.

UNEMPLOYMENT IN INDIA

Any discussion on the labour force in a country involves reference to unemployment and underemployment. Since 1931 the Indian Census Operations have tried to enumerate unemployment in India. It should be pointed out here that in a vast country like India it is not possible to arrive at accurate estimates of unemployed and underemployed people. In 1931 Census the respondents were asked to provide data about employment through a separate schedule. However, in spite of several reminders very few respondents returned the forms and therefore the quantum of an employment could not be measured. A most systematic effort was made in 1941 Census. The respondents were asked two separate questions : 1. Are you in search of employment? 2. If yes, how long have you been in search of it? However, the collected data could not be tabulated due to war time budgetary cuts. In Ajmer,

1. Pribram, K., *Encyclopaedia of Social Sciences*, Vol. XV, p. 147.

Marwar, Gwalior, Hyderabad, Travancore and some other cities, tabulation of information on unemployment was made in terms of age and education of unemployed persons and the duration of unemployment. Similar tables were prepared for the provinces of Bombay, Bengal and Berar as well as the Central Provinces.

In 1951 Census, Census Superintendents were given the option to include an additional question on employment. However, incomplete and inadequate reporting was made and that too only in Uttar Pradesh, Mysore, Bombay, Saurashtra and Kutch. Thus, the attempt was not successful. In the 1961 Census two specific categories were provided for the classification of non-workers: 1. Not employed before but seeking employment for the first time; 2. Employed before but now out of employment and seeking employment. The number of unemployed persons enumerated was added to the number of workers to obtain the number of persons in the labour force. Then, labour force participation rate was computed according to the Census data. This analysis was fraught with two problems. Firstly, the reference period was very wide and secondly, the term seeking work was not defined. Therefore, the quantum of unemployment was underestimated. The counting was absolutely low. Since then several surveys have been conducted to measure the quantum of unemployment in the country. The scope of these surveys however has been generally very limited. The National Sample Survey has attempted to estimate the quantum of unemployment in successive round. The seventeenth round was made in 1961-62. Similar attempts have been made by the Planning Commission.

The Second Five Year Plan recorded the first official estimate of the quantum of unemployment in India. Estimates of the backlog of the unemployed were obtained by comparing the additions to the labour force during the plan period of Third Plan and Fourth Plan. By examination of these estimates it was concluded by Dantwala Commission that the estimates of Planning Commission were inaccurate. It was pointed out that the unemployment situation in rural areas was not properly estimated. The Committee of Experts on unemployment estimates recommended attempts to measure the number of the unemployed by different segments of the labour force. It asked Planning Commission to give up such efforts. Therefore, Committee on unemployment known as Bhagwati Committee was appointed to assess the number of unemployed and underemployed and to suggest remedies. The following table depicts the preliminary estimates concerning employment and underemployment for 1970 prepared on the basis of data collected by Bhagwati Committee.

TABLE 15.1

Unemployment and Underemployment in India, 1970

(In millions)

Employ-ment	*Total*	*Male*	*Female*	*Unem-ployment*	*Total*	*Male*	*Female*
Rural	7.7	3.2	4.5	Rural	23.5	12.2	11.3
Urban	1.3	0.8	0.5	Urban	3.4	1.8	1.6
Total	9.0	4.0	5.0	Total	26.9	14.0	12.9

Following the recommendation of the Expert Committee on Unemployment estimates, a multi-dimensional approach was adopted by National Sample Survey in the 27th round. During the 1971 Census, a special card was issued to the Graduates and the holders of technical diplomas and certificates. These special cards were sent to about 3.5 million Graduates and Post-graduates, Of these, only 2.2 millions returned it duly filled in. The following table shows the percentage of unemployed graduates and post-graduates in 1971, computed on the basis of the above partially acquired data:

Table 15.2

Percentage of Unemployed Graduates and Post-Graduates, 1971[1]

Subject	*Graduates*	*Post-graduates*
Agriculture	13.3	7.3
Veterinary Science	6.7	1.5
Medicine	5.3	2.0
Engineering and Technology	11.5	4.6
Science (other than above)	19.2	10.1
Arts	15.1	10.4
Commerce	16.4	7.1

The eleventh and twelfth rounds of National Sample Survey disclosed that the incidence of unemployment in rural areas among male agricultural labour was four times than of the other rural males. Among the female agricultural workers it

1. *Technical Manpower Bulletin*, New Delhi: Council of Scientific and Industrial Research, April 1972, p. 21.

was as much as seven times of that of the other females. Thus, agricultural labourers are the worst victims of unemployment and underemployment in India. Similar is the position of landless labourers. They have no protection against economic crisis. Again, in rural areas the incidence of unemployment of the educated is higher as compared to the urban areas. The rural residence has also been a handicap since urban residence and long period is required for searching a job. Besides unemployment, underemployment is very much visible among the above mentioned classes in rural areas. In fact agricultural sector in India suffers from surplus labour. In the urban areas the trend of increasing educated unemployment and underemployment is on the increase as is clear by the following data in mid-1981.

UNEMPLOYMENT IN MID-1981

The number of job-seekers in the country, whose names are there on the live register of employment exchanges, increased by more than one-and-a-half lakhs during the first five months of 1981, from 1.62 crores on January 1 to over 1.63 crores on June 1, according to figures furnished by the Labour Ministry.

The comparative figure at the beginning of last year was 1.43 crores.

Among the 22 States and nine Union Territories, West Bengal leads with more than 26 lakh unemployed, followed by Bihar with 21 lakh.

Nagaland has the least number of 5,500 unemployed.

The figures for other states (in thousands) are: Andhra Pradesh (1,479.6), Uttar Pradesh (1,427.1), Kerala (1,362.3), Maharashtra (1,284.9), Tamil Nadu (1,156.5), Madhya Pradesh (884.1), Karnataka (620.1), Gujarat (494.4), Punjab (475.7), Orissa (460.3), Haryana (371.4), Rajasthan (367.7), Assam (324.7), Himachal Pradesh (151.7), Manipur (114.3). Tripura (71.4), Jammu and Kashmir (50.8) and Meghalaya (10.2).

Among the territories, Delhi has the largest number of registered unemployed — more than 29 lakhs.

It is followed by Chandigarh with (in thousands) (64.9), Pondicherry (39.3), Goa (32.3), Mizoram (14.8), Andaman and Nicobar Islands (10.1) and Lakshadweep (4.4).

The number of graduate and post-graduate registered job seekers at the beginning of this year was 13.89 lakh and 1.34 lakh respectively.

Among the graduates, people in the arts group are the largest (6,76,000), followed by those in science (3,10,700), commerce (2,19,100), engineering (2,25,000), medicine (14,800), agriculture (11,400) and law (4,800).

Both graduate and post-graduate job-seekers with employment exchanges are going up since 1978. Graduate registered unemployed went up from 10.74 lakh in 1978 to 12.08 lakh in 1979 and to 13.01 lakh in 1979.

UNEMPLOYMENT IN 1991

Number of Job Seekers

Number of job-seekers on the live registers of employment exchanges increased from 178.38 lakh as on 31 December 1981 to 363 lakh on 31 December 1991. Table 15.3 gives registrations, vacancies, placements and job-seekers on the 'live register' for the period 1981-1990.

National Sample Survey Organisation

National Sample Survey (NSS) was set up in 1950 with a programme of conducting large-scale surveys to provide data for estimation of national income and related aggregates especially relating to unorganised sector of the economy and for planning and policy formulation. Today, it is a major fact-finding body and occupies a unique position in the nation's statistical system. It carries out annually socio-economic surveys covering various facets of population. It also undertakes field work of annual Survey of Industries and carries out sample checks of area and yield of crops to improve quality of estimation of agricultural production prepared by the states, besides updating the urban framework for selection of samples in urban area. Its personnel strength is now about 6,000 in 170 offices is spread over throughout the country.

It was reorganised in 1970 by bringing together all aspects of survey work into a single unified agency known as National Sample Survey Organisation (NSSO) under the Department of Statistics. The activities of NSSO are guided by a Governing Council with requisite independence and autonomy in the matter of collection, processing and publication of data. Besides the Chairman, the Council comprises five academicians, six data users in the Central ministries and state governments and six functionaries of the Department of Statistics. It is headed by the Chief Executive Officer, who is also the member-secretary of the Council. NSSO has four functional divisions, namely: (*i*) Survey Design and Research Division, (*ii*) Field Operations Division, (*iii*) Data Processing Division, and (*iv*) Co-ordination and Publication Division. Each division is under the charge of a Director.

Table 15.3

Activities of Employment Exchanges

Year	*Exchange (including UEIGBX)*	*Registrations (Thousand)*	*Applicants Placed in (Thousand)*	*Applicants on the Live Register (End of the Year) (Thousand)*	*Vacancies Notified (Thousand)*
1956	143	1,670.0	189.9	756.5	296.0
1971	437	5,129.9	507.0	5,099.9	813.6
1976	517	5,619.4	496.8	9,784.3	815.6
1981	663	6,276.9	504.1	17,836.1	896.8
1982	692	5,862.9	473.4	19,753.0	819.9
1983	726	6,755.8	485.9	21,953.3	826.0
1984	745	6,219.0	407.3	23,546.8	707.8
1985	800	5,821.5	388.5	26,269.9	674.7
1986	821	5,535.4	351.3	30,131.2	623.4
1987	835	6,011.7	334.4	30,247.3	600.9
1988	840	5,963.2	328.5	30,050.2	543.3
1989	849	6,575.8	289.2	32,776.2	600.2
1990	851	6,540.6	264.5	34,631.8	490.9
1991	854	6,235.9	253.0	36,299.7	458.6
1992	860	5,300.6	238.7	36,758.4	419.6
1993	887	5,532.2	231.4	36,275.5	384,7
1994	891	5,927.3	204.9	36,691.5	396.4

The subject coverage of the socio-economic surveys conforms to a well-defined cycle of the surveys extending over a period of ten years. Survey on consumer expenditure, employment and unemployment, manufacturing establishments and enterprises and trading establishments and enterprises in the unorganised sector are to be repeated once in five years, while subjects like land-holdings, livestock holdings, debt and investment are to be

Table 15.4
Employment in the Public Sector by Industry

(Lakh Persons as on 31 March 1996)

	1981	1983	1984	1985	1986	1987	1988	1989	1990	1991	1992
1	2	3	4	5	6	7	8	9	10	11	12
A. By branch											
1. Central Government	31.95	32.66	33.11	33.29	33.46	33.50	33.81	33.95	33.97	34.10	34.28
2. State Governments	56.76	60.38	61.54	62.80	64.73	66.66	67.81	68.29	69.79	71.12	71.90
3. Quasi-Governments	45.76	50.40	52.74	54.96	56.74	57.95	59.48	59.99	61.73	62.22	63.93
4. Local bodies	20.37	21.11	21.30	21.64	21.90	22.14	22.11	22.38	22.23	23.13	21.98
Total	154.84	164.55	168.69	172.69	176.83	180.25	183.21	184.44	187.72	190.57	192.10
B. By industry											
0. Agriculture, hunting etc.	4.63	4.76	4.89	4.98	5.26	5.57	5.54	5.55	5.49	5.56	5.73
1. Mining and quarrying	8.18	8.84	9.27	9.74	9.66	9.42	9.56	9.56	9.66	9.99	9.87
2. & 3. Manufacturing	15.02	16.34	17.17	17.61	18.15	18.62	18.67	18.63	18.70	18.52	18.61
4. Electricity, gas and water	6.83	7.21	7.33	7.60	7.85	7.89	8.49	8.69	8.97	9.05	9.16
5. Construction	10.89	11.20	11.20	11.46	11.81	11.85	12.14	11.46	11.34	11.49	11.51
6. Wholesale and retail trade	1.17	1.18	1.24	1.31	1.31	1.34	1.39	1.50	1.50	1.50	1.57
7. Transport, storage & communications	27.09	28.26	28.64	28.94	29.29	29.70	30.11	29.74	30.23	30.26	30.64
8. Finance, insurance, real estate etc.	7.48	8.72	9.14	9.83	10.30	10.56	10.95	11.23	11.54	11.94	12.14
9. Community, social & personal services	73.55	78.06	79.81	81.23	83.21	85.29	86.35	88.11	90.19	92.27	92.87
Total	154.84	164.57	168.69	172.70	176.84	180.24	183.20	184.47	187.62	190.58	192.10

Note : Totals in A and B differ due to rounding off.

Source: Ministry of Labour.

Table 15.5

Employment in the Private Sector by Industry

(Lakh persons as on March 31, 1996)

1981	1983	1984	1985	1986	1987	1988	1989	1990	1991	1992	
1	2	3	4	5	6	7	8	9	10	11	12
0. Agriculture, hunting etc.	8.58	8.47	8.19	8.07	8.22	8.48	8.44	8.68	8.76	8.91	9.12
1. Mining and quarrying	1.30	1.20	1.13	1.13	1.11	0.91	0.93	0.96	0.99	1.00	1.07
2. & 3. Manufacturing	45.45	46.56	44.73	44.21	44.48	44.10	43.95	43.83	44.57	44.81	45.66
4. Electricity, gas and water	0.35	0.37	0.39	0.39	0.40	0.40	0.41	0.39	0.40	0.40	0.40
5. Construction	0.72	0.68	0.66	0.70	0.69	0.58	0.50	0.69	0.68	0.73	0.78
6. Wholesale and retail trade	2.77	2.75	2.76	2.77	2.77	2.77	2.83	2.86	2.91	3.00	2.96
7. Transport, storage & communications	0.60	0.59	0.57	0.54	0.54	0.52	0.51	0.51	0.52	0.53	0.54
8. Finance, insurance, real estate etc.	1.96	2.07	2.14	2.19	2.21	2.29	2.38	2.34	2.39	2.54	2.66
9. Community, social & personal services	12.22	12.83	12.89	13.09	13.32	13.59	13.97	14.29	14.60	14.85	15.27
Total	73.95	75.52	73.46	73.09	73.74	73.64	73.92	74.53	75.82	76.77	78.46

Relates to non-agricultural establishments in the private sector employing 10 or more persons.

Note: Coverage in construction, particularly on private account, is known to be inadequate.

Source: Ministry of Labour.

covered once in ten years. Thus, out of a cycle of ten years, per-assigned subject are allotted for seven years while there years are kept as 'open rounds' (two full-year round and two half-year rounds) to cover special topics of current interest to meet the demand of data users. Integrated with the main topics of a round, annual survey on consumer expenditure was reintroduced from 42nd round (July 1986 — June 1987) with a relatively smaller size of one-fifth of the usual quinquennial round during the intervening period between two quinquennial rounds on the subject. From 45th round (July 1989 — June 1990) it was decided to extend the scope of annual survey to cover employment-unemployment as well.

Table 15.6

Estimates of Employment in Organised Public and Private Sectors

(Lakh persons as on 31 March, 1996)

Year	*Public Sector*			*Private Sector*			*Public and Private Sectors (Total)*		
	Male	*Female*	*Total*	*Male*	*Female*	*Total*	*Male*	*Female*	*Total*
1990	165.22	22.50	187.72	61.88	13.94	75.82	227.09	36.44	263.5
1991	167.10	23.47	190.57	62.42	14.34	76.76	229.52	37.81	267.5
1992	167.81	24.29	192.10	63.67	14.79	78.46	231.48	39.08	270.56
1993	169.01	24.86	193.87	62.80	15.51	78.31	231.81	40.37	272.18

* Quick estimates.

Notes : (*i*) Includes all establishments in the Public Sector irrespective of size of employment and non-agricultural establishments in the Private Sector employing 10 or more persons.

(*ii*) Excludes Sikkim, Arunachal Pradesh, Dadra & Nagar Haveli and Lakshadweep as these are not yet covered under the programme.

Source: Ministry of Labour, DGE&T.

QUESTIONS FOR EXERCISE

1. Discuss the problem of industrial unemployment in India. Suggest remedies.
2. Describe various differentials of Industrial workers in India.

16

Population Problems

On the assumption of a round figure of 6,000 million as the world's population and an inhabited land area of 135.16 square kilometres, India accounts for about 2.4 per cent of the world's land area and 14.6 per cent of its population. In terms of population, India occupies the second place among nations of the world, the People's Republic of China estimated to have 1,000 million population, being the first. But if one were thinking of the Indian sub-continent comprising India and Pakistan, its population would be more than that of China, while in respect of persons per unit of area, this sub-continent would be quite as densely populated as any other comparable area in the world. Along with the People's Republic of China, this may be regarded as holding the key to the world's demographic growth.

In his book *India At the Time of Akban* W.H. Moreland put the population of this sub-continent at 100 million at the time of Akbar's death. On the strength of this estimate, the population of India, as she is now constituted, would have been about 92 million around the year 1600. In the course of three centuries, these 92 million increased by a little over two and a half times to 238.4 million in 1901. This must appear a very slow rate indeed compared to the fact of India's more than doubling her population in 50 years with a base as large as 252 million in 1921. Although this does no more than conform to the general world trend in the current century, the absolute magnitude of India's population and the size of her annual population growth in the context of her social and economic situation and her rate of economic growth, present a great multitude of problems.

The Great Divide

The year 1921 has been aptly called the Great Divide which left behind the era of extensive famines and epidemics. The three decades beginning with 1921 registered slowly increasing growth rates, caused possibly more by assured food supplies than by any rapid improvement in public health and medical services, although the government, during this period developed, an efficient machinery for quickly containing and quenching epidemics. An extended network of communications facilitated accumulation of reserves of food at strategic points and assured their effective distribution at short notice. This and international collaboration reduced the threat of famines and minimised rigours of the Bengal and Madras famines of 1943 and the Rayalaseema situation in 1946-47.

Recurrent famines, epidemics and pandemic malaria had carved up the country as it were between themselves in two distinct regions. A malaria map of India, reproduced in the All-India Census Report for 1941, came as a shock to those to whom the era of famines and malaria is already a fading memory. It described the whole of North and Central India together with the thick spine of the Deccan plateau down to the northern tip of Tiruchirapalli as subject to recurrent famines, while whatever was left east of this tract, from the eastern-most point to the extreme west and from the northern-most point to the extreme south, was shown in the grip of an endemic scourge. What was more, the tracts of recurrent malaria were almost contiguous to those of recurrent famines and epidemics like plague and small-pox and experienced recurrent crisis in population growth between 1881 and 1931. It is no accident that it is roughly this tract, formerly ravaged by both epidemic and scarcity, with recurrent bursts of famine, that has shown the highest reaches of increase in 1951-1961 (21 to 30 per cent), for already in 1941-1961 it had shown a growth rate approaching 2 per cent per year. A much lower rate of growth (up to 20 per cent) is noticeable in the central and eastern tracts, the northern irrigation and the southern coastal belts, formerly in the endemic malaria and cholera zones of varying intensity and therefore subject to spates of recurrent crisis, relative stagnation or variable increase between 1881 and 1931. It is possible that this latter area will attain still higher rates of growth before showing a decline. It will be recalled that the census count in 1961 surpassed even the most generous of expectations, having exceeded by more than 8 million the highest estimate ever made before the census.

International migration being negligible and natural fertility still having its way, the birth rate has remained fairly constant over the decades subject only to second order effects of mortality changes on the sex-age composition of the population. The growth of India's population has thus been determined almost solely by variations in mortality, while fertility has remained uncontrolled. While the birth rate has always been a little over 40 the death rate has declined from 47 to 21 per thousand between 1921 and 1961. Infant death rate has declined very considerably during recent years, although the level is still high. According to the 14th Round of the National Sample Survey, infant death rate was 153 per 1,000 live births for males and 138 for females, giving an average of 146 for both sexes. Deaths during the first month of life form about 45 per cent of the total infant deaths, of which 25 per cent occur under one week. The remaining infant deaths are divided about equally between the periods 1-6 months and 6-12 months. Deaths in infancy are mostly accountable to exposure (broncho-pneumonia), malnutrition and weaning diarrhoea, infections and parasitic diseases, as well as such congenital causes as immaturity, birth injuries and malformation.

High Bereavement Rate

Arthur Geddes held everybody under a debt by looking at infant deaths and mortality at higher ages in supremely human terms as bereavement rate. He was closer to the secret of India's unchanging and high fertility than any other demographer when he observed that "a map of regional types thus constitutes a map of essentially differing or contrasted impact upon the heart and mind, upon the social and personal 'psychology' of given population groups. To map the areas of differing human impact thus forms a first and vital step in exploring the changing, fluctuating social psychology of a people. The next step is to discover the actual response, the psychological-reaction to the impact of experience."

It is possible that this high bereavement rate is responsible, on the social and psychological as well as on the personal and human level, for an average of more than 6 children still being born alive per woman of unbroken marriage during the reproductive age. This fear of loss may be responsible for a psychological recklessness to which the compulsions of ensuring a minimal supply of family labour during the peaks of agricultural operations lend a special edge. When to this are added the starkness of the rural scene and the attendant apathy and fatalism that has prevailed for so long, the natural desire to look up to sons for support in old age, the scarcity of wage employment for women and the lack of old age pensions and social security or insurance benefits, one appreciates why the age specific fertility rates for currently married women should rule a high plateau between 230 and 260 in the age span 20-30, or the fertility rate should still be as high as 173.6 for all ages.

Two Opposite Sets of Effects

An accelerating expectation of life at birth in a situation of uncontrolled fertility leads to two opposite sets of social and economic effects. To take the darker side first, it has made for large accretions in the younger dependency age group of 0-14 because one of the important results of an increase in life expectancy is a decrease in the infant death rates and deaths at young ages. It has also made for greater savings of life at old ages beyond 60. Either way, it has resulted in increasing the dependency load on working adults in the age group 15-59. The first effect of a rising expectation of life therefore has been not only an increase in the dependency load on the adult working male or female in the family but increased national allocations over a whole area which achieve no immediate gain in economic growth, *viz.*, child and maternity care, public health, hospital and maternity amenities, primary and secondary education and therefore on educational housing, teachers and teachers' training, over food and other consumer goods, often necessitating imports and frittering away of valuable credit or foreign exchange. This could be done in India only by diverting scarce resources from sectors of savings and economic growth to sectors of consumption. To this extent the nation is certainly deprived and called upon to make greater sacrifices of future goals to the immediate problem of living. On the other hand a rising expectation of life has brought in lasting economic and social gains. A longer life has introduced stability in economic climate, favoured augmentation of human skills, productivity per worker, technical know-how, longer and larger returns from educational investments, particularly scientific and technological, and greater savings and continuity of economic effort in national life. It has made for greater real assets, both human and material, and has been responsible for far-reaching schemes of social and health security, old age, accident and premature death pensions, rapid expansion of individual life insurance and other safeguards all in the space of the last decade. The reduction of maternal and general mortality has made for greater employment of women in the wage sector, and extension and continuity of individual economic enterprise.

Need for Family Limitation

All this might have brought in much richer harvests had it been attended by a rapidly declining fertility thereby reducing dependency and much avoidable "infructuous" expenditure both on the national and the individual plane. Indeed such a realisation, however instinctive or inchoate, has given family limitation, to judge by the results of recent surveys, universal currency in recent years as a desirable personal and national goal. Regardless of whether the State accepts family limitation as being at the very centre of all national planning, which indeed is what our Government has done, it is the millions of individual decisions taken in the context of millions of individual family plans and aspirations that will determine the success of the movement and yet preserve human dignity and the supremacy of flexible individual choice, so valuable in a working democracy.

The introduction of insurance, securities, old age pensions, annuities and medical amenities among the salaried, business and professional classes has paved the way, in recent decades, for small families in these social groups. The widening of the organised industrial base and the increasing employment of women in the manual and white-collar wage sectors have served to moderate the desire for more children not only because pregnancy interferes with earnings and continuity of service but because an improving survival rate affords greater satisfaction in parenthood by reducing the bereavement rate. Nothing stimulates the desire for family limitation more than the prospect of a fuller and richer life in which the individual more and more comes into his own.

Ever since Japan entered the modern industrial age in a big way, her birth rate has responded fairly closely to the ups and downs of business cycles. Deliberate family limitation became part of Japan's life as early as 1920. It is not a product, as is often wrongly imagined, of post-World War II. The McArthur regime introduced unprecedented measures of democracy in Japan: the demolition of the cult of the Emperor, the land reforms, the breaking of trusts, reforms of inheritance and personal laws, franchise and elections, equality of the sexes, economic emancipation of women. These instruments of change, apart from the baby boom which may be expected after any war in which a nation has been deeply involved, were an invitation to rapid population growth. Japan's answer to this threat was a change in the eugenics law which legalised abortion. But what is significant is that abortions are on the wane since 1956. There was growing awareness that drastic methods may boomerang, that, however attractive on the short run, they make for unstable internal class relationships, may even generate psychosis and jeopardise a nation's strength in the event of a war. The usual humane methods consistent with human dignity and individual preference now prevail.

Population Distribution

Even as there are areas of high density where a greater proportion of the population is concentrated in a comparatively small proportion of area, the distribution of population generally conforms to natural features. It is usual to divide India into 7 natural regions: the Himalayan, the Northern Plains, the Central Indian Hills and Plateaus, the Peninsular Hills and Plateaus, the West Coast, the East Coast and the Islands.

The region of lowest density is the Himalayan. The Northern Plains region has always been the most populous. The region of highest density, excepting for Kerala, is still the Indus Jamna-Ganga Doabs and the West Bengal basin. Stemming from the narrow strip of Gurdaspur, Amritsar, Jullundur and Ludhiana in the north-west, the broad belt of Uttar Pradesh merges with North Bihar and finally with West Bengal, the density in the entire region being seldom below 500 per square mile and often above 1,000 in spacious bands astride the river.

The Central and Deccan Hills and Plateaus, delineated by Mohindergarh (Punjab) in the north to the Nilgiris (Madras) in the south, Santal Parganas in the east and the Arabian sea in the west, are well under a density of 500 in the entire territory, except for the districts of Ahmedabad, Kaira, Baroda and Surat in Gujarat, Greater Bombay and Kolhapur in Maharashtra,

Hyderabad, Guntur, Krishna, West Godavari and Srikakulam in Andhra Pradesh and Bangalore in Mysore. Within this territory again, there are three large continuous areas with still lower density (all below 200 per square mile), that may be described as the western desert and lowlands, the Madhya Pradesh teak and scrub forests and southeastern hills and upland forests. The first consists of the desert districts of Rajasthan bounded by Ganganagar in the north, Sirohi in the south, Nagaur in the east and Jaisalmer in the west and the lowland districts of Kutch and Surendranagar of Gujarat. The second and central area starts with Tonk of Rajasthan in the north-west and embracing Chitorgarh, Bundi and Kota of Rajasthan stretches across the northern, central and eastern districts of Madhya Pradesh. The third area straddles four States and covers Adilabad (Andhra Pradesh), Chanda (Maharashtra), Bastar (Madhya Pradesh) and Koraput, Kalahandi and Baudhkhondmals (Orissa).

The West and East Coasts again are tracts of high density, the peaks being reached around Bombay-Thana, in Kerala, along Thanjavur, Chingleput and Madras and again in Krishna and the East and West Godavari districts.

The Himalayan region contains a little over 3 per cent of India's population in less than 14 per cent of India's -area, the Northern Plain region just under 37 per cent of population in just over 22 per cent of India's area, the Central and Peninsular Hills and Plateaus — the great heartland of India — contain a little over 19 per cent of population in a little over 27 per cent of India's area, the Deccan Hills and Plateaus a little under one-fifth of India's population in just under 22 per cent of India's area, the West and East Coast hold 11.2 per cent and 9.7 per cent of population respectively in a little under 13.5 per cent of India's area each.

Urban Growth

To one who follows the above account it will come as no surprise that the greatest absolute concentrations of urban population occur in the Gujarat (Cambay plain surrounded by Kathiawar and Gujarat uplands); a long and broad band surrounded by another wide band of lower concentration encasing the Tapti from Nagpur in the east to the Gujarat coast; in the triangle formed by Nasik, Bombay and Gujarat; the Krishna valley of Maharashtra continued into the entire stretch of Mysore's Malnad, extending in lesser concentrations to the. Maidan and the Hyderabad core, and except for brief gaps in the West Coast to the whole of the West and East Coastal belts, including the whole of Madras joining up with Bangalore through the Hosur Gap; and the southern half of West Bengal which proceeds in a diagonal band up the club handle of Burdwan district to Dhanbad and Hazaribagh of Bihar. There is again the solid quadrangular tract embracing north-western Uttar Pradesh and almost the whole of Punjab. There are tracts of secondary but often heavy concentration as in the desert and uplands of Rajasthan; the Malwa, traditionally the great passage-way between the capital and the western seaboard in Cambay; the Narmada-Tapti Doab, traditionally the great internal frontier of India, the homeland of cotton and an important exchange tract between the north and the south; and the great Deccan tract which has grown rich on kingdoms and cotton. Finally, there are the isolated tracts of modern urban growth like Singhbhum, Sundargarh, Durg, Bhopal, Gwalior or Jabalpur.

This again provides the clue to the historic aspect of India's urban growth. As may well be guessed, a large number of towns would still be exalted villages in which the landed gentry would build up their own elite, seek their own company and urban amenities, consolidate their leadership and ensure the advancement of their progeny. A second and large group of towns would be large agricultural and contact marts, engaged in recent years in proliferating into small and medium organised industrial activity. These two groups would very naturally dominate the heartland of India, even encroaching on the large, navigable, continental rivers. A third group would consist of trade and commerce and mercantile towns which would again very naturally concentrate on the West and East Coasts and the prosperous valleys and estuaries of the large rivers. With this group will naturally go a section of the service and administrative towns on account of the opportunities of cultural contact that the mercantile and trading centres afford and the thickening of administrative activity that these tracts demand, but it will be readily conceded that this category of service and administrative towns will have the best distribution throughout the country. A fourth group would consist of the great metropolitan areas, some of which are bound to be at strategic points conveniently spaced on the coast and some others at the meeting ways of trans-continental trunk communications, such as Delhi, Hyderabad and Bangalore. The fifth group would be centres of industrial activity,' either resource located or conditioned by the economies of power, transport and communication, or allocated on considerations of national, regional or local importance and proximity either to raw material, power, communication or markets.

Although the urban population has been growing rather rapidly but in view of its small proportion to the total population it makes no effective impression on the demographic or socio-economic situation of the country as a whole. The functional classification of India's towns also suggests why the rate of urban growth should still be modest and why the urban pull of migration from the rural areas should still be weak. According to European and American experience and even that of Japan it is manufacturing that exercises the strongest, most persistent urban pull Besides, manufacturing alone is capable of a rapidly multiplying universe. In India the number of manufacturing cities and towns is still small compared to urban areas with other predominant functions which cannot fail to weaken the urban pull. An analysis of growth rates over the decades shows that the growth rate of manufacturing towns is slightly higher as a whole than that of any other category, but only slightly, and no functional category of town can claim regional prominence in the matter of growth rates. In other words, no matter what predominant function they fulfil, towns which are on power, road and railways arteries appear to show a higher rate of growth than those which are not, suggesting thereby that manufacturing activity may be making itself felt, however weakly, through the incrustation of other functions.

The main trend of the increase seems to be that big cities are becoming bigger owing to immigration thus disputing, while making more than full use of, the opportunities of maximisation of investment and resources offered by large cities. This concentration and congestion of urban population in a few cities brings about a peculiar type of closed circuit migration from urban to urban and certain other kinds of turnover migration between rural and urban areas, apart from impeding flow of rural to urban migration to lesser cities and towns, which ought to expand at a much more rapid rate. The performance of twelve cities, Greater Bombay, Calcutta, Delhi, Madras, Ahmedabad, Hyderabad, Bangalore, Kanpur, Nagpur, Pune, Lucknow and Howrah, clearly brings out the greater attraction of migrants to this class of towns probably on account of better amenities and scope for business, trade and service.

Towns — Urbanised Villages

But although a little more than 57 per cent of India's urban population lives in towns of more than 50,000 each, the fact remains that many of the small towns are not much more than urbanised villages particularly in social and economic organisation and outlook, which affect the demographic trends. The characteristic urban outlook and mode of living, which is associated with the word urban in Western countries may obtain in some measure in the cities with a population over 1 million but not to any great degree in other towns. Even in respect of literacy, the cities stand out far apart from the non-city urban and rural areas.

It may be worthwhile to run over briefly the broad areas in which rural-urban differences in social and economic organisation and outlook exist and those in which they are less evident. Differences exist in the field of literacy and the differences widen in higher levels of education. In marital status, the proportion of never married is distinctly higher in urban than rural areas, the complementary rate of married being lower in urban than rural areas, but the numerical smallness of the differences between rural and urban proportions still suggests an essential homogeneity in the social outlook of the population in the matter of marriage although the age distribution of married persons in rural and urban areas shows that the practice of marrying late is gaining ground in towns.

A Major Difference

A major rural-urban difference is still to be found in the low urban proportions of females per 1,000 males and difference in age distribution between the sexes. The low ratio implies an unstable, migratory population, a substantial amount of single households, congestion in housing and concentration of male population of working age. An analysis of household composition data in advanced industrial districts revealed that while married sons are as a rule appreciably fewer in urban than in rural areas, as a reflection of the urban mentality, it is curious that other married male relations which may mean fathers, uncles, brothers and so on are often proportionately more numerous in urban than rural areas. This indeed is evidence of how little 'living together' or the joint family has weakened even in the cities of advanced industrial districts. It is also evidence of the load of dependency in urban areas which weakens the motivation for advancement and status seeking.

Fertility Pattern

In the matter of birth and death rates in urban areas several conclusions seem to emerge. First, that neo-natal death rates are still very high even in such cities as Bombay, Calcutta, Madras and even Delhi suggesting thereby that although these cities have about the best provision in the country for sanitation, care and treatment of infants, they also have slum areas with conditions favourable for a high infant rate. Secondly, there was still no evidence of any reduction in the fertility level in towns each with population of 1 lakh and over. If at all, there was a slightly upward change. Even the million plus cities showed average characteristic of high fertility levels. Bombay alone presented a picture appreciably below the level of the high fertility group, but it was still higher than the level of Western countries of low fertility. Even the New Delhi levels were well above those of Bombay. In short, the averages for the six million plus cities showed that excepting for Bombay the fertility pattern of fecund women was not much different from those of other towns having less population. Essentially family growth conformed to a high fertility pattern.

Migration

An analysis of migration statistics even for avowedly industrial districts confirmed that migration from outside the State is still negligible except in Assam, West Bengal, Delhi and the industrial areas of Bombay, Thana and Ahmedabad. Except for technically qualified personnel in industrial locations, inter-State migration still plays no major role in the greater part of India. Secondly, migration into most of these urban areas tends to be evenly distributed between short and long term.

Further analysis of migration data by duration of residence is apt to upset many notions based on the experience of urbanisation in the Western world, where nothing like the Indian volume of floating or rapid turnover migration in towns has been in evidence. By floating or rapid turnover migration is meant a situation where the volume of population migrating out of a city in a given period is comparable to the volume migrating into it and either exceeds or approximates the decadal increase in population composed of net immigration and natural increase. Such a situation obviously obtains in such high industrialised areas as Greater Bombay, Calcutta, Madras, Hyderabad, Thana, Poona, Hooghly and Rampur. Places like Delhi, Kanpur and Ahmedabad are not very far behind. The top industrial layer of urban India is, therefore, very much in this process, thereby exposing the precariousness, vulnerability and instability of industrial skill, experience, knowledge and human worth in the principal metropolitan centres of the country. The statistics also underline the lack of a true industrial proletariat who have staked their lives in the city and severed their roots in the village. It is only in the urban areas of districts like Bangalore, Ludhiana, Vadodra, Coimbatore, Chingleput, Singhbhum, Burdwan, Howrah, 24-Parganas, Sehore and others where we seem to have a stable and numerous resident population whose progeny also continue to live in the self-same town and where the rate of natural increase can be distinguished from and is comparable to the proportion of decadal immigration.

Immigration

The differential rates of in-migration by rural and urban origin at once suggest that areas which import more mill hands than white collar workers have more or rapid turnover of immigrants of rural origin, notably Greater Bombay, Calcutta, Madras, Kanpur, Ahmedabad, Hyderabad, Singhbhum, Dhanbad, Burdwan, Howrah, Hooghly, 24-Parganas, Gorakhpur, Lakhimpur, Kamrup or Ranchi. The high proportion of immigrants of urban origin in places like Delhi, Madras, Hyderabad, Bangalore, Vadodara, Chingleput, etc. seems to accord with the general experience of expansion of non-factory, trade, transport, communication and service establishments and also of manufacturing concerns requiring high technical skill like factories turning out precision products and chemicals. The districts like Bangalore, Thana, Poona, Chingleput, Sehore and Gwalior are illustrations of the proportion of immigrants of urban exceeding that of rural origin.

The circulating migration of urban population from town to town leads to several conclusions. The absolute volume of this type of-circulating temporary migration of urban population and its proportion to rural born immigrants being quite high, it is obvious that this population will offer substantial resistance to the stream of migration from rural to urban areas, reducing eventually both its volume and velocity. The natural increase among the resident and migrating urban born population will reap obvious advantages over rural born immigrants in point of education, outlook, aptitude, technical skill and even urban housing and will tend to push back incursions into urban livelihoods by rural migrants. Thirdly, the extent of circulating urban migration suggests that a fair proportion of the total pool of urban population has to keep continuously on the move in search of opportunity and better employment. This means that the home towns themselves offer only limited openings for advancement, and what is available elsewhere must be disputed by those who are already in other towns and, therefore, comparatively out of reach of rural born competitors. All this may have the effect of rolling back still more resolutely the stream of rural migrants into urban areas.

Technical Competence

It is not often realised that in urban areas, of even reputedly highly industrialised districts, the proportion of persons with any kind of certified vocational or technical training is often much lower than for urban India as a whole. The bulk of the factory operations in them are without any approved technical training or academic competence, which means that the old established industrial areas rely more on practical job experience of a mechanical nature than on intellectual and technological competence so vital for higher levels of growth. In the matter of non-technical diplomas, non-technical university degrees, the all-India average is often higher than what one finds in the so-called highly industrialised districts, suggesting the possibility in the current decade of a greater flow from other urban areas to industrial districts of trained operatives and white collar workers in managerial and executive jobs. Even in the matter of technical diplomas and degrees in specialised fields, it is surprising how few districts are anywhere near double the value of the all-India averages, that important industrial areas like Calcutta, Madras, Bangalore, Poona and Dhanbad should be so close to the Indian average, or that districts like Kanpur, Ajmer, Coimbatore, Chingleput, Howrah, 24-Parganas, etc. should be around half or less than half the all-India average. Again, except for the metropolitan city districts, the urban areas of even highly industrial districts enjoy no more than tenuous superiority over non-industrial districts in offering educational facilities to students. At the same time the high proportion of unemployment among persons holding technical degrees in districts like Bombay, Delhi, Hyderabad, Bangalore, Ludhiana, Thana, Pune, Vadodara, or Emakulam is also a sign of the constraints prevailing in the employment market of even those districts and cities which we usually associate with industrial progress.

In working for rural-urban differences one cannot fail to, be struck by the weak and in some cases tenuous differences that even highly industrialised districts possess from what is shared in the State or even all-India level. It would hardly be an exaggeration to say that none of them, except for Greater Bombay and Calcutta, and in, odd cases, Delhi, betray any significant departure from the pattern obtaining for the State as a whole. Even the rural urban differentials are weak in the majority of cases, except for sex-ratio and age-sex composition.

Nature of Urbanisation

This brings us to the question of the nature of urbanisation in India. The census data may come as a shock to those who would like to believe in wide rural-urban differences or who would imagine that the ordering of life in urban India was very different from that in the rural areas. Common labels or names have a way of hiding genuine differences and nothing can be more misleading than to think that urban in India is the same as in Europe or Asia. It is important to appreciate the widely different historic contexts of the growth of urban area in the West and India. There is little correspondence even between the India of today and the Europe of the pre-industrial Revolution era for even in the latter the towns were in chronic short supply of labour, while the population base was much too small to present a threat of surplus or difficulty of transfer from agriculture to non-agriculture. Any analogy with the USA has to be ruled out at the start. What happened in Europe in the second-half of the eighteenth century and throughout the nineteenth has no parallel to the Indian situation. Firstly, no country in Europe started with more than a mere fraction of India's population. Secondly, their urban population base was, again, a mere fraction of that fraction and nothing comparable to the 26 millions of urban population with which India started in 1901. The pull that the city or town exercised on the rural areas of Europe in the era of the Industrial Revolution was due not only to the low urban population base but also to the low density in the countryside and the low rate of natural growth. The low population base in the countryside led to many early improvements in agriculture and farming and to the scraping off of savings for industrialisation. To this was added the benefits derived from the colonies by way of raw materials and the competition for utilisation of manpower at home and the colonies. The low rate of natural growth in the towns constantly demanded an inflow of labour from the rural areas to man the growing industries. Improvement in agricultural practices and the investment on industrial growth and on cities and townships has been of an unprecedently high order. It seems that from now on the natural growth of urban population will work as a repellant as well as a pull to migration from rural areas. The amenities available in the town by way of educational and mechanisation of farming also rendered a large rural population surplus which now formed the hard core of an urban proletariat which had no means of getting back to the countryside. But the pith of the matter was the low urban population base which cried out for expansion all the time, because the natural rate of growth of this population was wholly inadequate to meet the growing demand for labour.

A Repellant to Rural Migration

There is foreseeable demands of industrial expansion in the current decade, particularly when we remember that the gross capital investment per capita in the industrial sector is apt to be quite high. While this is by no means intended as a suggestion that the rural-urban flow will slow down or be pounded back, the absolute volume of natural increase in tire urban population itself may well have been at the back of the slow rate of urban growth, despite the fact that the investment on industrial growth and on cities and townships has been of an unprecedently high order. It seems that from now on the natural growth of urban population will work as a repellant as well as a pull to migration from rural areas. The amenities available in the town by way of educational and other facilities will contribute towards a higher level of technological efficiency in the younger generation which may tend to push back the stream of rural migration. On the other hand the lack of pronounced rural-urban differentials may tend to reduce the force of outward push from the village. Even now, as we have seen, urban life in most districts is largely an extension of the essential pattern of rural life. There will be a steadily widening and deepening reserve pool of labour of all grades available in the city or town itself to respond to new opportunity.

QUESTION FOR EXERCISE

1. Describe Population Problems in India.

17

Family Planning and Family Welfare

Family planning programme makes a planned and scientific approach to the problems of family life and attempts to solve them. In a narrower sense it is concerned with the spacing and limitation of child-births in the family and with helping childless couples to achieve parenthood when medically possible. Through marriage guidance, genetic counselling, sex education both for the parents and children, etc., family planning aims to promote the happiness of married couples in relation to each other and the well-being of their children. In the Indian context, and, in the context of the population explosion in the world as a whole, family planning has came to be identified largely, with limitation of family size.

The world population in the middle of seventeenth century was about 500 million. It increased to 1,250 million by 1850. Within 100 years, it: increased from about 1.2 billion to 2.5 billion. In mid-1962 it was 3,155,000,000. Fifty million people are added each year. About 57 per cent of the world's people live in Asia. Of the world's 10 largest countries 5 are in Asia — Mainland China (1000 million), India (930 million), Pakistan, Indonesia and Japan. The world growth rate is about 1.8 per cent a year. There is, however, a wide disparity in the rates of growth. The growth rate for the United Kingdom is 0.5 per cent a year, for Japan it is 1 per cent, for Latin America, Oceania and for most of the Asian countries like Ceylon, Taiwan, and Malasiya, it is nearly 3 per cent and for Brazil it is 3.4 per cent. At the present rate of growth, the world population by 2000 AD may be 8 billion or over. Such a situation cannot be viewed with complacency, especially in 'developing countries.

India ranks second in the world in relation to population, next only to China. With an area of little more than 2 per cent (2.4 per cent of the total land area of the world, India has to support about 14 per cent of the world population.

Concern for the number of children each family may have and measures to control births received attention in India (as in some other countries also) centuries ago. Many methods of preventing conception are referred to in the works of ancient writers. They are not all magical; some of them consist of use of herbal decoctions, tampoons and external applications including use of salt solution which is a well known spermicide. Long periods of voluntary abstinence is also one of the traditional methods.

Table 17.1

Population Differentials in India

Differentials	1951-61	1981	1993
1. Birth Rate	41.7	37.2	28.9 (S.R.S. 93)
2. Death Rate	22.8	15.0	9.3 (S.R.S. 93)
3. Total Productivity	5.97	4.5	3.6 (S.R.S. 92)
4. Infant Mortality Rate (Per 1000 Live Birth)	146	110	74 (S.R.S. 93)
5. Rate of Protected Couple %	10.4 (1970-71)	22.8	45.4 (31-3-94)
6. Cumulative Number of Birth Control (In millions)	(0.04)	43.4	168.8 (31-3-94)

The Beginnings

In more recent times a number of persons and organisations have urged the necessity of practicing birth control. In 1916 Sri Pyare Kishen Wattal published his book, the Population Problem in India advocating family limitation. In 1921 Prof. Raghunath Dhondo Karve advocated birth control. In 1923 Prof. N.S. Phadke started the Birth Control League in Bombay Presidency. A similar league was formed in Poona with efforts of Prof. G.D. Kulkarni. The Neo-Malthusian League was formed in Madras a few years later. On the 11th June, 1930, the Mysore Government issued orders to open the first Government Birth Control Clinic in the world. In 1932 the Senate of the Madras University accepted the proposal to give instructions on contraceptives and in the following year the Government of Madras agreed to open birth control clinics in the Presidency. In 1932, the All India Women's Conference at its Lucknow session recommended that "men and women should be instructed in methods of birth control in recognised clinics". The National Planning Committee, set up by the Indian National Congress in 1935, under the Chairmanship of Shri Jawaharlal Nehru, strongly supported family planning. At the invitation of the All India Women's Conference, Mrs. Margaret Sanger visited India during 1935-36 and stimulated interest in the country, in family planning.

On December 1, 1935, the Society for the Study and Promotion of Family Hygiene was formed with Shrimati Cowasji Jehangir as its first President. Dr. A.P. Filial, a vigorous advocate of family planning, conducted training courses in 1936, About the year 1937 birth control clinics were opened by the "Birth Control World Wide" in Uttar Pradesh and the Matru Sewa Sangh in Ujjain. In 1940 Dr. P.N. Sapru successfully moved a resolution in the Council of States for the establishment of birth control clinics. About this time Shrimati Rena Dutta toured extensively to organise a birth control campaign on behalf of the Family Planning Association, London, with varying success. By 1940 the Society for the Study and Promotion of Family Hygiene had become the Family Planning Society incorporating the Bhagini Samaj Birth Control Clinic in Bombay. World War II interrupted organised activities in the field of family planning.

However, a number of publications on family planning and related subjects appeared during this period.

The Health Survey and Development Committee under the Chairmanship of Sir Joseph Bhore, appointed in 1943 by the Government of India, recommended provision of birth control services although mainly for health reasons. Some members of the Committee considered the giving of contraceptive advice on economic grounds justifiable. Others appreciated the importance of the relation of population to the economic resources of the country but felt that action on promotion of contraceptive practices by the State is only justified if supported by public opinion.

Post-Independence Efforts

In 1949 the Family Planning Association of India was formed in Bombay under the Presidentship of Shrimati Dhanvanthi Rama Rau. Under her leadership the Association blossomed into a national organisation with branches throughout the country. Under joint leadership of Mrs. Margaret Sanger and Smt. Dhanvanthi Rama Rau the International Planned Parenthood Federation (IPPF) was started in 1952 in Bombay. Smt. Dhanvanthi Rama Rau was elected President of International Planned Parenthood Federation in 1960.

In March, 1950, the Government of India appointed the Planning Commission. In the following years Advisory Panels of the Commission on Social Welfare and Health discussed the problem of population growth. On April 11, 1951, the Advisory Panel on Health Programmes appointed a Sub- Committee on Family Planning. The members of this Committee were: Dr. Sushila Nayar, Shri R.A. Gopalaswami, Dr. Gyan Chand, Dr. A.C, Basu and Shrimati Dhanvanthi Rama Rau. This Sub-Committee strongly recommended that family planning should be recognised officially in order to safeguard the health and welfare of mothers and children and to aid the national economy by reducing the birth rate concurrently with the death rate in order to stabilise the population. Dr. Abraham Stone was invited to India under the auspices of the World Heath Organisation to advise on the establishment of pilot studies on rhythm method of family planning.

In December 1953, the Planning Commission recommended that a programme of family limitation and population control should (*a*) obtain an accurate picture of factors which contribute to rapid increase of population, (*b*) gain fuller understanding of human fertility and the means of regulating it, (*c*) devise speedier ways of education of the public and (*d*) make family planning advise and service an integral part of the services in hospitals and health centres. The programme was primarily directed to the building up of publip understanding and support and promotion of advice and service on the basis of the knowledge existing at the time. The demographic as well as medical and biological studies were taken up. The Government of India offered assistance in the shape of subsidised grants to States, local authorities, voluntary organisations and scientific institutions. The experience showed that Government supported family planning programme was welcomed by the masses of people. Thus, early in the First Plan promotion of family planning was adopted as public policy.

While recommending family planning programme it was stated in the First Five Year Plan: "It is apparent that population at a level consistent with the requirement of national economy should be stabilised. This can be secured only by the realisation of the need for family limitation on a wide scale by the people. The main appeal for family planning is based on consideration of health and welfare of the family. Family limitation or spacing of the children is necessary and desirable in order to secure better health of the mothers, and better care and upbringing of children. The measures described to this end should, therefore, form part of the public health programme." The Third Plan stated that the greatest stress has to be placed in the Third and subsequent Five Year Plans on the programme of family planning and that the objective of stabilising the growth of population over a reasonable period must be at the centre of planned development.

In pursuance of this population policy the programme to moderate fertility was expanded during the Second and the Third Plan periods. The major activities envisaged were: (*a*) education and motivation for family planning, use of non-official organisations for diffusion of knowledge and practice, (*b*) provision of services integrated with rural health services including facilities for sterilisation, (*c*) training, (*d*) supplies, and (*e*) research. These efforts are aimed at reducing birth rates as expeditiously as possible so that people experience the urgently needed benefits of economic growth.

The Operational Goal

The operational goal of the family planning programme is to create for 90 per cent of the married adult population of India the three basic conditions needed for accelerating the adoption of family planning by couples, viz. group acceptance, knowledge about family planning, and availability of supplies and services.

Group Acceptance: Each individual should know and feel that the immediate society or community to which he belongs has agreed, as a group, that having a small size family is the normal and desirable behaviour for the members of that group. Without such a feeling, any couple will hesitate seriously to adopt family planning; with such a feeling most couples will proceed to obtain the necessary information needed for them to conform to the norms of their group.

Knowledge about Family Planning: Information of two types is necessary. Firstly, knowledge that having a smaller family is valuable, for various personal reasons. Secondly, people should have knowledge about specific methods of birth control, including intra-uterine contraceptive device, contraceptive methods and sterilisation operations.

Availability of Supplies: A couple wishing to have simple contraceptive supplies should be able to get them inexpensively within easy geographic distance, without questions being asked and without other psychological barriers being interposed such as inconvenient time of day, having to wait, or lack of privacy.

Distribution of contraceptive supplies is sought to be arranged wisely through village panchayats, mid-wives and through other local depot-holders, as well as through various health and rural development workers. Commercial distribution of contraceptives is also of extreme importance, and purchase in the market is often preferred by the people themselves. Rubber and chemical contraceptives and IUCD are now manufactured in India. Steps have been taken to produce condoms in the public sector to foster marketing through commercial channels and consumer co-operatives.

Organisation at the Centre and States

In 1952, a family planning cell was formed in the Directorate General of Health Services. A Family Planning Programme Research and Planning Committee was formed in 1953. This was replaced by the Central Family Planning Board in September, 1956 and the Central Family Planning Council in 1965. There are also three expert committees, namely the Demographic Advisory Committee, Expert Group on Scientific Aspects of Family Planning of the Indian Council of Medical Research and the Communication Action Research Advisory Committee. States have family planning boards at the State level and committees at the district level. The State Governments, have appointed special family planning officers.

The current pattern of financial assistance to local bodies and voluntary organisations provides for 100 per cent assistance by the Government on all programmes of family planning, inclusive of contraceptives, sterilisation facilities, education, research and training. Overall assistance to State Governments is 90 per cent.

Community Education Programme

The extension education wing of the programme is yet to be fully developed. However, a great deal has been done to increase people's general awareness of family planning. The Ministry of Health and Family Planning and the Ministry of Information and Broadcasting have jointly published information material on the subject of family planning. The Films Division produced some films on the subject, apart from the films produced by the Family Planning Association of India and by some of the State Governments. These materials are available in English, Hindi, and the regional languages. Some feature films produced in private sector have won national awards as good feature films.

Among the educational methods used in the field, one which appears to be very promising is that of identifying local leaders, training them and using them as channels of communication.

Honorary Family Planning Education Leaders: For helping in identification of natural groups and natural group leaders, and their use as channel of communications, Honorary Family Planning Education Leaders, are appointed on an honorarium of ₹ 4,000 per annum at the divisional level Such leaders are required to cover 4 to 5 districts, to address meetings to disseminate information, to encourage the participation of the people and of responsible officials and non-officials in the area, and to mobilise public opinion in favour of family planning. They form committees and try to help organise a network of groups at all levels in cities and villages. Subsequently, it was decided to appoint leaders at district level on an all inclusive honorarium of ₹ 2,000 per annum.

Divisional and District Family Planning Education Leaders have reported on groups and meetings which were attended by a large number of persons. It is proposed to extend the Honorary Family Planning Education Leader Programme further, by appointing leaders at State, district and block levels.

Pariwar Kalyan Sahayakas: Additionally, the Government propose to enroll *pariwar kalyan Sahayakas* and *sahayikas* (family planning helpers) to disseminate information on family planning. The goal is to have such workers in every village and town in the country. Village midwives are also being involved in the programme.

Training of Personnel

The Medical Council of India has recommended that medical students should undergo a short course of training in family planning during the period of their internship which they are required to spend in a health unit for participation in practical public health administration. The Inter-University Board at its Thirty-seventh meeting at Tirupati in February 1962, informed that the replies received from universities, indicated that family planning is already a subject which is dealt with in the under-graduate course and wherever necessary in other courses, and that the attention of the universities was being again invited to the fact that courses in family planning and subjects of allied nature should be given to all students both medical and non-medical. The Indian Nursing Council at a meeting in November 1957, approved the proposals to include training in family planning in the basic courses for nurses and midwives. All schools for health visitors having the necessary facilities, are now giving instructions in family planning.

Special Courses: Under the Directorate General of Health Services, two family planning training- and research centres for potential instructors have been established, in Bombay and in Delhi. There is also a training centre in Ramanagaram. The All India Institute of Hygiene and Public Health also conducts courses on family planning. In the States, 23 regional family planning training centres have been established to provide training for workers within the States. In order to provide additional personnel for village level work, training centres were opened during the Third Plan period by voluntary organisations to train "family welfare workers." One centre each has been opened in Hyderabad, Madras, Nagpur, Allahabad and Delhi. In order to provide a long term solution to this need, expansion of facilities to provide the regular training course-for auxiliary nurse-midwives is being encouraged.

Touring Training Teams: Teams have been sanctioned in each State for providing on the spot training in family planning to health personnel posted in hospitals, dispensaries and primary health centres who cannot leave their area for training at central or regional centres. These teams are now being integrated into a Central Family Planning Field Unit in each State. The Field Unit provides a nucleus for the State Family Planning Bureau.

Fellowships: A fellowships programme has been developed to provide for studies in India and abroad in the fields of demography, medical and biological research and communications methods applicable to solution of problems of family planning programme implementation. During the past years, of the 38 fellowships, 15 were offered by the Ford Foundation, 10 by the Population Council, 5 by the Worchester Foundation and 8 by the Government of India. Total of 43 persons (26 during 1962-63) have been awarded fellowships in demography, communications, and physiology of human reproduction.

Research

Demography: The demographic research programme includes (*a*) continuous survey of population situation in India including estimated projection of population growth, (*b*) studies on internal migration with special reference to industrialisation and urbanisation, (*c*) *ad hoc* field studies on regional basis on factors related to family size, on base lines data regarding knowledge, practices and attitudes about family planning, and evaluation of family planning programme effects, (*d*) studies on interrelationship between social, economic and population changes, and fertility and mortality patterns in different regions, (*e*) studies of income and economic aspects of population growth, (*f*) development of existing training and research centres and demographic training in universities and (*g*) dissemination of information on population matters and co-ordination of efforts in the field of demography.

Nine Demographic Research Centres have so far been established in the country with the help of the Government of India, viz. Demographic Training and Research Centre, Bombay; Demographic Research Centre, Indian Statistical Institute, Calcutta; Demographic Research Centre, Institute of Economic Growth, Delhi; Demographic Research Centre, Department of Statistics, Government of Kerala, Trivandrum; Demographic Research Centre, Dharwar; Gokhale Institute of Politics and Economics, Poona; Indian Institute of Population Studies, Madras; University of Lucknow and University of Patna. Besides the studies undertaken at these nine centres, financial assistance is also being offered for *ad hoc* studies wherever necessary.

Medical and Biological Aspects of Reproduction: In the last few years basic research on reproduction has greatly increased.

Institutions which have been particularly active in the field include the All India Institute of Medical Sciences; Central Drug Research Institute, Lucknow; Indian Cancer Research Centre; Zoology Department of Delhi University; Banaras Hindu University; and others, and several medical colleges. Important work is also being done in the departments of animal science at Anand and Izzatnagar. Applied research in this field is also being done at the All India Institute of Hygiene and Public Health and the Family Planning Institute. A special course in reproductive biology has been organised by Delhi University's Zoology Department. Several other institutions are strengthening the training in this field.

Present studies cover the entire scope of reproductive biology — roles of the nervous system and of different endocrine glands, reproductive mechanisms in the male and in the female, immunological aspects of reproduction, and genetics. Careful studies are also being made in laboratories and clinics,' on specific contraceptive methods. The country now has a sound basis for studying present methods of contraception and producing knowledge which may lead to improvement in methods.

Communications and Action Research: The general goals of the communications and action research programme are to provide better understanding of basic factors which influence the acceptance of family planning; to collect and make available relevant knowledge and experience for improving the educational aspects of the programme; and to apply such knowledge and skills in developing, testing and demonstrating improved patterns of programme operation.

For this purpose, pilot projects of various types are being initiated at several institutions, namely, Family Planning Institute, Demographic Research Centre, Bombay; Kerala University; Gandhigram (Madras); Indian Statistical Institute; Planning, Research and Action Institute (Lucknow); Lady Hardinge Medical College, Delhi; and the Central Health Education Bureau, Delhi. These projects provide a source of objective observations and fresh ideas about different problems of programme implementation and provide field laboratories for working out and evaluating educational and organisational methods.

The Central Family Planning Institute

This Institute was established In 1962 by pulling together a number of centrally supported activities in the Delhi area such as the Family Planning Training Centre and Family Planning Communications and Action Research Centre. The amalgamation of these activities and designation of this complex as Central Family Planning Institute has facilitated more efficient functioning. The approved organisational plan of the new Institute includes major divisions for reproductive biology research; education, training and social research; statistical studies; population genetics and hormones development and the study of contraceptive methods and their effective use. Establishment of this Institute meets the vital need for a major technical agency concerned with scientific research and training on the various aspects of family planning in India.

Sterilisation Cases and IUCD Insertions

Facilities for free sterilisation operations are now available on a fairly wide scale, in several hospitals, maternity centres and other medical and health centres in the States and Centrally Administered Areas. The Government of India sanctions for the employees special casual leave when they undergo sterilisation operations. This facility has been further extended to the industrial employees also. Besides free transport and casual leave, compensatory allowances are also given by the Central and the State Governments to the persons undergoing sterilisation or IUCD insertion. In order to extend sterilisation facilities throughout the country, the State Governments are: (*i*) strengthening the staff of teaching medical Institutions for training of doctors in the technique of sterilisation operations; and (*ii*) strengthening The staff of hospitals upto *taluk* level for conducting sterilisation operations.

Maharashtra has initiated sterilisation camps. The psychological impact of these camps towards acceptance of family planning is considerable amongst the general population.

Studies on Knowledge of and Attitudes to Family Planning

Studies on family planning knowledge, practices and attitudes done so far give strong evidence of potential receptivity to the idea of family planning. These studies were done in and around

Delhi, Calcutta, Patna, Lucknow, Kanpur, Ludhiana, Hyderabad, Madras, Bangalore, and Trivandrum. About 70 per cent women of 35 years and above with 4 children appear to be ready to learn family planning methods. Between 10 to 20 per cent married women in rural India are reported to have some knowledge of contraceptives. Castes and religion do not appear to be directly related to the acquiring of knowledge of family planning. Education, age, number of living children and the health of the mother seem to be significantly associated with such knowledge. Except for a small minority there is no organised religious opposition to the family planning programme; even among objectors the opposition is mostly towards certain methods and not to a small-size family. Although it can be seen that an appreciable number of people fed the need for limiting family size, it appears that fewer people realise that this feeling is shared by many others in their groups. Also, there is little knowledge about how contraceptives could be easily obtained.

While proceeding with the campaign to reduce births, some have raised doubts that the campaign may effect quality of the people. It would be necessary to view this issue a little more closely. On one hand our knowledge about biological quality is rudimentary, and it is still not possible to control or modify genetic action. On the other hand, there is no doubt that environment can suppress many hereditary qualities but human control over envim uncut is gradually increasing. With advancing scientific knowledge, man has gained more and more control over his environment and has been able to develop more efficient means to influence both mortality and fertility.

The question that arises here is whether a family planning programme tends to eliminate some of the desirable qualities in the genetic pool? Scientific efforts so far have not confirmed any large effect on genetic quality from the differential fertilities observed in modernised societies.

In countries in which birth rates fall, it has been observed that, as equality of opportunity spreads throughout a society and as general level of living rises, the differences in respect of fertility behaviour of social groups tend to disappear. In the initial stages, of course, the birth rate falls first in the higher socio-economic group. This seems to be the natural, inevitable process of transition. It is now clearly evident in India. Probably, the existence of the model-of a smaller family in higher economic groups is an essential factor in the process of adoption of the same norm in the lower groups. What is essential is to accelerate the process of diffusion of small family norms from higher into lower economic groups.

Factors Favouring High Fertility

In the earlier stage of development of India and of other countries, introduction of scientific technology and systematic economic development has not only lowered mortality, but has been a strong force favouring higher fertility. Some factors in traditional Indian culture like the special preference for sons, lower level of marriage age, and the universality of marriage support high fertility. High mortality rate among children, although it is now considerably lowered, makes people aware of the chances of such losses, and this awareness tends to favour higher fertility.

Factors Favouring Lower Fertility

Urbanisation and industrialisation have been important factors in lowering fertility. The small family norm, adopted by the higher economic groups is spreading. Some aspects of culture also favour the idea of family planning. Religious taboo on sex during certain times, high moral value placed on abstinence and celibacy, etc., are some of the factors in view. The potentialities for building upon the favourable factors noted above are considerable. The relative readiness of the general population to accept newer social norms might be further accelerated by systematic educational methods. The factors for and against higher fertility are, in many cases, susceptible to influence by planned governmental action. Legislative action is known to have great impact on social conditions. Measures like compulsory education, raising the age of marriage and reform of laws of inheritance will indirectly give strong support to family planning programmes over a period of time.

Changes have Occurred

It must be realised that we are dealing with a dynamic and changing situation, not a static one. Since the turn of the century, the crude birth rate in India has declined slightly. At the same time, mortality rates have fallen radically. As a result, for every 1,000 persons today, the proportion of widows is less and the proportion of living couples in the childbearing age has considerably increased. This change in population composition would have been expected to produce a considerably higher birth rate than is now observed. The fact that the birth rate has not risen suggests that some important changes towards a smaller family pattern have actually occurred on a fairly wide scale. Recent studies indicate that active diffusion of family planning practices into the lower economic strata of the population is occurring. In some urban populations, the birth rates are now definitely lower than in rural populations. Well-organised family planning action programmes, making use of the insights in human behaviour and experience, have produced a remarkable rise in uptake of family planning methods especially of condoms and of vasectomy.

In the process of planned economic growth in India, family planning has been recognised as an "essential element in the strategy of development". National planners, government servants, legislators and citizens, are now applying the same principles of rational national planning to this social movement. So far, they have taken many steps. There is scope, however, for further intensive action towards fertility reduction in India.

It is known that it is biologically and socially quite possible for rapid changes in fertility rates to occur. It is also known that many factors in India now favour decline in fertility and that the decline has started showing itself. What is needed now is the acceleration of the process of change by the fullest possible mustering of knowledge that is now available, and the most energetic and closely organised application of such knowledge in the field.

FAMILY WELFARE

Family is a social institution. It has been both a producing and a consuming unit. It provides the kinship group which makes it possible to form basic human relationships. It meets emotional, cultural, recreational and various other vital needs of its members. Family is an institution which also gives education for family life.

During the last 150 years, a number of forces have been released in the Indian society which have affected the institution of family. Its structure, functions and relationships of its members with each other, have undergone a change. The family also, over all these years, experienced difficulties in coping with some of the functions that it performed in the past and lost some of them in the process of adjustment. Many things that were done in the family and by the family are today done in the community and by agencies which may be called substitute agencies. These substitute agencies perform functions which once belonged to the family. Redistribution of functions is taking place between the family and the agencies and services in the community.

Table 17.2

Expected Targets by 1997

	Indicator	*Goals to be Achieved Up to end of VIII Plan*
(a)	Crude Birth Rate (per 1000 population)	26.0
(b)	Infant Mortality Rate (per 1000 live birth)	70
(c)	Couple Protection Rate	56%

The family is no longer the joint family of the past and even those families that answer the basic qualifications of the joint family that have been stipulated, such as holding properly jointly and living under the same roof with a common kitchen, present a different picture today. A large number of family units are what are called nuclear families in some cases with a base far away.

Impact on Members

Impact of democratic way of life is clearly visible on the family members and the institution of family. Members of the family are playing modified or new roles. They have become more individualistic. Meek submission to authority of elders cannot be always expected now. Members of the family cherish new aspirations for education, careers, and have a desire to live life in a way, much different than the way their parents or grandparents lived. The members of the family do not any more spend the time together as they used to do in the past. They work in places away from home and have interest companionships also away from home. The family life is no longer that close-knit. Anxiety, tensions, insecurity, loneliness are increasingly haunting members of the family. The traditional set of social values also got recast in the process and some of the over the other. Influences of western culture and age are unmistakably seen.

Rural Areas

While these changes referred to above may be clearly noticed in urban areas, in rural areas some of these changes are still imperceptible. But the reaction has set in. There is a kind of restlessness followed by eagerness to assume roles different from the roles traditionally expected of various members of the family. Education, need to leave ancestral home to find employment in factories, necessity to take to avenues of earning living other than those in family tradition, mobility facilitated by fast modes of communication, contact with cities and towns, etc., all these together have contributed to the changes that have taken place or are taking place in rural families in India.

Family in Flux

The family all over India is in a flux. The degree of impact of newly released forces on the family may vary in different parts of the country and in rural and urban areas. Accordingly the jointness and closeness in the families might have suffered in varying degrees. The problems faced by individual members of the family accordingly also vary in nature and intensity.

Status of Women

The status of women in the last 150 years has improved. Women in most of the sections of the Indian society now increasingly seek employment and this is also usually away from home. This has become possible by relative emancipation of women as a result of several reform movements, liberal education, right to vote, women's participation in Indian freedom movement, the legislation that gave Hindu women the new rights in relation to property, divorce, adoption etc., and equal rights of citizenship women enjoy with those of men under the Constitution. New fields of activities for women were thus opened. Consequently, they have come to cherish a desire for expression of their capacities outside the four walls of the home. The changing role of the women has brought changes in family relationships. Women's employment has effected child raising patterns in families. Supplementary services to take care of children have thus become more necessary.

Education, health, nutrition, employment opportunities, recreation have become concerns more of the community than of the family. The community can effectively deal with them now than an individual family.

The general poverty in the country, changes in family relationships and other factors have made it difficult for the family to shoulder responsibilities for the aged, the handicapped and the other dependents. The functioning of the family in these areas has been disturbed. Its members have been naturally going through stresses and strains.

Supportive Services Needed

The attitudes of people in general to the family, attitudes and relationships of the members of the family to and with each other, the functions of the family and the resources and capacities of the' family to meet its needs have thus undergone changes. Supplementary services in support of the family have become necessary if family life involving varying ages, different sexes, different relationships, different generations and different roles is to function smoothly and with optimum satisfaction to the all concerned. Families in all the parts of India need support and protection. This can come generally through State policies and directly from social services and social welfare services including family welfare services.

Area of Concern to National Policies

The State has to see that the basic needs of the people like food, shelter and clothing are met. In addition to this, educational, health and recreational services need to be provided for all. Housing is another subject that needs attention in this context. Today basic needs of a large number of individuals are not met satisfactorily. Educational, health, recreational services are inadequate. Employment opportunities are not enough. Social services and social welfare services, provided to employees in private and public sectors, cover only a small percentage of the total population. Scholarship schemes, programmes for women, children and Backward Classes, income tax relief, etc., are all meant for mitigating material poverty and poverty of opportunity. All these measures, however, do not touch even a fringe of the total problem. It will take some time before the minimum decent standard of living would be ensured to most of the nearly 10 crore Indian families. This number of families will go up as years will pass by. The difficulties of families arising out of low per capita national income and unsatisfactory sharing of wealth, can only be solved by greater production and equitable distribution of goods and services. This is an area of concern to general national policies. This aspect of family welfare will have to be continually kept in mind by the national leaders who draw up economic, fiscal, industrial and employment, educational, health, housing policies of the country. While formulating national policies, legislating new acts and expanding and operating social and social welfare services, the needs of the family, its integrity, its efficient functioning and optimum well-being of its members must be kept in view. Much needs to be done in this direction.

Many of the services that are thus of significance to the family, are services that are basically needed by the entire population of the country. Housing, health services, employment opportunities, education, nutrition etc. are common needs and cannot be viewed as exclusively in the service of the family. But the family does derive strength from these all and this must be remembered. At present these services do not reach all the families in the country. Non-availability of these services to all families creates many difficulties for the family.

Sharing of Burdens

Such services, well organised and free or on moderate charges within the reach of the families, reduce the burdens of family expenditure on health, education, housing, recreation, and open educational opportunities to deserving students from families with small means. Pensions, provident fund schemes, and recently introduced old age pension schemes and allowances for the handicapped also reduce the financial hardships both of individuals and their families. The socio-economic programmes of the Central Social Welfare Board, Griha Kalyan Kendras, etc. seek to supplement the family income by providing (part-time) employment to women in needy families These measures must have lightened the financial burdens of the families though in a very small degree. It would, however, be better, if all these measures were implemented in a co-ordinated manner with a major emphasis on the welfare of the family.

Family Always Needed Support

It is not only now that the family is in need of special type of help. It needed help of all kinds and at all times. It needs more help now because of rapid social and general changes. Some of the special needs of the family were once met through mechanism provided in the joint family, the caste and the *Jajmani* system. External help was given to improve conditions affecting a particular family. Shelter, food, medical help, etc., were given to meet the needs of a family in distress on humanitarian considerations. Friends in the community and elders in the family gave advice and help which led to better relationships in the family. Besides, the general tendency was to keep family matters in the family and not to discuss them with others. But all this help was on an *ad hoc* basis. It never took the form of an organised network of services working for welfare of the family. Such measures are needed today in view of the changed conditions in terms of the composition of the family unit, the changed roles of the members of the family, and the new needs of the family and its members, and because families are inadequate to meet them. It is necessary to have services to help the family to function at its best. These services can have a stabilising, protective and promotive influence on the family. Such services can be broadly classified as follows: (1) those which contribute to the family's economic security like compensation for financial burdens, (2) those which deal with the problems of adjustment and relationships, and (3) those which protect its members in case of a special need or a family breakdown. These areas are by no means independent of one another. Work in relation to economic security and community social services is to be done by the State and the community together. Material help of small size and socio-psychological help to resolve problems essentially arising out of-attitudes, interpersonal relationships, including those caused by differences in ages and experience can be given by a special type of family welfare service. Such a family welfare service also usually helps families to cope with stresses and strains of socio-economic changes, changes in the value systems, impact of democratic way of life, technology, urbanisation and industrialisation, etc. The goal of a family welfare service should be, therefore, to contribute to harmonious family inter-relationships, to strengthen the positive values of family life, to promote healthy personality development and to ensure satisfactory social functioning of various members of the family.

Understanding Changes

Historically it could be said that in India the family was allowed to drift for over a century and a half. The British had the policy of non-interference in the religious and social life of Indian people. Yet during the British days Acts on subjects like age of consent, widow remarriage, child marriage restraint, children in trouble, guardianship, abandonment of child, etc., were passed or appropriate legislative provisions made. After Independence the Hindu Code, Hindu Succession and Adoption Act, etc. were passed. They all affected the families, in some ways may be for the better. Along with this, number of social and economic forces were released that made impact on family life. After partition, number of families went through holocaust, Comprehensive assessment of the changes all this might have brought in the institution of the family, its structure, functioning, relationships in it in all communities is not fully available. And whatever is known, cannot be said to have guided the policy makers and those responsible for the implementation of policies.

Traditional Pattern of Helping the Family

In Indian society traditional organisations still continue to help the family. This work is done through what may be called caste or communal or language group organisations run by different groups. They give help to families in the field of education, health, housing, medical, care, etc. In various communities there has been a tradition of giving material relief to the families in distress. There are thousands of such organisations. They render variety of services. An exhaustive list and adequate information on these organisations is unfortunately not available. All these organisations and agencies could be reoriented and equipped to render supportive services to families in the local communities in the modern sense. From the caste and language group approach they could be oriented to the local community approach. The Hindus, the Muslims, the Christians, the Parsees, the Jews and others all have such organisations. Even if the assistance continued to be given to the families on the basis of religion, caste and language group criteria, better and efficient work could be ensured. The Parsec community has organised good supportive services to the Parsee families. But it must be admitted that until all these services are merged into a national network and put on secular footing ensuring minimum level of material assistance to the needy families, for material assistance is what most of them render, these organisations will continue to cater to the members of the respective religious, caste, and language groups in the present manner.

Currently families are exposed to hazards arising out of divorce, death of the bread winner, absence of bread winner away from home, juvenile delinquency, desertion, marital conflicts, poverty, unemployment, ill-health, imprisonment of the earning members of the family, difficulties arising out of physical handicaps in oneself or in members of the family, drinking, gambling, indebtedness, infidelity, inability to take decisions, conflicts arising out of inter-caste and inter-language group marriages, general family disharmony, etc. In all these situations marked by social and emotional problems families need help as they feel inadequate to meet the situations satisfactorily by themselves. The family-social welfare agencies can do this work of helping the families in such situations.

A Recent Development

Individual members of the families are being helped for decades but helping them with focus on the family is a recent development. Family welfare agencies which have been started recently are trying to put much of this help in proper perspective. Their work is difficult as the basic needs of a large number of families are not fulfilled. Affluence might not remove difficulties like tension, unhappiness, problems of inter-personal relationships from which the family suffers, but it does make work of the family welfare worker more limited on the side of material assistance and more intensive on the socio-psychological side.

Newly Started Services

Family welfare agencies started by voluntary organisations since 1950 attempt to meet these needs. But these agencies work in a very limited sphere. All their efforts have not yet grown to their lull stature and they serve small number of clients in the metropolitan cities. They also do not reach a large number of population in cities. All over the country they handle not more than 5,000 cases. Many people do not even know about the existence of these services.

Information is available only about the activities of nine family welfare agencies. Their names and addresses are listed here :

1. Liaison Committee for Organisation of Parsee Charities, A.A.l. Institute Building, Chikalwadi, Tardeo, Bombay-7.
2. Family Planning Training and Research Centre, Government of India, Sardar Vallabhbhai Patel Road, Bombay-4.

3. Delhi Council for Social Welfare, 31, Netaji Subhas Marg, Delhi-6.
4. Family Welfare Agency, 10, B.D.D. Chawl, Delisle Road, Bombay-11.
5. Family Life Institute, Association of Moral and Social Hygiene in India, 4, Rouse Avenue, New Delhi-1.
6. Family Counselling Bureau, Bapnu Ghar Committee, Maharashtra State Women's Council, 12, Annie Besant Road, Worli, Bombay-18.
7. Family Welfare Agency, Nagapada Neighbourhood House, Byculla, Bombay-8.
8. Family Counselling Bureau, Association for Moral and Social Hygiene, Maharashtra State Branch, Bombay-1.
9. Family Service Centre, 5, Convent Street Off Wodehouse Road, Bombay-1.

These family welfare agencies deal with problems of adjustment and relationships. Occasionally they arrange financial assistance, medical aid, etc. and refer appropriate cases to other agencies. In doing this they use resources available in the community. In urban areas the problems they deal with seem to arise out of several factors, but some of these are:

1. inadequate housing,
2. working wife-mother,
3. late marriage,
4. idea of companionship in marriage,
5. an undefinable process of democratising,
6. a demand for a capacity for response between the partners, intellectual and temperamental compatibility,
7. changing roles and expectations of different members of the family.

Problems arising as a result of these and many other factors are experienced to a large extent by the middle classes, which have to contend very hard to cope with the socio-economic changes. This is not to say that other classes do not face such problems. As a matter of fact there is an increasing demand for family counselling from families from all strata of society. It is also not necessary to assume that there is now more maladjustment in the family than before. There is less willingness to tolerate such maladjustment. People are no longer prepared to suffer silently, if remedies were available.

Aims and Objects

The study of the aims and objects of the family welfare agencies reveals that the agencies realise that the family is a social unit which is most important in the growth and development of effective individuals and the family life should therefore be strong and wholesome. According to them every individual is an integral part of the family. Every problem of the individual, they, therefore, look upon as a problem of the family. Most of them work with the following objectives:

to help individuals to overcome problems of adjustment in their relationships in the family;

to impart family life education, which would enhance the members' competence to raise or to maintain such standards of conduct in family relations as would make the family living a happy and wholesome experience for all;

to foster healthy development of the family, to keep it strong, and stable and to help it stay together;

to ensure life of mutual love and affection which will provide security to all its members;

to organise courses in family life education so that members realise their rights, duties, and obligations and adjust themselves through understanding; to provide family counselling, medical-aid, financial assistance, legal aid, and case-work service in adolescent problems, mental problems and parental problems;

to provide shelter, counsel, help to women in distress;

to arrange for marriage counselling and pre-marriage counselling; and

to help families experiencing difficulties, to understand, to face and to resolve their problems through competent guidance.

The purpose of family welfare services was very well stated by I Grade Putra Kamayana at the International Conference on the Family in Delhi (11-17 December, 1966) in the following words: "It is generally recognised that the main purpose of family social welfare services is to strengthen family ties and relationships and to safeguard its integrity and enhance and maintain members' capacities to fulfil the respective responsibilities and discharge their functions properly. Invariably they are also aimed at enabling and facilitating the family members to participate in the social and economic life of the country and to contribute their share to national development." This statement would be worth keeping in mind while assessing the work done by various agencies working for the welfare of the family in India and whose aims and objects are similar to those implied in this statement.

A Pioneering Agency

The first family welfare agency was started in Bombay in 1950. It was started as a co-operative venture of the Tata Institute of Social Sciences and the Indian Conference of Social Work. The purpose of the agency was to contribute to harmonious family inter-relationships, to strengthen the positive values in family life, and to help in satisfactory social functioning of various members. The agency recognised the value of case work service to the family in resolving various difficulties and maladjustments that arise in it. As a field of social work, family welfare, however, is still scarcely known.

Nature of Requests

To render multiple or multi-purpose service to the family more on social than on economic front of the family life, is the aim of family welfare agencies. These agencies make an effort to clarify family relationships, deal with problems which are sometimes inter-related to monetary difficulties. They give emotional support and general help to the family to help itself. The requests made to them so far, were related to adoption, family adjustment, placement of women and children in institutions and families, medical-aid, rehabilitation of families in distress, marriage counselling, pre-marriage counselling, family counselling, reference to child guidance clinics, vocational guidance, etc.

Difficulties of Agencies

The family welfare services which started work only 17 years ago experience a number of limitations. One such limitation is absence of mental health services or their inadequacy. Counselling is yet to be adopted to Indian cultural setting. It further needs different orientation. As a part of educational or public health services family counselling services might be well received and welcomed. Generally people do not come forward to receive counselling. They have the same resistance as people have to the use of mental health services. This is however breaking down slowly. Further there is lack of personnel, standardised tests, knowledge of existing services and limited ability of the clients to communicate. Education of the people on counselling needs to be undertaken without further delay. Training of personnel for counselling in India has to be organised in Indian setting.

Problems of adjustment and relationships are experienced in rural families the same way as in the urban families. However, they are, where awareness prevails, not recognised as such.

There appear to be no spokesmen for the cause of the family. Value of significance of the family for happiness of the individual and of the society needs to be better appreciated. Legislation must protect and strengthen it. Social, economic and cultural conditions must be conducive to the development and maintenance of healthy family life.

Co-ordination

Work of governmental agencies and voluntary organisations in relation to the welfare of the family needs to be co-ordinated. Integration of services working for the family and its members with a focus on family and with the objective indicated earlier, is necessary. In difficulties that do not arise out of individual action or in all difficulties that are beyond the capacity of the individual or the family to overcome alone, help is needed. Today, it is provided in a haphazard manner and in an inadequate measure. Governmental and non-governmental agencies are doing more than before; but the work has just begun. Whatever is being done is required to be integrated and co-ordinated so that it might be more useful.

Need for family welfare is accepted. Action is being initiated. No one agency can meet all the needs of the family. It is but natural, therefore, that pooling of socio-economic and psychological resources of a community on behalf of the client and his family should become an integral part of family case-workers' task.

Guiding Developments

Impact of changing conditions on the structure and functioning of the institution of family must be continually studied. The government, administrators of various welfare programmes and people in general need to be educated in the importance of the family as an institution so that little would happen at their hands which would adversely effect the family, and positive efforts would be made to promote efficient functioning of its members. This will also enable members of the family to have an opportunity to develop their capacities to the foil and derive a sense of fulfilment.

Some of the changes that have engulfed family might have been initiated unconsciously and some deliberately. But they all could be understood, directed and intelligently controlled by the planners, legislators, administrators keeping in view the ultimate objective of the welfare of the family.

QUESTIONS FOR EXERCISE

1. Trace the history of Family Planning in India.
2. Describe the Agencies of Family Welfare in India.

18

Population Policies

According to The Ad hoc Consultative Group of Experts on population policy, set up by the Population Commission of the United Nations Economic and Social Council, Population policy means, "Measures and Programmes designed to contribute to the achievement of economic, social, demographic, political and other collective goals, through affecting critical demographic variables, namely, the size and growth of population, its geographic distribution (national and international) and its demographic characteristics."[1] Further, it has been pointed out that population policy should include measures and programmes likely to affect critical demographic variables as well as those specifically designed to do so.[2] In defining population policy Berelson has outlined the following three principal characteristics:

1. It includes the action taken by government in the form of a statement of position, laws, decrees or administrative programmes.
2. It covers population events.
3. It refers to both the intentions and consequences designed to alter population events.

Thus, population policy is characterised by the three components of population change, viz., fertility, mortality and migration. Thus population policy of a country refers to the governmental measures with reference to population change. It

1. United Nations Economic and Social Council, Population 'Commission, *Report of the ad hoc Consultative Group of Experts on Population Policy* (E/CNI9/267), 23rd May, 1972, p. 6.
2. *Ibid.*, p. 6.

decides the goals to be achieved in the fields of fertility, mortality and migration. This may be understood in more details as follows:

1. Policies Influencing Mortality: Mortality is an undesirable characteristic of population. Therefore population policies aim at reduction of mortality. This has been done particularly through the concept of public health and the national programmes of eradication of 'mass killers', the epidemics Small pox, Malaria, Cholera, etc. The World Health Organisation has defined health as, "A state of complete physical, mental and social well-being and not merely the absence of disease or infirmity."[1] This definition of health has decided the goal of public health in different countries. The public health campaigns have led to unprecedented decline in mortality. It has been pointed out by a United Nations Public Health report that not a single pandemic has occurred since 1918 when influenza caused 25 million deaths in the world. According to the United Nations Secretariat, "As might be expected, all Governments have formulated policies designed to reduce morbidity and mortality, and none has considered acceptable a policy of permitting survival rates to remain low in order to prevent further increase in rates of National Population Growth."[2] In 1974 the United National World Population Conference in Bucharest adopted checking of mortality level as the goal of World Population Plan of Action. It was resolved that, "Countries with the highest mortality levels should aim, by 1985, to have expectation of life at birth of at least 50 years and an infant mortality rate of less than 120 per thousand live births."[3]

2. Policies Influencing Migration: These are concerned both with internal and international migration. Internal migration is a constitutional privilege in most of the countries. The policy towards internal migration seeks to relieve population pressures. In most of the countries today metropolitan reasons have very high population growth rates. Therefore, the Governments aim at reducing this pressure. However, it has been reported by the United Nations that most of the developed countries do not have

1. As quoted in John J. Hanion, *Principles of Public Health Administration*, St. Louis: C.V. Mosby Company, 1960, p. 363.
2. United Nations Secretariat, "Population Policies and Programmes", *The Population Debate: Dimensions and Perspectives*, Vol. II, New York: 1975, p. 589
3. United Nations, "World Population Plan of Action," *Studies in Family Planning*, Vol. 5, No. 12, December 1974, p. 385.

any policy to discourage migration to urban centres. The less developed countries also generally do not depict such policies. Therefore, it has been pointed out that such population policy must be adopted.

Most of the countries today have well defined policies concerning international migration. Rules for entry and exit from the countries are becoming more and more elaborate. Governments are imposing increasing restrictions on international migration. An example of such restriction may be seen in Great Britain at present, particularly concerning immigration of Asians. An Immigration Act adopted in 1971 was enforced in January 1973 to introduce a uniform system of immigration control for all the countries. This Act aimed at discouraging immigration. Similar population policy concerning immigration may be observed in Australia. Again, sometimes restriction on emigration are imposed to control 'brain drain', such as found in India these days.

3. Population Policies Influencing Fertility: These may be classified as anti-natalist.

(*i*) *Pro-natalist policies*. Thomlinson has described three approaches to an affective pro-natalist policy:

(A) To accept existing values and attitudes and eliminate or diminish the economic liability of having children.

(B) To modify the norms by glorifying values concerning reproduction. This includes such legal measures as lowering the minimum age for marriage and reinstating the old custom, of divorce on the basis of infertility.

(C) To relax the taboos on illegitimacy.

All the above mentioned three approaches were adopted by Hitler in Nazi Germany. Pro-natalist policies have existed since ancient times in one form or the other. They could be seen in Germany, Italy and Japan between the two World Wars period. Sweden has had a highly developed population policy maintaining lowest birth rate in the world. In France, various measures were adopted in pursuance of the pro-natalist policy in the Code de law Famille of 1939. In 1962 a natality committee was appointed in Israel, which in its report in 1966, recommended the Grant of Financial Aid to large families and restriction on induced abortions. Japan reversed her anti-natalist policy by implementing several programmes having demographic implications such as the Eugenics Protection Law of 1949 which made abortion easily available.

(*ii*) *Anti-Natalist Policies:* Anti-Natalist Policies aim at limiting the growth of population. This aim is as old as the ancient Greek State. Both Plato and Aristotle emphasised the value of the quality of population and sanctioned anti-natalist policy. This was again emphasised by the famous Essay of Malthus published in 1798. It was further accepted by John Stuart Mill when he declared in 1821 that, "The great problem is thus to find out how to limit the number of births."[1] Margarat Sanger championed the cause of birth control in more recent years. Anti-natalist policies may be both direct and indirect, short term and long term. The direct anti-natalist policies include provision of contraceptive services, liberalisation of abortion laws and raising age at marriage.

(A) *Provision of Contraceptive Services:* One finds both optimistic and pessimistic approaches towards the population check by provision of contraceptive services. Arguments are available on both the sides. Therefore, it has been concluded by Davis, "The need is not to abandon the family planning programmes, but to put equal or greater resources into other approaches."[2] However, it is undeniable that today family planning programmes are getting whole-hearted support everywhere. It has been accepted as a basic human right that persons can decide the number and spacing of their children. On December 10, 1967, the Human Rights Day, it was affirmed by Heads of States or Prime Ministers of twelve countries, "We believe that the objective of family planning is the enrichment of human life, not its restrictions, that family planning, by assuring greater opportunity to each person, frees man to attain his individual dignity and reach high full potential."[3] The Population Council of New York has recently pointed out that in 1974-75, 81 countries have family planning supportive policies covering 94% of the population of the developing countries. India was the first to adopt a family planning programme in 1952 followed by China and Hong Kong in 1956.

---

1. John Stuart Mill as quoted in Ralph Thomlinson, *Population Dynamics: Causes and Consequences of World Demographic Change*, *op. cit.* p. 61.
2. Kingsley Davis, "Population Policy: Will Current Programmes Succeed?", in Ashish Bose, *et al.* (Eds.), *Studies in Demography*, *op. cit.* p. 389.
3. Issued by Secretary-General U. Thant of the United Nations, "Declaration on Population", *Studies in Family Planning*, No. 16, January 1967, p. 1.

(B) *Liberalisation of Abortion Laws:* This has been the measure adopted by Japan during the period 1948-1958 in which her birth rate was reduced to 50% of the normal birth rate. "Today, 60 per cent of the world's population live in countries where abortion during the first trimester is legal either for social and economic reasons or on 'request' without any specific indication. Another 16 per cent live in countries where abortion is permitted on extended medical grounds, for eugenic indications, and/or for humanitarian reasons, such as those associated with rape or incest.[1] In 1975, several developing countries were found to have liberal abortion laws, including China, India, Singapore, Hong Kong in Asia, Uruguay in Latin America and Tunisia and Zambia in Africa. Liberal abortion laws however can be effective only with the provision of medical infrastructure, as found in most of the European countries.

(C) *Raising Age at Marriage:* Raising age at marriage cuts down reproductive span. Thus it reduces fertility. For example, it has been calculated that the increase of three years in marriage age has resulted in three to four per cent cut in the birth rate in India. The birth rate may be reduced by 25 to 30 per cent by raising the female age at marriage in India to 19 years or more. However, this measure will be effective only when the law relative to it is uniformly enforced through a country.

(*iii*) *Indirect Anti-natalist Policies*: Besides the above mentioned direct anti-natalist policies, there are some indirect anti-natalist policies such as incentives to check population growth, dis-incentives to child birth, improving the status of women, social and economic development, urbanisation, nutrition and health services, social security and population education. These may now be discussed in details as follows:

(A) *Incentives:* Incentives have been defined by Rogers as, "Direct or indirect payments in cash or in kind that are given to an individual, couple, or group in order to encourage some overt behavioural change.[2] Incentives are offered to the individuals, couples or groups, they may be in cash or in kind. They, may be immediate or deferred. As a general rule incentives have been

1. Margot Zimmerman, "Abortion Law and Practice", *Population Reports*, Series, E. No. 3, March 1976, p. E-25.
2. Everett M. Rogers, *Communication Strategies for Family Planning*, New York: The Free Press, 1973, pp. 152-224.

valuable indirect anti-natalist measures. However it has been pointed out that they are unethical and seem to be an exploitation of poverty. There is ample scope for cheating and fraud. The motivational aspect is neglected. However, these defects may be overcome.

(B) *Disincentives:* While incentives are positive rewards, disincentives are negative rewards. While incentives impel, disincentives restrict. The variety of disincentives may be visualised by the following disincentives provided in Singapore in 1968. (*i*) Couples with a large number of children would not have priority over newly-wed couples in the allocation of subsidised public housing, (*ii*) Under the Employment Act; no paid maternity leave would be given after the third child, (*iii*) The subsidised accouchment fees in Government Maternity Hospitals were modified so that higher fees were charged for higher parity confinements. Other disincentives, which came into effect on August 1, 1973, were announced by the Singapore Government in order to discourage large families. Accouchment fees, maternity leave, priority points for public housing and income-tax relief were all adjusted to encourage each family to have no more than two children. Disincentives have been criticised on the ground that they penalise innocent children. The population also resents them. Therefore, generally they are used in exceptional cases and certainly not as much as incentives.

(C) *Improvement of the Status of Women:* Several studies have pointed out a close relation between high fertility and low status of women. On the other hand, improvement of the status of women has everywhere led to decrease in fertility. Improvement of the status of women requires higher standards of education, higher socio-economic status, exposure to urban environment and greater interest outside the home. All these factors have led to fall in fertility rates. Improvement in the status of women is also linked to higher age of man, affecting fertility adversely. It also gives women an opportunity to exercise their discretion in number and spacing of children.

(D) *Social and Economic Development:* As may be clearly seen in the developing countries, lower social and economic status leads to higher fertility rates. It also results in high death rates. On the other hand, as is clear in the example of developed countries, social and economic development leads to reduction in birth rates. Thus, it is an effective indirect anti-natalist measure.

(E) *Urbanisation:* As a general rule fertility is low in urban areas as compared to the rural areas. Therefore, an indirect anti-natalist policy includes the urbanisation of rural communities. This does not necessarily require rural emigration to cities. Urban mentality may be created even in rural areas with good results.

(F) *Nutrition and Health Services for Children*: An important cause of more child birth is the high infant and children mortality rate. Provision of Nutrition and Health Services for Children leads to reduction in the infant and child mortality. Thus, the need of high rate of fertility is considerably reduced.

(G) *Social Security*: An important reason of large number of births is the desire for a son for reasons for social security as may be found in India. The provision of social security measures against sickness, unemployment, invalidity, old age and death may be useful in restricting birth rates. This has been observed in Tea Gardens of South India where social security measures were known as restricting birth rates.

(H) *Population Education*: Population education at school to the children and out of school to adults has been found to inculcate an appreciation of population problems and awareness to the need of population control. This facilitates the adoption of family planning measures. Therefore, it has been adopted on a large scale in developed countries. However, the impact has not been very clear in the developing countries as yet. In India the National Council of Educational Research and Training has recently incorporated population education in the syllabi of school education. Voluntary agencies like Family Planning Association of India have also undertaken population education programmes for school children and the out of school youth.

ROLE OF THE UNITED NATIONS

United Nations has played a significant part in determining the population policies of developed and developing countries. In 1946 the Population Commission was set up by the Economic and Social Council and a Population Division was established in the Department of Economics and Social Affairs. Since then different organisations have tried to influence population control in. different countries. These include the Asian Population

Conference 1963, Second World Population Conference 1965, World Health Organisation Programmes since 1965, UNICEF schemes in 1967, FAO 14th session in 1967, UNESCO programmes since 1966, ILO programmes since 1967, World Bank soft, loans for population activities, United Nations Fund for Population Activities (UNFPA) in 1969. The above mentioned organisations and their programmes have resulted in the effective role of the United Nations in the fields of Population Statistics and Projections, Population Studies and Research, Population Policies, Family Planning Training and other educational activities in the field of population.

In 1974 United Nations celebrated World Population Year (WPY). A World Population Plan of Action was announced by member states. The original plan was revised several times and finally adopted by most of the developed and developing countries who are members of the United Nations. It highlighted the need for rapid social and economic development more necessary than population control. It represents the agreement of the 136 member nations. A summary of its most important features will give an idea about the role of the United Nations and the World Population Plan of Action.

1. The need for economic and social development as well as a more equitable distribution of wealth was emphasised.
2. Though all nations recognised that the population growth is high, most nations did not regard this as a cause for alarm.
3. While the critical nature of population growth was questioned, the inter-relationship of population growth to socio-economic development was emphasised.
4. The sovereignty of each nation to determine its own population policy without external interference was accepted.
5. Countries which considered their birth rates detrimental to their national progress were invited to consider the advisability of setting up quantitative goals and implementing policies which might lead to the attainment of these goals by 1985.
6. There was resentment that population was considered to be a problem of the poor nations and the need to view it from the global point of view was emphasised.

7. Surprisingly, family planning was not considered as an agent of change to speed up the development process. The provision of family planning services was supported more on grounds of basic human rights than on demographic grounds.
8. It was recognised that the resources of the world were getting depleted and the issue of differential resource utilisation was raised.
9. The need to consider the role and status of women in the context of development was highlighted. The question of the relationship between fertility and the status of women was considered secondary to its importance in the scheme of human rights.
10. Because of the magnitude of the population problem, the need for international assistance to carry out population activities was highlighted.

POPULATION POLICY IN INDIA

India's population policy may be studied in the following four periods, demarcating different approaches to the population problems. There have been shifts in the approach and the emphasis. There have been gaps in the policy and programmes. A brief review of these different periods is as follows:

Pre-Independence Period

The British reluctance in framing a population policy for India has been pointed out by Chandrasekhar in the following words, "Till the early twenties the British measured the prosperity of their rule, to some extent by the magnitude of the net addition to India's population. The degree of satisfaction over and the justification of the British rule in India was directly in proportion to the substantial increase in the population that the Census revealed every decade."[1] This reluctance on the part of the British rulers was partly due to controversy over birth control in Britain and partly due to the policy of not interfering in local matters. During the two World Wars, Indian elite showed concern about the population growth. This was mostly concerning the density of the population. The 1931 Census revealed population growth but

1. S. Chandrasekhar, *Population and Planned Parenthood in India*, London: George Allen and Unwin Ltd., 1955, p. 75.

it was controversial whether India was over-populated. The Neo-Malthusians were of the opinion that India was over-populated. In 1916 P.K. Wattal supported family planning movement in his book, The Population Problem in India. The first birth control centre in Bombay was opened by R.D. Karve in 1925. Ravindra Nath Tagore strongly supported the family planning movement. The following were the main landmarks towards progress in this direction during pre-Independence period:

1. In June 11, 1930, the Government of Mysore opened the first Government Birth Control Clinic in the World.

2. In 1931 Madras University started instructions in methods of birth control.

3. In 1932 the Government of Madras agreed to open birth control clinics.

4. In 1932 the All India Womens Conference at Lucknow recommended instructions in methods of birth control in recognised climes to all men and women.

5. In 1935 the Indian National Congress set up a National Planning Committee under the chairmanship of Jawaharlal Nehru. This committee emphasised the need of birth control measures. It suggested raising of the marriage age, sterilization of insane and diseased persons, maintenance of vital statistics and periodic demographic surveys.

6. On December, 1995, the Society for the Study and Promotion of Family Hygiene was founded.

7. In 1939 the Birth Control Worldwide in Uttar Pradesh and the Matri Seva Sangh in Madhya Pradesh established birth control clinics.

8. In 1940 P.N. Sapru successfully moved a resolution in the Council of States for the establishment of birth control clinics.

9. In 1940 the Society for the Study and Promotion of Family Hygiene changed its name to the Family Planning Society.

10. In 1943 Famine Enquiry Commission called the Woodhead Commission, gave an adverse report to the practice of birth control.

11. In 1945 the Government of India set up the Health Survey and Development Committee under the chairmanship of Sir Joseph Bhore. This Committee recommended birth control services for the promotion of the health of the mothers.

Besides the above development, an important influence in population control during this period was the support of M.K. Gandhi to this movement. He declared, "There can be no two opinions about the necessity of birth control. But the only method handed down from ages passed is self-control or Brahmacharya. It is an infallible sovereign remedy doing good to those who practise it. The union is meant not for pleasure but for bringing forth progeny.[1] M.K. Gandhi, however, did not support other birth control measures, along with so many National Leaders. Secondly, they thought that independence and not population control is the main problem. However, the elite pressed the government to propagate and encourage information on birth control and its practice.

The Period From 1951 to 1975

This period was the period of five year plan. A brief resume of population policy developments during this period is as follows:

1. First Five Year Plan (1951-1956): The Draft Outline of the First Five Year Plan, published in July 1951, had a section on Population Pressure: its bearing on development, recognising that there is a pressure of population in India which requires a population policy as essential to planning.

2. Second Five Year Plan (1956-1961): It was maintained that the rate of population growth was a key factor in development and planning. The need for curbing the birth rates was accepted though population control programme was not considered as an alternative to socio-economic development.

3. Third Five Year Plan (1961-1966): It accepted the objective of stabilising the growth of population over a reasonable period as the centre of plan development.

4. Fourth Five Year Plan (1969-1974): It viewed population also from the point of view of social change. It insisted upon family planning as an essential and inescapable ingredient of development.

5. Fifth Five Year Plan (1974-1979): It included family planning in the context of the National Minimum Needs Programme. It incorporated the National Population Policy announced in April

1. M.K. Gandhi, *Young India*, 26 April, 1928, as quoted in Chandrasekhar, *Population and Planned Parenthood in India, op. cit.*, p. 50.

1976. It laid down target for a birth rate of 25 per thousand, and a population growth rate of 1.4 per cent, by the end of the sixth plan period. Table 18.1 shows outlay and expenditure of family planning programme in different plan periods.

The Period of Emergency 1975-77

During this period the Government of India, under the four-point programme of Mr. Sanjay Gandhi and the twenty-point programme of Mrs. Indira Gandhi made concerted and firm efforts towards mass sterilisation, in a bid to check population growth. The entire State Machinery was utilised for this purpose. Incentives were given for sterilisations. Camps were organised and even cases of forcible sterilisation were not rare since most of the government servants were asked to bring cases for sterilisation, under the fear of losing yearly salary increments and even the job. Riots were witnessed at several places in the country in protest against the use of force for sterilisation. Information about other methods of birth control was widely disseminated and a successful movement was launched to check population growth. However, in the absence of sufficient propaganda in favour of family planning movement and due to the widespread illiteracy, superstition and religious conservatism, the movement could not succeed but rather resulted in the fall of the government in the following elections.

It was for the first time in the History of Independent India that some thought was given to the politicies of the Family Planning Programme. It was decided that eight per cent of the central assistance to State Plans would be earmarked against the performance of the family planning programme. The Policy Statements included long term measures such as raising the age at marriage to 18 for girls and 21 for boys, and improving the levels of female education. A legislation was proposed with the provision that any violation of the age of marriage law would be treated as a cognisable offence. The measures for family planning included a system of graded monetary compensations based on the number of living children at the time of sterilisation with ₹ 150 offered when the couple had two living children and ₹ 100 and ₹ 70 when the couple had three and four or more children respectively. Group incentives were introduced in order to bring about greater involvement. A multimedia motivational strategy was outlined. Family planning was recognised as a multifaceted problem requiring the contribution of all the Ministries to the implementation of the programme. A long term programme for population education of the younger generation was accepted as a supportive measure. Legislation was proposed for compulsory sterilisation of a couple after they had a certain number of children. Each State was given the option to frame its own legislation in this direction. They were advised to enact such legislation for those who had three or more children. The Union Government announced modification of the service/conduct rules of Central Government Employees for family planning purposes. The principle of compulsion was accepted, in spite of the fact that the Indian delegation strongly contested the propriety of coercion at the World Population Conference at Bucharest in 1974.

Due to the above stringent measures, spectacular results were achieved. An increase of 95.9% in sterilisation was noted in 1975-76 over the year 1974-75. A further increase of 216.2% was noted in the succeeding year 1976-77. Of these the percentage of males sterilisation was as much as 75%. The achievements of targets was spectacular. 106.4% target was achieved in 1975-76, 90.9 in 1976-77. It was estimated that 29.12 million births were averted by March 1977. The performance of different States in 1976-77 was: Bihar 229.0, Madhya Pradesh 374.3, Uttar Pradesh 209.4, West Bengal 224.3, Gujarat 158.5, Haryana 425.3, Maharashtra 153.5, Punjab 299.8%. Delhi surpassed all other areas with target achievement of 477.6% sterilisation in 1976-77, All these States had achieved spectacular improvement upon their performance in former years. This spectacular success was appreciated all over the world. The role of incentives as well as disincentives was equally important in this process. For example, under the Uttar Pradesh Essential Articles and Things (Restriction on Grant or Supply to Unplanned Families) Order, 1976, the following items were linked with acceptance of sterilisation: the issue and supply of rationed articles; licences and permits under any order issued under any section of the Essential Commodities Act or Under Rule 114 of the Defence and Internal Security Rules; Licence or permit for the allotment of a scooter or motor car from the discriminatory quota of the State Government; and permits for public carriers, autorickshaws, taxis; a permit for a building under the Uttar Pradesh Buildings Act, 1972, or issued by any Development

Authority; allotment on rental basis of a house owned by the State Government or by any Development Authority; free medical aid; concession in educational fees, stipends; reservation of seats in medical colleges or other technical institutions; facilities regarding payment of dues of electricity charges in instalments.

The stringent coercive measures adopted resulted in a lot of torture upon the public. This was not reported during the period of emergency due to strict censor over the press. However, soon after the lifting of emergency, *Times of India*, April 1, 1977, reported, "Then suddenly the near-butchery began. The handling of the programme went from one extreme-apathy, niggardliness, bad planning, poor organisation and general maladministration to the other coercion, quotas, bureaucratic overzealousness, fear and brutality.... The national population policy (NPP) promulgated a year ago, seemed (and seems still to many people), despite the many fine sentiments it expressed to have been framed only to legitimise the assault on human dignity that was euphemistically called sterilisation campaign."[1] The ruling Congress was defeated in March 1977 particularly on the issue of the excesses of the family planning programme particularly in the Northern States.

Post-Emergency Period

The Janata Government, after coming into power, announced that coercion would not be used to implement the family planning, programme which was now renamed as the Family Welfare Programme. Therefore, all the rules and regulations with element of compulsion were dropped. However, the importance of family planning movement was equally emphasised. Sterilisation was now referred to as 'voluntary sterilisation' and the word 'expectations' was substituted for the earlier word 'targets'. The Government accepted many of the measures included in the National Population Policy announced by the previous Government, such as raising of the age of marriage, integration of services for maternal and child health with the Family Planning Programme, popularisation of Family Welfare Programme etc. Some of the measures taken by the Government include emphasis on the voluntary nature of the programme, securing the cooperation of rural cooperative institutions, system of graded

1. A.S. Abraham, "Voluntary Family Planning: Still as Important as Ever," *Times of India*, April 15, 1977.

compensation for sterilisation, etc. This lukewarm policy resulted in considerable decline in the performance level of different states towards family planning expectations. A general decline was noted everywhere. It was clear that the programme has received a serious setback due to political reasons and the prospects of its success were rather bleak.

However, the Indira Congress staged a quick comeback, in the year 1977. This change of government has again set the ball rolling though the government is very cautious not to use coercion anywhere. New incentives are being introduced. For example, recently the Uttar Pradesh Government announced an additional yearly increment to the salary of teachers having two or lesser number of children and undergone sterilisation. Similar steps have been taken by other State Governments. The Central Government Servants have been also offered incentives for family planning purposes. More advertisement is being given to the methods of birth control Abortion has been legalised and service for it is now available in most of the urban areas at cheaper rates. Steps are being taken to increase the supplies of other means of birth control.

Family Welfare

India's population rose from 36.11 crore in 1951 to 84.63 crore as per the 1991 Census. On 2.4 per cent of the world's land area, India supports more than 16 per cent of the world's population. The population is increasing by about 1.7 crore every year. The average annual exponential growth rate has fallen for the first time after independence to 2.14 per cent in 1981-91 from 2.22 per cent in 1971-81. As per the Sample Registration System (SRS), the annual natural growth rate of population has come down to 1.94 per cent in 1993 from 1.91 per cent in 1991, the birth rate has gone down from 29.2 in 1992 to 28.7 in 1993 and the Infant Mortality Rate (IMR) has come down to 74 per thousand live births in 1993 from 79 in 1992. The Family Welfare Programme in India aims to provide family planning services within the broader context of maternal and child health care. It disseminates information and education to enable couples to make voluntary and informed choices regarding the size of the family and spacing through contraception.

The National Health Policy (1983) set a goal of Net Reproduction Rate (NRR) of Unity, corresponding to CBR of 21, CDR of nine and natural growth rate of 1.2 per cent for 2000 AD. It has been stated in the Eighth Five Year Plan Document that NRR-I would now be achievable only in the period 2011- 16 AD. The population of India is expected to cross the one billion mark by 2001 as per the projections made by the Standing Committee of Experts on Population Projections. As per the UN Population Projections (Medium Variant), the India's population would overtake that of China by 2035 AD, when India's population will be 1.545 billion as against China's population of 1.516 billion.

Achievements

The National Family Welfare Programme was launched in India in 1951 with 'the objective of reducing the birth rate to the extent necessary to stabilise the population at a level consistent with the requirements of the National Economy' (First Five Year Plan Document). The achievements of the Family! Welfare Programme since its inception are summarised below:

S. No.	*Parameter*	*1951-61*	*1981*	*1993*
1. Birth Rate	41.70	37.2*	28.7	(SRS 1993)
2. Death Rate	22.80	15.0	9.3	(SRS 1993)
3. Total Fertility Rate	5.97	4.5	3.6	(SRS 1992)
4. Infant Mortality Rate (per 1000 live births)	146.00	110.0	74	(SRS 1993)
5. Couple Protection Rate (per cent)	10.40 (1970-71)	22.8	45.4	(31 March 1994) (Provisional)
6. Cumulative Number of Births Averted (in million)	0.04	43.4	168.8	(31 March 1994)

Refers to period 1971-81.

It is estimated that if the averted births had taken place, the average annual exponential growth rate of population during the 1981-91 decade would have been of the order of 2.71 per cent as against 2.14 per cent actually registered in 1991 Census. The Eighth Five Year Plan has laid down following goals to be achieved by 1997.

Indicator	*Goal to be achieved by the end of the Eighth Plan*
(a) Crude Birth Rate (per 1000 population)	26.0
(b) Infant Mortality Rate (per 1000 live births)	70.0
(c) Couple Protection Rate	56.0 (per cent)

Among the states, there is considerable variation in reducing the growth of population *e.g.* States like Kerala and Tamil Nadu with crude birth rates of 17.4 and 19.5 respectively have performed very well. On the other hand, the crude birth rates in Bihar (32.0), Madhya Pradesh (34.9), Rajasthan (34.0) and Uttar Pradesh (36.2), which constitutes about 40 per cent of India's population, are higher than the national average of 28.7 per thousand population in 1993. Similar variations are seen in respect of the infant mortality rates. At one end of the spectrum, Kerala has an IMR of only 13 per thousand live births whereas it is as high as 106 in Madhya Pradesh and 110 in Orissa. Total fertility rates in Bihar (4.6), Madhya Pradesh (4.4), Rajasthan (4.5) and Uttar Pradesh (5.2) are significantly higher than the all India average of 3.6 (SRS: 1992).

In keeping with democratic traditions of the country, Family Welfare Programme seeks to promote on a voluntary basis, responsible and planned parenthood with two child norm, male and female, or both, through independent choice of family welfare methods best suited to the acceptors. Family welfare services are offered through total health care delivery system. People's participation is sought through voluntary agencies, opinion leaders, people's representatives, government functionaries and various other structures and influential groups. Imaginative use of mass media and inter-personal communication is resorted to for explaining various methods of contraception and removing socio-cultural barriers. As a result, the number of acceptors of various family planning methods have started increasing over the years.

Implementation Machinery

Family Welfare Programme implemented through the state governments with cent per cent Central assistance. In rural areas, services are provided through the network of sub-centres, primary health centres and community health centres. Establishment of sub-centres programmes has been made hundred per cent Centrally-sponsored scheme (except the salary of male health worker and construction of sub-centre building) from April 1981. Against the requirement of 1.34 lakh sub-centres, there are 1.31 lakh sub centres functioning as on 30 September 1993. It is proposed to establish 17,030 sub-centres during Eighth Plan.

Birth Control Methods

During 1994-95, 42.90 lakh sterilisations were performed in the country. The number of IUD insertions during the same period was 62.40 lakh. Besides, there were 171.13 lakh CC users and 47.46 lakh OP users. Nirodh, besides being provided free, is also sold under the social marketing programme which is being operated through a network of over three lakh retail outlets of 11 leading consumer goods, pharmaceutical and oil companies. With a view to make condoms available in rural and far-flung areas at reasonable prices, scheme of distribution of condoms through Public Distribution System has already been implemented in many states. It is estimated that 45.4 per cent of 15.5 crore eligible couples, whose wives are in reproductive age group of 15-44 years, were protected by one or the other approved family planning methods as on 31 March 1994 averting 16.88 crore births since inception of the programme.

Medical Termination of Pregnancy

It Is estimated that about one-fourth of the maternal morbidity and mortality are due to illegal abortions. In order to prevent these health hazards to women, the Medical Termination of Pregnancy Act, 1971 was promulgated. Under this Act, medical termination of pregnancy can be done in pregnant women upto 20 weeks, if pregnancy is likely to result in birth of a congenitally malformed child or continuation of pregnancy is likely to harm the mother in the existing circumstances and in cases of contraceptive failure.

Research studies in India have shown that vacuum aspiration is a safe and effective method for terminating first trimester (three months) pregnancy. During the last few years studies on first trimester MTP using antiprogestin compounds like RU 486, alone or along with prostaglandins are being carried out to see whether these could provide a safe, effective non-surgical method for termination of early pregnancy. It has been observed that about 10-15 per cent of abortion seekers came during second trimester of pregnancy. A wide variety of methods have been investigated for second trimester NTP. Whatever is the method used, second trimester of pregnancy termination is not as safe as first trimester pregnancy termination. All available data indicate that in order to minimise health hazards, women should come for termination soon after she misses her period. To avoid the recurrence of an unwanted pregnancy, women should be provided with concurrent contraception : IUDs, OCs, Condoms, etc., or sterilisation. Since inception of the programme in April .1972, 97.5 lakh terminations upto December 1994 were conducted under NTP Act.

Maternal and Child Health Care Programmes

The National Health Policy (1983) in context of the global objective of 'Health for All by 2000 AD' has inter alia set the following normative goals relative to maternal and child health care: (*a*) reduction in infant mortality to less than 60 per thousand live births; (*b*) reduction in maternal mortality to below 200 per one lakh live births; (*c*) reduction in child mortality (0-4) to less than 10 per thousand population. As a part of the overall strategy to achieve these goals, the following specific programmes have been under implementation as cent per cent Centrally-sponsored schemes : (*i*) Universal Immunisation Programme (under implementation since 1985-86), for reducing mortality and morbidity due to six vaccine preventable diseases, namely, diptheria, pertussis, tetanus, poliomyelitis, measles and childhood tuberculosis. The primary target group for this programme is infants and pregnant women. When the immunisation programme was launched in 1985, IMR for the country as a whole was 97 per every thousand live births. The intensification of immunisation programme has contributed to a significant decline in IMR in the last few years. The decline has been particularly pronounced in 1990 as compared to earlier years. During that year the IMR declined (by 11 points) to 80 per thousand live births from 91 in 1989; and (*ii*) Oral Rehydration Therapy (ORT) Programme (under implementation since 1986-87) for reducing mortality and morbidity due to dehydration caused by diarrhoea. The primary target of this programme is children under five years of age. Diarrhoea diseases are a major health problem in the country especially among children below five years of age. On an average, a child suffers three episodes of diarrhoea per year. The National Diarrhoeal Diseases Control Programme, initiated in the Sixth Plan, was, therefore, intensified in the Seventh Plan with a conscious decision to promote Oral Rehydration Therapy; and (*iii*) Prophylaxis Schemes (under implementation since Fourth Plan period), against nutritional anaemia among pregnant women as well as children and against blindness due to Vitamin 'A' deficiency among children under three years of age. Nutritional anaemia is one of the major public health problems especially affecting pregnant women and pre-school children. Anaemia affecting the mothers also affects interuterine growth of the foetus. Similarly, nutritional anaemia among pre-school children makes them susceptible to disease and death. Vitamin 'A' deficiency is widely prevalent in the country among the pre-school children.

Child Survival and Safe Motherhood

The package of services under Child Survival and Safe Motherhood Project are to be expanded under two major components: (a) child survival component under which the ARI control programme will be expanded along with provision of the kit based supply of drags. In addition essential newborn care for ensuring survival of newborns is being introduced. Exclusive breastfeeding is being promoted as an intervention for child survival; and (b) safe motherhood component under which first referral units will be set up in the six states of Assam, Bihar, Madhya Pradesh, Orissa, Rajasthan and Uttar Pradesh.

SPECIAL SCHEMES

All India Hospitals Post-partum Programme

All India Hospitals Post-Partum Programme (AIHPP) was introduced in 1969. It is a hospital-based maternity centered approach to family planning. The primary objective of the post-partum programme is to improve the health of the mother and children through MCH and Family Welfare Programme which included ante-natal, neo-natal and post-natal services; immunisation services to children and mothers; and prophylaxis against anaemia and blindness. The programme is based on the following rationale: (*a*) that women who have recently delivered are of proven fertility, and are at risk to become pregnant again rapidly; and (*b*) at the time of delivery and during the lying-in-period, they are generally more receptive to adopt one or the other family planning method. The post-partum programme offers necessary facilities to such women. It has proved to be an efficient way of delivering family planning services. The programme now covers 550 medical colleges and two post-graduate institutions. With a view to provide MCH and family welfare services in rural and semi- urban areas, as well as to improve the health of mothers and children, the postpartum programme has been extended to 1,012 sub-district hospitals.

Post-partum Pap Smear Test Facility at Medical Colleges

In order to detect cervical cancer among women acceptors and non-acceptors of various family welfare methods, the PAP Smear Test Facility Programme has been introduced in all the medical colleges of the country. Under the scheme, a post of a cyto-technician as per state government's scale of pay and financial assistance and contingencies provided. The cytotechnician is required to work under the overall guidance and supervision of the professor of pathology of the medical college. The programme has been extended in a phased manner in 105 medical colleges all over the country. The state governments have sanctioned the programme in 80 medical colleges only.

Sterilisation Beds Scheme

Under the scheme, beds are provided to voluntary organisations/ local bodies/institutions on the basis of their performance of previous years and on the recommendations of the state government and regional director of health land family welfare of the respective state. Maintenance grant under this scheme at the rate of ₹ 3,000 per bed per annum is provided to each institution subject to a minimum performance of 75/60 tubectomies per bed per annum for government institutions and local bodies/ voluntary organisations respectively. A total of 3,610 sterilisation beds have been reserved under the scheme.

CRITICAL EVALUATION

Population explosion in developing countries is a matter of international concern. For India with 16% of the world's population and 2.4% of the global and area, it is a problem of serious magnitude. Its current population growth rate of 2.03% (SRS, 1989) with an annual addition of 1.6 crore presents a formidable scenario. India's population size has increased from 34.2 crore at the time of independence to 84.4 crore as per the 1991 Census. Already, there is tremendous pressure on our resources for providing even the basic needs, such as food, housing, education, health, to the country's large population. If the present growth of population is unchecked, the demand for even basic facilities and services would far outstrip their supply and there would be a serious impact on our socio-economic development, the quality of the lives of the people and the environment. Indeed, population control has to be the foremost national priority.

Although India was the first country in the world to launch the National Family Planning Programme in 1951, over the years many other developing countries, like Thailand, Indonesia, China, Sri Lanka etc. have achieved a much greater degree of success in controlling population. China has an annual growth rate of 1.44% (1989) and Indonesia 1.59% (1989). The National Health Policy adopted by the Parliament in 1983 envisages that by the year 2000 AD, the Net Reproduction Rate would be Unity, with the population growth rate at 1.2% birth rate of 21 per thousand, death rate of 9 per thousand, infant mortality rate at below 60 per thousand live births and couple protection rate of 60%. The latest figures available indicate that while due to the efforts made in providing better and more extensive health care, the death rate has come down to 10.2 per thousand, the birth rate is still very high at 30.5 per thousand. The population is increasing at an unacceptable rate of 2.03%. The infant mortality rate has come down, but is still high at the rate of 91 per thousand. The couple protection rate at 44.1% is also much below the target. A sustained national effort is, therefore, called for to achieve the goal of balanced population profile by the turn of the century.

The family planning programme in India is being promoted on voluntary basis, as a people's movement in keeping with the democratic traditions of the country. The two children norm is being promoted through independent choice of the family planning method best suited to the acceptor. The programme in the field is implemented by the State Governments and Union Territories Administrations and there is very wide disparity in the success rate. While it has had considerable success in the southern states, specially Kerala and Goa where the birth rate has come down to about 19 per thousand, its impact in the large northern states like UP, Bihar, Madhya Pradesh and Rajasthan, has been limited and the birth rates in these States are still in the range of 33 to 37 per thousand.

It is realised that the people respond to the family planning programmes more readily, if they are assure! of the survival of their children. Therefore, for many years family planning is being paused as a part of the Integrated Programme of Family Welfare with special attention to the health and well being of the family, specially mothers and children. A vast rural and urban infrastructure has been established to implement the Family Welfare Programme in the country. Immunisation Programme has been universalised to ensure better prospects of child survival which in turn would create the right psychological ambience for the small family norm. The desire for large families, specially male children in the prevailing socio-cultural and economic milieu, characteristically low status of women, low female literacy, early marriage of girls and high infant mortality rate are stumbling blocks in the progress of the Family Welfare Programme. The lack of popular commitment and will inhibit its faster tempo. The Programme is perceived as a Governmental programme, devoid of popular participation. Quality and out-reach of its service-delivery network are deficient in many parts of the country. Over emphasis on terminal methods lead to inadequate coverage of younger couples with high fertility potential. Communication systems are not effective enough to dispel the prevailing apathy, ignorance and misconception about the programme among the masses.

Confronted with the grim prospects of population explosion and the inadequacies of the present strategies, radical and innovative strategies are called for to revamp the programme and bring about a more rapid decline in fertility. Population Control and Family Welfare Programme need to have a national consensus, cutting across political, religious and cultural differences. It needs to be based on active community participation and has to be transformed from a Governmental programme into a people's movement. A differential need based strategy needs to be developed in the 206 low performing districts in the country which are mostly in the four North Indian States, viz. UP, Bihar, Madhya Pradesh and Rajasthan to create an immediate impact. The status of women and female literacy are key factors for fertility decline, as seen in the State of Kerala and elsewhere. Age of marriage of girls is yet another crucial factor. In the four large North Indian States mentioned above, the average age of marriage for girls is well below the national average of 18.3 (1981) and the statutory minimum age of 18 years. Studies indicate that if the average age of marriage of girls in India is pushed up by two years, it may result in lowering the birth rate by about 25%. Besides, a comparatively higher age of marriage would bring down maternal and infant mortality.

Information, Education and Communication (EEC) effort is vital to the Population Control Programme. Fortunately, there has been a quantum jump in female literacy (24.8% in 1981 to 39.42% in 1991) during the last decade, thanks to specific measures undertaken by the Government Population education should be a part of school and college education. It should also form an important ingredient of adult education and non-formal education. Communication strategies should be so devised as to be effective enough to bring about altitudinal changes and dispel apathy, ignorance and misgivings about family planning and small family norm. All non-governmental organisations — private sector, voluntary agencies, private medical practitioners and practitioners of Indian Systems of Medicines, Local bodies and Panchyati Raj Institutions should be folly involved in a massive effort of community participation. The service delivery system and its out-reach should be expanded with emphasis on quality of service. A package of effective incentives and disincentives should be formulated specially for younger couples in high reproductive range who require spacing methods of contraception. New generation contraceptives should be introduced in the country to make an impact on younger couples.

Thus, there is an imperative need to develop an integrated multi-sectoral strategy to handle the population problem in all its demensions. Given strong political will, commitment of the people and vigorous implementation of revamped strategies, there is no reason why India should not be able to contain its population within manageable limits and open the way for utilisation of its resources for improving the quality of life of its people.

QUESTIONS FOR EXERCISE

L Discuss Population Policy in Indian context.

2. Describe the progress of Family Planning in India.

Bibliography

Agarwala, S.N., *India's Population Problems,* Tata McGraw Hill, New Delhi, 1977.

Asha A. Bhende, Tara Kanitkar and G. Rama Rao, *Teaching and Research in Population Studies*: Seventeen Years of UPS, Bombay: International Institute for Population Studies, 1976, p. 294.

Asha A. Bhende and Tara Kanitkar, Principles of Population Studies, Himalaya Publishing House, Bombay, 1978.

Bogue, Donald, *Principles of Demography,* New York: John Wiley and Sons, 1969.

Charles Emil Stangeiand, Pre-Malthusian Doctrines of Population: *A Study in the History of Economic Theory,* New York: The Columbia University Press, 1904.

Dandekar, Kumudini: *Demographic Survey of Six Rural Communities,* Bombay: Asia Publishing House, 1959.

Dandekar, V.M. and Kumudini Dandekar: *Survey of Fertility and Mortality in Poona District,* Poona: Gokhale Institute of Politics and Economics, Publication No. 27, 1953.

D.E.C. Eversley, *Social Theories of Fertility and Malthusian Debate,* Oxford, Clarendon Press, 1959.

D.V. Gloss, Introduction to Malthus, London: Frank Cass and Company, 1959.

Govt. of India, "Registration of Births and Deaths in India", ECAFF Seminar on Civil Registration and Vital Statistics, Copenhagen, July, August, 1966.

Govt. of India, Ministry of Health and Family Welfare, *Family Welfare Programme in India*: Year Book, 1975-1976, New Delhi, Department of Family Welfare (undated).

Gyan Chand, *Population in Perspective*, New Delhi: Orient Longmans.

Hutchinson, E.P., *The Population Debate, The Development of Conflicting Theories upto 1900*, Boston, Houghton Mifflin Company, 1967.

Joseph Spengler and Otis Dudley Duncan, *Population Theory and Policy*, The Free Press of Glencoe, 1966.

Kingsley Davis, *The Population of India and Pakistan*, New York: Russell and Russell.

Kingsley Davis, "*The Theory of Change and Response* in Modem Demographic History" *Population Index*, Vol. 29, No. 4 October, 1963.

Ralph Thomlinson, *Population Dynamics*, New York: Random House, 1965.

Sydney H. Coontz, *Population Theories and Economic Interpretation*, London: Routledge & Kegan Paul, 1968.

Shyrock, Henry, *The Methods and Materials of Demography*, Vol. I. Washington D.C.; U.S. Bureau of Census, 1971.

Sovani, N.V., and Kumudini Dandekar, *Fertility Survey of Nasik, Kolaba and Satara (North) Districts, Poona*: Gokhle Institute of Politics and Economics, Publication No. 31, 1955.

Srivastava, S.C., *Indian Census in Perspective*, Census Centenary Monograph No. 1, Office of the Registrar General, India, New Delhi, Chapters I, II and IV.

United Nations, *Mysore Population Study*, ST/SOA/Series A-34, New York, 1961.

United Nations, *Principles and Recommendations for National Population Censuses*, ST/STAT/Ser/M/27, New York, 1958.

United Nations, *Principles and Recommendations for the 1970 Population Censuses*, ST/STAT/Ser/M/44, New York, 1969.

United Nations, *Handbook of Vital Statistics Methods*, ST/STAT/Ser, F. No. 7, New York, 1954.

United Nations, *Methodology of Demographic Sample Surveys*, New York, ST/ TAO/Ser, c 1/4 119, Series M, No. 51.

The Determinants and Consequences of Population Trends, Vol. 1. ST/ SOA/SER. A/50, Population Studies No. 50, New York, 1973.

Aging of the Populations: Its Economic and Social Implications, ST/SOA/ SER/A/26, Population Studies No. 26, New York, 1956.

Visaria, Praveen, *The Sex Ratio of the Population of India*, Census of India, 1961, Vol. 1, Monograph No. 10.

William Peterson, *Population*, London : The MacMillan Company, 1969.

Warren C. Sanderson, "On Two Schools of the Economics of Fertility," *Population and Development Review*, Vol. 2, Nos. 2, and 4, September/ December 1976.

Zacharia, K.C., *Migrants in Greater Bombay, Bombay*: Asia Publishing House, 1968.